Defeated Masculinity

Post-Traumatic Cinema in the Aftermath of War

P.I.E. Peter Lang

Bruxelles · Bern · Berlin · Frankfurt am Main · New York · Oxford · Wien

Raya MORAG

Defeated Masculinity

Post-Traumatic Cinema in the Aftermath of War

"Rethinking Cinema"
No.4

The publication of this book was financially supported
by the Hebrew University of Jerusalem.

© Cover illustration
Sculpture by Itamar Jobani, *Invalid Topography.*

Éditions scientifiques internationales
Brussels, 2009
1 avenue Maurice, B-1050 Brussels, Belgium
info@peterlang.com; www.peterlang.com

ISSN 1379-8391
ISBN 978-90-5201-469-2
D/2009/5678/10

Library of Congress Cataloging-in-Publication Data
Morag, Raya. Defeated masculinity : post-traumatic cinema in the aftermath of war / Raya Morag.
p. cm. — (Rethinking cinema ; no. 4) Filmography: p.
Includes bibliographical references and indexes. ISBN 978-90-5201-469-2
1. Masculinity in motion pictures. 2. Defeat (Psychology) in motion pictures. 3. Psychic trauma in motion pictures. 4. World War, 1939-1945—Influence. 5. World War, 1939-1945—Motion pictures and the war. 6. Vietnam War, 1961-1975—Influence. 7. Vietnam War, 1961-1975—Motion pictures and the war. 8. Motion pictures—Germany—History—20th century. 9. Motion pictures—United States—History—20th century. I. Title.
PN1995.9.M34M67 2009 791.43'653—dc22 2008056114

CIP also available from the British Library, GB

Bibliographic information published by "Die Deutsche Bibliothek" "Die Deutsche Bibliothek" lists this publication in the "Deutsche Nationalbibliografie"; detailed bibliographic data is available on Internet at <http://dnb.ddb.de>.

For my daughters

Contents

Acknowledgements

Friends and colleagues have given important advice and encouragement during the years I have worked on this book.

I would like especially to thank Yeshayahu Nir for the privilege of being his Ph.D. student in the Communication & Journalism Department at the Hebrew University of Jerusalem, for his many years of assistance and intellectual generosity. Special thanks to Tamar Liebes for her continuous help and strong support. Thanks also to Hannah Naveh for her encouragement and comments on an early draft; to Moshe Zimmerman, for his help and support; to Régine-Mihal Friedman for always being there for me; to friends and colleagues who have contributed in different ways to this project: Elihu Katz, Etti Schely-Newman, Menahem Blondheim, Ilana Pardes, Ariele Hirschfeld, Alan Rosenthal, Aner Preminger, Tirtza Elnathan, Nurith Gertz, Orly Lubin and Gertrud Koch; and to Dominique Nasta, the editor of the "Rethinking Cinema/ *Repenser le cinéma*" series, for her invaluable help. Thanks to my colleagues and students in the Department of Communication & Journalism of the Hebrew University, and to my former colleagues and students in the Department of Film & Television at Tel Aviv University. I owe a special debt of gratitude to Thomas Elsaesser for his numerous books and articles which provided a source of inspiration, for lengthy and stimulating conversations over the years, and for his friendship.

Thanks to Liviu Carmeli of the cinématheque archive of the Department of Film and Television at Tel Aviv University, Harriet Kasow and Wendy Benhaim at the Media Library of the Hebrew University, and the staff of the Jerusalem Cinématheque archives and library for giving generously of their time to help me obtain the films necessary for my research. Special thanks to Gilli Mendel, the Jerusalem Cinématheque, for her help throughout.

I benefited from the expertise of Peter Lemish and Orit Friedland, who translated parts of an earlier version of this book from the Hebrew; and especially from Helene Landau's devoted work as translator and editor, which made this book available. She has read and discussed with me at length countless drafts, and the final product bears the mark of her careful and highly professional work. Thanks also to Marc I. Sherman for preparing the index; to Vicky Barda for helping with the pictures;

and to Émilie Menz and Alice de Patoul at P.I.E. Peter Lang publications.

To my friends with whom I shared this journey: Bilha and Israel Ben-David, Dina Bitton, Gary Bornstein, Ilana and Yehuda Hemel, Ruty Kononovich, Francesca Levi-Schaffer, Orit San-Gupta and Rafi Yaacobi; to my mother, Sara Kesar; and in memory of my late fathers Yitzhak Amami (Chomsky) and Shlomo Kesar; to my family, and especially my sister, Shiffi Shmueli, for her thoughtful comments and constant assistance. Finally, to my daughters, Reout and Rotem, for their patience, help, and love.

I was supported during parts of the writing of this book by Israel Foundations Trustees. I am also indebted to the Department of Communication & Journalism, to Smart Family Communications Foundation, and the faculty research funds granted by the Hebrew University of Jerusalem, which helped me bring it to fruition.

Earlier versions of some sections of this book have appeared previously in *The Seeing Century: Film, Vision, and Identity* and in *The Communication Review*.

Preface

Scene One: A lone man wanders through the Texan desert wearing a red cap and a dark suit faded from the sun. He has only the clothes on his back. He gazes at the empty, wide-open spaces. An eagle watches him from afar, waiting to see how it will end. He faints in the middle of a God-forsaken town and when he comes to a doctor asks him questions in a heavy German accent. The man is silent. The doctor looks at a business card he found in the man's pocket and asks, "Do you know which side of the border you are? Is it you? Or a relative of yours? I will call this number, maybe they can tell me who you are." The man is still silent. After awhile he is again seen wandering into the distance.

Scene Two: Against the sunset, a group of American soldiers return to camp after battle repeatedly singing a song from a TV show popular when they were children: "Who's the leader of the club that's made for you and me? M-I-C K-E-Y M-O-U-S-E. Who is marching coast to coast and far across the sea? M-I-C K-E-Y M-O-U-S-E. Mickey Mouse. (Mickey Mouse)."

Do these two scenes have anything at all in common? The first is from German director Wim Wenders' *Paris, Texas* (1984) and the second from expatriate American director Stanley Kubrick's *Full Metal Jacket* (1987). Ostensibly, from the details provided above they have nothing in common. In actuality, the subject of both of the two scenes, like this book, is the defeated male. The first scene depicts the collapse of the German male after World War II through displacement, and the bursting of the American dream held by second generation Germans. The second depicts a contrived victory and the concealed defeat of American soldiers fighting in the Vietnam War.

Over the years, I would get the same feeling when watching films belonging to New German Cinema and American Vietnam War cinema. It was as if despite great differences between the two, the texts had something very basic in common. After awhile I realized that in both cases the trauma of defeat was in the background, threatening to break out of the collective cinematic unconscious, but at the same time restrained by it. In both cases, the male characters were carrying the burden of the trauma of defeat on their bodies.

This book will describe the complex relationship between trauma and cinema in which textual processes are both different and amazingly alike. Resemblance between the two corpora is found not only through the experience of spectatorship, but also in the evidence of the power of cinema to mediate post-traumatic social processes that allow repression to be lifted and the past to be perceived. Showing a male isolated from all human contact, silent, lost in the infinite desert, or soldiers after a day of battle glorifying the leadership of a mouse are both meaningful political representations with far-reaching implications. In both cases, mediation of the past is carried out largely through the corporeal processing of memory: the films repeat the trauma through the body and through masculine sexuality. The wound etymologically hidden in the word "trauma" ceases to be figurative and becomes literal.

The world depicted in the films is discussed not only as a way of representing the bodily symptoms of post-trauma. These cultures are not immersed in their symptoms; in fact, the opposite is true. Both corpora reveal the enormous socio-cultural difficulties involved in recognizing the reality of the defeat, systematically dismantling the moral perspective that brought about the war while representing an alternative morality. These complex processes can only take place within the medium most able to represent the collective feelings lurking under the surface – cinema.

INTRODUCTION

Post-Traumatic Cinema

This work deals with post-traumatic cinema[1] in the aftermath of war. In order to describe the complex relationship between cinema and the trauma of military defeat, I will analyze two test cases: post-World War II New German Cinema (henceforth NGC) and post-Vietnam War American cinema. The enormous psychocultural difficulty in fully acknowledging defeat in the societies under discussion has three main cinematic expressions, the first of which is the belated reaction. These corpora acknowledged the trauma of defeat only after an extended latency period of several years following the end of each of the wars. The second cinematic expression is dual repetitiveness: the deferred reenactment is reflected in both the continuous production of films that emerged following the latency period (each is but another reenactment of the trauma, of mastering its inaccessibility), and in the repetitive nature of the film texts themselves. The third cinematic expression makes up the central thesis of this book: while defeat was repressed in these films, the defeated male is present. Cinema, therefore, is the primary axis of discussion in this book and the derivative of two additional axes – trauma and masculinity.[2]

While watching the canonic[3] narrative[4] films produced in these (post)traumatized societies I became conscious of the indirect and intriguing ways cinema in both countries was involved in processing the

---

1 I use the term "post-traumatic" as opposed to "traumatic" to emphasize the understanding of trauma as an experience based on inherent latency (Caruth, *Trauma Explorations*).

2 I henceforth use the term "masculinity" and not "maleness" to refer to the material aspects of corporeality, mainly the body, bodyliness, and sexuality. The term "male" will be used as an umbrella term covering both masculinity and other characteristics, such as behaviors, practices, attitudes.

3 I use two criteria to define canonization: films that were 1) well received by audiences, and 2) were discussed widely both in the public sphere and among scholars.

4 Despite the increased blurring of boundaries between fact and fiction in contemporary critique and production, for purposes of this study I distinguish between fiction and documentary films. I will analyze only fiction films since they depict more emphatically the traumatized collective unconscious because they are more accessible to mass audiences and elicit projection processes.

trauma of defeat. This led me to conclude that while it is obvious that the canonic narrative war films made in America from the late 1970s represent the trauma of defeat in the Vietnam War, it is less obvious, but equally true, that the canonic narrative films made in Germany from the 1970s and on – the New German Cinema – represent the trauma of defeat in World War II. Moreover, I became conscious of a distinct similarity in the formulation of trauma, notwithstanding the significant differences between the two corpora. The two show disparities *vis-à-vis* their societal and political-historical contexts and the wars themselves, as well as in the breadth of the defeat in each society: the collapse of the "Thousand Year Reich" was a total military and civic defeat, while that suffered in the Vietnam War, fought on foreign soil, was relatively much smaller. There are also disparities in the interval between the occurrence of the traumatic events and the first appearance of the films, with the NGC interval lasting until circa 1970,[5] about 25 years, and the American interval lasting until 1978, about 10 years after the popular realization of defeat. In addition, while most German directors were members of the post-war second generation, American directors experienced the Vietnam War directly, together with their own generation.[6] The two cinematic industries are also distinct: "art" films vs. popular-commercial films, wide use of literary adaptations vs. their absence, and government-subsidized industry vs. private investment intended to generate profit.

The central thesis of this book, namely that the defeated male takes the place of the defeat, is drawn from this asymmetrical and non-binary comparison. A multifaceted process of demasculinizationis evident in each corpus, demonstrating that the trauma of defeat determines the texts of these films more than any other variables, including militaristic, historical, industrial, and cultural contextualities.

I. The First Axis: Cinema

A. *Extent of the Defeat*

I have already claimed that the voices and the images of the defeats are unheard and unseen and are revealed only through representations of the defeated male. Full recognition of the extent of this cinematic repression can only be illustrated by understanding the extent of the defeat in both German and American societies.

---

5 Alexander Kluge's *Yesterday Girl* (1966) is commonly accepted as the first NGC film.

6 Only Oliver Stone was a Vietnam veteran.

The immediate results of its defeat were catastrophic for Germany. Some 3.5 million German soldiers died in the war, resulting in a loss of up to 39% of the men in some age groups. Over 3 million buildings and more than 55% of the buildings in major cities were destroyed. Between 1945 and 1949 millions of refugees and displaced persons wandered the roads, with some 6 million from Eastern Europe arriving in Germany without any possessions. Germans lived in temporary shelters and cellars, exposed to disease and crime. Industrial production nearly ceased and only sectors permitted by the Allies were allowed to be rebuilt at a slow pace. There was a severe shortage of basic commodities and foods supplies (Overy).[7]

American military casualties in the Vietnam War came to 58,235 dead and 300,000 wounded and handicapped. Between 500,000 and 700,000 Vietnam veterans suffered from post-traumatic stress disorder (PTSD)[8] and thousands of soldiers and yet-to-be-born children contracted cancer and/or birth defects due to exposure to Agent Orange. The total expense of the war has been estimated at $150 billion.[9] Though this study does not deal with the trauma sustained by the victors of the war, that is, the Vietnamese, I do think it is important to complete the picture of America's defeat by noting that between 1965 and 1975 about 4 million Vietnamese were killed, wounded, or missing in both North and South Vietnam. The United States laid waste to approximately a third of the agricultural land and over half of the country's villages.[10]

B. Power(lessness)

In both cinematic cultures under discussion there is a conspicuous gap between text and subtext: the representation of masculine identity and physique in the subtext is an ideological substitute for the repression

---

7 See this source for the results and statistics of the war beyond Germany's border (131-133).

8 PTSD was only official recognized by the American Psychiatric Association in 1980. According to Noy, in 1994 the association had not yet completed definitions for all the disorders grouped under trauma. Dissociative, somatic, and behavioral reactions to trauma were not included in that year's *Diagnostic and Statistical Manual of Mental Disorders* (*DSM-IV*), (17-18).

9 These statistics are from McLear; Olson; Jeffords (*Remasculinization of America* 121-125; note 29, 200); and Kutler.

10 Paraphrasing Ngo Win Long's description of the extent of the environmental damage, the area of Vietnam is less that 1/25 of the area of the United States. The area of Cambodia, Laos and Vietnam, together, is similar in size to France. Between 1965-1973, the United States bombed this area with seven million tons of bombs, three times more than the tonnage they used in World War II. Most of the bombs fell in South Vietnam (Kutler 591).

of defeat in the text. I will be demonstrating that together with this repression, with its political, historical, and social implications, cinema in both cultures was engaged in an ongoing subversive discussion of the defeat that tested the boundaries of masculine identity,[11] especially in terms of sexuality and gender, but less so in terms of class or ethnicity.

Weakening of post-war masculinity is concomitant with other social changes taking place in both societies. Germany in the late 1960s and early 1970s was challenged by the Student Revolt of 1967, the rise of the feminist movement, and the events of the German Autumn (McCormick, *Politics*; Fulbrook; Knight). America, too, at this time, was challenged by the student revolt; the Counter Culture; the rise of the feminist and anti-war movements; the Civil Rights Movement; and black militant and gay and lesbian movements[12]; together with a steady decline in the income of white working- and lower-middle class men.[13] Clearly, in both cultures cinema constructs the influence of changing gender relationships together with the influence of the trauma. Indeed, these changing relationships fuel the (re)formulation of masculinity in cinema during this period. That being said, in my view it does not seem possible that the comprehensive, intensive occupation with the trauma of the defeated male – as developed in the subtexts – can be related solely to these social upheavals. Rather, the representation of defeated masculinity reflects the intensive immediacy of such representations for the audiences, following an extended period of repression.[14]

---

11 Although portrayals of women exist in both corpora, I decided to deal exclusively with the defeated male. First, the non-hegemonic vanquished male is at the core of the discussion in these films. Second, it is my intention to provide additional tools for discussing non-hegemonic masculinity, given its relatively reduced status in current research. Masculinity studies in the last two decades, in my view, have reached a breaking point in terms of such research. Among other reasons, the widespread influence of cultural studies, with the dominance of post-colonial and queer perspectives, has blocked research from further elaboration on non-hegemonic masculinity that is white and straight.

12 Tuchman; Wood; Jeffords, *Remasculinization of America*.

13 Savran.

14 To my knowledge, the cinematic phenomena examined in this study were not present to as high degree in films produced in other victorious countries in World War II such as England, or those with limited victories, such as France or Italy. That is to say, there are far fewer expressions of the defeated male, such as demasculinization, negation of sexuality, bodily deformation, and negation of the gaze/ the look. Further in this vein, it can be said that presentation of masculinity in various Vietnam War films is significantly different from previous war films. While it is nearly impossible to determine the sole influence of the defeat in isolation from other developments, it is clear that defeated masculinity is a dominant theme in these films in comparison with films about World War II, for example.

C. *Repression of Trauma in Research*

According to Judith Lewis Herman, trauma research is characterized by episodic amnesia; that is, it has been discovered and repeatedly abandoned several times over the last hundred years.[15] As will be discussed extensively in this book in relation to each corpus, repression of military defeat characterizes not only the films, but also academic research relating to them. To date, the traumatic perspective has not been applied to either of the two corpora. Of the dozens of studies carried out on both NGC and post-Vietnam War films, none until now has analyzed the trauma of defeat as a distinct phenomenon. Though after the latency period (Caruth, *Unclaimed Experience* 10-24) both societies produced an extensive number of post-traumatic films, this has not been reflected in academic research.

II. The Second Axis: Trauma

A. *Trauma Discourse in Current Research*

Many factors have contributed to renewed academic interest in trauma during the last two decades. They include the view of the twentieth century as the "post-traumatic century," given the historical catastrophes perpetrated (Felman; Farrell); the ongoing discussion of the Holocaust (Felman and Laub); the Vietnam War (Lifton, *Vietnam Veterans*, "Survivor Experience," and "Psychology"; Herman, "PTSD"); and the events of 9/11 (Zelizer; Chouliaraki; Baudrillard, "L'Esprit"; Spivak). Other factors include the feminist movement placing trauma research on the social agenda in connection to rape and sexual abuse in the family (Herman, *Trauma and Recovery*); clinical research following the American Psychiatric Association's official recognition in 1980 of PTSD; public debates about false memory (Walker, "Paradox," *Trauma Cinema*; Radstone); disruption of the "social contract" (Foster, "Death"; Farrell) as seen in the AIDS crisis and destruction of the social welfare state; the spectacle of violence in the pathological public sphere (Seltzer); and "the millennium hysteria" of victim culture (Showalter, *Hystories*).

Various functions of trauma discourse – as cultural symptom, type of history, mode of our relationship to contemporary events, interpretative process, symbolic interaction, clinical symptom, and a corrective tactic within the framework of cultural attempts to establish moral criteria

---

15 As is widely known, the development of trauma theory since its inception is entangled with denial and repression. See Herman (*Trauma and Recovery* 22-33); Everly and Lating (10-15); Wilson; Leys ("Traumatic Cures," *Trauma: A Genealogy*).

(Farrell) – exemplify the myriad interactions between culture and trauma. According to Foster ("Obscene"), this discourse is the "magical resolution" to contradictory needs of contemporary culture: deconstructive analyzes vs. multi-cultural histories, and recognition of shattered subjectivity as the consequence of a "broken society" vs. validation of identity at any price. All of these make possible its use as a unified interpretative mode for a wide range of phenomena. At the same time, there is a need to limit the use of this interpretative mode as well as develop current trauma theory regarding the central questions which it encapsulates (as defined primarily from Caruth onward), and specific historical-traumatic emplotments, such as the trauma associated with military defeat.

Many writers have contributed to the development of trauma theory or to clarifying its involvement in different fields, both clinical and cultural. In my view, because of the duality inherent in the traumatic event (two periods of time and space, two types of experience/consciousness, two types of influences – on the body/on the soul, etc.), most, if not all, characterize trauma principally through oppositional categorization.

Caruth's definition of trauma as discussed in her books *Trauma Explorations* and *Unclaimed Experience* is based on contradictory concepts different from those traditionally accepted in research. She first distinguishes between fantasy and history(ical) memory; that is, not remembering vs. forgetting, but knowing vs. unknowing. The traumatic incident is examined through its inaccessibility, indirect referentiality, and late impact (*Nachtraglichkeit*),[16] making latency inherent to trauma. Secondly, she distinguishes between the encounter with death and the ongoing experience of survival. Other contradictory concepts she discusses are psychic temporality and chronological time and the real and the virtual.

According to Lifton, trauma is characterized by a number of tensions: between actual death and mental death associated with survivor guilt, between guilt and the happiness of survival, between being haunted by the traumatic image and traumatic enactment, between trauma that is indelibly imprinted and the possibility of being cured.[17] LaCapra adds the tension between loss and absence;[18] and Herman the tensions between the intrusive mechanism and numbing mechanism, the will to deny horrible events and to testify about them, remembering too

16 Belatedness.

17 "Survivor Experience"; "Psychology."

18 "Trauma, Absence."

much and too little, narrative memory and traumatic memory, testimony and trauma, and traumatic repetition as verbalization and as "wordless."[19] The trauma victim has also been characterized by tension between life in a world of trauma and everyday life (Van der Kolk and Van der Hart) and between having been a passive recipient to being a moral agent collaborating in one's cure (Young). Foster, in his discussion of abjective art in "Obscene" emphasizes duality in the positioning of the subject:

> On the one hand, especially in art, writing, and theory, this trauma discourse continues the poststructuralist critique of the subject by other means, for strictly in a *psychoanalytic* register there is no subject of trauma – the position is evacuated – so the critique of the subject seems most radical here. On the other hand, especially in therapy culture, talk shows, and memoir-mongering, trauma is treated as an event that guarantees the subject, and in this *psychologistic* register the subject, however disturbed, rushes back as survivor, witness, testifier. Here a traumatic subject does indeed exist, and it has absolute authority [...] *In trauma discourse, then, the subject is evacuated and elevated at once*. (123-124, Emphases in the original).

As a subject theory, trauma theory does not focus on passion and lack, according to the Freudian-Lacanian paradigm. Desire is converted into "memoro-politics" (Hacking), that is, questions of memory and referential crisis, and the Lacanian lack is replaced, in my opinion, by historical loss (LaCapra, "Trauma, Absence").

While there has been an increasingly greater interest in trauma discourse generally over the last two decades as described above, such discourse is at a very initial stage regarding cinema. A thorough discussion of the relationship between trauma and the feature film has yet to be developed.

B. Dual Absence of the Cinematic Signifier

Does the dual nature of the cinematic signifier – absent/present, according to Metz (42-57) – require a redefinition when discussing trauma? Does trauma cause an essential change in the process of denial/acceptance involved in cinematic spectatorship? It is common knowledge that the spectator watching a movie perceives the absent as present; that is, the world presented on the screen is only a representation, a reflection or image of the (absent) real world. When speaking about trauma, however, the question reaches far beyond cinematic illusion.

19 *Trauma and Recovery*; "Crime and Memory."

Beginning as we should from the perspective that cinema in general – and post-traumatic cinema in particular – is a manifestation of the social unconscious, as Fredric Jameson puts it in his seminal work *Political Unconscious*, we must distinguish between two levels of repetitiveness, both of which are a first expression of the traumatic event that has been repressed. On the first level, post-traumatic films that relate to the same historical-traumatic event create a body of work in which each additional film is a repetition (additional re-enactment). On the second level, as alluded to above, repetition is also expressed in the nature of the text and not merely in the repetitive production of more and more films. The repetitive structures that appear within each of the film texts in and of themselves actualize the repetitiveness phenomena. Both phenomena, which are the result of the acknowledgment of the trauma, and perhaps even representations of different facets of the traumatic event itself, indicate the duplication of absence. The direct connection to the referent occurs at the level of production/the illusion (the presence of absence [Baudry, "Ideological Effects," "Apparatus"]) but is impossible at the Real (the trauma is absent). To be more exact, in my view, when we are speaking of trauma as an object of cinematic representation, there is a dual absence: first, at the areferential level (disruption of the direct connection between the trauma and the referent); and second, at the referential level (the referent which is related to as absent/ present is not the referent of the traumatic event, rather its repetition, a first reenactment of the belated experience).

The subject of the trauma is, therefore, defined by the loss of historical referentiality, in accordance to LaCapra's theories. No wonder post-traumatic films create an unequivocal correlation between historical and traumatic representations. As will be clarified in the body of this work, it is my view that the more a film allocates space to an historical representation – in this case, of military defeat – the more it will lack representation of the trauma. The basis for this representation is not narrative remembrance, but traumatic memory; not chronological, but mental time; not the real event, but the virtual one. There is an immanent clash between representing history and representing trauma. The conclusion is that though (historical) trauma has no meaning without the historical events that created it (the taken for granted), these events will not be dominant in its cinematic representation. The first actualization of the traumatic experience – that is, the post-traumatic film – will be subjugated to the processes of the reenactment of the trauma and not to referential reliability. The "original" areferentialization will destroy the attempt for referentiality at the level of the absence which is perceived as presence. Far beyond Walker's analysis of the traumatic paradox in *Trauma Cinema*, I re-emphasize the inevitable split between historical and traumatic representation of trauma. That is, I claim that a film which lacks any concrete historical traces of the historical event that originated the trauma will adhere to a more fully and reliably traumatic representation, and vice versa. This observation will be the basis of my analysis of, on the one hand, NGC films, which lack any concrete historical references to the Nazi defeat whatsoever (but address it in the subtexts, as noted, through representations of masculinity); and American films, including those previously regarded in research as lacking historical "authenticity."[20]

The spectator experiences the crisis of referentiality, the crisis of indexicality, the loss of history, the dual repetition and dual absence. Based on a close textual reading, I shall prove that even though the spectator is exposed both to these experiences and to a highly (post)traumatic content in these films, s/he is not the (post)traumatized subject. Beyond the unavoidable level of post-traumatic interpellation imposed on him/her by the film, these corpora are unique in that they first and foremost construct the spectator as the moral other of the text.

III. The Third Axis: Masculinity

A. *Feminist Critique – A Survey*

After about thirty years of feminist critique of women's subjectivityies and their construction in cinema,[21] scholars reverted to an examination of the very same masculinity that had been perceived until then as "known and familiar" (from Neale's "Masculinity" to Adams and Savran). The attempt to deconstruct concepts familiar in feminist discussion of masculinity, such as powerful, complete, privileged, hegemonic, dominant, unified, and active, together with voyeurism, fetishism, sadism, and (reflexive) masochism, undermined existing conceptions. As Penley and Willis wrote in one of the first polemics devoted to this topic, the concept of masculinity is even more complex than assumed by feminist theory both because there are many masculinities, and because there is a need to examine the cultural structure of masculinity as well as the psychoanalytic structure of male sexuality in order to avoid reduction of both to monolithic and universal categories.[22]

---

20 E.g., *The Deer Hunter* (Michael Cimino, 1978) or *Rambo: First Blood* (Ted Kotcheff, 1982).

21 From Mulvey's "Visual Pleasure" and "Afterthoughts" to Grosz's *Volatile Bodies.*

22 Penley and Willis, for example, claim that the reason for changes in conceptualization of masculinities is pressure from feminism and from gays, the demands of late capitalism for a new type of worker-male, as well as the AIDS crisis with its political and cultural representation ("Male Trouble" 4).

Some studies described male hysteria (Showalter, "Male Hysteria" and *Hystories*; Adams; Di Piero), masochism (Creed; Savran) and masculinity as spectacle (Neale). Others, like Lehman, for example, were concerned with how the phallus controls and limits the representation of the male body, especially male sexuality. Lately, the on-going research into the crisis of masculinity by Hatty, Gardiner, and Adams and Savran has been encouraging continuing analysis of the contested boundaries of masculinity studies, as well as gay, lesbian, and queer studies and theory. Even so, the studies that have emphasized masculinity and/or the male spectator as cultural constructions, or even adopted the presumption that masculinity is a masquerade, have not probed these insights in the context of trauma.

To my knowledge, except in relation to gay or queer issues there are no cinematic studies dealing with a distinct corpus of films that constructs non-hegemonic masculinity, nor is there a theoretical perspective with which to discuss this phenomenon. By the term non-hegemonic masculinity I mean masculinity that has irreversibly lost its sexual and social power as a result of an historical traumatic event, is unable to represent the social order, and is torn from its traditional, including intergenerational, affiliations. Analyzing the two corpora under discussion suggests, that is, the loss or diminishment of traditional masculinity, gender turned back on itself, incoherence at the gendered core of (masculine) identity, and the failure to conform to the hetero-normative model. The masculinities discussed in this book are all deformed derivatives of a (mythical) hetero-normative prototype (which they radically subvert).

Kaja Silverman's pioneering work *Male Subjectivity at the Margins* focused on the marginal male principally in regard to American films made after World War II. Though the author does analyze a complete corpus and not just individual films or genre she limits the range of issues dealt with in feminist discussion of non-hegemonic masculinity. Her view of the returning American soldier as one who experienced "historical trauma as a force capable of unbinding the coherence of the male ego, and exposing the abyss that it conceals" (121) is more relevant when speaking of World War II from the American perspective than in relation to the wars analyzed in this book. This coherence is indeed an integral part of the discussion of World War II, given the political consensus regarding the American goals in this war which feeds, in my view, both the collective unconscious and definitions of masculinity. This is certainly the case of history told by the victors. Unavoidably, therefore, I believe that her study of masculinity is connected to consensual, nationalistic, patriarchal, and rehabilitative conceptualization that sustains the discussion of masculinity, marginal as it may be. The fundamental assumption of Silverman's discussion has limited relevance to the post-World War II German male or Vietnam War veterans, two representations of non-hegemonic masculinity *par excellence*. In the two latter cases, the films tell history (historical trauma), from the perspective of the defeated, as problematic as this may be in terms of consensus. Clearly, the trauma of military defeat is a much more extreme case of what Silverman termed "confrontation with lack." À la Rancière, the films she analyzed attest to only a temporary loss of trust in the dominant fiction; in contrast, the discussion of masculinity I propose entirely changes these former conceptions of non-hegemonic masculinity.

B. Gender as an Analytic Concept[23]

Using gender to analyze the social structure of male-female relations, to create conceptualization of the semiotics of the body, sex and sexuality, or any other meaning, emphasizes both its multiple meanings and the question of the advantages and disadvantages of applying gender as an analytic category.

In her seminal works *Gender Trouble* and *Bodies That Matter*, Judith Butler revolutionized ways of thinking about gender by deconstructing phallogocentrism and heterosexuality as imposed conceptions that naturalize masculinity. Exposing the naturalization at the heart of the gendering process emphasizes that gender is itself an effect of specific formations of power, institutions, practices, and discourses that establish its shape and meaning.[24] In seeking to analyze the repressed structuring of masculinity and to propose new tools for feminist study of non-hegemonic masculinity, the present study is aided by Butler's deconstructivist theory and Foucault's view of masculinity as discourse of power, with an emphasis on power(lessness).

At the core of this study is the male body and masculine sexuality as a means of constructing post-war identity. Until now the male body in NGC films has not been described as anti-fascist and anti-Nazi nor has masculine sexuality been described, comprehensively, as undermining the attachment between the hetero-normative, the patriarchal, and the national. Similarly, research carried out on Vietnam War films has not described the male body as abjected and emasculated in a comprehen-

---

23 Scott's pioneering work discusses the potential of gender as an analytic category. Hawkesworth expanded the scope of Scott's discussion, but warns of using gender as a mode of interpretation instead of as a analytic category (645-655, 687-713).

24 For critique of Butler's theory as another "ideology of reproduction," see for example, Hawkesworth. Vasterling critiques the non-humanistic subject that lies at the heart of Butler's view.

sive manner. Nor has it investigated masculine sexuality since it took for granted mythicization and was engaged in a naturalization process intended to preserve the soldier's patriarchal-nationalist power, that is, to deny his defeat. Just as the masculinity of the defeated non-hegemonic male has not been examined from this perspective, so too, the representation of the body and sexuality. Accordingly, I selected the concept of demasculinization to describe the loss of sexuality in terms of sexual power in both corpora.

IV. Cinema, Trauma, and Masculinity

A. Characteristics of Post-Traumatic Subjectivity

As will be demonstrated in length, an analysis of post-traumatic male subjectivity at the subtext of both corpora reveals a number of shared characteristics: defeated masculinity is positioned on the margins of the symbolic order or outside it; the order is undermined, devoid of the Name of the Father or Law; pre-trauma, the male subject is perceived as the preferred agent for representing the social order, while post-traumatic cinema is unique in constructing this affiliation as replete with tension, and exposing the male identity as unstable. Moreover, the films in these corpora do not raise the possibility of an alternative order: post-traumatic cinema does not describe re-emergence of the order that has collapsed as a result of the defeat and does not re-establish the Name of the Father. The male body that carries the burden of defeat is missing masculine power, is left non-sexual,[25] and deprived of gaze. Acquisition of language, in the Lacanian sense (whether speaking of the "new sensitivity" of NGC or the language learned during basic training in American cinema), and its use by the subject, have neither established nor renewed subjectivization.

Further, as I hinted above, these post-traumatic films are characterized by a moral dimension. Repression of the trauma of defeat and the presence of the victorious other, as well as self-perception of the male subject as victim and not as perpetrator in the overt text, appears to pull the ground from under the possibility of a true moral dimension in the cinema of the two cultures discussed. According to my claim, however, it is the presence of these subversive forces beneath the surface that challenge what at first appears to be absent – the moral dimension. The clearest potential for subversion is in the shaping of male subjectivity as

25 See Silverman in regard to the incommensurability between the penis and phallus in relation to collective loss of trust in the dominant fiction (*Male Subjectivity at the Margins* 1-121).

lacking phallic-sexual power, as not being affiliated with the symbolic order, as stripped of the power of the gaze. Challenges to the nationalist-male paradigm of each cinematic culture – Nazi and Native American masculinity respectively, as will be described later – are the primary basis of such subversion. I find that the male construction in post-traumatic films has become the agent of ideological statements of these cultures in relation to their traumatic past. In this sense, there are fascinating, important relations between the text and the subtext in the two cultures, acute also in terms of interpretation of questions regarding morality. As I will elaborate below, reading the subtext of the defeated subjectivity attests to a subject position of the survivor-perpetrator,[26] and not that of the victim.

B. *Feminist Reading of Non-Hegemonic Post-Traumatic Masculinity*

As Showalter claims in *Hystories*, "Feminists have an ethical as well as an intellectual responsibility to ask tough questions about the current narratives of illness, trauma, accusation, and conspiracy [...] If hysteria is a proto-language rather than a disease, we must pay attention to what it is telling us" (13). Studying the sometimes sadistic attempts to rehabilitate English soldiers suffering from what was then called shell shock, Showalter claims in "Male Hysteria" that because it had been repressed by the returning soldiers, contemporary women's literature helped define and understand the phenomenon during World War I (for example, through the character of Septimus Smith in Virginia Woolf's *Mrs. Dalloway*).

The genealogy of trauma also reveals the importance of feminist readings of trauma. According to Herman in *Trauma and Recovery*, contemporary understanding of trauma is grounded in a synthesis of research on women's history, shell shock, and sexual violence in the family; that is, ironically, it was possible to continue the Freudian denial of relating female hysteria to sexual abuse for only a limited period of time. The very same male-dominated institutions that assisted this denial, according to Herman, had to contend with defining male hysteria after three wars – World War I, World War II, and the Vietnam War – and eventually, from the 1970s, these definitions helped the feminist movement revive issues related to sexual abuse of women and children.

The trauma of military defeat in war is of social and scholarly interest to feminist research beyond previous (mostly non-feminist) theorization. The implications it has for social change, as well as for radical

[26] See Chapter 5 for a discussion of this term.

politicization of the discussion, are clear.[27] Moreover, post-traumatic films offer a unique challenge for feminist critique. The power relations involved in reading this corpora position the feminist reader together with defeated male; that is, they are both marginalized in relation to societal and textual hegemony. This is not, however, a subject position that requires that she identify with the survivor-perpetrator. The feminist reader does not collaborate with the defeated male against what appears to be textual hegemony. It is evident that first and foremost, conventional power relationships between the feminist reader and the hegemonic/patriarchal text are totally shifted in this case. The feminist reader is not the focus of the reading process; it is rather the subject position of the defeated male that must be the focus in order to reveal the moral position embodied in the films. The demand placed upon the feminist reader is a moral demand, one that positions her both outside and inside the text. She does not participate in negotiating power relations, but rather is part of an overall textual process that reveals the hidden negation of any hegemonic power, either of the past or of the present.

This book is divided into two parts. The first deals with post-traumatic New German Cinema after World II and the second with American post-traumatic cinema after the Vietnam War. Part I describes three models that characterize post-traumatic masculinity in NGC – Infantile Asexual, Utopian Bisexual, and Transsexual. Part II describes three models that characterize post-traumatic masculinity in American Vietnam War cinema – Asexual Hyper-Masculine, Homoerotic, and Impotent. The Epilogue restates the shared criteria of defeated masculinity in the two corpora and the characteristics of post-traumatic cinema.

---

27 See Brown.

PART I

POST-TRAUMATIC NEW GERMAN CINEMA AFTER WORLD WAR II

CHAPTER 1

Identity, Identification, and Sexuality

I. Three Complexes: Continuity, Authenticity, and Masculinity

A number of historical-cultural events accompanied the rise of the New German Cinema from the early 1970s and formed its identity as national cinema: the Hitler Wave (Friedlander)[1] of retro films that also characterized contemporary international cinema (Joseph Losey's *The Damned* [1963], Liliana Cavani's *The Night Porter* [1974], François Truffaut's *The Last Metro* [1980], among others); the events of the German Autumn of 1977;[2] the collective production of *Germany in Autumn* (1977);[3] the broadcast of the American mini-series *The Holocaust* in 1979 which became a media event;[4] and the Meidanek trial (1975-1981). All this culminated with the death of Fassbinder in 1982.[5]

It is widely recognized that in the late 1970s, that is, nearly thirty years after World War II, a number of NGC films first became popular among international audiences and only later in Germany. They included Hans-Jürgen Syberberg's *Our Hitler* (1975), Reiner Werner Fassbinder's *The Marriage of Maria Braun* (1978), Helma Sanders-Brahms' *Germany, Pale Mother* (1980), Volker Schlöndorff's *The Tin Drum* (1979), and Alexander Kluge's *The Patriot* (1979). This is when

---

1 The profits from German memorabilia rose to $50 million a year (Rosenfeld 100, 102 note 12).

2 The kidnapping of German industrialist Hanns Martin Schleyer, the hijacking of a Lufthansa airplane, the death of Baader-Meinhof members in prison, the murder of the Attorney-General, internment of persons suspected of having ties with the Red Army faction.

3 Created by eleven directors, including Fassbinder, Kluge and Schlöndorff as a reaction to the events of the German Autumn and to the hysteria, fear, and despair felt in German society.

4 On the TV series as a media event, see Kaes (*Hitler to Heimat* 27-33).

5 Elsaesser established Fassbinder's death as the end of NGC (*New German Cinema: A History* 310-311). See also his book on Fassbinder (*Fassbinde's German* 238) as well as the citation of the broad support for this conception ten years after Fassbinder's death (381 note 6).

the NGC triumvirate – R.W. Fassbinder, Werner Herzog, and Wim Wenders – was at its height.

Public debate about history and the shape of memory continued throughout the 1980s: the West German parliament debated extending the statute of limitations for Nazi crimes; in May 1985 President Ronald Reagan visited the military cemetery in Bitburg; on May 8, 1985, Richard von Weizsacker addressed the Bundestag to mark the fortieth anniversary of VE Day; the popular television series *The War War of the Bombers* was aired in 1985; the Historians' Debate took place in 1986-7 (see, for example, Evans), and the fall of the Berlin Wall in 1989 prompted discussion about unification (by such authors as Ludtke; Wege; Geyer, and others).

In this context, NGC of the mid-1980s can be characterized, in my view, as undergoing a process of antinomy: participation in public discourse that eventually can be understood, essentially, as distancing itself from this same discourse. On the one hand, NGC created monolithic-nationalistic productions (primarily for television), such as Edgar Reitz's *Heimat* (1984), or "national" oriented films such as Wim Wenders' *Wings of Desire* (1987) and Margarethe Von Trotta's *Marianne and Juliane* (1986). On the other hand, from the mid-1980s it lost its uniqueness as a national cinema in terms of the subjects it addressed, and became less a factor in shaping public discourse, as discussed earlier. This is also the case regarding the contributions of the directors who had played a major role in its formation in the 1970s, as well as their shift to international co-productions. Paradigmatic of this process, after Wenders completed *Wings of Desire* in 1987, he went on to become an international director. In my opinion, this film is indicative of the beginning of a process of simultaneous distancing from and involvement with Germany.

Examples of Wenders' distancing from national oriented discourse are films such as *A Notebook on Cities and Clothes* (1989), *Until the End of the World* (1991), *Lisbon Story* (1994), *Buena Vista Social Club* (1999), and *Million Dollar Hotel* (2000) filmed in such disparate places as Japan, Australia, Portugal, Cuba, and the United States respectively. If, as Corrigan claimed in *Displaced Image*, the first two decades of Wenders' creativity were characterized by movement thematically, stylistically, and geographically between the German and American cultures, then his productions from the end of the 1980s until the beginning of 2008 can be characterized by movement between continents and cultures. As such, his protagonist no longer travels on the East-West German border (*Kings of the Road*, 1976) and does not wander the Texas wilderness as part of displacement to the American geo-psychological space (*Paris, Texas*); rather, he is the utopian traveler, a man of the world, and not necessarily a German speaker with a German identity. The return to Berlin, to the German language, to work with Peter Handke as scriptwriter, and to the Expressionist style in *Wings of Desire* are indicative, as claimed above, of the turning point before the distancing, despite his making *Faraway, So Close* in 1993 as a sequel to *Wings of Desire*

Elsaesser claimed in his monumental monograph *New German Cinema: A History* that three problems defined the identity of NGC as a national cinema in its growth years: "[...] the question of continuity of German history, [...] the family as a problem of personal identity and patriarchal authority, and [...] legitimacy" (214). Does it suffice to characterize NGC as national cinema from the mid-1970s through the mid-1980s (before it distanced itself from public debates on the past) in terms of both the continuity complex and the authenticity complex?

Analysis of gender and sexuality is entirely absent in the perspectives of all influential NGC researchers, including Elsaesser, Corrigan, Kaes, Koch, McCormick, Rentschler and Santner.[6] Indeed, no such research to date has created concepts for examining the relationships between the German past and the present from the perspective of gender and sexuality. Here I am not referring to examination of the relationships between the genders during and after the war, but rather to an ideological examination of construction of masculinity in these films.[7] While research dealing with descriptions of the post-war family was carried out, it did not go beyond citing characterizations such as "the missing father," or, in the films of Fassbinder, for example, a "structure of lovers instead of husbands," to a full discussion of gender and its symbolic meanings.

How could the avoidance of discussion of gender in research of NGC, especially in a culture in which masculinity played such a problematic and disastrous role in its Nazi past be explained? Does the research bare traces of the cultural repression of its objects? For example, a careful examination of McCormick's *Politics of the Self* reveals that his writings about post-modernism in the German context ignore,

---

6 The gender perspective was adopted principally when discussing female directors, for example, in relation to the representation of women. Of course, I will not be discussing this perspective.

7 This examination is made, for example, by Huston and by von Saldern. In this work I analyze only films made by male directors. In 1989, nineteen female directors were involved in NGC, more than any other film industry in the world (Knight). My examination of the male portrayals created by these female directors did not find any significant differences from those directed by males.

nearly completely, discussion of World War II and the Holocaust. Although the author compares literature and cinema from 1968 to 1990 as part of what he describes as the "failure of the separation of the 'personal' from the 'political,'" he does not associate this failure with the trauma of the past. In McCormick's view, the films that depicted this separation – that is, a significant number of those produced in the 1970s – should be understood as postmodern reactions or criticisms of the roles that modernism and the avant-garde played in the arts and in politics of the twentieth century. In my view, this introduced bifurcation into discourse about repression as the sole alternative to preserving repression. The distinction he makes between the "politicized 1960s" and the "subjective 1970s" appears to be missing the point. This type of analysis explicitly takes upon itself the traces of repression that are within the objects of the analysis. McCormick's analysis completely ignores the subversion of these traces revealed in the films' subtext.

There are several reasons why NGC research has avoided discussing gender and sexuality: First of all, it has been influenced by socio-psychological repression of the trauma of defeat; secondly, the hegemony of the Mitscherlichian paradigm (described later) blocked the investigation of other topics. Thirdly, it avoided proposing conclusions regarding this large corpus of films because it presumed that each and every auteur of art films (as opposed to commercial films) was unique; and fourthly, it feared imposing an inclusive theoretical construct as a kind of "master narrative" of gender. Similarly, the research shared preconceptions regarding the unique conditions that led to the growth of NGC, which never saw itself as an ideological movement as opposed to other "new waves," and even considered the government subsidies shared by the directors their most salient common ground.

I claim that because of the relative isolation of each auteur in his world of art and their textual differences *vis-à-vis* genre, style, dramatics, and thematics, while as a group they are unaware of the unities they created, there is significance in the repetitive presence of the post-traumatic subject in their works. Moreover, despite the significant differences between their literary sources, their films are very similar in terms of the formation of masculinity and its subversiveness. The scope of this study, however, does not allow for examination of literary sources and their adaptation to film and in the following I relate to each film as the personal vision of its director.

Not only is gender a prominent component of the continuity complex, but it is actually a link in the chain between two other complexes – historical continuity, which means in this context unrelenting subversion of fascist-Nazi masculinity; and authenticity, the questioning of the renewed legitimacy of German culture. NGC is "legitimate German culture" principally because of this questioning\subversion; *inter alia*, the famous question Werner Herzog posed to Lotte Eisner in 1975 at the conclusion of his Munich to Paris pseudo-pilgrimage. Ironically, it was the film that Herzog carried with him when he "Walked on Ice" (following the literal and metaphorical meaning of the title of his diary of the journey), *Every Man for Himself and God Against All, or the Mystery of Kaspar Hauser* (1974), that caused Kaspar, the abandoned child, to become the key character of NGC. In my opinion, however, we are not speaking here of cinema written as a family melodrama whose central character is the abandoned child, but rather – and principally – the abandoned child as symbol of negation of socialization processes (principally sexual) as a counterbalance to the Nazi past, as I will elucidate below.

While describing the unique narratives characteristic of NGC – the individual with problematic relations with authority, and therefore a desire to revolt that ends in surrender or sacrifice; the protagonist "torn between homesickness and the longing for faraway places"; the utopia that comes with the return to "a childhood not yet lived"; and the choices that span from murder to suicide (Elsaesser, *A History* 216-217) – NGC research does not project on the entire corpus an understanding that these are male narratives that include an endless, always present, confrontation between Nazi and post-war masculinities. In my opinion, this masculinity complex is inherent in the definition of Germanness in NGC of the 1970s, as I will later prove.

II. Mourning Work, Undermining Melancholy

Adorno's question in "What is German?" – "What does coming to terms with the past mean?" (*Aufarbeitung*)[8] – is an inseparable part of research addressing the paradigm offered by Alexander and Margarete Mitscherlich. In their extremely influential 1967 book *The Inability to Mourn*, the Mitscherlichs described the collective outcome of this inability, which in their opinion was characteristic of post-war German

[8] In the introduction to the essay by Adorno, Hartman notes Adorno's reference to Kant and explores the psychoanalytic and political connotations of the German concept, including the materialistic metaphor: "Adorno uses '*Aufarbeitung*' to evoke (1) the personal and painful character of the consciousness that must emerge from Germany's 'Zero Hour'; (2) the psychoanalytic effort to confront and 'work through' the memory of offense and catastrophe; (3) the convergence, however distantly, of '*Aufarbeitung'* and '*Aufklarung*' (enlightenment, clarification); (4) a critique of the parallel notion of 'mastering the past' (*Vergangenheeitsbewaltigung*), which is tainted, verbally at least, by the idea of some ultimate repression" (*Bitburg* 115).

society. Because of "the way of German loving,"[9] and principally because of narcissistic identification with the Führer as an ideal-ego, the Germans found themselves after his death and after revelations of his monstrosity in danger of mass decline into depression and melancholy: his failure was a failure of their ego.

Abstention from psychological reaction to the downfall, from direct confrontation with the Holocaust, and from the loss of Hitler as Führer, that is, the de-realization of the past, as well as substitution of narcissistic identification with Hitler with identification with the Allies and adoption of the position of victimhood, were in the Mitscherlichs' view defense mechanisms against the threat of impoverishment and de-evaluation and against "guilt, despair and anxiety" (23). The outcome was political, social, and national stagnation that was also expressed in the economic miracle (and according to Santner, in the Historians' Debate). As is well known, the Mitscherlichs claimed that German society was ideologically and emotionally paralyzed by its inability to mourn and it is consequently clear that de-Nazification was forced upon it from the outside.

In his 1959 speech mentioned above, Adorno's concept was more extreme than that of the Mitscherlichs, since in his opinion there was no danger of German society falling into melancholy *en masse* because Germany had never abandoned its identifications with the old order. Following Margarete Mitscherlich's work, Santner claimed in *Stranded Objects* that the generation of the sons is characterized by blocked mourning; by its inheritance of the denial of guilt and the loss of opportunities to mourn; by fixation on parents; by existential feelings of incompleteness; and unrealistic, absolute yearning for security and intimacy.[10] The result was that for the second generation the depressive stance was one of the sole strategies for emotional survival.

The majority of NGC directors clearly belong to the second generation[11] and it is therefore no wonder that their films were studied in relation to the Mitscherlichs' paradigm. NGC researchers claimed

---

9 According to the Mitscherlichs, the special German characteristic of "uncompromising love of the unobtainable such that the unobtainable is lost" is a repetitive component of German history since the days of Roman Empire (6).

10 In *Stranded Objects*, Santner claims that the parents "were not" there, as all their mental energies were channeled towards forgetting and repressing, or they "were" there only to demand that the sons serve – by way of identification – as a corrective mirror of themselves (31-56).

11 Among the triumvirate, Fassbinder and Wenders were born in 1945 and Herzog in 1942. Kluge was born in 1932, Schlöndorff in 1939, Sanders-Brahms in 1940, and Von Trotta in 1942, to mention but a few of the prominent directors.

without reservation that the corpus is characterized by denial of the Nazi past and the Holocaust, and by the Germans' adoption of a position of victimhood. Consequently, the question should be in what ways did NGC directors – as the second generation – see themselves as "new" cinema and how were these characteristics (second generation and "new") expressed in their films?

In 1977, Wim Wenders wrote an essay about Joachim Fest and Christian Herrendoerfer's reactionary film *Hitler, A Career* (1977) entitled "That's Entertainment: Hitler:"

> And I speak for everyone who [...] after a long barren period, has started producing sounds and images again, in a country that has a profound mistrust of sounds and images about itself, that has therefore, over the last thirty years, greedily swallowed up all the foreign images it could, as long as they distracted it from itself [...] We, the directors of the New Cinema, have felt this lost most keenly: in ourselves as the absence of a tradition of our own, as a generation without fathers; and in our audiences as confusion [...] There are good reasons for this distrust, for never before and in no other country have images and language been treated with such a complete lack of conscience as here; never before and in no other place have they been so degraded to impart nothing but lies. (94-95).

Indeed, NGC developed against the background of rejection of the Nazi film tradition; as a continuation of Young German Cinema and the Oberhausen Manifesto of 1962 that emblazed on its flag a new aesthetic and political beginning; in opposition to the model of cinema as entertainment derived from the Allies' control of the local industry; and against the Heimat genre, which together with war films were the dominant genres of the 1950s.

A decade after Wenders' essay, Kaes wrote, "An uncompromising rejection of the National Socialist film tradition has in fact become the secret unifying force of the New German Cinema since the 1960s" (*Hitler to Heimat* 8). What is the meaning of rejecting Nazism, beyond Wenders' famous declaration and the collective opposition of the Manifesto to Nazi cinema, past genres, and *papas kino*?[12] What textual strategies did the second generation have to adapt in order to integrate

12 Though television series' are not the focus of this research, it is impossible not to relate to *Heimat*. The director, Edgar Reitz (born in 1932), among the signatories of the Oberhausen Manifesto, said after the showing of *Holocaust* in 1979, that the writing of Germany's history should be restored to German directors (Santner, *Stranded Objects* 75; Hansen 11). In my opinion, *Heimat* is not grounded in the "double bind of rehabilitation and mourning work" described by Hansen and others. Rather, in spite of the Reitz's declarations, he seems to act in accordance with the conventions of Nazi films and applies a variety of strategies of denial and nostalgic narcissism. See Chapter 1.

the rejection of Nazi cinematic tradition in (unconscious) preservation of the burden of the mental structures of the first generation? Here, in describing the complexities of the task of reconstruction of the post-conventional German identity in cinematic texts, Santner asks, "How [...] does one avoid the maddening binary opposition: schizophrenic dissolution of identity/narcissistic respecularization of identity?" (*Stranded Objects* 151). Although his research avoids presenting any unequivocal evaluative statements in regard to the involvement of NGC in mourning work, what can be learned from his analysis is that NGC neither confronts this binarism nor establishes a post-conventional Habermasian self.

I argue that as a corpus, NGC allows for more than reflection via the Mitscherlichs' prism of the first and/or second generation or via the Santnerian textual-ideological challenge. The opposition posed by Santner does not seem to me to be binary – these are not two extremes exclusive of one another, just as we are not speaking of a dialectic. NGC films are "new" in the sense that they describe the destroyed/absent/disintegrated/marginal-in-the-social-order self as part of the opposition to the omnipotence of Nazi masculinity. In my opinion, the deeply melancholic, specular-narcissistic self always exists in a context that undermines this melancholy. NGC does not destroy the context of the melancholy, but constructs it in such a way as to create for the spectator a strong, uncomfortable feeling that accompanies the viewing process (e.g., the house exploding at the end of Fassbinder's *Maria Braun*; Travis's [Harry Dean Stanton] return to the desert after he reabandons his son at the end of Wenders' *Paris, Texas*; or the hen's obsessive repetition of the dance in the amusement park at the end of Herzog's *Stroszek* [1977], a reverberation of the empty cyclical movement and suicide of the protagonist). These three endings conclude a complex process of identification that is part of a melancholic mode of viewing with a different tone. The melancholy is neither desired nor longed for; just the opposite; and presenting it as the context for the schizophrenic or specular self (if we apply Santner's terms) does not construct it as the sole viewing mode. Integration of identification and alienation structures, characteristic of NGC, all the more clearly sharpen the role played by marginal-specular masculinity in these post-traumatic films, as I will describe below.

As I hinted at above, in spite of its significant contribution to the understanding of psychocultural processes in post-war Germany, the Mitscherlichs' paradigm prevented later research from raising additional issues, whose legitimacy was discounted. In addition, it negated scholars who diverted from what was considered essential: discussion of the dilemma of "mourning work or melancholy." The research searches for traces of denial, describes elegiac structures, and discusses victimhood. Accordingly, no NGC scholars have considered the possibility of additional reflection within, but beyond this paradigm.

I claim that gender representations in this corpus serve as a very special type of counter-narrative: on the one hand is the absence of representation of the Nazi past, World War II, and the Holocaust, while on the other, is the presentation of a prominent male alternative to the fascist-Nazi model.

The uniqueness of this counter-narrative is embedded in presenting an alternative that does not involve either direct mention of the fascist-Nazi masculine model or presentation of the trauma of the Nazi past, including the defeat; moreover, it does not include a construction of an alternative type of masculinity with a specific substance rather than one whose entire authenticity is derived from rejection of familiar Nazi masculinity.

At the explicit level, NGC texts undermine, as noted, the melancholy mode prevalent in them, while at the same time, at the subtext, they present clear subversive attitudes toward the past. The post-textual outcome is not a clash between the dominant and repressed tales, which the reader realizes through the very act of reading, but rather is a clear statement about the past on all textual levels. That is to say, this is not a case of interpreting the subtext according to the logic of oppositional reading (à la Stuart Hall). Rather, there are tensions in the film texts between the melancholy mode and masculinity's attempt to establish another, even utopian, mode; and tensions between spectacular narcissism and subversion of it.

III. Gender and Excesses of the Past

Up to now, presentations of the Nazi past in NGC research have only been discussed within the paradigms of mourning work, oedipalization, and displacement,[13] though the latter, after all, is a corollary of the mourning work paradigm. In addition, to the best of my knowledge, trauma as a paradigm has not been discussed in research beyond the level of the specific film;[14] for example, in discussions of the trauma of survival on the home front shared by the mother and the daughter in Sanders-Brahms's *Germany, Pale Mother*; membership in Baader-

13 E.g., by Santner in *Stranded Objects*; Elsaesser in *A History* and "Historical Imaginary; Kaes in *Hitler to Heimat*; McCormick in *Politics of the Self*; and Linville in *Feminism, Film.*

14 By Kaplan in "Mother/Land"; Kaes in "Presence of the Past"; Kosta in *Recasting Autobiography*; Keene in "Mothering Daughters"; and Linville in *Feminism, Film.*

Meinhof that ends with death in prison in *Marianne and Juliane*,[15] or of the anxious atmosphere of the 1970s following the arrest of members of Baader-Meinhof as presented in Fassbinder's episode in *Germany in Autumn* (1977).[16]

The collective trauma of the Nazi defeat itself is not portrayed directly in the principal films of the leading NGC directors. NGC did not create war films[17] and the war/defeat is mentioned elliptically, partially, and marginally in only a few of the films. For example, Fassbinder used audio and visual images from the battlefield in *Lili Marleen* (1981); identified the protagonist, Hans Epp, as a veteran of the French Foreign Legion in the opening scene of *The Merchant of Four Seasons* (1972); showed scenes of bombings, rebuilding, and American soldiers in *Maria Braun*; and included two veterans (Hermann [Klaus Löwitsch] and Willi [Gottfried John]) in that movie and Nazi soldiers in *Despair* (1978). Alexander Kluge used the knee of the dead private as a metaphor in *The Patriot*. Werner Herzog had German soldiers serving on the Greek island near the end of the war in *Signs of Life* (1968) and the allegory of the defeat of Aguirre (Klaus Kinski) in *Aguirre, Wrath of God* (1972). Wenders introduces a former Nazi and has him sing the "Jew Rosenthal Song" and mention the murder of a Jew in *Wrong Movement* (1974); shows a souvenir candle shaped like a bust of Hitler at the amusement park in *Kings of the Road*; and war footage of Berlin being destroyed and scenes of divided Berlin in *Wings of Desire*. H. Sanders-Brahms shows images of explosions, Berlin's destruction, the rape of the mother by Allied soldiers, and the return of the father, a Nazi soldier, at the end of the war in *Germany, Pale Mother*.

Is the extreme marginality of the defeat in NGC narratives enough to refrain from questioning the representation of the trauma? Yet, in spite

---

15 By Kaplan in "Discourse"; Seiter; and Linville in "Retrieving History."

16 By Corrigan in *Displaced Image* and Elsaesser in "Subject Positions."

17 To the best of my knowledge, *Das Boot*, Wolfgang Petersen's 1981 blockbuster, is among the few war films produced at that time. Aside from the chronological placement of the plot at the end of the war, the film ignores totally the context of the Holocaust and the defeat. The plot describes the life of sailors in a submarine as they attempt to survive natural disasters and a British destroyer. The opening speech of Lt. Thompson is symptomatic of the discourse of this type of text, which belongs clearly to the revisionist films (and also includes episodes from the Nazi documentary *Baptism of Fire* [1943]): "[O]nly in a magnificent democracy such as ours could a simple person become a genius of the greatest army of all times [...] How would we win the war without his genius? [...] to the Führer who showed the old, stupid, British bulldog, Winston Churchill, where exactly to shove his cigar" (quote from the film). The sinking of the submarine at the end of the journey is not presented, therefore, as part of the historic defeat, but rather as a dramatic event that invites the viewer to another emotional climax.

of the centrality allocated to discussion of representation of history and German identity, leading studies written from the 1970s to the 2000s did not discuss or devote even a single chapter to the lack of representation of the collective trauma of the Nazi defeat.[18]

This absence of representation is not part of the endless discussion about the historical return of the repressed. Even in *Stranded Objects*, Santner, whose research focused prominently on the problematic complexity of the discourse relating to mourning work and memory, did not devote space to this extreme absence (*Beruhrungsangst*)[19] or to the clarification that I believe is required: Do NGC films that directly ignore the trauma of the defeat of Nazism deal with it, after all, indirectly in a meaningful manner? That is, can we find an expression that by its nature does not require "finding traces," but rather the opposite?

The assertion that NGC is characterized by denial of the Nazi past and the Holocaust and by adoption of victimhood (although never associated with moral judgment regarding the collaboration of NGC in these socio-cultural processes)[20] is such a research cliché that it appears there is nothing to be added. But is this, indeed, the case?

Even if they strove to reach conclusions in regard to the entire corpus, these scholars principally focused on describing traces of denial and repression via analysis of a few films that expressed some form of representation of the past; for example, identifying elegiac procedures, Holocaust denial, and the absence of Jewish characters in Edgar Reitz's *Heimat* (Santner, *Stranded Objects*), or the analysis of Nazism as a cinematic spectacle in Fassbinder's *Lili Marleen* (Elsaesser, "Subject Positions").

---

18 Including those by Franklin; Sandford; Santner, *Stranded Objects*; Corrigan, *Displaced Image*; Rentschler, *West German Film*; Klaus, 1984; Elsaesser, *A History*; Kaes, *Hitler to Heimat*; McCormick, *Politics of the Self*; and Linville, *Feminism, Film*.

19 Fear of touching on the sensitive topic in Germany history.

20 As intimated above, a very good example of this is Santner's stance in his book both toward Syberberg's *Hitler – A Film from Germany* (1977) and Reitz's *Heimat*. In spite of his criticism of their works as "elegiac narcissism" (*Stranded Objects*, 149-157), he cites their contribution to creation of an "elegiac space" (150-152). Although he selected Christa Wolf's *Kindheitsmuste* as an example of a successful expression of the "Benjaminian mode of anamnesis and mourning," he does not emphasize that it was a radical replacement of forms of mourning work in comparison with the films of Syberberg and Reitz (156). I believe that he refrained from making a strong statement in regard to the degree of collaboration of these films in denial processes regarding the Nazi past just as did other researchers. See Kaes (*Hitler to Heimat*, and "History and Film") for an example of a similar research method.

Though few films in the corpus address the past, Nazis crimes, or the war/the defeat (and even then, the exceptions prove the rule), it is my view that there is merit in discussing the entire corpus; that is, to reflect upon it, as I will describe below, within the accepted paradigm, but not according to it. In fact, the extreme rarity of representations of the past points to the need for an examination of this rarity. As intimated above, it is not my intention to engage in additional research regarding traces of denial-repression-victimization-lack of mourning work-melancholy in films that describe the German family as a victim of the war (H. Sanders-Brahms' *Germany, Pale Mother*), describe the rise of Nazism (Schlöndorff's *The Tin Drum* or Fassbinder's *Despair*), or examine in this light the allegory of a crazed leader (Herzog's *Aguirre* or even his *Fitzcarraldo* [1982]). It is not my intention to continue on the path of "finding traces," as fascinating and important as that may be, but rather to propose an alternative. By examining the entire corpus, and not a few selected films that present the past, I conclude that NGC was involved in an endless confrontation with Nazism and the war: its representations of masculinity are the primary expression of NGC's opposition to the past, and are a counter-weight to the rare representation of the historical past itself.

I claim that the representations of masculinity – unstable, marginal to the social order, with asexuality or perverted sexuality and dysfunctional couplehood – serve as a counter balance to structures of denial-repression-victimhood. As a psychocultural representation that subverts the *Alltagsgeschichte*,[21] by negation of the symbolic foundations of everyday life, this construction of post-war German masculinity is a response to the absence of historical representation of the past.

The material that has been repressed from the German narrative is not displaced, as in the genre of melodrama, for example, to the *mise-en-scène*, but rather to gender. That is, this displacement is directed to the masculinity of the characters, and not to the general domain of their acts and actions. In an almost allegorical sense, the male body and its sexuality (with its values, attitudes, and sexual orientation) is the conflictual center of the German narrative in relation to its past. The German narrative of NGC is not able to integrate the weight of the past within it and is not able to contain it. As an elastic discursive category, gender enables such inclusion. The importance of structuring gender as an elastic category in these post-traumatic films is derived from the symbolic connection heteronormativity has with the patriarchal. Since such a connection was of course meaningful to the extreme in the Nazi

21 Everyday history.

world, its subversion, as I will describe later, is among the most important manifestations of the representation of the past in NGC, a representation that enables the trauma of the defeat to be present.

IV. Mutant Sexuality

Judith Butler's claims in *Gender Trouble* as well as in *Bodies That Matter* that compulsory heterosexuality is an hegemonic, cultural construction could be supported all the more strongly by contextualization, especially historical. In his book *Nationalism and Sexuality*, George L. Mosse studied modern nationalist influence on respectability (behaviors, manners, morality, and sexual attitudes) in modern Europe in general and Germany in particular. His primary thesis is that nationalism imposed respectability from above, while the family was the agency of sexual control from below. As a result,

> […] respectability, taken for granted, now became vital for the very existence of bourgeoisie society; […] it provided an important cohesion for the existing order […] It was part of the appeal of nationalism, and subsequently of racism and fascism, that they promised to support respectability against the chaos of the modern age. (180).

Respectability that emphasized heterosexuality adopted a stereotype of beauty "without desire" for women and men, sublimation of sensuality toward leaders and the nation, manliness as transcendent of baser desires, and provided, according to Mosse, the mechanism that imposed control and promised defense. The covenant between nationalism and racism reached its height as one between nationalism, respectability, and racism. Since Nazi Germany undertook the ultimate efforts to shape and control human sexuality, as Mosse claimed, the attempt to cinematically subvert the covenant between heteronormativity/respectability and nationalism is clearly important.

NGC responded strongly to this covenant. This was not just the case in the oeuvre of Fassbinder, known for its sexual excess that by definition undermined Nazi respectability[22] and subverted the direct relation between racism and sexuality. Rather, NGC subverted this covenant in oeuvres of directors whose sexual persona was not as overtly involved in the conception of sexuality portrayed in their films (e.g., Wenders, Herzog, Schlöndorff, and Kluge).

NGC as post-traumatic cinema subverts respectability in its bourgeoisie-conservative version (as described by Mosse), not only as a

[22] That is, undermined all that was defined, according to Mosse, as "decent and correct."

counter-weight to the covenant struck in the past with nationalism and Nazism, but also – and principally – as a result of the failure to realize promises of social cohesion, control, defense, realization of the ideal of masculinity, and national continuity. In opposition to the nationalistic-racist version of respectability, NGC presents what I term mutant sexuality, that is, negated and\or perverted sexuality that shatters all possibilities for past covenants, a result of fracturing identification with the Hitlerian imago.

In the following section entitled "The Hitlerian Imago" I will discuss at length the concept of mutant sexuality in order to define through it the nature of the primary symbolic construction of NGC: sexuality whose representation concurrently reveals its deconstruction. This unique representation establishes a spectrum with infantile asexual masculinity at one extreme, as portrayed by the abandoned child (most prominently represented by Werner Herzog's Kaspar Hauser (Bruno S.) in *Every Man for Himself and God Against All, or the Mystery of Kaspar Hauser* and Volker Schlöndorff's Oskar (David Bennent) in *The Tin Drum* and their "mirroring" adults.[23] At the other extreme is transsexual masculinity following a sex change that represents a Fassbinerian range of options for deconstruction, and whose key figure is Erwin/Elvira (Volker Spengler) in *In a Year of Thirteen Moons* (1978). While proposing and analyzing three models of post-traumatic German masculinity, I will claim that the male body in NGC bears the burden of the historical past: the body remembers.

V. Three Models: Infantile Asexual, Utopian Bisexual, Transsexual

A. Characteristics of Post-Traumatic Masculinity

The male protagonists in the post-traumatic films affiliated with these three models of masculinity live on the margins of the social, familial, and sexual orders. The films depict no change in their marginality and in fact do not usually describe the social order itself as primary. When it is described, heteronormativity, the bourgeoisie, and the

[23] For example, Wenders' Bruno (Rüdiger Vogler) and Robert in *Kings of the Road*, Zimmerman (Bruno Ganz) in *The American Friend* (1977), Philip (Rüdiger Vogler) in *Alice in the Cities* (1974), and Herzog's Woyzeck (Klaus Kinski) and Stroszek (Bruno S.) in films whose titles are their names (1979; 1977), and Stroszek (Peter Brogle) in *Signs of Life*. See elaboration on this concept in Chapter 2.

patriarchal are represented in an extremely ironic context.[24] The marginality of the male in relation to the symbolic order is also connected to the absence of the Name of the Father, which is revealed both in the absence of fathers in the narratives[25] and in the multiplicity of fathers.[26]

Similarly, the films almost never proffer the option of a future construction of non-marginal masculinity. At the most, it is hinted at in a note found fluttering in the wind. In *Kings of the Road*, for example, after a bitter confrontation, the two protagonists finally admit to the absence of women in their lives. After Bruno has left, Robert finds his note declaring that everything must be different from now on. Their joint odyssey did not bring them to the Woman; however, their separation signifies that perhaps there is still hope. In the oeuvre of other directors, even more extremely, the body that remembers leads the protagonist to his death (usually actual death, but occasionally a symbolic one). For example, in *Stroszek*, Stroszek's suicide in the Native American park reproduces both the trauma of his life in Berlin and the broken promise of couplehood symbolized by his endless cable ride up and down the mountain; in *Paris, Texas*, Travis's body leads him back to the desert; and, as I will discuss later, at the end of *Kaspar Hauser*, Kaspar's body is shaped as a body that remembers after his death.[27]

---

24 As in Fassbinder's *Why Does Herr R. Run Amok?* (1970), *Martha* (1974), *Lola* (1981), *The Merchant of Four Seasons*, *Despair*, and *Chinese Roulette* (1976); *Woyzeck and Stroszek.*

25 For example, Robert's father in *Kings of the Road*; Alice's in *Alice*; Maria's in *Maria Braun*; the father who commits suicide in Fassbinder's *Mother Kuster's Trip to Heaven* (1975); the murdered father in his *Jail Bait* (1973) or in his *I Only Want You to Love Me* (1976); and its displacement on the Jew Mendelson in *Lili Marleen*.

26 As with Hunter's two fathers of in *Paris, Texas*, Oskar's two fathers in *The Tin Drum* Renate's two fathers in *The Merchant of Four Seasons* or even Angela's two fathers in *Chinese Roulette*.

27 Similarly, Stroszek goes crazy in *Signs of Life* at the sight of the valley filled with thousands of windmills, an image full of movement and life that stands in total opposition to what his body remembers – the monotony of being imprisoned in a military fort; Zimmerman's sick body in *The American Friend* leads him to his death; Bloch (Arthur Brauss) vomits repeatedly in Wenders' *The Goalkeeper's Anxiety of the Penalty Kick* (1972).

In my opinion, NGC is unique, especially in light of the "remasculinization" process characterizing films made in the 1950s, as described by Fehrenbach ("Rehabilitating"), Jeffords "Remasculinization of Germany," Moeller ("Remasculinization," "Last Soldiers"), and Poiger. These scholars analyzed the moral rehabilitation of German masculinity as a major part of this process. The difference in comparison to NGC narratives is clear. Whether we accept or reject the validity of their "remasculinization" (it seems incomplete because the German soldier is absent in these films), emphasizing the integration of the male/father into couplehood and the family ap-

Bodies lacking sexual socialization (Infantile Asexual), isolated from heterosexual couplehood (Utopian Bisexual), and unwilling to accept a clear sexual identity (Transsexual) need to create for themselves a possible history in order to be part of the social body. Instead, the films present the impossibility of hegemonization of the body in this manner: Kaspar, Oskar, Stroszek, Bruno, Robert, Elvira and all the others who carry the burden of their bodies/sexuality-ies are cut off from the social body without any option for change.

For example, during the autopsy at the end of *Every Man for Himself and God Against All, or the Mystery of Kaspar Hauser* Kaspar's feet are exposed beyond his covered body and look exactly as they did before he met the townspeople; i.e., before socialization – infected, neglected, the soles of someone who walked barefoot his entire life. The abjected status of his body is part of his asexuality that remained unchanged despite his development in other domains of socialization that enabled him to create for himself a temporary bodily history (like eating and dressing). This bodily history did not at any stage include sexuality. The extreme bodily abjectification in the final scene – including the removal of the brain – projects retroactively, of course, upon the very same temporary bodily history and obliterates it entirely. This process happens, in my view, to each and every male NGC character.

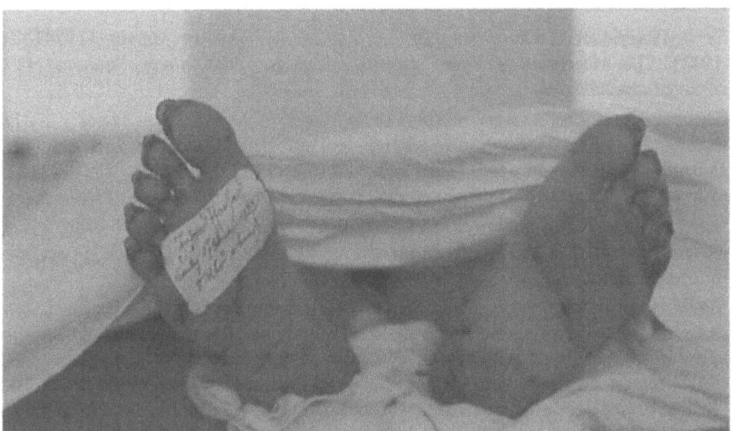

The remembering body, *The Mystery of Kaspar Hauser*

---

pears to pave the way for the extreme demasculinization in NGC films as belated acknowledgment in the 1970s, possible only after an additional 20 years.

Thus, to provide another example, in Fassbinder's *In a Year of Thirteen Moons*, Elvira is aware of the irreversibility of bodily history that she created for herself through the sex change operation, an irreversibility of significant meaning in terms of understanding the relation between the past and the present. It leaves her simultaneously a man and a woman, and a non-man and a non-woman. She is also with and without a past and has no attachment to the social body; this abjected historical situation leads her to death.

In Wenders' *American Friend*, symbolic mortality is imposed on Zimmerman and as the plot of the Highsmith-Wenders mystery develops, his bodily history changes and is rewritten: first as a sick person with a fatal blood disease that is never fully revealed; later as the man he murdered on the train (after he symbolically assumes his identity by giving the dead man's ticket to the collector); and finally, as a man dying in an ambiguous manner. Though it is uncertain if it was imposed upon him or his choice, Zimmerman moves between being an "inventor" of his terminal bodily history and adopter of the bodily history of the dead. Both are symbolic acts that prove beyond a doubt his separation from his own body, from his wife and family, and from the symbolic order. As the number of murders he commits rises, his physical condition worsens so that his body leads him to death. In this film, too, there is a failed attempt to stop the process by establishing temporary bodily histories that might have allowed the protagonist to take part in the social order and\or regain couplehood.

As claimed above, all three models of masculinity share the marginality of the male in relation to the social order; the absence of the Name of the Father; subversion of the hegemonization of the social order; the body that remembers, which leads the protagonist to his death; and the impossibility of creating a bodily history that will lead to integration with the social body. Masculinity in all of the models, however, is not active. It is either disconnected from the action or in the end leads itself to such: Hermann Braun in Fassbinder's *Maria Braun*, for example, is sent to prison after confessing to a murder he did not commit (simulation of activity), and the deal he makes with Oswald (Ivan Densy) (an act only mentioned in the film) in the end leads to his death. Woyzeck in Herzog's film of the same name (1978) passively surrenders to abuse by the camp commander and the doctor. The deterioration of his body after the medical experiments he underwent leads him to commit murder. Similarly, Kurt Raab, the Herr R. of Fassbinder's *Why does Herr R. Run Amok?* is characterized by silent and passive reaction to his oppressive and degrading environment, until he murders his wife, son, and a neighbor and then commits suicide at his workplace. Like the other NGC protagonists who commit murders,[28] the act does not change the murderer's place in the world, a fact that leads him, and them, either figuratively or symbolically to their deaths. Lack of activity is inherent in post-traumatic masculinity and although it is sometimes structured as movement on the spectrum from passivity to activity and back (as in the case of Stroszek in *Signs of Life* or Travis in *Paris, Texas*), there is no essential change.

As a result, the males are not presented in any of the models as subjects of the social-bodily order or of the private bodily history to which they are bound in one way or another. Even if the narrative leads them to subjectivization, as it did to Travis in *Paris, Texas*, Stroszek in *Stroszek*, and Fox (Rainer Werner Fassbinder) in Fassbinder's *Fox and His Friends* (1975) as part of salvation through journey and meeting with the other, it is but a temporary state, destined for trouble. The unstable masculine subjectivity seeks to hold on to a world that in advance has denied it the possibility to represent or affiliate with the social order.

The neurotic-psychotic relations the characters maintain with their masculinity traverse the differences between the directors, the genres, and the styles. In NGC as post-traumatic cinema the defeat does not exist (where were they and what did characters like Hermann, Willi, and Hans do in the war?), but the defeated male does. The connection created in the films between marginality and non-representation of the symbolic order and mutant sexuality is the central strategy for disruption of the covenant between nationalism and respectability, as part of negotiation with the past. The protagonists of NGC reject any possible attachment between themselves and the Nazi past, on the one hand, while on the other, manifest the trauma of defeat through the very same strategy – demasculinization/mutant sexuality.

I claim that negation of the fascist-Nazi body and inscription of the trauma of defeat on the male body determine the boundaries of discussion in post-traumatic films. That is, the boundaries of the psychohistorical discussion of the past are not genre-dependent. So far, analysis of the past through films defined as historical was only partial and failed to recognize the unique forms of representation of the past in NGC. Therefore, I propose an analysis of the entire corpus. This implies an emphasis placed on post-trauma framing (and not on the period described by the diegesis) that to a great degree eliminates the importance of temporal

[28] Bloch in *Goalkeeper's Anxiety*, Zimmerman in *American Friend*, Hermann Hermann (Dirk Bogarde) in *Despair* or Ricky (Karl Scheydt) in Fassbinder's *The American Soldier* (1979).

and spatial boundaries depicted in the corpus – Canada, Peru, Australia, Texas, or Paris, to name but a few. The obsessive repetition of the characteristics of post-traumatic masculinity is not dependent on the place or on the period described in these films. Rather, precisely because of the extreme variance between NGC directors in terms of the diegesis, the similarity of how they approach the Nazi past and the defeat – through construction of gender and sexuality – is so prominent.

The central function of representing sexuality as destructive and mutant enables NGC, through its opposition to the past, to engage in the process of mourning work that begins – in all the models – with regressive-melancholic structures and continues through negating them or being rescued.

B. The Hitlerian Imago

Post-traumatic NGC cinema obviously illustrates through presentation of sexuality in the three models of masculinity the way in which primary identification with Hitler is constructed in the oeuvre of the second generation; and, therefore, re-conceptualizes identity constructions at large. Discussion revolving around the Mitscherlichs' paradigm,[29] however, completely ignored the very structures of sexual-gender identity that seem to me essential to understanding the construction of masculinity in NGC, with all its political implications.

What is the meaning of negation of the Nazi body in terms of sexuality? What is the relationship between representations of sexuality and the other characteristics of German masculinity (marginality, passivity, negation of fatherhood, inability to represent the symbolic order, the body that remembers that leads the protagonist to his death)?

According to the Mitscherlichs, "Hitler […] established his 'image' as that of an unmarried man living exclusively for his people, that is, for his children, or his brothers and sisters" (*The Inability to Mourn* 211). But in his 1970 *Society Without the Father* A. Mitscherlich expanded Hitler's psychoanalytic analysis in a new direction:

> The mass leader […] is much more like the imago of a primitive mother-goddess. He acts as if he were superior to conscience, and demands a regressive obedience and the begging behavior that belongs to the behaviour pattern of the child in the pre-Oedipal stage […] The tie to the Führer, in spite of all the protestations of eternal loyalty, never reaches the level, so rich in conflict, where the conscience is formed and ties with it are established [….] Having never experienced firm object ties, the [...] individual

[29] Principally by Santner, *Stranded Object*; Elsaesser, *New German Cinema: A History*, "Historical Imaginary"; and Linville, *Feminism, Film*.

> [...] is governed by pre-Oedipal wishes, external stimuli, without being able to organize these into a memory, in the sense of a consciousness, a self. (283-285).

In this book A. Mitscherlich describes the influence of the mass leader on the personality of the individual as causing loss of morality due to the lack of a super-ego and unwillingness to assume responsibility. He focuses on types of consciousness and cognizance and/or their absence in mass societies, which, in my view, limits his analysis regarding the non-maturation of individuals who were followers of the Führer. That is, he does not develop the full implications of his insights regarding inhibition of primary development and regression in analysis of masculinity, femininity, and sexuality. In the following analysis I will continue where he left off and merge these two seemingly contradictory concepts of Hitler's image offered by the Mitscherlichs and by A. Mitscherlich and what I consider the unavoidable implication of this merging, namely a unique structure of identification with Hitler's image that was shared by the films of the second generation. This structure is the result of Hitler's adherence to the maternal imago and his demand to negate identification with the Father while channeling attraction to the Mother towards the cult of the Father/Big Brother and towards symbols of the Nation, the Race, and the State.

In my opinion, the regressive and mutant structures of sexuality applied by second generation directors to their protagonists are the primary expression of the presence of this structure. NGC presents it in order to deconstruct the processes entailed and subvert the spectator's identification with the Hitlerian imago.

Subversion of this multifaceted identification is realized in the corpus in two ways: first, through attempts by the protagonists to escape from this identification structure by searching for their lost childhood, by moving from silence to language, and by establishing couplehood; second, through display of the tragic consequences of being absorbed by this identification structure. The male who denies Nazi masculinity and the complex identification structure it entails reveals a subject position that is vacuous and despairing. The horrific failure of masculinity reveals the destructive effects of this identification; in other words, displaying melancholy in this context involves undermining it.

The substitutive love object – Hitler as the primitive Mother and the cult of the Father – leads masculinity to self-negation in the most extreme manner. First and foremost, NGC constructs sexually immature masculinity. Second, even when sexuality does appear, as noted, the result is always failure. This can be seen in attempts to break out of infantile asexuality in order to make contact with the woman (*Paris,*

Texas and *Stroszek*); to establish couplehood (*Woyzeck*, *The Merchant of Four Seasons*, *Martha* [Fassbinder, 1973] and *Despair*), or to love homosexually (*Fox*). Failures include breakup of relationships, violence, murder and/or suicide.[30] Third, the outcome is desubjectivization. Even when the camera serves as an extension of subjectivity at the height of the drama, the protagonists of post-traumatic NGC lead themselves to loss, and the result is presentation of a vacuous subject. For example, in *American Friend* the camera follows Zimmerman after the murder as he runs the length of the train until reaching the locomotive where he shouts – cries; in *Chinese Roulette*, the camera circles the husband and wife hugging in the final scene before the murder/suicide; in *Aguirre*, the camera circles the raft filled with bodies and monkeys as the current sweeps it away, while the voice of Aguirre declares his fantasies of conquest. Finally, this vacuous subject position will dominate the films: Zimmerman will die bereft of identity after breaking off relations with his family, wife, and the "friend"; in *Chinese Roulette* Mr. (Alexander Allerson) and Mrs. Christ (Margit Carstensen) will be revealed naked even of pretence at the end of the drama, not only through the *mise-en-scène* but through the sound.[31] The Fassbinderian subversion of conventional closure places the male and female subject positions within marriage as an alternative option that is tragically replaceable and therefore negates subjectivity.

30 For example, in *Paris, Texas*, Travis again parts with his wife and child and returns to the desert; in *Fox*, Fox is robbed of his lottery winnings by his lover and then abandoned by him. At the moment of his death he is robbed again by two boys while his former friend steps over his body and continues to walk by; in *Despair*, Herman, whose wife commits adultery in his presence, offers a homeless man a deal in exchange of identity with the intention of changing his life, but murders his "double"/ himself and is captured by the police.

31 The last shot shows the estate from a distance; shots are heard from within the house without any clarification of who fired and who was shot. Then an ironic-tragic song is heard on the soundtrack: "Are you ready to marry? To be loyal to your partner until death do you part?"

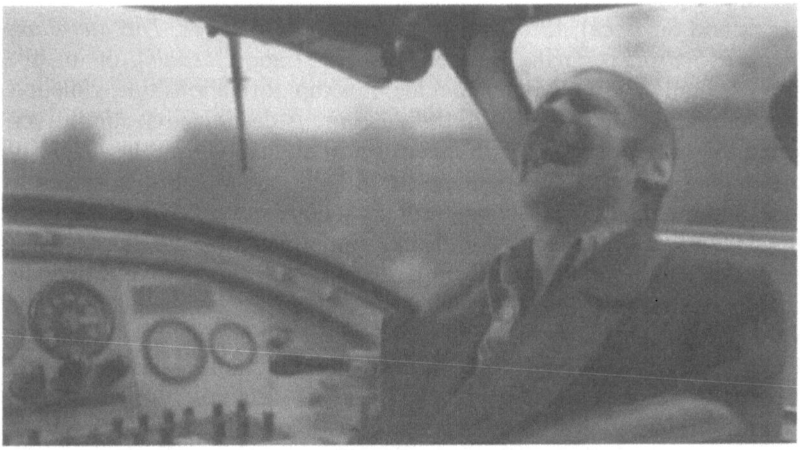

Desubjectivization, Zimmerman in *The American Friend*

The connection that Hitler created between his image as a maternal imago (and not as an ideal father figure) and as "the loyal son of a loving mother" (Elsaesser, *A History* 241) – thus representing the primal love object, one previous to the oedipal – is not only the clearest source of the hold of Nazism on the masses and the structures of their regressive personalities,[32] but also the source of regressive and perverted sexualities.

The sexual regression revealed in post-traumatic NGC is the result of the complexity contained within this image. In contrast to other researchers who related only to representation of the "son" or to the "phallic mother," I suggest that the multifaceted complexity of the Hitlerian image is the key to understanding the sexuality portrayed in NGC. This image includes the phallic mother, "her son" and also the cult mediated Father/Big Brother; that is, the image negates mature sexuality (Hitler is not the Father, but the son), represents primordial sexual attraction to the Mother; and, concurrently, channels this attraction to patriarchal phallic symbols.[33] Pre-oedipal identification is inte-

---

32 Discussed extensively in the research in connection to a "society without the father" and "the inability to mourn."

33 Linville's criticism (*Feminism, Film*) of misogyny and matrophobia in the Mitscherlichs' book is theoretically limited. First, she disregards the complexity of the image; second, she misses taking note of the fact that the Mitscherlichs not only point to "gender transformation" (from male-father to woman mother) in the context of the key-image discussed, but their discussion does not suggest the simultaneous existence of more than one possibility for gender and sexuality. Here I suggest an examination of the complexity of the Hitlerian image as described in their various studies as one construct.

grated – through its displacement to patriarchal symbols – into identification with the Father figure. Yet, this displacement creates a problem in that the potential for phallicization has been negated in advance. The result, in my view, is extremely ambivalent: pre-oedipalization together with phallic symbolization without phallicization. The trope of the son therefore embodies this ambiguity in all its complexity.

Furthermore, this self-negating identification structure is queer in nature: The imago of the Führer as the mother-goddess involves gender transformation; his pretence of being her son involves both gender continuity and gender duality, since he is concurrently the mother and the mother's son. The demand to displace primal attraction to the Mother with phallic paternal symbols (while phallicization, as noted, has been negated in advance) exacerbates the queerness since these symbols are both phallic and paternal. All together this complex structure erupts in the films of the second generation as what I call "mutant sexuality."

The result is not only hidden homosexuality and manic-depressive personality structures (according to the Mitscherlichs), but is primarily movement along a spectrum of sexuality that by definition negates the possibilities of mature and healthy sexuality: on the one extreme of the spectrum is sexual asocialization and fixation of the adult male in infantile asexuality. This is the result of simultaneous attraction to the maternal and paternal figures, including a lack of identity differentiation; midway on the spectrum is utopian bisexuality, relationships between men motivated by a common desire for the maternal aspect of the Woman, realized through an Odyssean journey. At the same midpoint are representations of heterosexual and homosexual couplehood that are not indicative of breaking away from pre-oedipal patterns and development into mature sexuality; rather, their violent disintegration is indicative of the regressive and the immature. At the opposite extreme of the spectrum, mutant sexuality is realized as failed transsexuality; that is, as a (failed) attempt to transcend the blending of the pre-oedipal with the cultic simulacra of phallicization by means of a sex change operation.[34]

C. *Couplehood*

Protagonists in the canonic films of the leading NGC directors are, as noted, characterized by their failure to achieve mature sexuality and the violent disintegration of their interpersonal relations. Relationships with

[34] That is, the merging of pre-oedipalization and simulacric imitation of "father" and "husband" performed by Elvira in *In a Year of Thirteen Moons*. See extended discussion in Chapter 4 below, especially the analysis of the scene in which Elvira, the transsexual, meets his wife and daughter.

women are usually short term and often end in calamity – murder (actual or symbolic) or suicide.[35] There are no hetero-normative models of masculinity in NGC. Rather than being representative of the possibility of mature sexuality, hetero- and homosexual couplehood represent movement on the scale between asexuality and transsexuality. As an inherent part of the crisis of masculinity, the films negate both hetero-sexual and homosexual couplehood.

The (defeated) German male has lost his affiliation to the fundamental structures that imposed heteronormativity: oedipalization, social institutions, the symbolic order, and the social body. Therefore, as part of subtextual opposition to respectability (and nationalism), relatively few post-traumatic films present hetero-normative relationships, and the crises in such relationships are always presented as part of the crisis of the social order. For example, in *Maria Braun*, Hermann and Maria (Hanna Schygulla) are married for less than two nights because of the war and never consummate their marriage after its end; in *Signs of Life*, the collapse of couplehood is the result of the trauma of the war; so too, in *The Merchant of Four Seasons* and *Lili Marleen.* None of the films portray masculinity as sexual; for example, in *Maria Braun*, Bill (Greg Eagles), an American soldier, becomes Maria's lover, followed by Karl Oswald, a character I do not consider representative of German masculinity since he was not in Germany during the war; in *Martha*, the husband's masculinity is presented primarily through vampire-like biting or other grotesque actions; and the asexuality of Alfred Matzerath (Mario Adorf), the husband in *The Tin Drum*, involves emotional abuse.[36]

---

35 For example, in *Why Does Herr R. Run Amok?* Kurt Rabb murders his wife and commits suicide; in *American Soldier*, Ricky murders Rosa; in *Merchant*, Hans, who dreams about the woman who was the "love of his life," hits Irmagard, and commits suicide; in *Martha*, Helmut abuses Martha who becomes disabled and dependent upon him; in *The Goalkeeper's Anxiety of the Penalty Kick*, Bloch murders Gloria and waits to be captured by the police; the protagonist in *Woyzeck* murders Mary; Stroszek in the film of the same name commits suicide after Eva disappears with a truck driver.

36 See my analysis of these relationships in my article "Not a Dirty Secret."

In *Fear Eats the Soul* (Fassbinder, 1974), masculinity per se is not discussed, rather that of the Moroccan-German guest worker. Emmy's husband died sometime ago, and the film revives, principally, the sexuality of the aging German woman both as an ironic comment on the absence of German masculinity and on racism (in regard to the presentation of Ali's sexuality).

It is interesting to note that the only male in NGC whose mature sexuality is present in the film is a terrorist, Katharina's lover in *The Lost Honor of Katharina Blum* (Schlöndorff and von Trotta, 1975), who was pursued by the new government.

Most of the films that present heterosexual or homosexual couplehood were created by Fassbinder, and the characteristics I noted earlier appear in his oeuvre more intensely than in those of any other NGC director. In my view there are two reasons for this: first, he directed forty-two films over the span of sixteen years. Such productivity increases the importance of his work to the corpus. Second, undoubtedly, is the fact that Fassbinder was homosexual. Certainly this sexual orientation enabled him as a second generation director to more widely represent heterosexual couplehood, whereas his two colleagues in the triumvirate and other prominent directors distance themselves from it. Fassbinder's decision to position strong women at the center of his (melo)dramas, is a result of the same phenomenon: the sexuality and dominance of women replace the post-war male and echo his failures. Homosexual relationships are disrupted as well. In this sense, Fassbinder does not differentiate between hetero- and homosexual couplehood, and the worldview dominating couplehood in his films is permanent: "I abuse and/or I am abused; therefore I exist." At the same time, homosexuality is not described as the ultimate orientation, or as a choice that might rescue masculinity (or the femininity that replaces it). In films such as *Fox*, *The Bitter Tears of Petra von Kant* (Fassbinder, 1972), and *Despair*, homosexuality is more a way of describing the protagonists' detachment, withdrawal from reality, and sense of loss than of presenting a preferred form of sexuality. With that, in 1970s Germany, while giving voice to homosexuality undermined Nazi conceptions, the homosexuality portrayed is regressive and not sexual, and in fact directed attention to the failure of masculinity (without relating to sexual orientation).

Midas and Dionysus, Poussin's huge painting of a naked male that serves as the background in *The Bitter Tears of Petra von Kant*, stands in the *mise-en-scène* in contrast to the female nudity of store window mannequins principally because of the presence of what is absent (male sexuality). But the painting also serves to complement these mannequins, for instance, in the shot where they are shown hugging in *Petra's* (Margit Carstensen) bed after the collapse of her relationship with Karin (Hanna Schygulla). Like them, Poussin's painting symbolizes that which is missing from the relationship. In this sense, for NGC as a whole and for Fassbinder in particular, it can serve as an appropriate metaphor for relations between the absence of male sexuality and couplehood.

How does NGC structure the relationship of the spectator *vis-à-vis* the sexuality of the couple? Discussions of the Fassbinderian melodrama to date have not emphasized the centrality of couplehood as a textual strategy that estranges the spectator from the melodrama as a counter-reaction to Nazi respectability. In *The Bitter Tears of Petra von Kant*, as in *Chinese Roulette*, as will be described below, the *mise-en-scène* serves to undermine the spectators' identification processes and support those of alienation directed to concepts of couplehood (not necessarily those of female homosexuals).

Poussin's reproduction is ironic both toward the female homosexual hysteria of Petra in her relationship with Karin, who is bisexual, and in relation to Petra's own heterosexual past:[37] With its Renaissance excess, the painting apparently symbolizes the factor that undermines Petra's fulfillment of her passion: the threatening sexuality of Karin's male partner. But this threat is only iconographic, since the camera never leaves the room and Karin's heterosexual world, like Petra's first marriage, is solely imaginary, both for Petra and the spectator. The film does not present Karin's bisexuality as the only factor sabotaging the relationship, as their couplehood is burdened with other kinds of oppression (age, class) and is in itself presented more through the lack of sexuality than active sexuality.

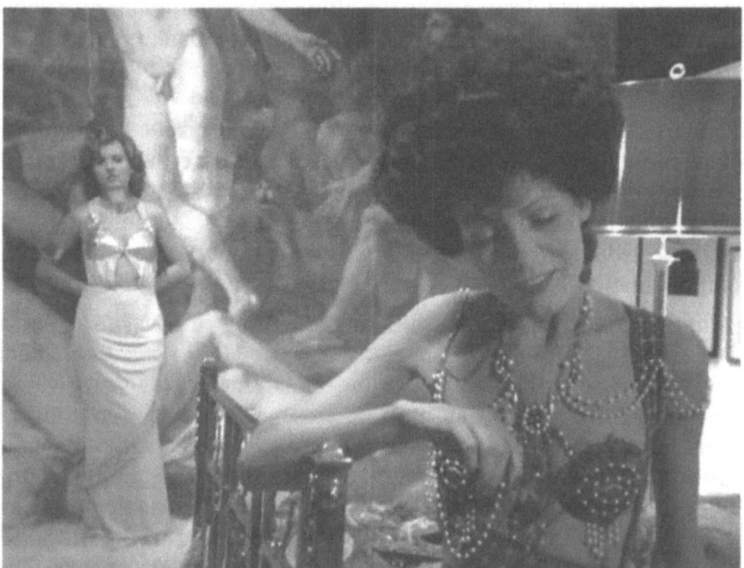

Failure of German couplehood, *The Bitter Tears of Petra Von Kant*

[37] Kirby made the point that Dionysus at the center of the reproduction is a bisexual character. In his 2002 documentary film *My Fassbinder, The One and Only: The Willing Victims of Reiner Werner F.*, Rosa von Praunheim interviewed actresses who had worked with Fassbinder. Hanna Schygulla, Ingrid Caven, Irm Hermann, Barbara Valentin, and others claimed that Fassbinder was bisexual.

The male body is not the sole body imagined. Posing replaces sexual interaction between Petra and Karin and/or Petra and Marlene (Irm Hermann). The estrangement of the spectator from the *mise-en-scène*/the drama is based on rupturing his/her potential look: First, the point of view shot disrupts the system of suture. As spectators, we first see the thing seen and only after the fact can we identify the person seeing; for example, the shot of the mannequins hugging in bed is followed by a shot of Petra's mother looking in that direction. Second, as described by Corrigan in "Transformations," the characters leave and enter the frame and often move to its outer limits and stand there. Third, the track shot from Marlene's typewriter to Petra's bed and back ruptures the continuity of the space. The spectator is not invited to participate in a simple exchange of gazes because such exchanges between the characters (Petra and Karin, Petra and Marlene, Petra and Gabi [Eva Mattes]) are never eye to eye. The *mise-en-scène* places Petra and Karin in close physical proximity without intimacy. Imagined male bodies, imagined (hetero)sexuality, posing, preventing eye contact, and lack of physical intimacy are indicative of the inability of NGC characters to establish relationships of couplehood and family.

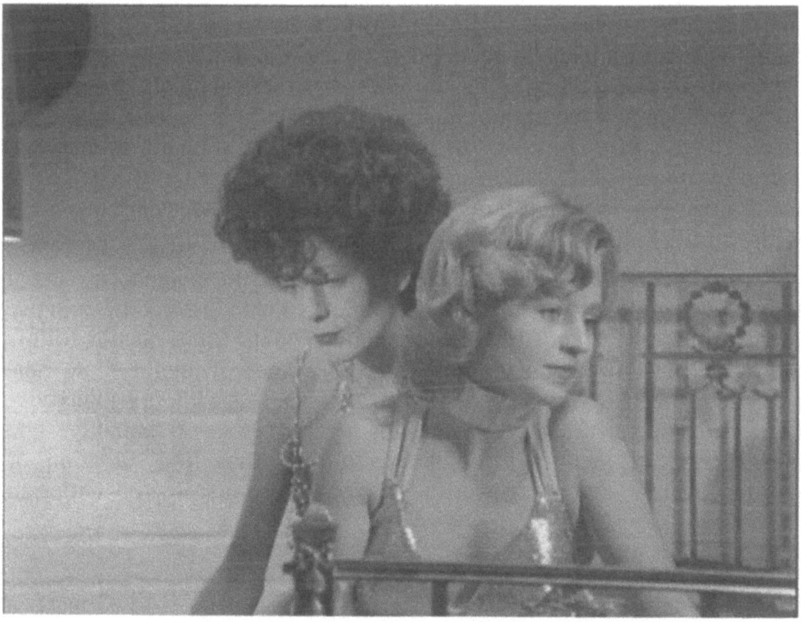

Lack of eye contact, *The Bitter Tears of Petra Von Kant*

Irrespective of the appearance of Petra's daughter and mother at Petra's birthday party, the family is not the center of the drama; at best, the substitute family, Petra, Karin, and Marlene,[38] and principally, the two couples (Petra and Karin and Petra and Marlene) play this role and cause hysterical disruption of identity. Petra is characterized as a subject without subjectivity in terms of her profession (since Marlene does her work), in terms of her social role as a mother and as a daughter, and in terms of her sexuality. The ostentatious exhibitionism of her relationship with Karin is a substitute for the absence of authenticity.

What is the nature of the spectator's view that is part of the gaze but frustrated from making eye contact? Is sexual identity defined by the sexual gaze? Does it mean sexuality? The film abounds with substitutes for sexuality that actually define it: the iconography of the (absent) sexual male body and the frozen sexual female body sculpted according to the conventions of a mannequin; the poses of the characters; and the theatrics, costumes, and soundtrack (a mixed bag of the Platters and Verdi). As in the fragile *mise-en-scène* in *Chinese Roulette* (in which the characters are split and multiplied as they are reflected in the glass furniture), *The Bitter Tears of Petra von Kant*'s excessive *mise-en-scène* requires that the spectator move beyond passive glancing, in contrast to the character of Marlene, who represents the spectator.[39] On the other hand, Michael Ballhaus' camera prevents any possibility of parting with the gaze without frustrating it with the lack of eye contact. The passion of the characters (who are not making eye contact) is captive within the excess of the *mise-en-scène*, of the sound and the dramatic events, and therefore remains asexual. And thus the spectator, even at the height of the drama when Petra has a nervous breakdown or when Marlene leaves with Karin's doll, is alienated from the anti-erotic situation.

Actually, the Fassbinderian film points both to metaphoric sexual impotence and to sexual substitutes, both of which construct the collapse of identity. As I claimed at the beginning, NGC films do not follow Santerian binarism ("schizophrenic disappearance of identity" or "narcissistic respecularization of identity"). As a subject without subjectivity Petra is characterized through the obstructed excess of sexuality. The construction of identity through substituting roles (the variation of mother-lover or daughter-lover is remarkably similar to the Hitlerian

[38] Petra fulfills the role of mother-lover for Karin, who was abandoned in childhood when her father murdered her mother and committed suicide.

[39] As noted by Johnson and others.

identifications described earlier) subverts any possibility for a healthy relationship.

These principles of characterizations – obstructed mutant sexuality and distorted substitutes for couplehood that lead to desubjectivization and thwart the possibility of spectator identification – are, in my opinion, fundamental characteristics of NGC.

Kirby emphasized the return of history in the film through fashion and display.[40] In my opinion, Fassbinder presents the characters as captive to cycles of changes in their sexual orientation and cycles of oppression, no less than in cycles of exploitation. As I claimed, the return of history is not connected to identifying traces of fascism but, rather, the trauma of defeat is constructed in representations of desubjectivization of femininity and masculinity. These representations embody the complex nature of the second generation's identification with the Hitlerian image while being radically subversive toward it.

From the above analysis, it is clear why the Infantile Asexual Model, whose central figure is the abandoned child,[41] is in many ways the paradigmatic model for the construction of masculinity and appears as a psychosocial platform in these post-traumatic films.[42] The non-differentiated sexual identity of the abandoned child is the essence of male identity in NGC, which, as noted, is the result of identification with the complex Hitlerian image, interwoven with opposition to it. This model does not involve channeling sexuality towards the cult of the Führer, but rather obstructing it. The sexual identity of the NGC protagonist is characterized by perpetual and distorted sexual ambivalence – namely, mutant sexuality.

Thus, as a paradigmatic model, it is possible to identify the basic characteristics of the Infantile Asexual Model in the two other models. As we proceed, however, I will describe the films according to their affinity to the model most relevant to them, while emphasizing their place on the sexual spectrum. For example, I will analyze *Kings of the Road* in the context of the Utopian Bisexual Model, though it is based on an experience of infantile asexuality (the absence of women in the life of the two male buddies and the journey each makes to childhood). Similarly, *In a Year of Thirteen Moons* describes the experience of the

---

40 Petra's designs and costumes in her view refer to fascism, to styles popular in the late 1920s and the 1930s.

41 The Mitscherlichian syndrome of emotional deficiency in childhood was described in 1950 (Sampath 1-2 note 5).

42 In *A History*, Elsaesser wrote, "This is a film history conceived as family melodrama, whose key figure is [...] the abandoned child" (215); but, as noted, he does not venture beyond a thematic discussion to a discussion of gender or sexuality.

double abandonment Erwin underwent as a child, but it also presents his radical transformation to Elvira. This extreme makes it the sole film affiliated with the Transsexual Model.

The Utopian Bisexual and Transsexual Models of masculinity are attempts to be saved from the destructive reproduction of the trope of the son. These attempts are in and of themselves widespread subversive acts against the tyranny of identification with the Hitlerian image in its transfer to the second generation.

Moreover, and aside from the shared characteristics of the films created by these directors, it is impossible to ignore the differences in their constructions of masculinity. In my opinion, the source of these differences is their uniqueness as auteurs: the Utopian Bisexual Model is more central to the oeuvre of Wenders, while the Transsexual Model is unique to Fassbinder.

The following description of the models will point out the tension between these constructions of masculinity which, despite the differences in the styles of the auteurs, very clearly manifest the unique and unified relationship NGC had with the Nazi past: the negation of the Nazi body; the presence of the defeated male; disruption of the connection between heteronormativity, respectability, the patriarchal, and nationalism; subversion of the Hitlerian trope of the son through mutant sexuality; and construction of identification structures that will enable the spectator's position to shift from identification with regressive-melancholic structures to their subversion and to mourning work.[43]

---

43 If the spectator is a member of the third generation, as the moral other of the text s/he must identify with the demand of the film not to fulfill sexuality or to raise a new generation. See Chapter 5.

CHAPTER 2

The Infantile Asexual Model

I. Description of the Model

Masculinity according to the Infantile Asexual Model is characterized by its reproduction of the experience of abandonment; by psychological, social, linguistic, sexual, and bodily regression; by an indistinguishable gender identity that involves nonexistent and/or convoluted sexuality; by attachment to a self-destructive family unit; by anti-oedipalization, and by contorted bodies.

Both Herzog's *Every Man for Himself and God Against All, or the Mystery of Kaspar Hauser* (*KH*) and Schlöndorff's *The Tin Drum* (*TD*), the two paradigmatic films of this model, illuminate the extreme consequences of being abandoned by parents, an experience that characterizes, autobiographically, the generation of directors under discussion and is described in the films as fundamental to growing up in post-war Germany.[1] Textually, Kaspar Hauser and Oskar portray both the development over time from childhood to adulthood and the absurdity of being at the same time both the child and the adult. This portrayal of time preserves the experience of abandonment.[2] The experience is not, for example, only an extended separation from the parents or a doubtfully imposed return to them. Alice (Yella Rottländer), in Wenders' *Alice in the Cities*, had been abandoned by her father and then by her mother, who left her with a strange man, Philip (Rüdiger Vogler), who had himself not seen his own parents in nine years. Her mother disappeared and Alice was abandoned again by Philip at the police station after they had established a surrogate father-daughter relationship. The

---

1 The major canonic films affiliated with this model are Herzog's *Signs of Life*, *Even Dwarfs Started Small* (1970), *Stroszek* and *Woyzeck*; Wenders' *Goalkeeper's Anxiety*, *Alice*, *Wrong Movement*, *Kings of the Road*, *American Friend*, *Paris, Texas*, *Wings of Desire*, *Faraway, So Close*; Fassbinder's *Why Does Herr R. Run Amok?*, *The Merchant of Four Seasons*, *Petra*, *Fox*, *Chinese Roulette*, *In a Year of Thirteen Moons*, *Lola*, and *Veronika Voss* (1981).

2 The two films are based upon well known stories, proverbial symbolic in nature: Kaspar Hauser on the historic story from 1828 (Sampath) and *The Tin Drum* on Gunter Grass's 1959 novel.

adult who became a father (biologically and/or symbolically) abandons his child (who also symbolically represents the child within him) and then reabandons him. As such, this is a complex structure that symbolizes both the great need and the great difficulty facing Germany's second generation in becoming the child/adult-son/father without ever having fully experienced any one of these affiliations in the past.

The repeated cases of abandonment include mirror relations between adults and children, as we see in other films, such as *The American Friend*, *Paris, Texas*, *The Bitter Tears of Petra von Kant*, *Why Does Herr R Run Amok?*, *The Merchant of Four Seasons*, and *Chinese Roulette*.[3] But, in contrast to these and all other films included in this model, neither *Every Man for Himself and God Against All, or the Mystery of Kaspar Hauser* nor *The Tin Drum* propose options for healing the abandonment experience, not even temporarily. Rather, as noted, they reproduce it. There is no salvation from abandonment: not through imposed adaptation (Kaspar) and not through relinquishing the revolt against the parents (Oskar); not via multiple father substitutes (Kaspar, Oskar) nor via becoming a father (Oskar), and not via multiple surrogate mothers (Oskar).

Other characters in these films are also abandoned children: for example, the daughter of Frau Gabler (Brigitte Svoboda) and the deaf child that was found dead in *Goalkeepers Anxiety*; Mignon (Nastassja Kinski) in *Wrong Movement*; Alice in *Alice in the Cities*; Hunter (Hunter Carson) in *Paris, Texas*; Amadeus (Ihr Sohn) in *Why Does Herr R. Run Amok?*; Renate (Andrea Schober) in *The Merchant of Four Seasons*; Gabi (Eva Mattes) in *The Bitter Tears of Petra von Kant*; Angela (Andrea Schober) in *Chinese Roulette*; and Lola's out-of-wedlock daughter Marie (Ulrike Vigo), in *Lola*. In NGC, however, the abandoned child principally represents the adult images of itself; e.g., Stroszek (Bruno S.) in *Stroszek*, Woyzeck (Klaus Kinski) in *Woyzeck*, Philip in *Alice in the Cities*, Bruno (Rüdiger Vogler) and Robert (Hanns Zischler) in *Kings of the Road*, Travis, in *Paris*, *Texas*, Sam (William Hurt) and Henry (Max von Sydow) in *End of the World*, Fox in *Fox and His Friends*, and Erwin in *In a Year of Thirteen Moons*. As noted, the children are resonant, mirroring the adults, and in any event serve in the narrative as a symbolic structure of the masculine (or feminine) position. Thus, the narrative structure of the abandoned child is found in the plot

---

3 By "mirror relations I refer to relationships in which the abandoned child, by his/her very presence in the narrative, mirrors the abandonment experienced by the adult as a child. Such a presence becomes a metaphor for the ongoing presence of this experience in the life of the adult.

or the story as part of the characters' tales about their past, as in *The Bitter Tears of Petra von Kant* or *End of the World.*

This structure not only creates entanglements within the plot (as in *End of the World*, in which Henry flees from the Nazis without his parents and is lost by his son, Sam. In turn, Sam's son loses Sam because Sam was searching for Henry), but is also substantive. For example, the Angel Cassiel (Otto Sander) in *Faraway, So Close* wants to be a human, to experience time. Twice he saves the girl Raissa (Aline Krajewski) and earns the right, but just when he wants to find a woman, as he declares to Peter Falk, he is called upon once again to save the girl. And so his masculine plans are foiled and he becomes an angel again. Here the abandonment of the child and/or saving him/her involves the loss of masculinity. The Infantile Asexual Model confronts the experience of abandonment with the loss of masculinity and sexuality. In contrast, as will be described later, the Utopian Bisexual Model confronts the experience of searching for the woman with the loss of masculinity and sexuality.

As opposed to the other children in NGC, Kaspar Hauser and Oskar do not symbolically mirror adults who were abandoned children in the past (such as Alice is to Philip in *Alice in the Cities*, Hunter is to Travis in *Paris, Texas*, or Gabi is to Karin in *The Bitter Tears of Petra von Kant*); but rather they are at the dramatic center of the narrative. As I mentioned, the experience of abandonment involves regressive asexuality or sick sexuality: Kaspar, who preserves childlike qualities during his socialization, keeps his indistinct sexual identity. In death he returns, as I described above, to the pre-childlike/abandoned situation in which he was found. Oskar at the age of three turns into a post-traumatic Peter Pan and remains so until age twenty-one.[4] His sexual maturation involves incestuous relations both with his future mother Maria (Katharina Thalbach); with his symbolic mother, his neighbor; and grotesque sexual relations with Roswitha (Mariella Oliveri).

This regression is multidimensional, whether presented by the film as characterizing the positive hero, like Kaspar, and therefore signifying the gap between him and the oppressive environment; or whether characterizing a positive hero who very slowly accepts the monstrous de-

[4] Only after the death of his mother and his two "fathers" does Oskar throw the drum into the grave of Matzerath, his father, while over the soundtrack we hear his voice saying, "Yes, I must, I want to grow up!" Of course, this statement is not realized in the world described. Just the opposite: Kurt, his brother/son, receives a drum from Oskar at the age of three. That is to say, the regressive choice remains a valid option for growing up and for being an adult in Germany. The image of the grandmother in the field that opens and ends the film supports this cycle.

mands of the environment, as does Oskar (thus signifying the tragedy of the rebel who is a product of his environment). A change in one of these dimensions – socialization, psychological development, sexuality, language acquisition, body image – is temporary, partial, and contorted.

In both *KH* and *TD*, the excess of contorted bodies is the most subversive expression of anti-Nazi masculinity. The bodies of Bruno S. and David Bennent are countertypes to the Aryan body that was based on the Greek statutes of Winckelmann, redesigned in those of Arno Breker, made popular through the films of Leni Riefenstahl, (*Triumph of the Will* [1935] and *Olympia* [1936]), and eventually attained cult status in Nazi culture.

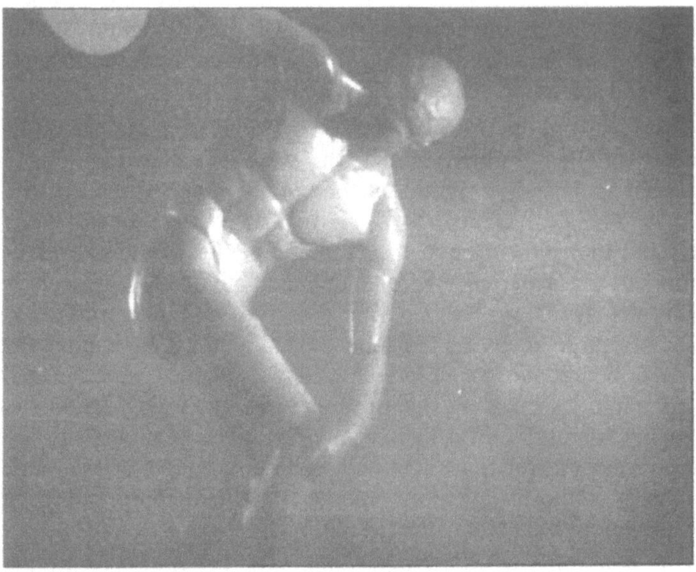

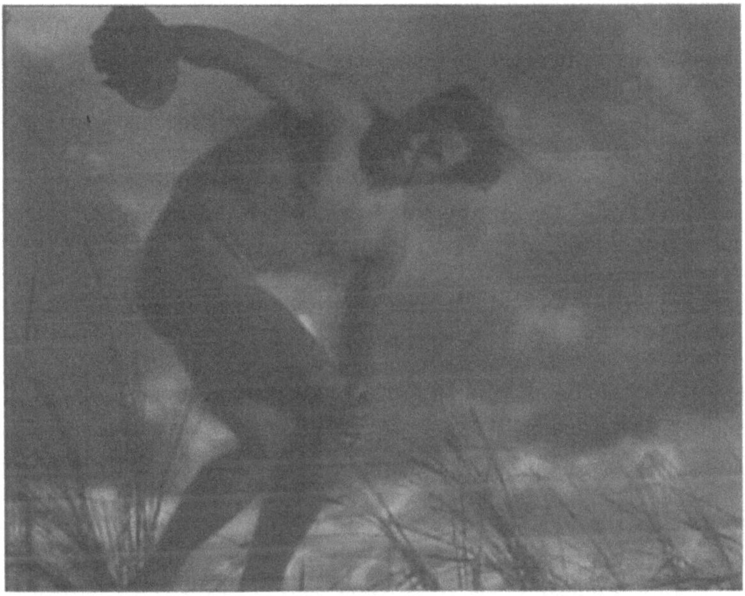

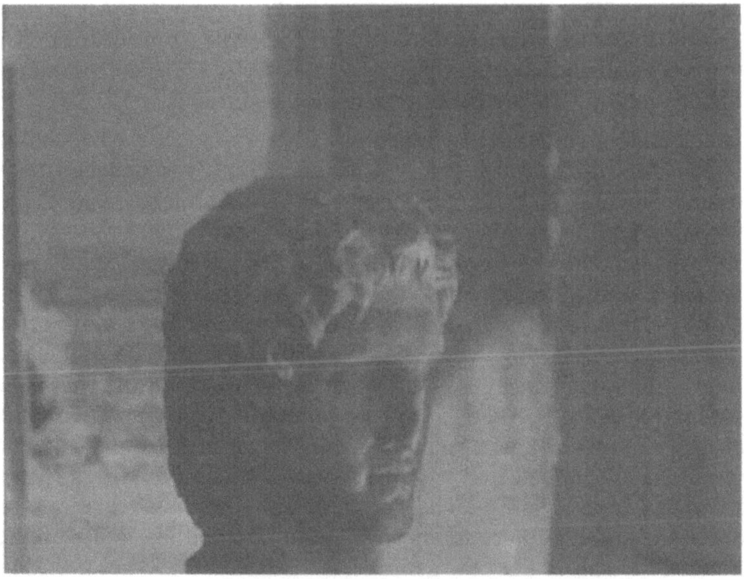

The fascist Nazi body, *Olympia*

First, an extreme distorted excess subverts the Aryan ideal of beauty (as described by Mosse, *Nationalism*; Mangan). The bodies of Oskar and Kaspar are unusual in this respect. While Aryan masculinity paid tribute to the muscular, athletic, tough, white, "pure" body, Kaspar is barely able to walk, control his muscles, or coordinate his limp limbs. When he is placed in the city square by the father figure with his arm extended, his stance is an extreme grotesque reference to the sculptured cast of the Aryan body. In the space in which he is presented/"placed" the most prominent image is the absence of bodily dominance in the sense of strength and control.

Second, the Aryan body is not an individualized image. In contrast, Kaspar and Oskar's bodily uniqueness defines them as individuals. This is conspicuous because the individualization is not a celebration of the human body, but rather otherness that fills the viewer with horror, aversion, and confusion.

Third, the Aryan "perfect human body was based on the principle of performance (*Leistungsmensch*), action, and invulnerability to injury. With his low stature and stunted growth, Oskar ridicules these principles. From the moment he decides to fall down the stairs in order not to grow, literally as well as metaphorically, and not to become part of the adult German world, he is defined by bodily vulnerability.

Fourth, in both cases the image of the body subverts the Aryan body image constructed as "resistant to decay." Deconstruction of the Aryan body through distortion, negation, and derision is the most prominent textual opposition to the nationalistic ideals it represents.

The abandonment experience neurotically reproduced by the characters (fear and withdrawal together with attraction), the defeated body, asexuality, mutant sick sexuality, and extreme violent relationships unavoidably lead to discontinuity of the family unit; that is to say, the family unit becomes self-destructive. NGC narratives are clearly anti-sagas. The few that include more than one generation negate the family dynasty in different ways: In *TD*, for example, a baby, Kurt, was born to the renewed family following the mother's suicide at the end of the Nazi period, but this baby was Oskar's brother as well as his son. That is, he too was born into the perverted reality of symbolic incest and two father figures. These developments contradict in every manner the potential that could have been realized with the re-establishment of Alfred (Mario Adorf) and Maria's family. The secretive acts of sexual relations between Oskar and his future mother when both he and his father are her lovers lead the son of the new generation, Kurt, to be another grotesque reproduction of the previous one. There is no continuation of the family unit in any of the films that typify this model, even when children are physically present in the few family units, as in *The American Friend*, *Why Does Herr R. Run Amok?*, *Chinese Roulette*, and *The Merchant of Four Seasons*.

Anti-oedipalization is prominent in the two films under discussion as well. As will be described later, both undermine the Freudian-Lacanian developmental model through opposition to the symbolic order, regression to the pre-oedipal, and how they relate to language.[5] This can be seen in both the plethora of multiple father figures (actual, imagined, and surrogate[6]) and the domination of the father as savior/murderer.

II. Kaspar – The Genderless Body

Every Man for Himself and God Against All, or the Mystery of Kaspar Hauser (Werner Herzog, 1974).

1828. First seen in a dark basement, Kaspar Hauser is shown tied to the floor, dirty, with his body covered with wounds, fed water and salt, a toy horse by his side. A father figure in a dark coat teaches him to write his name, releases him from the basement after sixteen years and drags him a long distance to the square of a nearby town where he places him in a statuesque position. The town's residents are unsuccessful in learning about his origins and in understanding his very unusual nature. He learns to sit, eat, and speak in the house of Professor Daumer (Walter Ladengast). Later, in the circus, he is displayed as a riddle. After two years, he still believes in his own inner world, one that is close to nature and cut off from that of the townspeople. Then, in a surprising act, the father figure hits Kaspar; after a while, he stabs him. The autopsy reveals deformities in Kaspar's brain and liver. The town clerk announces: "This explains it all!"

To the best of my knowledge, none of the leading researchers of Herzog's work[7] have related to *Every Man for Himself and God Against All, or the Mystery of Kaspar Hauser* as having an anti-Nazi physical counter image at its center. Past attempts to interpret the mystery of Kaspar Hauser associated him with German Romanticism and/or Weimar Expressionism; with literary sources whose dominance is denied emphatically by Herzog; with the character of Jesus; with the figure of a

---

5 Kaspar speaks anti-logical language and the language of dreams while Oskar prefers to drum and/or to scream.

6 In *KH*, the father figure in the dark jacket, Daumer, the Lord, the professor of logic, the blind old man; in *TD*, Matzerath, Bronski (Daniel Olbrychski), and Oskar.

7 Cleere; Sandford; Silverman ("Terrible Fall"); Franklin; Benelli; Corrigan (*Films*, "Producing Herzog," "Original Tradition"; Elsaesser, ("Anthropologist's Eye," *A History*); Horak; Koch ("Blindness"); Mayne ("Herzog").

passive rebel that failed, representative of the intensive public debate that was taking place during the 1960s and 1970s concerning the possibility of change in Germany; or as a character who opposes social-patriarchal-cultural oppression. Discussions of Kaspar's unclear sexual identity and maturity that should have led to discussions of sexuality only produced further attempts to understand the secret of the "negative fairytale"[8] or the *anti-Bildungsroman* outside the context of Nazi imagery, which I suggest is essential to understanding this film.

Lehman, who studies representations of the male body in culture, claimed male feral child narratives[9] "serve as a locus for examining sexual difference and the role that language plays in it" (39). While I agree with his theory that gender-related subjects are a central aspect of these narratives, I find that specific cultural context is absent from Lehman's commentaries. He goes on to claim that Herzog's film was based on the 1832 publication by Feuerbach,[10] though Herzog omitted any reference to what Feuerbach called in the original book, "Kaspar's refusal to accept his culture's gender definitions" (qtd. in Lehman 47). That is, Herzog totally ignored the domain of sexual development. This representative denial in the research also appears, for example, in Sampath's *Kaspar Hauser: A Modern Metaphor* (1). The author surveyed the evolution of the motif of Kaspar Hauser in twentieth-century literature and noted that Kaspar's representation changed after World War II (137);[11] though she does not suggest what I regard as an inevitable explanation for this change.

In my view, Herzog's narrative is, indeed, *Rousseauistic Zivilisationspessimismus* (à la Sampath); however,[12] the film is not just the

---

8 See Sampath.

9 The author also discusses François Truffaut's *The Wild Child* (1969) and Hugh Hudson's *Greystoke: The Legend of Tarzan, Lord of the Apes* (1984).

10 The uniqueness of Herzog's approach, as I will describe below, is prominent against the background of the adaptations of the original book, similar to that of the director Peter Sehr who called his film *Kaspar Hauser – Crimes Against the Inner Life of a Human Being* (1993). As previously hinted at, I relate similiarly to other NGC cinematic versions of literary sources, such as *The Tin Drum* and *Woyzeck*.

11 First, he no longer appeared as an attractive youngster; second, only a few works continue to suggest that he has magic powers.

12 It is widely known that in 1974 Herzog made a pilgrimage in the snow from Munich to Paris, where Lotte Eisner was living, documented in his book *Of Walking in Ice*. Called by him "our collective conscience," he did so in hope of delaying her death for as long as possible (qtd. in Rentschler, *West German Filmmakers* 115). He showed her *The Mystery of Kaspar Hauser* and asked for her opinion of the film as "legitimate German culture." A cinematic historian of Expressionism, Jewish immigrant, friend of Fritz Lang and Friedrich Murnau, personal assistant of Henri Langlois, Eisner gave her blessing to the young German director and assured him that his

director's aspiration to return to pre-scientific, pre-linguistic modes,[13] just as it does not omit or totally ignore sexuality-related representations. Herzog chose to present a character that is not only nonsexual, but genderless.[14] This was not meant as repression, but as a post-traumatic reaction to the trope of the son, which *KH* embodies in its extreme.

The meaning of designing a grotesque world is not only to create a free carnival spirit, a world in which the characters "evoke and distort our familiar conception of reality," (Cleere 12) but to present a counter symbol to what the Nazis called asocials, "People who could not be integrated into the community of the Volk, and who lacked the generally accepted norms that guaranteed so called productive work within a settled community, be it the family or the state" (Mosse, *Image* 178).

In contrast to the character of Oskar, the uniqueness of Kaspar is, as noted, his being not only asexual, but genderless. This construct is not only an effect (in the Butlerian sense) of the identification with the trope of the son described above, but serves as evidence of the tragic outcome of being subsumed within this complex identification structure. The effect is the substantive nature of genderlessness. Stated another way, since this figure is not meant to represent queerness but anti-fascism\Nazism, what is lacking is the "essence" of gender. Though Kaspar can be placed, at least physically, closer to the masculine end of the feminine/masculine spectrum, he shows no awareness or reaction to it. During Count Stanhope's (Michael Kroecher) party, he disappears and is found embroidering. In conversation with the maid Kathe (Brigitte Mira), he inquires about the role of women, a subject totally foreign to him and devoid of any connotations. Aside from these references that signify unawareness of the differences between the genders, Kaspar avoids the attributes the townspeople associate with him, includ-

film was indeed "legitimate German culture." In *A History*, Elsaesser claimed, "By endorsing continuity, bestowing the right of inheritance, mediating between fathers and sons, enemy nations and two rebel film movements, Lotte Eisner, thanks to Herzog, became the super mother of the New German Cinema and of a film history conceived as family melodrama, whose key figure is, precisely, the abandoned child" (215). Herzog dedicated *KH* to Lotte Eisner (and "to the better part of Germany that had to leave"), as did Wim Wenders at the end of *Paris, Texas*.

13 The subject is discussed extensively in relation to Herzog's production and is fed by the declaration of the director about his preference of the visual over the oral and his desire for illiteracy. See, for example, Peucker ("Literature"); van Wert.

14 This is not a pre-Butlerian binarism based upon a definition of gender identity expressing innerness/the soul, in contrast to definition of the sex as physical. Following Grosz, my aim is to focus on this binarism as an open category. Grosz offers a way out of the Butlerian impasse by insisting on the positively of morphology and the stylization and "open materiality" of the specific body (191).

ing those regarding gender. As in his reactions to all the other areas, he remains loyal to his inner truth without hierarchies and categorization.

In my opinion, this is not a case of what Butler calls in *Gender Trouble* a "pregendered person" (3). Rather, the absence of gender created in Kaspar what she calls a repetitive stylization of the body, a distinguishable "bodily identity" (96) that cannot be seen as a transitional stage. As the dramatic events of the plot prove, Kaspar does not progress to a new stage. In spite of the socialization process imposed upon him by the townspeople, Kaspar remains asexual and indubitably genderless. Changes in bodily coherence, learning skills such as sitting and eating, and the change in perception of "falling" (as he describes his relation to reality) are understood as connected more to the outer surface of his body-essence. Just as there is no change in his genderless essence, or his asexuality, so his consciousness continues, in spite of the socialization process, to be based on intuitive sensual experience. The integrative, positive perception of the self is not dependent on bodily non-integration at any stage, and together with asexuality and genderlessness signifies an unchanging wholeness. The bodily integrity of Kaspar is seen in how he presents himself as an alien body and preserves his genderlessness and asexuality.[15] The body preserves his deficiencies as coherence. In other words, genderlessness and asexuality are structural components of the coherence of that which is absent. This is not a case of a body that is not sexed in a pre-cultural, pre-discursive stage (Butler 258); rather, it is a body that had already established its identity.[16]

The excesses of the body mediate the past; that is, the symbolic imagery of the powerless body simultaneously creates awareness of the horrific identification with Hitler as "son" and acknowledgment of the Nazi defeat.

A. The Subject [Op]position Through Radical Pose

As noted, Kaspar is first discovered in the town square standing in the statuesque position his unnamed father figure has placed him, one hand stretched out holding a letter. This position – frozen, strange, non-functional – is more than a physical expression of his lack of control over his body and alienation. He is filmed from behind in a high angle shot, which reveals a symmetric composition that contrasts with his physical asymmetrical strangeness. As indicated previously, this posi-

15 See Mary Douglas, "the boundaries of the body become [...] the limits of the social *per se*" (qtd. in Butler, *Gender Trouble* 13). Emphasis in the original.

16 Irene Meijer and Baukje Prins noted Butler's "theorizing of abject bodies as disruptive challenges to what counts as fully human" (285).

tion is the diametric opposite of the statuesque Aryan stance – Breker's statues emphasize the tension of the arms, with legs separated; a position of readiness that promises security and "preparedness for war" (Mosse, *Nationalism and Sexuality* 174).[17]

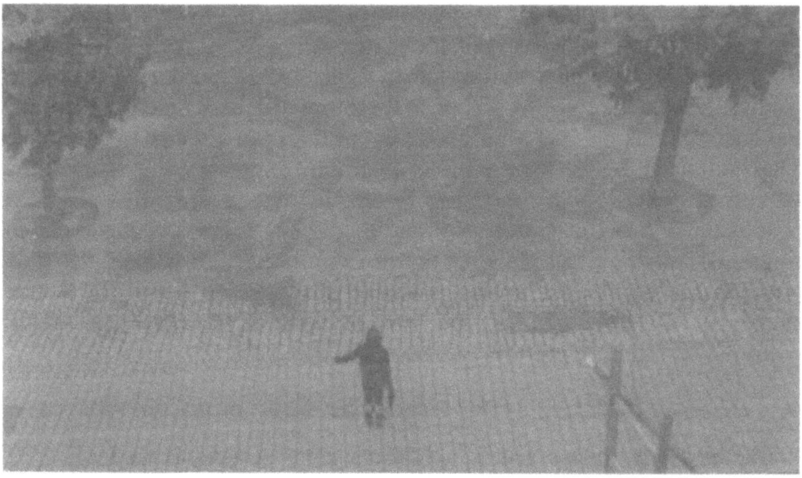

Total opposition to the statuesque Aryan pose, *The Mystery of Kaspar Hauser*

In the circus together with the other "attractions," all of whom represent different sides of Kaspar's own enigmatic nature, he is positioned by the townspeople in the same pose in which he was first seen in the square; that is, he has become identified with this pose. Moreover, though the way he holds his body underwent change during the two years he was in the town, he himself returns to the original pose after the second murder attempt, when he is stabbed in the chest. This repetitive behavior appears at first glance to be Kaspar's regression to the pre-socialization stage; in actuality, however, it is radical positioning that illustrates his objection to any attempts to transform his non-integrated body into a social one. Herzog also uses this pose in *Stroszek*, where, following the collapse of his American dream, when Eva (Eva Mattes) leaves him, Stroszek stands in the snowy field, his checkered coat and hat emphasizing his estrangement and unstable mental condition. His instinctual physical positioning signifies upcoming death.

[17] See there photographs of the statues (171); and note 38 (215) that describes a very popular Nazi book that devoted eleven chapters to a description of the Nordic racial look – high and slender, wide shouldered with narrow hips, rosy skin, and light hair that darkens with age.

Is Kaspar's really a pre-socialized body? As I hinted above, his is not a neutral bodily surface upon which culture acts (à la Butler). In fact, his non-integrated body symbolized by the pose does not lack a history; it actually has a central symbolic historical meaning: since Kaspar himself retreats to this pose when the father figure attempts to murder him, his reaction is at odds with his passive positioning in the town square and in the circus. It is instinctive and traumatic. The pose links his liberation from the dark basement by the father figure to his murder by the same person. Kaspar's return to this pose therefore signifies redemption from the basement as no less a traumatic event than the attempt to stab him. The contorted body, frozen in its position, expresses the trauma involved in contact with the father figure. In other words, this physical pose is the anti-oedipal strategy through which the film relates the father figure as redeemer to the father figure as murderer. Of course, the film presents the entire redemption process with extreme irony. As Butler suggests, "Discrete genders are part of what humanizes individuals within contemporary culture" (*Gender Trouble* 139).

B. Disempowerment of the Gaze. The Gape as an Alternative

In the town square scene, neighbors stare at Kaspar through their windows. His look, however, avoids reflection on his surroundings: it is frozen, vacant, directed to the space immediately in front of him and never shifts beyond the view made possible by his pose. The shot of Kaspar's look is replaced by one of a cow tied to a tree; but the spectator does not experience it as a subjective (point of view) shot since Kaspar's facial expression does not change. Does the omniscient camera serve as a substitute for his gaze? The photography in much of the film subverts the convention by which the omniscient camera and the protagonist exchange places. Indeed, in this scene and in those following, the omniscient camera reveals the surroundings beyond Kaspar's frozen range as a substitute for his look, but does not replace it. More the case, the photography embodies the difference between the "unlook" of Kaspar and the looks of the townspeople. The film refrains from attributing to Kaspar reflection on his surroundings.

Similarly, it is inherently understood that Kaspar is not capable of eye contact, as is illustrated in the scene in which one of the townspeople asks him questions. While Herzog shows the townspeople gazing at Kaspar, for example during Count Stanhope's party, Kaspar's reaction – more precisely his lack of reaction – negates the power in their gaze, retroactively making it gazeless. The camera constructs his isolation from the world by disempowering the gaze directed towards him. In other words, Kaspar denies his surroundings their power by being impervious to them. His isolation in terms of framing within the conversation does not deny him his subjectivity.

Much like when Stroszek takes leave of the prison director in *Stroszek*, Kaspar does not return the looks of the pastor and the professor during their conversation. Herzog refrains from using a shot reverse shot during a later conversation Kaspar has with the professor when he tests Kaspar's ability to think logically. But in this scene, when the professor asks questions the camera focuses on him and Kathe with a two-shot. The cut to Kaspar shows him looking straight ahead while the professor's speech is heard off screen. Only at the end of the scene does Kaspar turn to him, but when the professor rejects his answer, Kaspar turns away and lowers his head. The next shot again shows only the professor continuing his speech.

Despite his distinctness, Kaspar is not a fascinating spectacle: first, as noted, because the film does not construct him as part of the power relations involved in the exchange of gazes; second, because spectators react with repulsion and confusion (Kaspar's fractured, flabby, distorted, frozen body invites afetishization); and third, because the absence of sexual desire in Kaspar's body eliminates the option of viewing his body as both an object of deterrence and of fascination: fascination is impossible. Clearly, breaking the conventions of traditional photography[18] and the use of editing to create separation between Kaspar and his onlookers change the power relations post factum, breaking the gaze of others, as noted, and constructing the Kasparian look as part of extra-social subjectivization. Fourth, Kaspar's look is unique since it is not only without reflection or power, but is a gape; that is, it involves an expression of astonishment that cancels distinctions between inward and outward looks. Rupturing the gaze and replacing it with the gape strips the private sphere from the public, and turns the body into a means of separating the self from the social body.

---

[18] Both the role of the camera as omniscient vs. its role in subjective shots, as well as filming a dialogue.

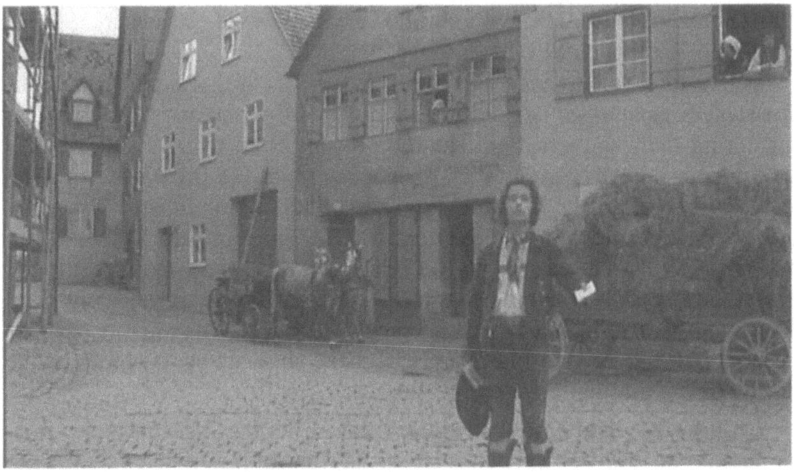

Kaspar's gape, *The Mystery of Kaspar Hauser*

In my view, the film emphasizes Kaspar's "unlook"\gazelessness as an anti-oedipal element. The non-seeing eyes and the swollen, injured feet appear to be oedipal variations, but actually Herzog uses these motifs principally to undermine them: the son will be murdered by his symbolic father, and not the opposite, before his sexual identity is established. He himself will become a riddle in the circus and outside it. The murder will force upon him re-abandonment in a type of achronological use of the oedipal narrative. These transitions are not presented as a development in linear time, but rather as a return to the starting point that, too, is essentially atemporal and puzzling.[19]

In sum, the radical corporeality of Kaspar is a multi-layered historical-cultural reaction that includes negation of the fascist-Nazi body, preservation of anti-oedipal bodily history, genderlessness, and asexuality. It also includes a unique distinctiveness that attests to individualism and undermines the Nazi perception of the connection between body and soul,[20] "regressive" positioning, gaping as retroactive undermining of the gaze, and abjective re-abandonment.

---

19 *KH* ends with the town clerk mumbling, "A beautiful protocol, an exact protocol," a paraphrase taken from Buchner: "A good murder, a real murder, a beautiful murder" (Horak note 15).

20 See Butler, who asked in *Gender Trouble*: "From what strategic position in public discourse and for what reasons has the trope of interiority and the disjunctive binary of inner/outer taken hold? In what language is 'inner space' figured? What kind of figuration is it, and through what figure of the body is it signified? How does a body figure on its surface the very invisibility of its hidden depth?" (134).

In the Herzogian film, the spectator participates in the unique structure of the intersection of gazes. In becoming linked to the gaze of the townspeople, s/he can also be said to retroactively lose his/her spectatorial power. The transition between perceiving Kaspar's distinctiveness as a spectacle and its removal from any social context causes the spectator to participate in the processes of rupturing constructed by the film, the most central being the break from identification with the past.

C. *"Catalogue of Asocials"*

In *Image of Man*, Mosse discussed the use made by the Third Reich of the racist catchphrase "catalogue of asocials." I will use the phrase in a contradictory manner to characterize what I described above as Herzog's anti-Nazi and anti-racist corporeal world in *KH*. This also holds true in regard to his other films, such as *Signs of Life*, *Even Dwarfs Started Small*, *Stroszek*, and *Woyzeck*, and, moreover, explains his ideology of casting, as I will now describe.

Herzog's use of characters that are eccentric, deviant, freaks, outcasts (to name but a few of the terms used in the research to refer to this phenomenon)[21] is based on their physical characteristics. Through his casting and its ensuing imagery, by investing meaning in the physical and the bodily, Herzog contests corporeal representations of the Nazi past with all their ideological overtones. Furthermore, liberation of the body from control of the social order and making it anti-social has meaning precisely because of the bodily excess of these protagonists (the dwarfs in *Even Dwarfs Started Small*, Stroszek in *Signs of Life* and in *Stroszek*, Woyzeck in *Woyzeck*; and thus, to a certain degree, the aborigines in *Where the Green Ants Dream* [1984], and *Nosferatu* [1979]); and justifies, in my view, the ideology of Herzogian casting.

21 For criticism regarding the exploitation of Bruno S., the Native Americans, and others and the extreme nature of production conditions, see for example Corrigan ("Producing Herzog" 12-13), Horak (30), and Koch; See Les Blank and Maureen Gosling's documentary film *Burden of Dreams* (1982) regarding production of the film *Fitzcarraldo*. There Herzog spoke about the curse encompassing the jungle as a place where God's work of creation has yet to be completed; whose nature is "an excess of harmony that paralyzes and collective murder"; of enormous growth and all-engrossing absence of order that leads to a feeling that the wild jungle is a surrogate for the eccentric body of the human character in other films. The obscenity of the jungle that Herzog mentions is but an expression of the same physical anti-eroticism. In this sense, the ship is a parallel with the mechanical amusement park in which, for example, Stroszek dies or the van that goes around in circles. That is, all the physical elements of the world of the protagonists reflect their unstable mental condition. See also Herzog's own documentary film *Klaus Kinski, My Friend* (1999) that was made after Kinski's death in 1991, following their problematic collaboration in five films.

Many scholars have written that Herzog describes the deviant as signifying authenticity. In "Blindness as Insight" Koch, however, presented an opposite approach (79-84). She accused him of neo-romantic regression and fraud because of the prophetic/pastoral role he took upon himself in representing the world of the disabled.[22]

The following table is my characterization of Herzog's oeuvre as a split discourse:

Style	Modern	Pre-Modern/Neo-expressionist/Neo-Romantic
Genre	Fiction	Documentary
Dominant mode	Verbal	Visual
Relation to language	Induce speaking	Silence
Materialism	Transcendent	Sensual
State of characters' Consciousness	Meaning	"Being"
Text accessibility	Transparent	Sealed
Diegesis formation	Filmic	Pro-filmic
Ideology of casting	Actor as the focus	Role as the focus
Icons	Klaus Kinski	Bruno S.
Central trope	The space	The body
Character clarification	Exterior world	Interior world
Source	Taken from literature	Origins in the landscape/nature
Nature of the diegesis	Manipulative	Authentic
Relationship between film and director	Persona dependent	Autobiographical

The shift between the quasi-documentary and the fictional, the external and the internal worlds, the body and the space, and so on, is not actually movement between them. In his attempt to understand how the subject is constructed, the spectator is exposed to a split discourse that is not necessarily either binary or dialectical. The Herzogian film structures "excessive" subjectivity that projects itself on the space/landscape/surroundings and its style does not allow the spectator a definitive understanding of these projections (even when they are revealed as metonymic). The question of "what precedes what?" (subjectivity projecting on the physical space or vice versa) is not answered. On one

22 Many other scholars were involved in this controversy.

hand, the use of photography intensifies the problem of interpretation, since it appears to be a problem of hermeneutics; on the other, it strengthens self-reflexivity by revealing the dominance of acontinuity on all textual levels. Are the space/landscape/surroundings that repeatedly appear (for example, wheat fields and the cow in *KH*) perceived as external to the character? Or internal? Is it possible to construct a "*mise-en-scène* [that] seeks to create a point of view, without the point of view shot as its basis"? (Elsaesser , "Anthropologist" 154) As claimed earlier in regard to the photography in *KH*, the gape as an inclusive strategy constitutes the reply.

The answers to these questions, however, do not lie in interpreting one film, paradigmatic as it may be, or in an attempt to impose narrative complexity where it doesn't exist ("what precedes what?"). It also does not lie in a hermeneutic emphasis on filling in the gaps, or even in imposing an ideological interpretation (i.e., is the film "regressive" or "radical"?). In my opinion, Herzog's split discourse strategy demands finding the answer at the symbolic level; none can be found at any other level of the film text.

Herzog's protagonists are not only crazed men of illusions. Their enigmatic subjectivity, as described above, is dependent to a great extent on their physical abnormality and all it entails. The body-gesture-body language-positioning-corporeality (henceforth the Body) appears to make the work of hermeneutics and the consequent political stance of Herzog researchers most challenging. There is a need to focus attention on the Body as a textual foundation that includes the spectrum described in the table. Composing the relations of the Body with the *mise-en-scène*, the space, the point of view, and the narrative becomes the central method of structuring the subject.

Interestingly, it is through Herzog's emphasis on the visual, his cancellation of causation in the narrative, and his subversion of other organizing principles that the spectator tends eventually to construct deviant subjectivity through the Body. Thus, distorted bodily excess, asexuality, and the corporeality of the body lead the viewer inevitably to a symbolic-historical interpretation. I maintain this is true even if, or perhaps because, Herzog rejected this option and insisted in his interviews on a substantive enigma.

The body, like the subjectivity it carries, is not enigmatic. It is a mediator of the past – with the identifications and imagery entailed in the past. The body, that is, makes counter-history a valid option.

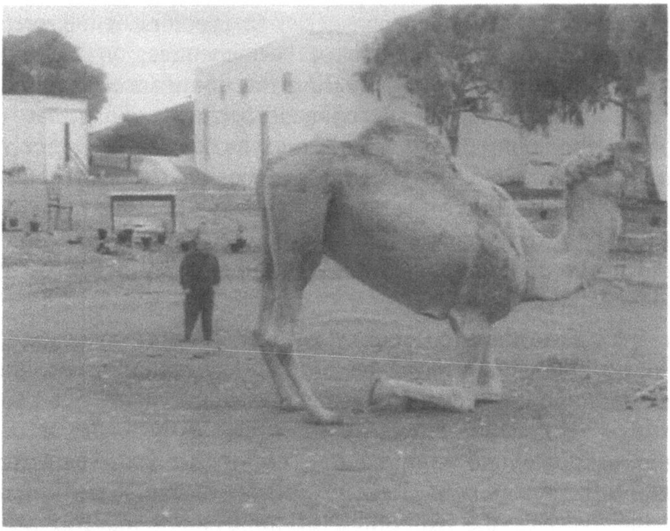

Distorted anti-Nazi body, *Even Dwarfs Started Small*

The two types of Herzogian protagonists (the overreachers and the underdogs) are characterized not only through their definition of the human. Extreme bodily excess and asexuality are the primary signifiers of the process they undertake: any attempt to go beyond the limitations of their bodies ends in loss. These physical, conscious, and spatial boundaries determine the limits of the confrontation of the self with the social order.

In *Signs of Life*,[23] which takes place in 1942 on the Greek island of Kos, Stroszek, a German soldier, is injured and deemed unfit to return to battle. Placed in an abandoned castle on an isolated island, his incapacity is projected on his surroundings – the castle becomes a closed space, a prison. This feeling also prevents him from having conjugal relations with his Greek wife. Herzog emphasizes the projection of illusionary visions of the unfit self which causes him to be crazed at the sight of a valley filled with thousands of windmills,[24] to hide in the castle, and to

---

23 See also van Wert on the connection between *Signs of Life* and the short documentary film *Last Words* (1968) that Herzog made the same year. The author claimed that the short documentary films involve autobiographical events and provide Herzog both with a therapeutic break from the complicated productions of his fiction films and the chance to reach the broader TV audience.

24 For further discussion, see Peter Buchka's documentary film *Haunted Screen: German Film after WWI* (1998) that sketches a portrait of Werner Herzog. The windmill sequence was shot in Crete on the Lasithi Plain where there are 10,000 windmills (Peucker, "Invalidation" 229).

see himself as commander of the Eastern Mediterranean front. "Since no one wants to duel with him, Stroszek started to mock the city. It is in a state of virginity, ready and inviting someone to bomb her. This is the lust of every city [...]."[25] Imprisoned within his body (the castle and the windmills symbolize two extremes, frozen vs. active), the protagonist simultaneously tries to become a celebrated soldier and "to bomb the city's virgins." Thus, Stroszek's failed masculinity is realized both in his failed performance as a soldier and his failed sexuality.[26]

Stroszek's failed performances in *Signs of Life* are projected more on his surroundings than on physical deformity. Herzog's later protagonists – like the dwarfs, Stroszek and Woyzeck – illustrate the process described earlier in which the body leads the protagonist to his death principally through physicality; though the isolated island in *Even Dwarfs Started Small*, frozen Wisconsin in *Stroszek*, and the military base in *Woyzeck* all provide metonymic space that intensifies the distorted excess of the body.

Having a distorted body prevents redemption by means of potential sexuality. In *Even Dwarfs Started Small*, Hombré (Helmut Döring) has difficulty climbing into the double bed because of his height; in *Stroszek*, Eva's pimps abuse Stroszek's body, after which she abandons him; in *Woyzeck*, Woyzeck, whose body is abused ceremonially by the captain (Wolfgang Reichmann) and the doctor (Willy Semmelrogge) (medical experiments, starvation), embraces murder, a counter balance to his increasing estrangement from his weak, shivering, and contorted body. The repeated stabbings of the knife in Marie's (Eva Mattes) body – stressed by Herzog through a series of shots – enlivens, albeit in a distorted manner, the corporeality he lost as a result of his abuse, both actual and imagined.[27]

The bodies of the dwarfs, Stroszek, and Woyzeck carry with them the signs of imagined boundaries no less than signs of actual ones. Thus, Stroszek prepares a statute of himself for Eva, a statue which expresses his "distorted soul," caused by their "no longer sharing a bedroom,"[28] and Woyzeck imitates the strange man who attached himself to Marie's body from behind. When a protagonist imagines his body as another's –

[25] Quote from the film.

[26] See, for example, the totally reverse usage of the same scene by the Italian director Gabriel Salvatores in *Mediterraneo* (1992), in which sailors are stranded on an island cut off from the war.

[27] Herzog's stance in the film in regard to his protagonists is always positive. Even when Woyzeck becomes a murderer, the process is described without moral judgment and as unpreventable because of the oppression he experienced.

[28] This is a quote from the film.

as an object or as another male in the act of objectification – it signifies the tragic result of this imagined self-objectification.

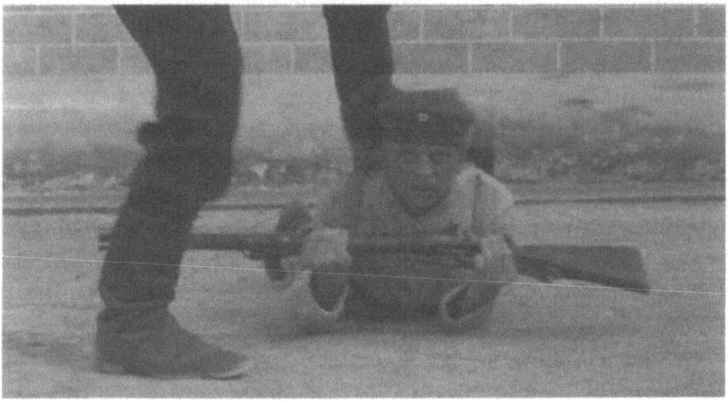

The contorted, abused body leads to death, *Woyzeck*

I conclude that the central trope of these films is not cyclical movement,[29] but rather the corporeality itself that leads to loss: abnormality, convulsions, frozenness, deterioration, lack of control, and imagining sexuality through self-objectification.

The Bodily perception and the "asocial catalogue" that is based upon it are related to the mythological character of Tantalus, the Titan "from whom the fruits and the pure water retreated at the moment he sought to satisfy his hunger and thirst." According to Shoham, two poles signify the spectrum of insurgence: the Sisyphean rebel who becomes Prometheus and the Tantalic rebel who becomes Icarus.[30] The corporeality of the Herzogian protagonist is more like that of Tantalus-Icarus than that of Sisyphus-Prometheus. Shoham places the Sisyphean rebel in the psychological developmental stage that he calls "separation" and the Tantalic rebel in the oral, "consolidation" stage. Kaspar, the dwarfs, Stroszek in *Signs of Life* and in *Stroszek*, and Woyzeck are all Tantalic rebels.

29 As claimed by Sandford; Peucker ("Invalidation," "Literature"); Corrigan ("Producing Herzog"); Benelli. They described, for example, the car that circles the courtyard of the institution in *Even Dwarfs* or the van and hen that go round in circles in *Stroszek*.

30 According to Shoham, in contrast to the Sisyphean insurgent, the Tantalian rebel does not seek involvement in his surroundings. "[....] he longs for direct contact with the absolute; for the immediate sensation of contact with the other, to return to the sensation of grace of the womb and enduring presence of the early orality" (108, my translation).

In sum, the uniqueness of Herzog's creative world is realized on two levels: First, as noted, in his choice to present radical counter images to those of the Nazis; and second, in his concrete design of the asocial body as one that represents the destructive inscription of history on the body. Precisely because these bodies are failed and unable to overcome their limitations they can mediate the despectacularization of the images of the past. Like all NGC (anti)heroes, Herzogs' carry the burden of the past on their bodies.

III. Oskar – The Body, The Drum, The Voice

The Tin Drum (Volker Schlöndorff, 1979).

In 1899, Oskar's grandmother sits in the middle of a field hiding his grandfather under her dress. Many years later, when Oskar is three-years old, while watching the affair between his mother Agnes (Angela Winkler) and her cousin Jan Bronski (Daniel Olbrychski), apparently with the encouragement of his father Alfred, Oskar decides not to grow up, and engineers a fall down the basement stairs. At dinner one night Alfred and Jan collaborate to make Agnes eat eels caught using the head of a dead horse, after which she vomits for weeks. When she discovers she may be pregnant, she commits suicide. In 1939, Oskar drags his "Uncle" Jan to the Polish post office, where he is shot. At age sixteen, Oskar begins his sexual games with Maria, an adolescent girl hired to help around the house who Oskar discovers is sleeping with his father. When the Nazi army advances to the Russian front, Kurt, his brother/son, is born. Oskar joins two dwarfs, Bebra (Fritz Hakl) and Roswitha, and they entertain Nazi soldiers. Roswitha is killed and Oskar returns home. As the Russians arrive, to cover traces of his Nazi past Alfred swallows the Iron Cross Oskar gave him, chokes, and dies. At age twenty-one, at his father's grave, Oskar throws away the drum and announces he wants to grow up. The family – Maria, Oskar, and Kurt – leaves while Oskar calls to his grandmother who is sitting – again – in the field by the side of the railway tracks.

A. Abandonment and Sexuality

As in the case of the actor Bruno S., to a significant degree David Bennent established the role of Oskar through his corporeality.[31]

Superficially, and in contrast to Kaspar Hauser, who was an abandoned child deprived of gender and sexuality, Oskar is not asexual, and he portrays a different version of the abandoned child. First, he is characterized sexually. Second, he was the one who decided to abandon his fathers/mother (the climax of which is his participation in the deaths of all three). This decision pre-empts being abandoned, or more precisely, is a result of it, in the broadest sense: it is commonly understood that Oskar decides not to grow up (physically) because of his revulsion towards his family and the adult world of Germany.

In contrast to Kaspar Hauser and other NGC children, most of whom are homeless,[32] Oskar's abandonment does not relate to physical space because he remains at home with his parents. Abandonment of physical space is displaced to his body; that is, Oskar abandons his future body. He also substitutes the physical (body) in favor of the audial (the drum, his shattering voice). Since the audial substitute he chooses is part of his distorted body, there is in fact no difference in this regard between him and Kaspar. Oskar, too, embodies the experience of abandonment: "homelessness" is replaced by "bodylessness."

The difference between the *TD* and the *Mystery of Kaspar Hauser* abandoned child paradigm is found, as noted, in sexuality. Oskar abandons his two fathers, Alfred and Jan, signifying first of all, opposition to the sexuality of the adult world in which both Jan ("my uncle and my father," as Oskar calls him) and his father are his mother's lovers. The decision to harm his future body, the abandonment, happens after he observes the erotic relationship of his (three) parents while sitting under the dining table. But, although the body that destroys itself separated

---

31 *Stroszek* is a pseudo-autobiography of Bruno S. following his release from a mental institution. Sandford described how Schlöndorff became acquainted by chance with David Bennent (the twelve-year-old son of the actor Heinz Bennent), who was physically like a four-year-old boy. According to Sandford, Schlöndorff had decided previous to this meeting that for the sake of audience identification the role of Oskar would not be played by a dwarf (46). See there Gunter Grass's 1978 painting of David Bennent, including the drum and eel. Schlöndorff described the "authentic element" that Bennent brought with him to the role of Oskar, since the two had similar problems. In this respect, "He is the opposite of a child actor who everyone thinks is touching. He has no pity, no tact at all, no sentimentality" (177).

32 For example, Alice in *Alice*, Mignon in *Wrong Movement*, Hunter in *Paris, Texas* and Gabi in *Petra*; and their mirroring adults, Karin in *Petra*, Fox in *Fox*, Hans in *The Merchant*, and Erwin/Elvira in *In a Year of Thirteen Moons*.

itself in advance from the familial body, the final result is reproduction: Oskar becomes part of the intergenerational transfer of the destructive sexual-familial structure.

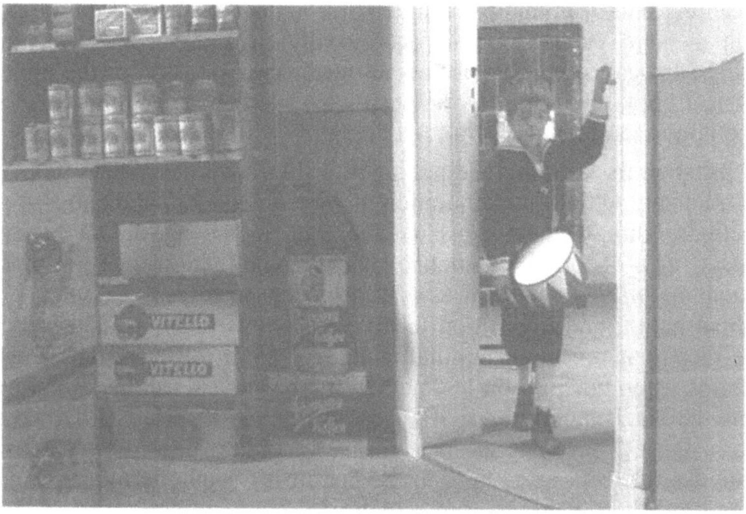

The abandoned bodyless child, *The Tin Drum*

As Oskar's sexuality develops it becomes distorted, just like the environment from which he has separated himself. Forced to be the son of two fathers, he became one of two fathers of his own son, Kurt, who is perhaps his brother. As a child he pays the price of the perverted familial sexual structure that includes a husband and lover, while as an adolescent he reproduces the same perversion when he and his father are Maria's lovers, and, later, when he and Bebra are Roswitha's lovers. That is, sexuality is the main factor that undermines his previous rebelliousness.

Oskar's sexuality is not a deviation from the Hitlerian trope of the son. After all, he is emblematic of this identification structure portrayed in cinema of the second generation: Although he is Kurt's father, he is presented first not as a father, but rather as the son of his symbolic mother, Maria. His behavior is directed by a desire to be imbibed within the female body (and its metonymic substitutes – an abundance of dark hiding places like his grandmother's dresses, under the dining table, Maria's bed, the neighbor's blanket). That is, his behavior represents a primordial sexual attraction to the mother that is preserved by intergenerational transference of sexual patterns.

Retaining the physical body of a three-year-old means giving preference to pre-oedipal identification over the oedipal (e.g., crib, continuous supervision). Oskar's first scream when he falls down the stairs becomes his surrogate language, along with the drum. That is, the sounds of screaming and drumming – nonverbal in nature – keep him in the pre-oedipal stage even as he chronologically matures. Ironically, these bodily surrogates which presume an imaginary extension of the limited physical body retain him in the destructive sexual stage from which he sought to separate himself through the fall.[33]

Oskar shifts from pre-oedipal identification with the mother (climaxing tragically with his collaboration in Agnes's suicide) and anti-oedipal reactions (climaxing with his collaboration in the murder of his two fathers) to a distorted situation of latent sexual acting. In spite of his sexual maturity, this latent sexual behavior preserves the same pre-oedipal nature and opposition to the Father. His body, which was the sole means of revealing familial and social truth (Oskar drums and/or screams when he spies on his mother and her lover, and his drumming turns the Nazi march into a Viennese waltz and the Heil Hitler salute into a dance), becomes the sole means of hiding this truth. Thus, he continues to sleep, as a child, in the bed of his symbolic mother Maria when his father is absent. But, actually, by hiding under her dress he is not seeking refuge, and their childish play with candies becomes sexual foreplay.

B. The Drum: Phallic Substitute, Nazi Weapon

Throughout his childhood, Oskar observes his environment with a voyeuristic gaze. The positioning of the camera reveals Agnes' and Jan's affair even when Oskar is at the top of the church spire or in the clothes closet, and is, of course, not able to share its view. In this sense, Oskar's omniscient consciousness moves between all-knowing voyeurism and audial witnessing (drumming, screaming). Oskar's audial reaction (including the transition from being a witness to being a witness participant through the splintering of the glass) is, as noted, a substitute for his physical disabilities and an expression of revolt. Even when he matures sexually, he pretends that this audial reaction is his sole mode of corporeality. The drum, however, is no longer an extension of his rebelliousness[34] and has become a false means of preserving false childishness.

33 Even Kaspar Hauser describes his life as a "terrible fall." See Silverman.

34 Schlöndorff calls this "*Verweigerer*" – rebel/refusenik (qtd. in Sandford 159).

The oedipal and sexual conflict between the son and the father takes place when Oskar discovers that his father is also having an affair with Maria. In this scene, Oskar enters the house and sees the two having sex on the living room sofa. When Maria shouts to Alfred "Get out now! Get out," Oskar places the drum on his father, lies on it, and does not let him up. Maria shouts, "No! No! No!" but Alfred can't remove himself from Maria and reaches orgasm. In contrast to what happened in his early childhood, Oskar does not react by drumming or with a scream; the audial extension of his corporeal disability is useless in the world of sexuality. Rather, by placing himself on his father he physically continues Alfred's sexual movements using the drum as a phallic substitute. Thus, in this scene, Oskar is himself and is also his rival. Perversely, the drum not only divides and unifies them, but also signifies Oskar's phallic abilities: the invisible corporeal change that has begun within him. In other words, in contrast to his childhood, at this stage the drum is not the extension of a body that has not grown, but rather of a body that has secretly matured sexually. Bodily movement signifies the imagined sexuality that Oskar experienced when he was part of the symbolic incest of the primal scene. In fact, his imitation of Alfred is a physical expression of his phallic ability disguised by the drum. In an absurd way, without his father knowing, Oskar has imposed on them a reproduction of the destructive familial structure of two lovers and two fathers, and symbolic incest.[35]

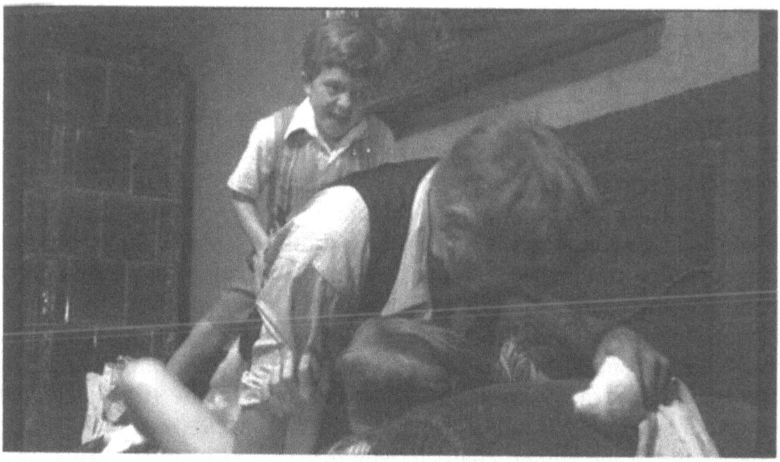

Oskar, his father, and Maria, *The Tin Drum*

[35] In a certain way, this is an inheritance from the past, since Jan, too, was Agnes's cousin.

Thus, corporeal distortion imprisons Oskar in the reproduction of the destructive familial sexual structure and leads him to accept his father's pragmatic Nazi values. The film constructs his false sexual identity in parallel with the Nazi conquest of Europe. The family, it will be recalled, celebrates the birth of Kurt, his brother/son, together with the impending approach of the Nazis to Moscow. No wonder, then, that upon Kurt's birth Oskar escapes the family to become an entertainer for the Nazi troops using the same performance instrument – the dissonance between his low height and ear-shattering voice. The drum that opposed the rise of Nazism in the parade becomes his principal weapon. Nazism uses the imaginary boundaries of Oskar's body in reverse: not as a substitute for physical disabilities but as powerful abilities. The fact that the imaginary and real regression of Oskar finds its solution both within the Nazi family unit and Nazi propaganda (including the romantic triangle with Bebra and Roswitha) leads the spectator to recognize Oskar's multifaceted monstrosity. The body that remembers, indeed, leads Oskar to his symbolic death as a rebel.

Despite the appearance that the film presents an turnabout in its depiction of regression to pre-oedipal childlikeness as a result of Oskar's announcement at Alfred's funeral that he is ready to grow, Kurt's throwing a pebble at him, the family departure, Oskar's call to his grandmother, and the final cyclical image of the grandmother in the field attest, in my opinion, to the impossibility of being saved from regressive constructs.[36]

IV. Two Faces of Revolt, One Body

Kaspar and Oskar, the two paradigmatic cases that construct the Infantile Asexual Model, represent the spectrum between being an abandoned child and one that abandons. Each exemplifies a different type of revolt against the paternal and the symbolic. It appears that the experience of being abandoned is not only an autobiographical experience of this generation of directors who are representative of all those who grew up in Germany during the Nazi period, but is also the central fantasy of the second generation: the fantasy of not growing up in a German family; abandoning it/being abandoned by it and/or murdering the parents/being murdered by them. The two paradigmatic films affiliated with this model of masculinity create a connection between the absence of the Name of the Father, characteristic of NGC, as claimed earlier, and

---

[36] On the differences between the Schlöndorff's film and the Gunter Grass novel, see, for example, Hall. Among the differences, the author notes that in contrast to the film, the novel does not end with the defeat of Hitler.

its ultimate manifestation (to murder/be murdered) as a consequence of the abandonment experience. Retaining the experience of abandonment preserves the adult in infantile asexuality or distorted infantile sexuality. In any event, sexuality – or its total absence – does not rescue the abandoned child/adult from the experience of abandonment and does not make possible the continuation of the family unit.

The attitude of each of the films towards its protagonist is different. Kaspar is a positive hero who symbolizes the unpreventable, necessary regression linked to an inner truth of opposition to the narrow-minded and oppressive middle class. Due to his sexual maturity, Oskar is an ambivalent hero, a monstrous child; the regression associated with his character is not radical, but rather part of his complicity with the family. As noted, he represents the German family in which even the rebel eventually comes to take on its character. The trope of the son – even in its most extreme appearance in the life of Oskar – carries with it meanings far beyond the Spirit of '68.

In spite of the difference in the nature of the revolt, in the personality of the rebel, and in the attitude of the film toward him, the two films share not only the themes discussed but also the strength of the imagery of the body. The distorted body remains – in the end – the principal symbol, whether speaking of mythicization of the German abandonment narrative in *Every Man for Himself and God Against All, or the Mystery of Kaspar Hauser*, or of allegorization of a period as in *The Tin Drum*.

V. Redemption through Mirror Relations: *Paris, Texas*

I claimed earlier in this chapter that neither *Every Man for Himself and God Against All, or the Mystery of Kaspar Hauser* nor *The Tin Drum* offer rescue from abandonment, but rather fixated on it and became fixated within it. Similarly, Herzog's and Fassbinder's other films represent an identity devoid of any possibility of redemption. In contrast, the films of Wim Wenders not only actualize the characteristics of infantile asexual masculinity (reproduction of abandonment, regression, asexuality, bodily excess, attachment to the self-destructive family unit, and anti-oedipalization), but also enable redemption for the abandoned adult/child through mirror relations. In other words, in contrast to his colleagues in the triumvirate, Wenders structures the role of the cinema as comforter through his use of multifaceted reflexivity as a mediator between identity options. *Paris, Texas* is an extraordinary realization of the Infantile Asexual Model: more so than his previous films, such as *Goalkeeper's Anxiety*, *Alice in the Cities*, *Wrong Movement*, *Kings of the Road*, *The American Friend* – and still more so than those that came later, from *Wings of Desire* through *Million Dollar Hotel.*

A. Father/Son – Mother/Wife

Paris, Texas (Wim Wenders, 1984).

Paris, Texas *describes the journey of Travis after four years of wandering the Texas badlands, to a reunion with his son Hunter in the city and their joint journey to Jane (Nastassja Kinski), their wife mother who lives in Houston. In the background is the breakup of the family unit due to jealousy and obsessive love on the part of the husband, and the wife's immaturity. Travis "kidnaps" Hunter from his brother Walt (Dean Stockwell) and his wife Ann (*Aurore Clement*), who are raising him, and renews the connection between Hunter and Jane. Following a confrontation with Jane at the peepshow parlor where she works, Travis realizes it is impossible to undo the past and so returns to the desert.*

In 1986, approximately two years after the release of *Paris, Texas*, in his book *America*, Baudrillard made a comparison between America and Europe: "What is new in America is the clash of the first level (primitive and wild) and the 'third kind' (the absolute simulacra). There is no second level. This is a situation we find hard to grasp, since this is the one we have always privileged: the self-reflexive, self-mirroring level, the level of unhappy consciousness" (104). As a joint French-German-American effort, *Paris, Texas* adds "the second level," reflexivity, to Travis' journey from the primitive and wild[37] to the absolute simulacra.[38] The heart of the journey from the Texas desert to the simulacra of the Houston peephouse is Travis's schizoid experience.[39] The overall textual schizoidity is manifest in the paternal being split between Walt and Travis as well as in the maternal being split between Ann and Jane; however, above all else, the split is constructed at the end of Travis's

[37] "The desert is a sublime form that banishes all sociality, all sentimentality, all sexuality. Words, even when they speak of the desert, are always unwelcome. Caresses have no meaning, except from a woman who is herself of the desert, who has that instantaneous, superficial animality [...] Each night the earth plunges into perfectly calm darkness, into the blackness of its alkaline gestation, into the happy depression of its birth" (71).

[38] Most Wenders scholars claim that reflexivity is central in his work.

[39] In his book *The Divided Self*, Laing described the schizoid existential condition as being derived from ontological insecurity. Its primary characteristics are anxiety that leads to isolation and total loneliness; self-absorption; absence of a sense of temporal continuity; loose ties with reality; the capacity to connect only to depersonalized experiences, to phantoms self-fantasies, and to an object of imagination or memory, but not to real people; the desire not to exist; and behavior limited to observation and fantasy.

journey between the feminine and the maternal in Jane's identity. This is the split of intergenerational unity between father and son (mirror relations): Travis's relinquishing of the feminine in favor of the maternal causes him to return Hunter to Jane, thereby creating a symbolic unification between the paternal figure and the son, between himself and Hunter. The mirror relations are expressed in the unification of Hunter-who-is-Travis (the childlike element that is in Travis) and Jane-who-is-the-mother-of-Hunter/Travis.

Redemption from abandonment is therefore limited – the final split between the feminine and the maternal is also reconfirmation of the schizoidity of the male subject (man/husband or son) and the father's re-abandonment of the son. In other words, the father (as a former abandoned child) attains redemption as a son through his own son. Relinquishing his fatherhood and masculinity means, of course, reaffirmation of his asexuality. The return to the desert is thus not like his first retreat to it. Travis is not the same man he was four years earlier. Although there is no continuity in the German family and there is no place in it for a father, in every case abandonment is the factor that determines the plot of the family drama for generations. But Travis symbolically leaves with Hunter the child within himself, and therefore his return to the desert is not an eternal regression. The Wendersian male learns to accept the childhood experience of abandonment through what appears at first glance to be a neurotic reproduction of a family pattern. On second glance, however, it turns out to be (irrespective of the loss of sexuality) an internal acceptance. From this stage on, his identity will be defined in terms of relinquishing masculinity/sexuality/fatherhood in favor of redeeming the child-that-is-within-him from the experience of abandonment.

The following is a description of the salient scenes that construct this process, focusing on the place of the spectator.

B. House of Mirrors Scenes

The peepshow parlor designed by Wenders-Shepard creates a context that the film undermines at almost every possible level. The peepshow as image is based on the tense relations between the context and its negation. In his book *The Theatre of the Absurd*, Martin Esslin described the image in *Diary of a Thief* that expresses the essence of Genet's theatre as

> [T]he image of a man caught in a maze of mirrors, trapped by his own distorted reflections, trying to find the way to make contact with the others he can see around him but being rudely stopped by barriers of glass [...] [Genet's plays] are concerned with expressing his own feeling of helpless-

ness and solitude when confronted with despair and loneliness of man caught in the hall of mirrors of the human condition, inexorably trapped by an endless progression of images that are merely his own distorted reflection [...] fantasies battening upon fantasies, nightmares nourished by nightmares within nightmares. (166-167).

In and of itself, the peephouse refers to Jean Genet's *The Balcony* (1960) (a work that was part of the cultural world of the film's scriptwriter Sam Shepard). In the play, Jean Genet describes a whorehouse in which the clients become addicted to their fantasies (a punishing judge, a leper healed by the Madonna, etc.). They position themselves at the center of their erotic dreams, a perverted continuation of their roles in the actual world. While in *The Balcony* these fantasies signify the relationship between governance and sex, the context of the peepshow in *Paris, Texas* is constructed to fulfill three other purposes: it is the basis for confrontation with the fantasy image of the woman; a means of raising the possibility of constructing a coherent male identity through this confrontation; and a means of questioning the essence of the cinematic apparatus.

Like in the opening of *The Balcony*, in *Paris, Texas* the ground is pulled from under the feet of the spectator. In the play it turns out that the bishop, dressed elegantly and speaking flowery theological language, is not a bishop at all, and the location is a whorehouse where he is acting out his sexual fantasies. Travis's first encounter with the peepshow is also based on mistakes related to viewing. It becomes clear that the peephouse allows for choice among fantasies (forty-two altogether) in which women act out the fantasies of men through voyeurism and exhibitionism without physical contact.[40] According to Haug, as long as sex continues to be a commodity driven by profit it is ambivalent: making it a service industry causes an endless stream of passions (55). That is to say, the satisfaction such sex provides only leads to further

---

40 Haug's observation on commodity aesthetics is interesting in this regard: "Prostitution remains on the level of simple commodity production, or rather a service industry, with the pimp as capitalist agent and the brothel as factory [...] In a situation of general sexual repression [...] the use value of mere sexual illusion lies in the satisfaction which voyeurism can provide. This satisfaction through a use value, whose specific nature is an illusion, can be called illusory satisfaction. The characteristics of this satisfaction through sexual illusion are that it simultaneously reproduces further demand alongside satisfaction, and produces a compulsive fixation. If guilt feelings and the angst they arouse block the way to the sexual object, then the commodity of sexual illusion acts as its replacement, mediating excitement and a certain satisfaction which might be difficult to develop in actual sensual and physical contact. This type of seemingly unhindered satisfaction threatens to cut off completely the possibility of direct pleasure [...] Thus a general voyeurism is reinforced, habituated, and determines the human instinctual structure" (55). (Emphasis in the original)

craving. Haug's words bring the difference between prostitution, whose "use value" is related to physical contact or direct sensation, and voyeurism, whose nature is an illusion, into focus. Under late capitalism, the ideal of commodity aesthetics is to provide a minimum of use value under the disguise of maximum seductive illusion. It appears that the peepshow represents one of the strongest powers of capitalist society.

In *Paris, Texas*, the peepshow is based on the relationship between voice and sight made possible by a one-way mirror and a telephone connected to a loudspeaker. The first meeting is based on errors of perception: the location (whorehouse or peepshow?), the identity of the blonde (Nurse Bibs [Sally Norvell] is not Jane), and the relationship between the voice and the mirror ("what do you [female] see? What do you [male] see? Nurse Bibs and the rubber horse."). Wenders places Nurse Bibs in the center of the frame/the mirror, but her view turns to the side, diagonally, while Travis, who is also in the center of the frame/the mirror, looks straight ahead and experiences the clash between his look and what appears to be her look at him, but is actually her look directed at herself. These errors in perception shape the central characteristic of the peephouse: it ruptures the simultaneousness of the look, of viewing.

As noted, Travis's encounter with the blond "nurse" and his first encounter with Jane in a "hotel" establish the context. In his second encounter with Jane, the film undermines this context. When Travis enters the booth named Poolside, he requests a blonde over the phone. This request includes the concept of the blonde, that is, objectification of the female subject, a concept constructed ideologically by the fantasies offered to clients. Travis uses this concept to find Jane; in fact, his search for the right woman in a place that creates an illusionary world of identity exchange is related to his other search for a coherent identity. The fact that he receives the wrong blonde is crucial to the second encounter. According to the laws of this simulacric world, it is too easy to transgress the boundaries between imagined and real. In the reality of the encounter, the ruse becomes reality (as in the end of *The Balcony*): a world of mirrors from which it is impossible to be saved.

Therefore, in a gesture parallel to the final scene with Pauline (Lisa Kreuzer) in *Kings of the Road* (when Bruno takes Pauline's tears and wipes them on his cheek), at the end of the first encounter with Jane, Travis wipes away his tears with the telephone – an act that symbolizes his recognition of the impossibility of any other contact. Then, at the end of the second encounter, he says, "I can't see you, Jane." An expression of the impossibility of escape from the world of mirrors.

C. First Encounter with Jane

During their first encounter Travis looks at Jane almost against his will (he shades his eyes). When Jane starts to undress, he stops her. This rupture of the fantasy/spectacle and voyeurism takes place within a context in which Jane does not know who he is and both of them are hiding their identities. Such concealment forces Jane to complete the fantasy of a prostitute in a "hotel," a role grounded in split identity. The equivalence between woman and spectacle, man and vision lasts even when Travis prevents her from acting out the fantasy. Up to this point in the scene, Jane appears to be enclosed within the *mise-en-scène* of the fantasy only from Travis's point of view. When the context of the fantasy is fractured and Travis interrogates her about the nature of her job – is she a paid prostitute after work hours? – the camera moves to the other side of the one-way mirror and the point of view is fractured. Until then the spectator has only seen Jane from Travis's point of view. From the point the scene is filmed in medium close-up and the space of the framed mirror becomes the space around Jane's face, the frame of the one-way mirror disappears and congruence is formed between the mirror and the film screen. Thus a contrast is created between the shots in which the frame of the mirror is seen and those in which Jane fills the entire frame, depicting not only change in the spectator's point of view but also, of course, in his/her transition from breaking the screen to congruence with it.

The spectator's awareness of the role of the camera is all the stronger after Jane appears in her room, stares into the mirror, and is reflected in it. When the camera is located in her room, penetrating the *mise-en-scène* of the fantasy, the laws of the house of mirrors are preserved and Travis is not shown. The question heard from the loudspeaker, "How much money do you make on the side?" reinforces not only the fact that there is intervention from an additional mirror (the cinema) but that an acoustic mirror is active as well. When the camera moves to Travis's side, Jane fills the whole frame and is again located in its center. At the end of the scene, the camera focuses on Jane with a medium close-up as she continues to speak without being aware that Travis has left. In contrast to earlier shots in which the spectator's position is that of Travis, here only the spectator views her. This element, including the last shot in which she speaks to the mirror, "to herself" (a double meaning as Travis has left), is further developed in the second encounter.

Does the camera position change the relationship between the subject and the object? In the context of the world of mirrors constructed in the first encounter, as claimed above, both Travis and Jane are deprived of their original identity. Travis is characterized as "not seen," that is, he lacks identity, while Jane's is borrowed. The context (fantasy, voyeurism, spectacular *mise-en-scène*, the *femme fatale* dressed in red and in full light, the man in isolation and relative darkness) determines the gaze and subjugation to sight and sound for the spectator as well. The camera that passes beyond the mirror and shoots Jane from the place that Travis is not able to see does indeed change the subject-object relationship, but not completely: Jane does not see him. Even though the camera is located with her, the one-way mirror context remains dominant. Her voice is still not an autonomous female voice, but is rather a phantasmatic echo – it has no independent existence since it is not connected to an independent identity. The fact that Travis is heard through her loudspeaker, as a continuation of the split between his body and voice (body not seen and voice heard), hints of the subversion that will take place in the second encounter. The fact that the spectator moves within the changing hierarchies of sound and image, and of seen/not seen, defines his/her subversive role.

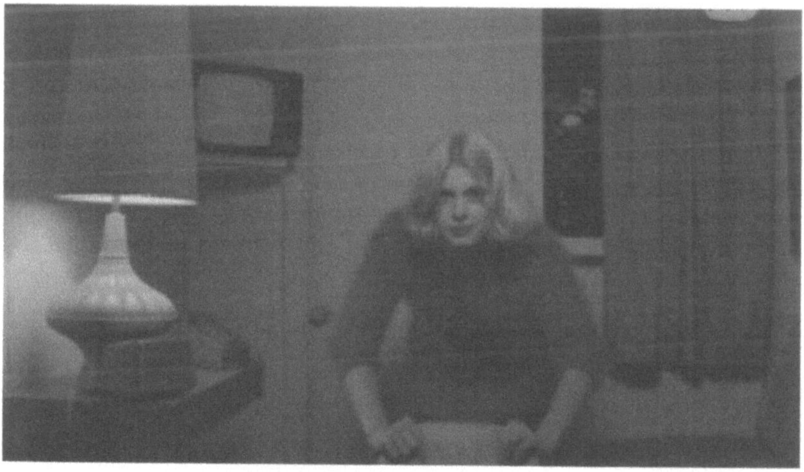

First encounter with Jane, *Paris, Texas*

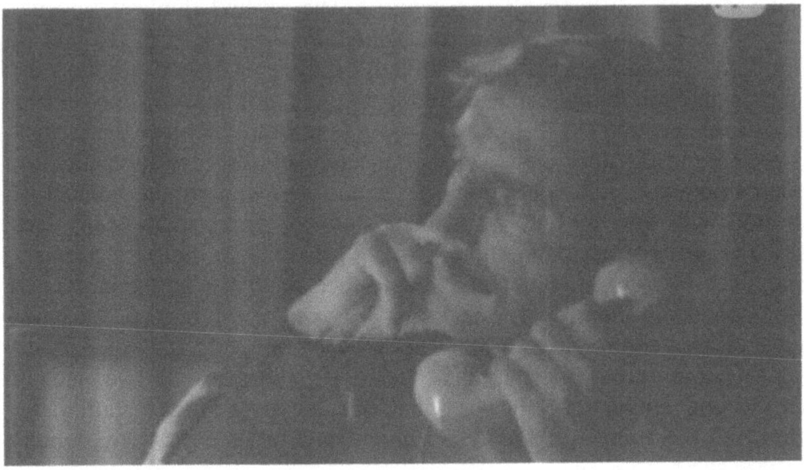

The spectator's position is connected to Travis and to Jane through their respective points of view. The spectator is part of the illusion, but is also aware of being alienated from it. The scene moves him/her between these opposing positions, all of which are within the patriarchal relations the protagonist himself tries to undermine.

In the second encounter will the spectator also find him/herself moving between these contradictory positions – being with the gaze or with the gaze that reflects upon itself? Participating in the cinematic illusion or being alienated from it? Is Jane the embodiment of the cinematic spectacle that does not return the gaze?

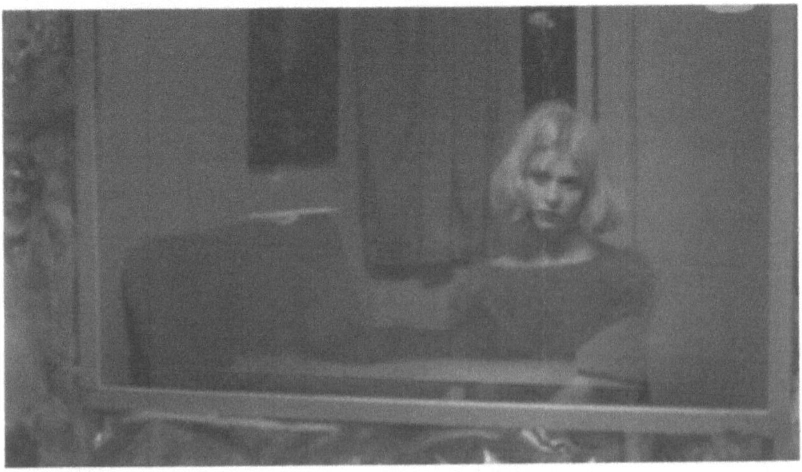

House of mirrors, *Paris, Texas*

D. Second Encounter

All previous relationships change when during the second encounter Travis turns his back to the one-way mirror and speaks to Jane without seeing her. Similarly, when Jane turns her back to the mirror after she recognizes Travis her position changes radically and she becomes a subject with an identity, a point of view of her own, and a voice.

The subject-object relationship is redefined here, since this breaching of the masks of identity also breaches of the laws of the world of mirrors. Discussing this reversal of relationships is central to understanding the woman as m/other in *Paris, Texas* and her being a juncture not only in terms of the crisis of displacement and of the American dream, but in terms of the trope of the son.

The pattern described in the first encounter becomes more complex in the second. On the one hand, Travis's gaze in relation to Jane is ruptured when he turns around and speaks to the mirror without looking at her. On the other, the spectator's gaze that sees Jane is retained. In contrast, Jane assumes that Travis sees her, an assumption that influences her reaction to his words until the masks are breached and their identities revealed.

In the second encounter, Travis cancels the gaze in favor of the look to enable a confrontation grounded on past issues of personal and familial identity. But the look, as described above, is disconnected from the eye, first of all in the simultaneous sense and then when it becomes absent and the confrontation is mediated mainly by sound.

The a-simultaneity of seeing, dominant in the first encounter and caused by the laws of the house of mirrors, is drastically reinforced in the second: Travis turns his back to the mirror, does not see Jane, but pretends that he does; Jane does not see him but thinks that he sees her. As the encounter continues, she turns her back to the mirror when she speaks: the only time she could have mastered her seeing, she prefers not to see him. The moment between their monologues is the sole time in which the a-simultaneity of seeing is ruptured, in parallel with rupture of the gaze (and power relations involved in it). In an attempt to override the laws of the house of mirrors, Jane turns off the light in her room and for a moment Travis's face is reflected, superimposed on her face. She sees him. A simultaneous reflection is created. When Jane gains sight, she also gains a voice of her own and delivers a monologue.

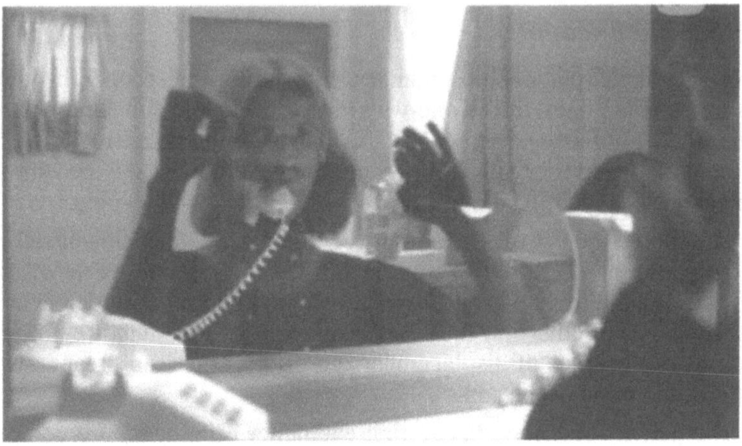

Mirror reflection in place of touch, *Paris, Texas*

How is the look connected with identity? When the simultaneity of seeing is created (the superimposed faces), Travis goes beyond observation and fantasy in order to feel ontological security. His attempt to construct a coherent identity is made through verbal interpretation of the personal familial crises while overcoming forgetfulness and repression. À la Laing, I claim that Travis interprets his part in their past relationship as ontological dependence on the other rather than couplehood based upon authentic mutuality. The outcome – a relationship in which the other is necessary for the existence of the self and simultaneously experienced as a threat – was total isolation, the complete blurring of identity. That is, Travis is describing a process of depersonalization that was part of his existential failure to be. This description is the climax of the re-subjectivization process described in the film, since during his time in the desert he does not give any expression to his subjectivity. During the second encounter, however, he tries to overcome silence in order to go beyond his schizoid existence. No wonder, then, that he decided to turn the chair around and not look at Jane. According to Laing, in a world full of dangers, to be seen means to be exposed to danger and the clearest defense is to make oneself invisible in one way or another. The schizoid wants people to look at him/her, as only thus can s/he ease his depersonalization and internal death. In other words, s/he needs other people to see him/her as a real live person. On the other hand, when the schizoid becomes aware of this, s/he will not be fully secure about other people's awareness. Here Wenders seem to be applying his version of the myth of Perseus and the Medusa head.

Even more, the fact that Travis turns around to recite his return monologue (fracturing the gaze, the look, and the a-simultaneity of looking) is an indication of the schizoid state in an additional sense: there is an assiduous split between the self and the body. The concrete expression of the self is Travis's voice. Laing (86) describes this in the following diagram:

(Self / Body)⇔Other

Self ⇔(Body Other)

That is to say, Travis's position during the monologue is in contrast to its content: the position prevents him from direct participation in relations with the other. The Self ⇔(Body Other) position leaves Travis's body to Jane's "look" (she thinks he is facing her).

In terms of the plot, we should remember that Travis decides to rea-bandon Hunter after his first encounter with Jane, as expressed in his recorded statement to Hunter, "I can't stay with you, I barely remember what happened, like a dark hole [...]." This is emphasized through a sound bridge between the end of the recording and Travis using the telephone in the peephouse. In this sense, the second encounter is principally an attempt to face the past and the other after the decision to re-separate has already been made. The attempt to move beyond the schizoid state through recall of the past is anchored in his pre-emptive decision to separate; that is, the look does not lead to an establishment of identity. This is the meaning of the statement: "I can't see you, Jane."

Sound is central to these scenes. Travis experiences the connection to the lost object of the m/other principally through the voice that enables more control over space than does sight. The image of the child swathed in the sonorous envelope of the maternal voice is dominant here. Doane describes how sound supports the phantasm of an imaginary body experienced by the infant:

> Space, for the child, is defined initially in terms of the audible, not the visible [...] The mother's soothing voice [...] is a major component of the 'sonorous envelope' which surrounds the child and is the first model of auditory pleasure. An image of corporeal unity is derived from the realization that the production of sound by the voice and its audition coincide. The imaginary fusion of the child with the mother is supported by the recognition of common traits [...] and [...] of their potential for harmony [...] At the cinema, the sonorous envelope provided by the theatrical space together with techniques employed in the construction of the soundtrack work to sustain the narcissistic pleasure derived from the image of a certain unity, cohesion, and, hence, an identity grounded by the spectator's fantasmatic relation to his/her own body. (573-574)

In an eight-minute monologue (in which screen time and real time converge), Jane tells Travis, "in this place every man speaks in your voice," thus describing their relationship in audial terms. She describes her conversations with other men as if they were with him and how she eventually relinquished his voice image. In other words, the monologue explains why she chose to work in a phantasmatic world that is controlled both by the voices of men and the fact she cannot see them. But *Paris, Texas* describes Jane's release from this world that symbolizes her dependence on Travis. When he addresses her by name she changes from an object of the gaze and a listener to a story told in the third person to a subject. Although they turn on the lights in order to see each other, Jane's release comes when she turns her face away from the mirror and finds her own voice.

When Travis leaves, the camera remains in the room with her. Following the cut, he is shot from the back, looking at the Hotel Meridian. The following shots show a caress, a smile of happiness, and a hug as Jane and Hunter are reunited (something that Travis cannot see, of course). Then there is a cut and a high angle shot shows Travis standing next to the street light with the car in the background. Are they looking at him? In this shot the exchange between the omniscient camera and Jane and Hunter's point of view potentially exists, and enriches the perception of Jane as a subject. In the last shots Travis is seen in his car; the camera is turned back and reveals the urban landscape, skyscrapers, street lights, and the highway; the dedication to Lotte Eisner appears.

E. Not a Son (Neither a Father nor a Husband)

The mutual caress is not part of the world of mirrors, as are schizoid isolation and limitation to fantasy, and even simultaneous looking is possible, as noted, only as a reflection that lasts a moment. The female point of view has preference at the end of the journey described in the film and the high angle shot from the Hotel Meridian clarifies, again, that in such relationships simultaneity is impossible. This shot establishes a definitive separation between Jane (and Hunter) and Travis. Before the separation, the film preserves at all levels the maternal child relationship, including displacing Travis's relationship with his mother to that of Hunter and Jane. At separation, Travis's moment of redemption from his abandonment, which had made him an eternal abandoned child and thus an asexual infantile adult, is signified in the film through the Hotel Meridian shot. That is, the moment of separation is also the moment of redemption. It is the climax of mirror relations, and also signifies the impossibility of normal couplehood. Travis's loss of masculinity and sexuality is no longer a result of his inability to master his abandonment, but the result of his awareness of the possibility of repairing this primal experience.

The family crisis is both that of American dream[41] and of the meta-process of displacement. In the Wendersian world that longs for emotional personal contact, it is ironic that the house of mirrors portrays the culmination of substitution and displacement. Destruction or rupture of all surrogates (the substitute family; the image of the perfect family in the home movie; the house of mirrors; *Paris, Texas* as a symbol; France and America as phantasmatic domains, etc.), leave a world in which only cinema renews the drama of phenomenological loss; and even more, cultural recovery. It is the confrontation with the simulacra, however, that enables both the Wendersian man and the woman to undermine the laws of the simulacra. And so, the crisis of the American dream is the beginning of the renewal of the German (cinematic) dream.[42]

The film's self-reflexivity is a counter balance to the absence of self-reflexivity in the house of mirrors.[43] Wenders uses this absence to reveal the male subject and to dramatize a discussion in cinematic representation. The unique image of the house of mirrors becomes, therefore, an allegory for the problematic existence of cinema in and of itself: a cinema that continuously asks questions – What is cinema? How can films come into being, except based on their very own impossibility? But more than this, the reflexivity – the "second stage" according to Baudrillard – is what assists the male subject in moving from voyeurism

---

41 Regarding the crisis of this dream, see Wenders' "The American Dream." The poem was written in 1984, near the time *Paris, Texas* was first opening in theatres (*Emotion Pictures* 116-146). In a 1991 speech, ("Talking") Wenders said the following: "I lived out my childhood dream of the 'Promised Land.' The dreamland of my childhood has become a nightmare; the happy images have turned into images of violence and a form of entertainment that sells ease, pleasure, and immediacy to the highest bidder [...] The landscapes of John Ford are now Marlboro Country, the American Dream has become a marketing campaign" (56-57).

42 To the best of my knowledge, no Wenders scholars to date have discussed the positive function of simulacra or its multiples in the world of Wenders. It may be that this is due to explanations given by Wenders in interviews, his writings about the shattering of the American dream, and his response to the traumatic production of *Hammett*.

43 In *America*, Baudrillard does not emphasize America as a dream or as reality, but rather as hyperreality: "It is a hyperreality because it is a utopia which has behaved from the very beginning as though it were already achieved [...] [T]he truth of America can only be seen by a European, since he alone will discover here the perfect simulacrum [...] The Americans, for their part, have no sense of simulation. They are themselves simulation in its most developed state, but they have no language in which to describe it, since they themselves are the model" (28-29).

and perception of the woman as fantasy to deconstruction of the spectacle. By the very act itself, he undergoes transformation from infantile asexual male reproducing the pattern of the abandoned child in his relationships to asexual male liberated from the dread of abandonment; that is, one who pays the price for his asexuality not as retribution but from choice. The meeting with the schizoid male, who becomes a subject as a result of the confrontation with the simulacra (i.e., with the woman as an image and with sexuality as an audio-voyeuristic fantasy), also leads the woman to a confrontation with the simulacra that previously reproduced her phantasmatic being and dependence on the male voice. This confrontation also enables her, as hinted above, to reconstruct her subjectivity.

Paris, Texas depicts the reasons for the familial crisis, gives expression to the process of remembering, enables the re-subjectivization of the woman, and demonstrates the symbolic exchange of child-adult/son-husband. For the male subject, escape from the schizoid state is impossible until his meeting with the simulacra world, which teaches him that fatherhood is only a momentary state, and that contact is accessible only through reflection. The unavoidable destruction of desire is, in the end, a central component of redemption, since it undermines the trope of the son. The man who leaves his son and wife is no longer split in the schizoid sense; he is no longer dependent on the traumas of the past. As claimed earlier, when Travis decides to give up his fatherhood and reabandon Hunter, he restores the child within him. The man who returns to wandering is not the same man who fled to the desert: he is no longer a "son of his mother." *Paris, Texas* opens for the second generation – for the first time in Wenders' oeuvre – the possibility of release from past identifications; a possibility that will be realized in future films.

What happens to the spectator? The change in the position of the camera, which causes a change in the point of view and in the relationship between sound and image, causes the spectator's fascination with "how it works."[44] The sense of lack of control of the visual in the *mise-en-abyme* of interspecularization is accompanied by the spectator's exposure to the gaze, as opposed to the protagonist who is not exposed to the gaze. The tension that affects the spectator in these scenes moves him/her from emotional identification to gaining knowledge (fascination with "how [the apparatus] works"). This tension is connected to the complexity of the image of the house of mirrors and the ever-changing hierarchical relationship between the image and the sound. But the

44 See Penley.

spectator does not only experience such shifts and excess of knowledge in comparison to that given to the protagonists. By film's end, the spectator participates in the reworking of past identifications together with them.

As noted, *Paris, Texas* is a turning point in Wenders' oeuvre, both in terms of saving the infantile male from the Mother and the process of subjectivization of the woman (transformation from an image of the phantasmatic woman mother to an actual mother, as well as from a voyeuristic exhibitionist object to a subject with a look, voice, and past of her own). The protagonists of Wenders' pre-*Paris, Texas* films were characterized by reproduction of neurotic-psychotic behavior connected to the Mother. In *Alice in the Cities*, *Wrong Movement, Kings of the Road* and *The American Friend*, in addition to a journey to the Mother, there is also a world of surrogates; except that the journey, in contrast to *Paris, Texas*, does not lead to the rescue of the main protagonist – and certainly not the women he meets. In *Alice* and *Wrong Movement*, this is the world of the substitute family. In *Alice in the Cities*, Philip Winter, estranged from his parents, unsuccessfully searches for his surrogate daughter's family. In *Wrong Movement*, Wilhelm (Rüdiger Vogler) also finds himself in a surrogate family: the group that accompanies him on his journey serves as a substitute for intimate interaction. These people have no reason for joining him and are obsessed with the journey itself. The height of surrogate behavior comes during their visit to the estate of Bernhard (Peter Kern) a supposed uncle, who joins them because of the same obsession that drives the arbitrary relations between the travelers.

In *Kings of the Road* and *The American Friend*, asexuality is not structured as part of belonging to the imaginary surrogate family, but rather as part of relations between men. In *Kings of the Road*, Bruno and Robert refrain from any close or sexual contact with women. In *The American Friend*, Zimmerman substitutes his relationship with his wife for visual games of sexuality suggested to him by his "friend," Ripley (Dennis Hopper). The transition from films that preserve the desire for the Mother and substitute it with different types of surrogate relations, to films that suggest the possibility of being rescued from these recurrent cycles takes place in *Paris, Texas*.

Wenders' films from the late 1980s and early 1990s – *Wings of Desire*; *End of the World*; *Faraway, So Close* – construct the male healing process in parallel to reconstitution of female identity: in *Wings of Desire* the eternal asexuality of the angel is exchanged for life on earth as a man who has fallen in love. *Faraway, So Close*, an ostensible sequel to *Wings of Desire*, develops a variation of "rescuing the child" that rectifies the abandonment experience. In *End of the World*, desire dies because the protagonists become addicted to their dreams (through an apparatus connected with the Mother); but in the end they – including the woman – learn to live without it\ without the Mother. Wilhelm in *Wrong Movement* is portrayed as not being involved in life, marginal to the symbolic order. The expected intimate connection with Therese (Hanna Schygulla) is revealed to be a connection with her daughter when he finds her naked in Therese's bed and slaps her. In the end, his inability to establish a connection with Therese leads them to separate in the middle of a crowd. As he leaves on his journey, Wilhelm refers to his mother, "It was as if I had to leave her behind in order to find her." His mother leaves him at the train station, but he then sees her in all the people he subsequently meets. The cinema of Wenders constructs the transition from this passive-obsessive pattern, so connected to the Mother figure and characteristic of the 1970s, to eventual liberation from it in the 1990s, after innumerable journeys.

CHAPTER 3

The Utopian Bisexual Model

I. Description of the Model:[1]

A. Masculinity in Wenders' Oeuvre – A Breakthrough

The utopian bisexual relationship is important in Wenders' 1970s films because, in the chronological sense, it enables his protagonists to make the transition in his 1990s films from the imaginary order to the symbolic, from yearning for woman as Mother to separation of the female from the maternal (that is, separate representations of the Woman and the Mother), and therefore the transition from infantile asexuality to sexuality. This process carries weighty cultural implications for the directors of the second generation and their German audience; that is, examination of the sexual representations in Wenders' 1990s films proves the extensive change that took place regarding past identifications. The process that began with utopian sexuality in 1970s films appears in his 1990s films as rescue from the trope of the son (the reproduction of regressive past identifications with Hitler).

As will be demonstrated in the following, Wenders' oeuvre should be defined as coherent and evolutionary – his early films adhere more to primordial processes than do the later ones. The Utopian Bisexual Model thus signifies a decisive shift in relations with the Nazi past and with the German defeat in World War II. As a description of the development of Wendersian masculinity will prove, this shift takes place in parallel with the abandoned child, but also transcends it.

The early oeuvre of Wenders from the 1970s through the mid-1980s has been characterized by its multifaceted transition from German to American culture; by the concept of America as "other"; by his obsessive use of the journey as a symbol; by chronological shooting, the anti-narrative, and an emphasis on silence as part of the "new sensitivity."

1 Major canonic films affiliated with this model are *Wrong Movement*, *Kings of the Road*, *The American Friend*, Nicholas Ray and Wenders' *Nick's Film – Lightning Over Water* (1980), Wenders' *Hammett* (1981), Wenders' *The State of Things*, (1982), Wenders' *Tokyo-Ga*, (1985), and *Wings of Desire*.

Wings of Desire (1987) marks a transformation that developed at the end of the 1980s and during the 1990s.[2]

Wendersian masculinity has been absorbed within this system of psychogeographical changes. In using the term "utopian bisexuality" I refer to the intimate fraternal relationship between two men, which is actually infantile homoeroticism without latent homosexual implications. This utopia is embodied in each man being the meaningful other for the other man through mirror relations, while simultaneously the Woman is the meaningful other for both of them. As most Wenders scholars have suggested, Wenders' men take part in an odyssey to the Woman, and desire for her is realized only through this journey involving a "buddy." I claim that the otherness symbolized by the buddy in this model is presented as a necessary stage in the realization of sexuality. At the same time, in the films of the 1970s, the possibility for a reflective mirroring friendship that will lead each one of them from the imaginary to the symbolic, from an absence of sexual relations to sexuality, from silence to language, is not realized; rather, it remains utopian. Therefore, from here on I will use the term "utopian bisexuality" to refer to these two components: the utopia that is unrealized erotic mirroring, and the utopia of the possibilities of couplehood that the relationship between the men may create for each of them in the future.

Although the model under discussion is characterized by the fact that the male reflective mirroring relationship remains an utopia and does not lead the protagonists to reach their Odyssean goal (the symbolic, the language, the Woman, etc.), I do want to emphasize that a retroactive consideration of the entirety of Wenders' oeuvre – including documentaries, writing, and even his photography – shows that the transition that took place from the 1970s to the 1990s was not only chronological, but transformative. It is not just a change in genre, style, and thematics.[3] Indeed, in the 1970s films Wenders' protagonist do not reach their goal, but viewing the transformation as a stage, or more precisely, a mode, enables us to see that these films lead to a means of confronting the past at a time NGC was mistakenly thought to be losing its importance. In this respect, the masculinity of the 1970s represented what appears to be

2 No longer is the crisis solely that of displacement (as in *Paris, Texas*), but the return to Berlin, the German language, and collaboration with Peter Handke is expressed in neo-expressionistic style. Minimalism is replaced by postmodern excess. The journey that began with *Wings of Desire* is no longer a journey in one space but one between continents; esoteric music is replaced by a rich, multi-layered soundtrack; and the spectator as traveler becomes a "man of the world" (Johnson; Geist [*Cinema*, "Mothers"]; Coates; Kolker *Films*; Corrigan ["German Friends"]; Elsaesser ["Spectators"]; Roger Cook, ["Angels," "Postmodern"]; Gemunden; Grob.

3 As claimed by Cook and Gemunden in *The Cinema of Wim Wenders*.

an impasse,[4] while in actuality the development of the presentation of masculinity enabled Wenders' cinema to rupture identifications with the Nazi past and propose alternatives. The desubjectivization of masculinity in his 1970s films, with its (a)sexuality, relations to the meaningful (male or female) other, and portrayal of the male body and the gaze, therefore, changes the overall film text, a psychocultural symptom connected to a hidden, powerful symbolic past.

Intimate erotic relationships do not develop between men who share the journey in films of the 1990s. *End of the World* represents this change paradigmatically: competition began and developed between the men (Sam [William Hurt] and Eugene [Sam Neill]) over the woman Claire (Solveig Dommartin), while the buddies (Eugene and also Phillip [Rüdiger Vogler], the detective) impose themselves not as partners in the journey, but as unwanted partners in the surveillance of Claire and/or Sam. The intimacy of the all-male journey of the 1970s films is replaced by the technological "intimacy" of video screens used to follow her/their tracks (that is, of Claire and Sam). In general, in Wenders' later films, as female subjectivity becomes more autonomous and ceases to be the representation of male desire, so relationships between the males lose their power and necessity. Accordingly, in *End of the World*, there is no representation of the all-male utopia. The anonymous group that characterized *Wrong Movement* retains in *End of the World* only some of its laws: Phillip trails after Sam, Claire, and Jean, and creates what appears to be a surrogate group; however, only Sam trails the mother.

The Woman is not only the cause of the desire at the heart of the male journey (as in the 1970s films); but the men in Claire's life actually have sexual relations with her and are not in need of intimacy with the buddy as a substitute. In *End of the World*, the sexual woman (Claire) is part of the man's journey, as is the mother (Edith [Jeanne Moreau]), but she is not connected to the mother. The "dreams camera," that is, this film's unique version of the split/multiplied look, is related to the mother but not to the Woman; and the return of the man (who carries the burden of having been an abandoned child) is a return to the mother and not to the Woman as mother. Like all NGC narratives, this one describes the destruction of the family unit, as mentioned previously: in this case, returning to the Mother involves her death. The apparatus (the dreams camera) that connects them is the reason for this death and the destruction. The mother's death nearly destroys both her son and his lover. Actually, they are addicted to her world through the apparatus that previously created a symbiosis with her, and weaning themselves from

---

4 This is what Santner termed in *Stranded Objects* "[a] maddening binary opposition: schizophrenic dissolution of identity/ narcissistic respecularization of identity" (151).

the dreams camera/mother enables them to become a man and woman once again. The death of the mother does not involve the Woman's death – just the opposite. Accordingly, Wenders' 1990s films manifest the end of withdrawal from the trope of the son (including the spectators' identification with it) together with gradual distancing from Germany.[5]

B. *Utopian Bisexuality – An Alternative Model*

In his famous 1977 essay about Joachim Fest's film *Hitler, A Career*, Wenders relates to the subject of "loss of the fathers" in German cinema: "I don't think that any other country has had such a loss of faith in its own images, stories and myths as we have. We, the directors of the New Cinema, have felt this loss most keenly: in ourselves as the absence of a tradition of our own, as a generation without fathers" (*Emotion Pictures* 94).

In this model, fraternal masculinity is created as a substitute for the problematic relations in NGC between the Father and the son. The Infantile Asexual Model includes the option for mirror exchanges in father-son relationships founded upon a similar experience of abandonment and its implications, while the Utopian Bisexual Model gives expression to a different element of the symbolic past. Not reproduction of the abandonment, but unresolved oedipal conflict: conflict with the buddy replaces conflict with the father. In both models abandonment imposes asexuality; the difference is that it is at the dramatic center of the Infantile Asexual Model, while the development of a relationship with the buddy is at the center of the Utopian Bisexual Model. Although the buddy is central, the fraternal does not define masculinity, but only signifies its boundaries: in relation to the family (*Wings of Desire*, *The American Friend*, *Hammett*, *The State of Things*), in relation to the passage of time as a decisive factor of male identity (the family past and the childhood in *Kings of the Road*, and the future in *Wrong Movement*, *American Friend*, *Nick's Film – Lightning Over Water*, *Hammett*, and *The State of Things*), and in relation to cinema as the medium through

5 In my July 2000 conversations with Wenders in Jerusalem, the director told me that from the time he was eight or so he only wanted "to live outside of Germany." After many years of residency in the United States and making films outside of Germany, he sees himself principally as a German director because of the fact that he "dreams in the German language," a language that determines his mind and his relations with the world.
See also the speech he made in relation to the same matter in November 1991"Talking about Germany," in which he claimed that the German language caused him to return home: "The German language is everything that our country no longer is, what it is not yet, and what it may never be" (Wenders, "Talking" 59).

which the protagonist shapes his life (*Kings of the Road*), *The American Friend*, *Nick's Film – Lightning Over Water*, *Hammett* and *The State of Things*).

Masculinity is defined by the absence of the Woman/the Mother, the presence of the buddy/negation of the Father, and the cinematic medium. The meeting with the buddy is based on projection onto the apparatus of the unfulfilled eroticism:[6] repair of the film projector and projection in *Kings of the Road*, visual games and reflexive cameo appearances by film directors Nicholas Ray, Sam Fuller, Peter Lilienthal, and Jean Eustache in *The American Friend*, and the (anti)production in *Hammett* and *The State of Things*.

The apparatus, however, does not only preserve utopian bisexuality; it also enables the presence of the sole fatherly element in the entire oeuvre of Wenders, also based on reflexivity: i.e., a photo of Fritz Lang in *Kings of the Road*[7] and his symbolic signature on the Los Angeles sidewalk in *The State of Things*, the appearance of Nicholas Ray as a father figure in *The American Friend* and as the dying Father in *Nick's Film – Lightning Over Water*,[8] and Yasujiro Ozu in *Tokyo-Ga* (1985).[9] Thus, the Name of the Father is not related to the symbolic order; rather, only to that aspect of it represented through its cinematic surrogates.

In the Utopian Bisexual Model, not only the eroticism of the buddies' relationship is displaced onto the cinematic apparatus, but so is the unrealized sexual desire for a woman. The framing of Jonathan Zimmermann in *The American Friend* works on three levels: on the literal level of his profession as a picture framer, a symbolic level of the

6 Regarding projection, Laplanche and Pontalis claim, "The subject sends out into the external world an image of something that exists in him in an unconscious way [...] projection is defined here as a mode of refusal to recognize (*méconnaissance*) which has as its counterpart the subject's ability to recognize in others precisely what he refuses to acknowledge in himself" (354). This claim, as we know, can also be ascribed to cinematic projection.

7 See Wenders' 1977 essay on Fritz Lang in *Emotion Pictures* (104-108). The reference to Lotte Eisner in the concluding titles of *Paris, Texas* are different than the reference to Lang "in the midst" of *Kings of the Road*. Lang appears in *Kings of the Road* in the prologue (the theatre owner recalls him and the *Nibelungen*); in the scene in the abandoned cement factory, when Robert cuts a "frame" out of a magazine in which Lang appears as himself in Goddard's *Contempt*; and in the epilogue where his picture is seen hanging above the head of the theatre owner. In many ways, in *Kings of the Road* Lang's presence has an uncanny nature. It appears that the fact that Robert – and not Bruno – is cutting out pictures of "the spiritual father" is not an accident in the context of the characters portrayed in *Kings of the Road*.

8 And so too in the scene in *Kings of the Road* based upon the allusion to his film *The Lusty Men*, a scene that establishes the protagonist's identity, as I will describe later.

9 See Alter's interesting article on Yasujiro Ozu as Wenders' cinematic father.

director's profession as one who fakes the world by fixing the flow in a frame, and on a literal/metaphoric level of the trap that Ripley, the American friend, sets (or does not set) for him. As the Highsmith-style detective plot progresses from framing as a profession to framing as a trap, the level of all-male eroticism becomes prominent, while the level of desire for a woman becomes foreign and distant. This happens simultaneously with multifaceted displacement of both eroticism and desire onto the same apparatus, sexual visual games. After the first murder (which reflects on the cinematic apparatus, as do all the subsequent murders because of the centrality of the actors who are film directors in the extra-diegetic world), it appears that the violence causes a release of this eroticism (and of the sexuality that underwent estrangement). But when it becomes clear that there is not only one murder but a series, the displacement processes gradually dissolve and death overshadows the protagonist's relationships with both his buddy and his wife.

The apparatus defines the protagonist in other road films in this model as well: it is the central means to mediate between him and the buddy, between him and his (a)sexuality; and is the sole means, as noted, of preserving the Name of the (cinematic) Father. The film imparts the role of mediator to the apparatus as the means of leading the Wendersian protagonists from their marginality in the social order to entering the symbolic. The imagined world of the visual games in *The American Friend*, of the films in *Kings*, of the film productions in *Hammett* and in *The State of Things* do indeed play an ambivalent role: It is disconnected from any reality and is also a realization of a reality that is revealed to be an illusion. The apparatus preserves the attachment of the protagonists to pre-oedipal regression or to death; but realization of the erotic and sexual projection on the apparatus as an identity construct develops over time. It dismantles the all-male relationships and leads to the heterosexual solution.

The Wendersian separation between the buddy and the father figure is established in *Wrong Movement*. More than the other characters who are chasing Wilhelm and so become part of the journey, Laertes[10] is the anti-buddy. His confession of Nazi party membership makes him a father figure, a ghost from the past. His bleeding body, like that of the wife of the industrialist and like that of her husband who is found hung, symbolizes the unique realization of these ghosts – a private sphere-of-death that echo the repressed public sphere-of-death. The Wendersian film constructs here, in my view, the separation between the characters capable of serving as a mirror of the self and those stripped of this role

---

10 This name of "the old man," as he is referred to in the film, is not part of the diegesis; rather, it only appears in the title.

and from the film. This construction will be developed in later road films.[11]

II. The Journey into Childhood: *Kings of the Road*

Kings of the Road (Wim Wenders, 1976).

Kings *describes the journey of two men along the length of the then East German border. One, Bruno (*Rüdiger Vogler*), has been living out of his van for the last two years and earns his living fixing movie projectors in villages along the border. Following an unsuccessful suicide attempt, Robert, who is separated from his wife, joins him. The two become friends during the trip, the climax of which takes place during Robert's visit to his father and their visit to Bruno's childhood home. At the end of the journey, at an abandoned army hut on the border, the two enter into a heated confrontation that leads to an exchange of blows. They argue about the absence of women in their lives. Promising to change, they part company the next morning. In the last scenes, Robert is seen on the train, while Bruno tears up the map following his visit to the last movie theatre.*

The male meeting is portrayed initially in modernistic style as a series of small gestures. Most are physical, for example the lending of a towel, but some are verbal. The erotic intimacy present at the beginning of the journey becomes multifaceted cooperation and eventually ends. As buddies they share childlike behaviors (the flight from the theatre in the middle of the film, stealing sunglasses); they share Bruno's work (the technical repair of the cinematic apparatus); and they symbolically share projection.

The high point of their partnership is the journey within a journey of each to his childhood, a journey that would be impossible without the other (e.g., when Bruno joins Robert, the latter completes the confrontation with his father by printing the newspaper; Robert proposes and makes possible the trip to Bruno's childhood home). The exchange of roles in the Odyssean journey is part of a widespread system of mirror reflections (e.g., Robert "drives" the truck; Bruno gives Pauline an abbreviated account of Robert's conversation with the man whose wife committed suicide, as if he were part of it). As a mirror to one another each also defines himself, as will be discussed below.

---

11 Wilhelm's response to Laertes ("Now I have you, Rosenthal") also includes, of course, the accusation as panic repetition of the past; that is, the murder of Rosenthal, the Jew, by Laertes. The escape of Laertes from Wilhelm's violence precedes and proclaims Wilhelm's own escape. The critique of the hopeless journey will lead *Wrong Movement* two years later to *Kings of the Road*.

The representation of their relationship as buddies is related, of course, to the paradigm of the American road movie and to the genre of the Western, but cannot be completely ascribed to them. The film defines the buddies ambivalently. While the conventional relationship between buddies is defined as a combination of action and power, in Bruno and Robert, action is replaced by (im)mobility, in spite of the movement of the journey, and power is replaced by asexuality. The film depicts these characteristics as existential (part of the road film genre). This quasi-existentialism, however, is actually a sexual masquerade. In principle, the journey is characterized by representation of dialectical relations, with sexuality displaced onto utopian bisexuality until the climax. *Kings* establishes heterosexuality as part of the unattainable desire for a woman against which the displaced action and power are measured.

This complexity in representing the relationship of the buddies has stylistic expressions that portray the development of masculinity toward fulfillment.

A. *Kamikaze: A Mirror Representation*

Robert, who attempted suicide by driving his car into the river in the opening scene, is rescued and begins his journey with Bruno. The scene depicts this failed suicide attempt as a symbolic act. The water, a feminine element, symbolizes the desire to be rescued from being absorbed by the Woman, a desire that motivates the journey and is shared by both men. No wonder that during the trip to Bruno's childhood home the motorcycle is replaced by a boat he rows to the island. In mythology, Hermaphrodite, whose parents were Hermes and Aphrodite, portrays both the fear of and longing for integration with the Woman. And thus, the scene of the attempted suicide is a type of *mise-en-abyme*: it establishes within the narrative the contradictory possibilities contained in the journey.

At the center of the scene that takes place in an empty cement factory, the nameless man whose wife committed suicide is introduced. The absence of a name is salient. It characterizes most of the secondary characters – the theatre owners, projectionists, teacher, child, and Robert's father. Both Robert and Bruno introduced themselves by name at a later stage; and the nicknames – Kamikaze and King of the Road – which they call each other are central to their pre-symbolic interaction and serve as a primary alternative for naming. Later the nicknames are described by both Robert and Bruno as letters on the path to acquiring reading and writing skills.

When the nameless man appears dressed in a coat stained with his wife's blood, Bruno wakes up and listens to the conversation as an audial voyeur. The man describes the suicide, cries obsessively, and then lies down on Robert's bed. The framing of the scene is a shot of a side view mirror hung diagonally, reflecting the movement of the clouds, a shot that reappears at the end of the scene. For Wenders, the desert, the open landscape, and even this empty frame of the clouds serve as projective images whose emptiness signifies their primacy. Because of the repetition of the empty frame at the end of the scene, the spectator is compelled to fill it through projection.

The representation of the nameless man, Kamikaze's "temporary tenant," refers to the similarities and the differences between them: the suicide is connected to Robert's failed attempt; and the coat the man wears, his wife's, is similar to the telephone cords that Robert repeatedly "discovers," which symbolically connect him to his wife. In this sense, the man serves as a mirror for Robert. He is located in the background of the frame between Bruno and Robert when the latter relates his dream. Later, Bruno throws stones at the building in a way that characterizes the man. Then the camera follows Bruno, who is crying-laughing at the top of the lookout tower. At the same time, the man is crying in the truck while Robert describes to him how the car his wife committed suicide in is being towed away. The verbal response that signifies Robert's world, edited in parallel to the preverbal (Bruno and the man), creates a correlation whose meaning is clear: the nameless man is a mirror to the two protagonists.

The film gives expression to the "kamikaze" motif during the first night shared by the two buddies in the truck. In this scene Bruno, who is reading a book, asks Robert to define the word "loon." His response is "crazy person" and "diver"[12] which, at the symbolic level, makes clear that what Bruno is reading defines the first meeting with Robert, who is both the "crazy person" and the "diver."[13]

Representing kamikaze at different levels as described above (objects, composition, editing, dialogue) relates, of course, to the facet of narcissism connected to death. In this sense, when Bruno ironically calls Robert "Kamikaze" at the end of their journey, it is an attempt to show that both of them are aware that regression to this facet of narcissism must not be part of their future subjectivities.

[12] A waterfowl called a grebe.

[13] At the beginning of the plot, Robert is seen as he rips up a still photo of a house, closes his eyes, and drives his car directly into the river. Bruno watches the suicide attempt from his truck and gives a towel to Robert who has escaped through the roof of his sinking car and gets out.

B. Home on Wheels: The Split/Multiplied Look

Robert's van is clearly connected to the look. It enables a splitting of the look that is essential for the journey: on the one hand, frontal shots of the van frequently place the protagonists in the center of the frame (that is, the window) with the passing landscape only implicated; while on the other, the side view mirrors multiply and reproduce the passing landscape since the photography shows the landscape both through the mirrors and beyond them. In this way, the landscape is included within the van, and the van becomes a part of the journey not only in the normal sense of movement, but also in the sense of the look.

The iconography of empty roads, geopolitical liminality, and indistinguishable locations are a reflection of the identities of the protagonists, which are also indistinguishable.[14] Moreover, through the splitting, the look eliminates the boundaries between "outside" and "inside." Thus, the images of the journey are enriched with splitting through different mirrors, and the windows themselves function as mirrors. In this way, the film subverts the essence of the point of view, and creates a continuous feeling of division that is perceived as almost part of the nature of the journey, since it is linked with the van. This split look is, of course, part of the reciprocal mirroring with which the film is so rich.[15]

The interminable movement of the van through the indistinguishable landscape represents the possibility of reaching the Woman, but also the impossibility of ever reaching Her. The split/multiplied look that does not give preference to either possibility or impossibility emphasizes that the van is a substitute for both. The split look is multiplied, but this multiplicity does not involve power or make the landscape distinct; rather it "distributes" the look throughout the space.

In terms of chronological development, the landscape in *Kings* determines the narrative. Wenders' style subverts other strategies connected to point of view editing: it refrains from reaction shots, and therefore undermines the importance usually associated with emotional reaction, and immediately cuts after the look turns aside. The spectator's identification, therefore, associates with the landscape. The importance of locations is clearly seen through the extensive screen time devoted to

---

[14] When speaking about "distinct" locations – Toter Mann, Friedlos, Mactlos – Robert dismisses them by claiming that "there are no such places"; Bruno responds "I've already been there." This means that there is nothing new, unique, or distinguished.

[15] Blurring of the boundaries between *Umwelt* and *Immenwelt* through splitting the look is a central aspect of Wenders' films in the 1990s. In his documentary film *A Notebook on Cities and Clothes* (1990), for example, the endless split between the monitors and the video screens fills a similar role of splitting/multiplying.

images of the land, the road, and the small villages along the route. But, even more, the endless space of the frame is omnivoyeuristic. Given that Wenders emphasizes the time between the events, attention is transferred from the story to the setting. The passage of time and the movement of the journey, including the type of events presented on the screen (minor activities not normally included in a film, like the time passing before entry into a room or the time it takes to go up a staircase) construct, together with the centrality of the landscape, the spectators' identification with the journey.

C. *Movie Theater Scene*

Pauline and Bruno's first encounter involve mistaken identities. Revealing their true identities, however, does not fulfill repressed expectations or reduce their anxiety, which reaches its climax when Bruno edits a loop and screens it over twenty times in a kind of compulsive repetition – whether as a substitute for dialogue or as its background. The loop includes a string of images of sex, violence, and loss taken from an American-German porno film showing at the theatre.[16] After about the tenth repetition, the camera focuses on Bruno, who has closed his eyes in pain. During their dialogue,[17] Pauline tells him about a woman who had had vaginal spasms in the theatre. Bruno in turn tells her about meeting the man whose wife committed suicide. The violent pornographic spectacle on the screen and the thundering sound of the announcer reflect this schizoid dialogue. The cinematic and personal language is only used here as a means of alienation as the characters retreat into their imaginary silence and melancholy. The sole moment of grace comes before their separation, when Bruno wipes away her tear and places it on his cheek: a moment of melancholy in the mirror-language of the body.

16 The loop shows a car and a house go up in flames, a naked woman moaning, and a rape taking place in the water, while the voiceover in German declares, "Brutality. Action. Sex. A film TV won't show."
It is difficult to decide whether this is a German or an American film because of the frequency of the dubbing, import of porno films and local productions of porno films. In any event, the stance of the film is identical in regard to these porno films. See also Sandford (*NGC*) on the state of the industry: "The film industry discovered [...] that there was one area that television, as a 'family medium' could not enter into, and that was sex [...] Later, as the moral climate became more permissive, it moved into the field of semi-pornographic 'revelations'" (12).

17 The inability to create intimacy is represented in the dialogue that takes place without eye contact, with the eyes directed at the screen. This is, of course, an additional rupture of the look that signifies the rupture of sexuality.

The fetishization of the erotic pornographic in this scene (which also includes photos of naked women on the screening room wall), ironically emphasizes the threat of castration and the need to confront the absence of sexuality. Between the image of the Woman as absent and her fetishized image, utopian bisexuality is a temporary subject position that signifies opposition to entry into the symbolic.[18]

In contrast to the other fourteen scenes in the film which show repair of projectors in movie theatres, the ones that take place in Pauline's theatre are unique both in terms of reflexivity and sexuality: the detailed mechanism of the apparatus is exposed; Bruno uses the apparatus to edit the loop and project it; the projectionist is seen masturbating; and the woman is revealed to be part of the apparatus – a cashier.

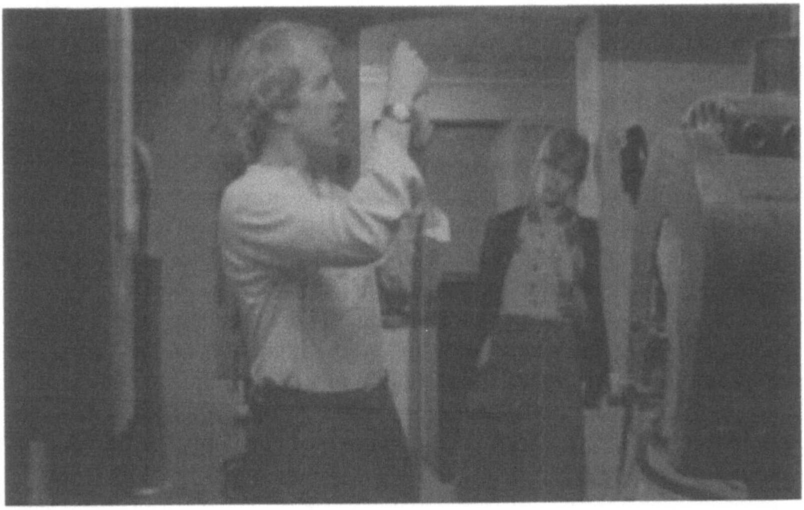

Movie theater scene, *Kings of the Road*

[18] The representation of the cinematic industry is also mediated, by raising the socio-political history (nationalization of movie theatres that belonged to members of the Nazi party, trials, confrontation with the imperialism of the Hollywood industry and ideology, etc.). This representation preserves, on the hand, the cinematic as substitute for reality; and, on the other, its collapse reflects the collapse of the reality in which it was active. This situation is given expression throughout the film, when the grandmother – both the one who heads the theatre with whom Bruno chats and Pauline's – is the central character connected to the declining status of the German film industry.

In *NGC*, Sandford noted that while in 1959 only 15% of the films were restricted from children under the age of 18, by 1969 the number had risen to 48% (156 note 6).

The reflexivity of these scenes can also be read at the psychoanalytic level, as alluded to previously. Penley quotes Freud's widely known claim, "It is highly probable that all complicated machinery and apparatus in dreams stand for the genitals – and as a rule male ones" (58). She argues in the chapter devoted to "bachelor machines" that in contrast to the "maleness" of the cinematic apparatus and the theories connected to it (e.g., Baudry, Metz), we should find a theoretical way to describe the cinema without eliminating the question of sexual difference; that is, to "bachelorize the bachelor machine."

Repair of the projector is a symbolic expression of Bruno's unfulfilled masculinity (similar to a scene juxtaposed through parallel editing in which Robert activates a printing machine). The screening of the loop creates a connection between the projection and asexuality: Bruno presents a spectacle of violence, sex, and loss, and in doing so projects the anxiety connected to his dependence on the Woman. In a more obtuse manner, however, repairing projectors and replacing projectionists in some theatres fulfills a similar role, that of distancing desire and reproducing utopian bisexuality. Projecting his lack of sexuality onto the porno loop and repeating it continuously (repetition, as noted, is an integral part of the mechanism of the cinematic apparatus) strengthens this lack of sexuality. By doing so, in contrast to the Freudian claim, the Wendersian film undermines the assumed commensurability between the apparatus and male sexuality.

What role does exposing the penis fulfill during the episode of the masturbating projectionist? When Bruno observes him, and the distortion created on the screen, the projectionist leaves and Bruno replaces him. This replacement has symbolic connotations regarding the repair, the screening of the loop, and the projection. At the same time, as part of the spectator's fascination of "how it [the apparatus] works,"[19] s/he becomes a voyeur in relation to the most unfamiliar place s/he could experience as a cinemagoer: the projection booth. Pauline and the spectator observe Bruno as he repairs, cuts, glues, and projects; the spectator continues and observes both the beams of light and the reactions of Bruno and Pauline as they watch the loop, and through the compulsive repetition of the loop, s/he participates both in the projection and in the intellectual fascination.

---

19 Penley, who describes spectator-screen relations in modernist reflexive films, suggests that films that present the possibilities of perception raised fascination with "how it works." The desire to know and to investigate is related to sexual fantasy of infantile, childhood inquiry, as is every intellectual process. The position of the spectator in this scene is constructed both on identification through projection and on fascination about "how it works."

Through the pornographic spectacle in this scene, the film refers to German commercial cinema, which during the years described produced pornographic films. Thus, the masturbating projectionist represents the spectators' attitude towards the porno industry, as well as towards the theater, as will be explained below. When Pauline told Bruno about the woman with vaginal spasms, she said, "My grandmother had to call an ambulance. They had to carry her and her lover outside. He was not able to pull it out from her." The story transforms the movie theatre in which the projectionist is masturbating to the site of real, live events (and sheds an ironic light on Bruno and Pauline's relationship). Bruno's story about meeting the man whose wife committed suicide focused the core of the schizoid dialogue on the impossibilities of sexual interaction. This is an additional indication of how sexual closeness to Pauline was blocked. This restraint is, as noted, part of utopian bisexuality. The film constructs the protagonist's anxiety through the stories (including the fact that one of them is a reworking of earlier events), a textual process similar to that of the previously told story of the loon.

When Bruno decides to stop repairing projectors, the regression to the imaginary, as expressed in his endless projection of films, also stops. (This is the way we should read the image with which the journey ends, the words *Weisse Wand*[20] which share Wenders' initials).

In the scene at the abandoned army hut near the East German border, Bruno says that he always felt loneliness "inside a woman." The stories told so far – the vaginal contractions, suicide, the loop showing rape and loss – are fully expressed in this climactic scene. It illuminates, retrospectively, the scene in the movie theatre and Bruno's relations with Pauline, on the one hand, and the materials he chose to edit and to project, on the other. The unavoidable conclusion is that because the projection is connected to Bruno's profession, it is part of the regressive constructs described in the film. When Bruno tears up the road map, he gives up the substitutive cinematic apparatus and begins a journey to the symbolic and to sexuality.[21]

At the level of spectatorship, fascination for the apparatus is connected to identification with Bruno. If we see projection as a defense

---

20 White Screen.

21 We should not forget that the van itself portrays this matter as the projectors and repair materials are kept in the rear. In this sense, Bruno takes "replacements" with him all through the journey. As I claimed previously, projection is part of the preservation of bisexuality and of narcissistic regressive fixations. No wonder then that the journey to childhood, to the house of Bruno, which involves the first step of liberation from the past, takes place on a motorcycle and not in the home on wheels that carries the projection equipment.

mechanism, the role of women is central. That having been said, Wenders does film Bruno distorting his face while watching the loop (in close up) and describes the melancholic relationship between Bruno and Pauline; that is, the spectator's identification with the apparatus, Bruno's projection, and his/her gaze at the masturbating projectionist are gradually revealed to be a process subverting the melancholia.

D. The Lusty Men

Kings alludes to Nicholas Ray's film *The Lusty Men* (1951), whose protagonist is a star rodeo rider, Jeff McCloud (Robert Mitchum), fallen on bad times after a riding accident. The opening scene finds him returning to his boyhood home, a small ramshackled farm in Texas, where he crawls under the old house and finds the toy pistol he left there as a small boy. Wenders wrote in his critique of *Kings of the Road* in *Emotion Pictures* that the scene in which Bruno returns to the place of his birth and discovers an old box of comics under the stairs is taken from this scene. The allusion is broad, as it reflects on Wenders' relationship with Ray as a father figure (which he will later address more fully in his documentary *Nick's Film – Lightning Over Water*).

The sequence on the island prefaces the climax of the journey to childhood described in *Kings of the Road* and is a key to understanding it. Here, Wenders' allusion to American cinema is the basis for constructing one of the more intimate and difficult moments of mourning and reminiscence experienced by Bruno during his journey. The story of *The Lusty Men*, as Wenders analyzes the possible interpretations of the title, raises connotations of obsessive longing, sexual desire, and the like. In *Kings of the Road*, these connotations are connected to specific disillusionment following the return to childhood and to the mother, which leads to their realization. In this, Wenders accepts Nicholas Ray's statement, "This film isn't a Western. It's really [...] about people who want nothing more than their own home" (112). The allusion functions beyond the specific reference and refers to the entire film, to Westerns as an expression of the childlikeness of men, to the role of men in Ray's films and, as noted, to Ray as the spiritual father.

Beyond that, when discussing displacement to American culture, it is clear that the American/Hollywood model of masculinity is ambivalent. As victors, the Americans controlled the German film industry and the masculinity represented in their films is actually what defeated German masculinity: As an imposed model for imitation (that is, not solely by choice), and in the absence of other models of masculinity, dependence on the American model included both admiration and resentment: this was a second surrender, this time psychological. No wonder that this is the nature of Wenders' reference to *The Lusty Men*, with its deep and unresolved ambivalence.

Does the ambivalent displacement to American masculinity models also express Germany's guilt over its defeat? Over the double surrender? Does the anti-American attitude which, as I will describe later, develops gradually in Wenders' films, function in place of mourning? It is clear that the ambivalent approach is prominent in Wenders's protagonists who are characterized by conventions taken from the Western, such as marginality and the absence of women. On the other hand, other clear characterizations of maleness in Westerns such as action and performance are not applied.[22] But, above all, as I will claim further, this very process of ambivalent displacement will be transformed later in Wenders oeuvre into a redefinition in regard to his relationship with Germany.

E. Primal Scream

In *Kings of the Road*, Wenders gives full expression to the connection between sexual and existential identity. The shared "desire for an unsatisfied desire" structures the relationship between the two men. The confrontation scene at the abandoned hut at the East German border expresses the film's demand for separation and distinguishability and the renewed entrance to the symbolic order, an entrance that fractures the imaginariness that characterizes the journey. It is also emblematic of the dialectical tension between utopian bisexuality and the possibility of future sexuality.

At the center of the film's narrative are two male characters, but only one female, Pauline, is physically present. Other women in the film are not physical present, but are present at every other level. This includes the "realistic" women (Robert's wife, whom he intends to talk with over the telephone, the woman who committed suicide, the dead mothers, and the elderly theatre owner who appears at the end of the film), the "fictional" women (in the porno loop and photos), and those who are somewhere in between (described in conversation).

The film subverts the binary opposition of presence and absence not only in relation to the female character, but also in the photography and the sound. The space in which the journey takes place repeats itself – forsaken, vacant towns lacking almost any sign of life, abandoned gas stations, stark landscapes, empty streets, small houses scattered by the roadside, utility poles, unchanging scenery, in spite of the advancing journey. The presence of the space and emphasis on the location has an illusive character. Robby Müller's photography undermines these

22 See Mulvey ("Afterthoughts"), Neale ("Masculinity") and Pam Cook.

relations, principally through the technique of delay. Thus, for example, when Robert exits from the rear of the van, the door closes and the shot leaves the viewer inside with the projector and the closed music box; the camera tarries with Paul as he collects the fallen candies instead of following Bruno and Robert as they ride away on his motorcycle, and the camera remains with Pauline as she stares outside when Bruno leaves. What is "present" and what is "absent" here? The sound emphasizes the silences and the intervals between the dialogues, which in and of themselves are no less a part of the dialogue.

The film uses several strategies to construct the transformation from utopian bisexuality to sexuality: the road film; the buddies' bisexuality (infantile asexuality, utopianism, imaginariness, substitutes of father-son relations, "return to a childhood not yet lived," mirror relations); subversion of the dichotomy of presence-absence in all levels of the film text (including the split/multiplied look); the kamikaze motif; projection as a means to enable regressions (pre-oedipal, narcissistic, death connected); and the apparatus (rupturing the identification between the apparatus and sexuality).

As claimed earlier, to date the Wendersian film has been principally interpreted in research through the paradigm of displacement; however, the famous sentence spoken by Bruno in the scene that takes place on the East German border, "The Yankees have colonized our subconscious," should be read, in my view, as a turning point in the film, beyond the paradigm of displacement. The entire dialogue in this scene turns around the anxieties of masculinity in the face of women and develops to include the declaration "Everything will be different from now on." In this sense, in my opinion, displacement to American culture, especially the dominant place given to the Western, is only one layer of the film's meaning.

In what ways does the Wendersian film transcend the Western? Willemen[23] claimed that spectacle and drama in the films of Anthony Mann tend to be constructed around the look at male characters. The spectator enjoys seeing the male exist in the city or in open spaces (walking, riding, fighting), or, more abstractly, in history. With this comes the pleasure of seeing him defeated and/or victorious through violent means, with both forms of pleasure based upon repressed homosexual voyeurism. In Willemen's opinion, especially when the male is presented in violent scenes, anxiety has evolved from gazing at the male, exactly as it evolved from gazing at the female. Underlying this view is the assumption that in a patriarchal/hetero-normative society, the male

23 Cited by Neale in "Masculinity" (8).

body can not be seen as an erotic object for another male's look/gaze. In her article on King Vidor's *Duel in the Sun* (1946), Mulvey presented two images of masculinities that appear in the Western that parallel two narrative functions: "married" (and thus integrated into society) and "non-married" (a refusal to enter society driven by nostalgic narcissism). In her opinion, the tension between the image of *social authorite* and that of *narcissistic authorite* defines the Western. Neale viewed nostalgic Westerns in terms of the theme of the loss of male narcissism. In his opinion, the intradiegetic and extradiegetic types of voyeuristic looks proposed by Mulvey appear at moments of competition in which the male battle becomes a pure spectacle and a fetishistic look is created in ritualistic scenes. He claims that the characters' look is not characterized by desire, but rather by fear/hatred/aggression. Therefore, only women are able to function as objects of the open erotic gaze.

The Wendersian film subverts the repressed homosexual voyeurism (Willemen), the tension between *social authorite* and *narcissistic authorite* (Mulvey) and the fear/hatred/aggression that is in the look (Neale). Instead, it proposes intermale eroticism and *narcissistic authorite* that negate themselves. In terms of style, emphasis on the "small events," as I described previously, totally subverts the violent-competitive spectacle of the Western. The principal point, however, is not subversion of all-American codes. The only time there is action, a fistfight, occurs in the climatic scene at the abandoned army hut. This scene, however, does not subvert the action of a Western; rather, it uses the genre to make a statement about German masculinity.

The Wendersian film uses American popular culture neither as an expression of a destination lost nor as a substitute home; that is, not to disassociate from Germany, but rather in order to subvert the fascist-Nazi masculinity of the past. Thus, the scenes in which the male body is exposed (for example, when they relieve themselves or undress) sharpen the codes of the Western in a subversive manner. Above all else, however, the subversion is used to strengthen the imagery of the anti-fascist male body (e.g., the direct frontal shot as the camera follows a fully naked Bruno).

What about the spectator's look? It suggests that in *Kings of the Road* there is a displacement of the possible voyeuristic/fetishistic look of the spectator both to the apparatus (projectors) and to the progress of the journey. Except that the journey never ends and the projection does; that is, the spectator could become a partner in the dismantling of the projection in both the erotic sexual and intellectual dimensions. Neither of the two protagonists exists in the position of "to-be-looked-at-ness" and the spectator does not look at either of them through the look of other characters. The film justifies the representation of the male body as part of "life on the road" and as part of the physical work involved in Bruno's profession as a projectionist/projection equipment technician. The transformation in the spectator's look is part of the film's rupture of identification.

Describing different forms of identification in *Kings of the Road* leads to the conclusion that they are complex and occasionally contradictory. The film constructs different identification forms – narcissistic and regressive, and that based on knowledge and investigation. These forms direct the spectator first and foremost to identification with the male journey, and the transformation involved.[24]

In contrast to the widely accepted interpretation that viewed Wenders' oeuvre as having developed from "indirect Germanness," and repression in the 1970s to a "return to Germany" with *Wings of Desire* in 1987, I do not see Wenders' early films as "indirect Germanness" based upon displacement, as is proven by the centrality of the Utopian Bisexual Model in his films. The Wendersian film does not use American culture (cinematic or iconographic) as a means of distancing itself from Germany, but rather as a means of constructing an initial stage – in the 1970s – for undermining past identifications with Hitler. The decision to separate from the male buddy and enter the symbolic order means Habermasian opposition to narcissistic patterns.[25]

Separation from personal history, elimination of all opportunities to mourn for the personal past,[26] a life style that expresses hunger for intimacy, and the overwhelming difficulty embodied in social-sexual marginality are represented by Bruno until the scene in the last movie theatre. The journey with Robert leads him to liberate himself from the defense mechanism, the projection, and to rebirth, signified by his primal scream after separating from Robert.

---

24 It should not be ignored that the viewer of Wenders' films accepts the actor as an intertext. Wenders relied on ten to twelve actors (and actresses) who over the years created both a system of references, and the Wendersian persona; e.g., Rüdiger Vogler. There is no doubt that the Wendersian spectator is aware of this persona, an awareness that is included in his\her reading of the reflexivity of the films under discussion.

25 As is well-known, Habermas opened the Historians' Debate with criticism of the historians Ernst Nolte, Michael Stürmer and Andreas Hillgruber, whom he claimed "place historiography in the service of a 'national-historical restoration of a conventional identity'" (qtd. in Santner, *Stranded Objects* 50). The "post-conventional" identity he proposed is connected with loss of the power of national symbols. He opposes the tendency to return to narcissistic patterns of identity formation, patterns that are indicative of a "refusal or inability to mourn."

26 Until the scene in the childhood home in which Bruno cries.

Robert represents the kamikaze-style of depressive position, fixation in relation to parents,[27] opposition to identification with the parent's generation (including unconscious ambivalent feelings), and separation from the parents (he returns to his father's village after eight years); but he is also rescued from these behavioral patterns by the trip with Bruno.

In contrast to Santner's claim in *Stranded Objects*, I claim that Wenders enables his protagonists to pass through the "narcissistic respecularization of the identity" stage in *Kings*, and by the end of the journey rescues them from it. The images at the end[28] include a feeling of closure because of the dramatic solution, a feeling that, as I previously claimed, will continue and grow stronger until the upheaval of Wenders' films of the 1990s.

Kings of the Road is unique among his films because of the diegetic use of the cinematic apparatus – the projector, the screening, the projection, the actor as projectionist, and the actor as film,[29] and not only as a metaphor for it (as in *Paris, Texas*, *American Friend*), or metonymies that include it (as in *Hammett* and in *The State of Things*). This uniqueness is revealed also as a *mise-en-abyme*; that is, as a statement of the Wendersian film on the possible double meaning played by the cinema as mental machine à la Baudry and the possibility of subverting it in order to be liberated from oppressive identifications with the Nazi past.

---

27 This fixation is expressed in the entirety of the reactions to the father, to the world of printing which represents him, and to verbal communication.

28 Including the intersection of the railroad tracks on which Robert travels with the road Bruno is traveling on. This is also the intersection of the visual and audio images; the song *Kings of the Road* is heard in two spaces of these different shots; Robert completes the journey armed with the child's notebook (symbolically – connected again to the world of the father, a world of words); the image of Bruno tearing up the road map next to the last movie theatre.

29 See the shadows theatre that the two of them create for the children in the movie theatre when the projector breaks down.

CHAPTER 4

The Transsexual Model

Discussion of the Transsexual Model[1] is based solely on Fassbinder's film *In a Year of Thirteen Moons*. As claimed previously, mutant sexuality characteristic of the masculinity of NGC is manifest at one extreme of the sexuality spectrum as transsexuality; that is, as an attempt to transcend the blending of the pre-oedipal with the cultic simulacra of phallicization by means of a sex change operation. *In a Year of Thirteen Moons* is the most extreme case of subversion of the second generation's identification with the Hitlerian image. In this sense, post-sex change masculinity represents Fassbinder's version of rupturing this identification. Because of (and not in spite of) its being the only such representation, it sheds light on the entire spectrum, beginning with the asexual masculinity of the Infantile Asexual Model, through representations of suicidal hetero/homo-sexualities and Utopian Bisexuality. Therefore, though transsexual masculinity appears only in this text, I will relate to it as a model. As discussed previously, principally because of the repeated presence of the textual structure of the abandoned child, the masculinities of each of the different models frequently overlap on the sexual spectrum, which depicts transition from asexuality (Asexual Infantile Model) to ruptured hetero\homo-sexualities and the fraternal substitutive masculinities (Utopian Bisexual Model). The sex change (Transsexual Model) is the climax of this process of rupturing the trope of the son through demasculinization. In other words, at one extreme of the sexual spectrum is the asexual abandoned child; at the other extreme is the transsexual male who negates sexuality by undergoing extremely corporeal (dis)embodiment. This spectrum demonstrates that NGC masculinity is being constructed as moving permanently toward asexuality. In this way, the films declare a clear opposition to the fascist body, to Nazi respectability, and to past

1 The term "transsexuality" will be used to refer to the masculinity of a man who has undergone a sex change operation in order to become a woman. See Prosser; Shapiro; Stone; and Griggs. I will henceforth use the term "queer" following Doty: "'[Q]ueer' might be used to describe the intersection or combination of more than one established 'non-straight' sexuality or gender position in a spectator, a text, or a personality" (149).

identifications as manifest in the trope of the son, while simultaneously acknowledging the Nazi defeat.

In a Year of Thirteen Moons (Rainer Werner Fassbinder, 1978).

*The plot describes the last five days in the life of the transsexual Elvira (formerly Erwin) Weishaupt. In the first scene she is dressed as a man, standing on the bank of a river. She pays a male prostitute to have sex with her, but he attacks her when he discovers she is a woman. She returns to her apartment and sees that her long-time partner Christoph (Karl Scheydt), who has been gone a number of weeks, has returned. They quarrel violently when he tells her he is leaving because she has become fat and ugly. She pleads with him to stay but he packs his bags and leaves. Together with her prostitute friend Zora (Ingrid Caven), she visits the slaughterhouse where Erwin had worked and the convent he was raised. There Sister Gudrun (Liselote Pempeit) tells about his time at the orphanage. Elvira meets Anton Saitz (*Gottfried John*), the man for whom she became a woman. She seeks his forgiveness for mentioning him by name in an interview, but Saitz barely remembers her. He has sex with Zora. Elvira cuts her hair and dresses as a man. She asks her former wife, Irene (Elisabeth Trissenaar), and daughter, Marie-Ann (Eva Mattes), to let her return to the family. She also looks, in vain, for past glory and comfort in the reporter who had interviewed her. But it is too late. In the morning she is found dead in her apartment.*

I. Description of the Model

The characteristics and meaning of transsexuality are the focus of continual controversy.[2] In sum, the research defines three optional relations: between transsexuality and heterosexuality, homosexuality, and transvestism; between gender and sex; and between the transsexual body and its discourse. The latter definition also reflects confrontations and/or overlapping between feminist, gay, lesbian, and queer studies.

In my opinion, the vectors of the discussion that I will propose further reveal transsexuality not only as a sexual identity that undermines conventional assumptions in regard to the commensurability of gender and sex, but also as a category in crisis. In *In a Year of Thirteen Moons* this crisis is exemplified by how it reveals Elvira's exceptionality.[3]

---

2 Butler (*Gender Trouble* and principally *Bodies That Matter*); Garber; Shapiro; Stone; Hausman; Ekins and King; Billings and Urban; Griggs, Prosser; Merck, Segal, and Wright.

3 As the following table will demonstrate, I will differentiate between Gender (soul) and Sex (body/soul); however, this is not pre-Butlerian binarism, based upon a definition of gender identity as expressing an "innerness"/the soul in opposition to defini-

Definition of the Transsexual Male-to-Female (MTF)

Binarism	
Heterosexuality, homosexuality, transvestism	Transsexuality
Heteronormativism	Denaturalism
Gender (soul)	Sex (body/soul)
Male	Female
Ontology / Epistemology	
Real, authentic	Unreal, Mimic
Born, attained through performance and citationality	Becomes a commodity
Substantive	Trans substantive
Subject	Trans subject
He/she	S/he
Genetic-chromosomal	Anatomical, morphologic, medicinal, cosmetic, stylistic
Being, core gender identity	being seen/ "passing"
The Body	
Coherent	Acoherent
Intelligible Body	Unintelligible body, abjected body
The Complete Body	The Body as prosthesis, made from body parts
Sexual difference	Sexual indifference
Bodily ego (Freud)	Fantasmatic-imagined body
The Gaze	
Gaze	Disembodied Gaze
The Effect	
Oppression, regulation, hegemony	Subversion

A. *An Unintelligible Body?*[4]

As noted, for example, by Corrigan (*A Cinema Without Walls*), Silverman (*Male Subjectivity at the Margins*), and La Valley in their discussions of *In a Year of Thirteen Moons* and even from a cursory reading of the plot or transsexual biographies, Elvira is exceptional in

---

tion of the "sex" as physical. Following Grosz, my aim is to focus on the surplus excesses of this binarism as an open category. Butler has not succeeded in defining this binarism in the transsexual context, in spite of the different approaches to the topic she took in her two books. In this regard, see also the criticism of Prosser.
The term "sexual indifference" is taken from Baudrillard's *Transparency of Evil*.

4 See Butler (*Bodies That Matter*) and Vasterling.

that in the years preceding her operation she never saw herself as having "the soul of a woman imprisoned in a male body."[5] Her motivation for the sex change is not clear; it was only a spur of the moment response to Saitz's statement that he could love her if she were a woman. Erwin responded by going to Casablanca for the operation; something that Fassbinder never completely explained.[6] The interpretation of the transformation to transsexuality (MTF) at the motivational level of the protagonist, at the level of the entire textual meaning, and also at the level of Fassbinder's oeuvre[7] is, thus, the central meaning of the film.

The film is characterized by excess of all kinds – of the body, representation of time, subplots, secondary characters, *mise-en-scène*, and sound. It appears, however, that much of the textual perplexity is concentrated in Elvira's body rather than in the *mise-en-scène* (characteristic of Fassbinderian filmmaking). Representing MTF transformation becomes all the more complicated because it is performed by a male, the actor Volker Spengler. Usually in cinema these parts become reflexive, demonstrating how an actor works on his role and reflecting on director-actor relations. In this specific case, because of personal events that preceded the production, this level of reflexivity is of minor importance. In the context of Fassbinder's life with his lovers, Spengler's collabora-

5 This assumption is found throughout most of the literature on the subject, including autobiographical research (e.g. Stone, Shapiro, Griggs). Fisk cites criteria to identification of "real transsexuals": "(1) A life long sense or feeling of being a member of the other sex; (2) the early and persistent behaviouristic phenomenon of cross-dressing, coupled with a strong emphasis upon a total lack of erotic feelings associated with cross-dressing; and (3) a disdain or repugnance for homosexual behaviour [...]." (qtd. in Billings and Urban 105]). Of course, Elvira does not fit any of these criteria. In world cinema we will find the total opposite representation; e.g., in *Southern Comfort* (Kate Davis, USA, 2000); *All About My Mother* (*Todo Sobre mi Madre)*, Pedro Almodóvar, Spain, 1999); *Transamerica* (Duncan Tucker, USA, 2005) and *Soap* (*Soap, En*), Pernille Fischer Christensen, Denmark, 2006), to name but a few well-known examples.

6 "[...] [A]nd Erwin said again that he loved him, and Anton said again that if Erwin were a girl, then […] Erwin left the brothel as if numbed, and then he did something very strange, something he had never given any thought to before. He hailed a taxi, had himself driven to the airport, booked the next flight to Casablanca, and there, without a trace of hesitation, had himself transformed into a woman in a comprehensive operation" (Fassbinder, *"13 Moons"* 188).

This is the place to note that sex change operations do, indeed, take place in Casablanca in the famous clinic of Dr. Burou (Stone).

7 It is well known that Fassbinder made *In a Year of Thirteen Moons* following the suicide of his lover Armin Meier. He dedicated this film, as well as *Fox and His Friends*, to "Armin and to all the others." There is an outstanding degree of intensity involved in the making of this film – Fassbinder was the scriptwriter, director, producer, photographer, editor and designer.

tion with him reaches its height as a doubled\failed replacement of Armin Meier.

The research mentioned above largely declares the film's and Elvira's excesses as unintelligible. According to Corrigan, for example, the film obstructs the spectator's search for semiotic coherence,

> Elvira's is a story that cannot be told, a body that cannot be represented [...] *In a Year of Thirteen Moons* is a movie about textual madness, about textualities that lose their ability [...] to balance the materials of signification with a sense of meaning [...] too many moons, too many lovers, too much sound, too much spatial clutter, and too many stories. (*A Cinema Without Walls* 68-69).

Accordingly, for the spectator, interpretation becomes a sadomasochistic task.

Is, indeed, Elvira's sexual identity, as Burgoyne claims in "Narrative," an "evacuation of truth [...] no index to the natural self"? Is Erwin/ Elvira, as La Valley claims, "a figure that goes beyond both genders by being both genders, or [...] by being neither"? (129) Is the body of Elvira an unintelligible body? Is its meaning embedded, at least, in utopia, acoherence, untruth? In contrast to the leading researchers, I would like to focus the discussion on the so-called unintelligible body as expressing the film's relation to the historical-cultural context, and, therefore, as actually highly intelligible. In my opinion it is a "binary excess" (for example, of gender sex; male-female; real-imitation), that reveals the film's attitude towards the historical-cultural context. What appears to be an indecisive identity seems to me to be decisive; lack of liberation from the personal past symbolizes liberation from the national past. In this regard the Fassbinderian film is coherent: the analogy between the secondary characters and Elvira is overt, as is the central riddle of her sexuality. The aesthetic complexity the reader has to overcome is central to the film's critical voice.

I claim that Elvira reconstitutes herself as an abandoned child. As Erwin, she had been abandoned three times: by her mother, who left her in a convent during the war;[8] by the family that wanted to adopt her; and by the nun (referred to by Fassbinder as a surrogate mother in *Anarchy*

---

[8] His biological father is unknown and his mother refused to reveal the details of his birth to her husband, Erwin's legal father, when he returned. According to Stoller, "male transsexualism was the predictable outcome of a particular family situation involving "too much contact with mother's body for too long and a father who is absent and so does not interrupt the process of feminization. The result is a son so strongly identified with his mother that he not only *wishes* to be like her, but comes to believe that he *is* like her, despite incongruous genitals" (qtd. in Billings and Urban 104. Emphasis in the original).

178). Elvira's relations are based upon compulsive repetition of the abandonment pattern: with Anton Saitz (irreversible victimhood) and with the homosexuals in the park (dressed as a man), with Christoph (weight gain, supplications, victimization, the financial deal), with her wife and daughter, with Zora (allowing Zora take her place with Anton), and with the reporter (reestablishing contact).

Rather than seeking – without success – mother substitutes (à la Herzog) or the maternal Woman (à la Wenders), the Fassbinderian abandoned child becomes a woman. He does not seek father and/or mother figures, but rather a figure that will relate to him as someone without clear identity. That is, his behavior reproduces the act that will eternalize his lack of clear identity. The neurotic pattern of affirming a lack of clear identity and of a-authenticity, of reproducing a-belonging, of a need for confrontation while failing to pass as either a man or a woman, structures the most extreme marginality of the German male born during the war. The tragedy of the attempt to artificially achieve love leads in a neurotic fashion to the destruction of identity and eradication of masculinity, until suicide becomes the final abandonment.

Christoph's rejection and departure causes Elvira's body to become transitional years after the period of post-operative transition has ended. Elvira transforms the real life test of "passing" into a way of life: in the opening scene, at the convent, the meeting with Anton Saitz, her return home, and her meeting with the reporter and his wife. Again and again she checks her "look" against the response of her surroundings (violence, uncertain identification, embarrassment, mockery, anxiety, alienation).[9] The dual life, articulated in her gender dysphoria[10] becomes more strident when Elvira, contrary to accepted distinctions between transvestites and transsexuals, dresses as a man. As proven in the opening and all other transvestite scenes, the cross-dressing appears to make the visual discrepancy even more conspicuous; and is, in fact, an additional step in the reproduction of the same pattern of behavior.

The opening scene shows Elvira in the park dressed as a man, battered and disgraced by a male prostitute. That is, the man who became a woman is disguised as a man in order to have sexual relations with

9 Ginsberg claimed that "passing" is "about specularity: visible and the invisible" (2). In many ways, the scene with Christoph's departure also proves that Elvira's attempt to "pass" as a woman/to be a woman for him was a battle lost in advance.

10 See Billings and Urban on the psychological phenomena that characterize the transsexuals following a sex change operation, as found in hundreds of patients: depression, suicides, prostitution (before and after the operation), continuous lack of economic independence, demand to restore what was done, sexual dysfunction, among others (108-110).

another man, and fails to pass. Silverman titles her discussion of this scene "Something's Missing" (*Male Subjectivity at the Margins* 247). I maintain that the penis is not what is missing. Has Elvira, who said she dressed as a man to make it easier for her to purchase sex, actually adopted heteronormativity and heterosexual desire? Is the phallocentric mindset actually the motivation for the sex change, her desire to be a "complete woman" for a man, and longing for middleclass couplehood (with Christoph), which are, à la Butler, heterosexual desires? Are not the desires of the so-called unintelligible body – to return to her work in the slaughterhouse or to go back to being a husband and father – desires of intelligibility? In my opinion, even her apparent heterosexual desires are constructed within the reproduction of the abandonment neurosis and unclear identity. The so-called unintelligible body functions as a critical power, challenging the norms that oppress and regulate its "unintelligibility."

According to Butler,[11]

> [T]he law requires conformity to its own notion of "nature." [...] Neither does s/he [Herculine] fully fall outside the signifying economy of masculinity. S/he is "outside" the law, but the law maintains this "outside" within itself. In effect, s/he embodies the law, not as an entitled subject, but as an enacted testimony to the law's uncanny capacity to produce only those rebellions that it can guarantee will – out of fidelity – defeat themselves and those subjects who, utterly subjected, have no choice but to reiterate the law of their genesis. (*Gender Trouble* 106).

Is this indeed the case? In my opinion, more than *Paris is Burning* (which Butler analyzed in *Bodies That Matter*), it is actually this Fassbinder film that presents a different transsexual subject position. If, according to Silverman, the importance of Fassbinder's cinema is that he provides a theoretical model for conceptualization of the look that includes the lack and does not deny it (which is impossible to do in the Lacanian perspective) (Silverman 80), then in my view the importance of *In a Year of Thirteen Moons* is its construction of a transsexual subject whose subjectivity, in all its facets, is not evidence of the impossibility of granting meaning to the character/body/text. Elvira's sexuality is not what Baudrillard describes as "lost in the theatrical excesses of its ambiguity" ("Transparency" 22); in fact, the recurrent failure of adapta-

---

[11] Here Butler relates to Foucault's analysis in the introduction to *Herculine Barbin*. In her words, Foucault romanticizes Herculine (Alexsina), the nineteenth-century French hermaphrodite, which contradicts his position in *History of Sexuality*. Though the discussion of the hermaphrodite is not entirely similar to the discussion of the transsexual, it reveals in the two cases the problematics involved in relating to the body as a "regulatory sexual regime" (101).

tion makes the body itself the source of meaning. Erwin's repressed homosexual desire for Anton Saitz[12] does not, as Butler claims in *Gender Trouble* and *Bodies That Matter*, change to heterosexual melancholia; but rather displaces the desire to be "a complete woman" for the desired man. But the sex change makes the neurosis not only central citationality (following Butler), but an irreversible condition. As such, through the excess of the abjected body, *le corps morcelé*,[13] the film undermines the impossibility of producing homosexual desire in a hetero-normative social order. Again and again Elvira, who embodies mutant sexuality, moves toward the reaffirmation of the abandonment neurosis and lack of clear identity. But the extreme nature of the abjective solution is an outcome of circumstances – the homosexual desire is driven by experiences of abandonment that began in Erwin's childhood during the Nazi period and by the fact that this desire is directed to Anton Saitz, a Jewish concentration camp survivor.

B. Not a Son

In *In a Year of Thirteen Moons*, Elvira commits suicide after a journey to her past, unable to express her suffering or to understand her "negative symbiosis"[14] with the German Jew. Elsaesser claimed in *Fassbinder's Germany* that we should understand the relationship between Elvira and Anton Saitz as a sociohistorical allegory:

> Erwin/Elvira and Anton are each other's mirror images of impossibility, making this love story embody the intolerably poignant confrontation of two human beings who are each other's 'other,' across a time shift and a history which is a personal disaster for both: the Holocaust for Anton Saitz, and the master-racial fantasies of National Socialism for Erwin Weishaupt [...]. Germans and Jews are henceforth tied together by such monstrous guilt and almost equally monstrous innocence, which together form a kind of inescapable 'symbiosis.' (204).

In my opinion, while Saitz's childhood biography is certainly representative of the period, Erwin's is not. Though he paid a personal price for the "master-racial fantasies of National Socialism," principally because he was born out of wedlock to a woman whose husband was missing for two years during the war, their "personal disasters" are

---

12 Like that of Franz Biberkopf (Günter Lamprecht) for Reinhold Hoffmann (Gottfried John) in Fassbinder's *Berlin Alexanderplatz* (1980). In my view, Franz Biberkopf, the protagonist of his television series, also embodies mutant sexuality, as he moves between violent heterosexuality, which includes the murder of his lover, and unconscious homosexuality.

13 The body in bits and pieces.

14 A term from Dan Diner (qtd. in Elsaesser, *Fassbinder's Germany* 205, note 25).

dissimilar even if they mirrored one other in the anti-Semitic Germany that made each redefine their Germanness. Are we speaking here of a different type of allegory? Further, do allegoric bodily inscriptions not only explain impossible love, but also substantiate Erwin's transsexuality? In my opinion, none of the researchers mentioned provided answers to these questions.[15]

The immediate meaning of Elvira's transsexuality is that Erwin ceases to be a "son" for his mother and her surrogates. Loss of (male) sexuality is unpreventable and derived from undermining the trope of the son. Here Fassbinder does away with the burden of past identifications in an extreme and entirely coherent manner. Reproduction of the abandonment neurosis and unclear identity in the film constructs the meaning of the abjected body. The body remains "unintelligible" in contradiction to both the masculine- and feminine-fascist-Nazi bodies. Thus, its meaning is anchored in loss of all sexuality, including transsexuality. Elvira's journey is not only to her past (to a childhood not yet lived, characteristic of NGC) and her inability to understand her past does not motivate her suicide. Elvira rejects options of identity and sexuality as a radical Fassbinderian statement against the Nazi past.

As I outlined at the beginning of the discussion on NGC, the trope of the son represents the complex identification mode of both first and second generation Germany: The imago of the Führer as the mother-goddess involves gender transformation; his pretence of being her son involves both gender continuity and gender duality, since he is concurrently the mother and the mother's son. The demand for primary attraction to the Mother and its displacement to symbols of the Father makes mutant sexuality the central symbolic construct in the oeuvre of NGC second generation directors. Fassbinder applies the neurosis of abandonment and unclear identity, including its transsexual corporeal implications, to create a film that dismisses in its entirety pre-oedipal identification with the Mother and channels this identification towards (failed) phallic-patriarchal symbols. The abjected body is therefore the horrific result of a double crisis: neither Mother, nor phallicization; that is, not being a son, and being a transsexual. This double crisis and Elvira's consequent mutant sexuality lead to her death. The attempt to construct what I called earlier "cultic simulacra of phallicization" (i.e., Elvira as Irene's husband and Marie-Anne's father;[16] and her transvestism when

[15] See also Koch ("Torments") who criticizes Fassbinder's anti-Semitism, a criticism I disagree with, as I hope will be clarified at the end of the analysis of the film.

[16] See the scene in which Irene asks him to request forgiveness from Anton Saitz for revealing his name in the newspaper interview. She addresses Elvira as Elvira when she refers to her current difficulties and as her husband, and by the male form of

she demands once again to be father and husband) cancels itself out as a result of the same process of rejection of options for identity and sexuality. Thus, the Hitlerian imago is replaced with the body of Elvira that is, in Fassbinder's words, "a terrible mirage" ("*In a Year of Thirteen Moons*" 193).

C. *Slaughterhouse Scene*

During their visit to the slaughterhouse, before meeting Anton Saitz again, Elvira tells Zora the story of their relationship. In many respects, this scene symbolizes the excess of the irreversible sacrifice of identity. More perhaps than in any other Fassbinder film, this scene manifests the image of the invisible: the slaughterhouse is not a conventional image for the spectator, familiar to him on a daily extra-diegetic basis. He/she becomes witness to the industrial slaughter of cattle. During most of the scene the camera is positioned above a tub of blood, close to the bodies of the cows. After the cows are hung upside down on the hook and move down the assembly line, the center of the frame shows the blade as it slits their necks and the blood as it flows into the giant tub. During the rest of the scene Fassbinder, who, it will be remembered, is also the cameraman, maintains proximity and horrific intimacy, showing the body cut and bleeding and filming the hide being peeled off, the organs removed, and the head severed.

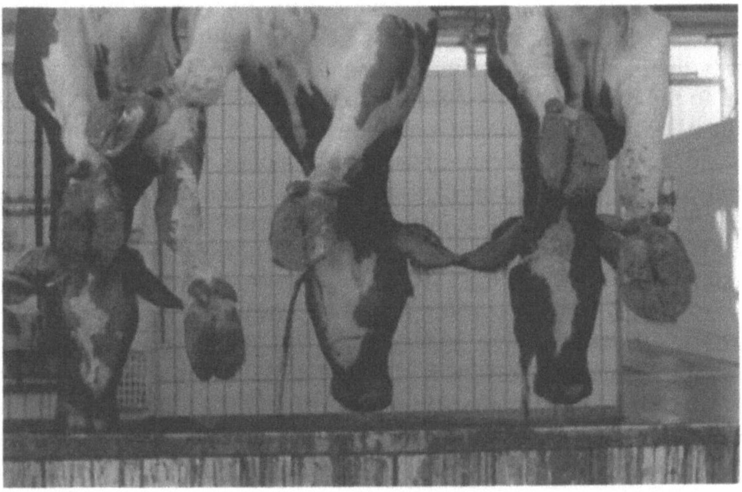

Lost masculinity and the disgusting dead, *In a Year of Thirteen Moons*

---

speech, when she seeks the protection of her husband in the face of Anton Saitz's revenge. For her part, Elvira, fully responds to the exchange of forms.

An inevitable, though not unequivocal, analogy is made between Elvira's body and those of the animals. The body is struck, abused, striped of its signifiers, led to destruction. But, even more, the extreme abjected image – repulsive, rejected, abhorrent – serves to define the impossibility of Elvira's passing as a male. As a woman/transsexual, Elvira cannot return to her job as slaughterhouse butcher even though during her retransitional stage of unclear identity following Christoph's departure she longs to "get a job in my old line of work" (Fassbinder, "*In a Year of Thirteen Moons*" 11). The slaughterhouse workers do not accept what is for them an unintelligible desire, deride her, and chase her away. Therefore, the slaughterhouse clearly symbolizes lost masculinity – in an extreme, subversive manner the film makes the connection between lost masculinity and the disgusting dead in a way that projects both on Elvira.

In my opinion the scene, with its variety of physical sensations, fuels the corporeal fantasies of the spectator in regard to off screen events related to Elvira's body: the sex change operation and sexual relations she has both as a prostitute and with Christoph. In this sense, the scene has more to do with Anton Saitz and her bodily sacrifice, than with Christoph, whose relations with Elvira are, as noted, a reconfirmation of the neurotic pattern of her relations with Anton Saitz, the beginning of her passing as trespassing.

The slaughterhouse scene is a portent of the destructive pattern that repeats itself in meetings Elvira has with different people during the last five days of her life. That is, the body that has endured excessive suffering is led/leads itself to its own death.

D. *The Gazeless Body*

The so-called unintelligible body of Elvira, dependent on the looks of others for its identification as transsexual, is constructed by the film as gazeless, beginning with the failure of the first passing in the opening scene. Negation of the look and the gaze climaxes in the convent scene. When Elvira goes home to Irene and Marie-Ann in one of her last attempts to return to the past (actually to reproduce in a destructive compulsive manner the behavioral pattern that led her surroundings to reject her), the conversation takes place almost without look or gaze. I will describe this process, similar to that of Kaspar, Oskar, Travis, and other NGC protagonists, which creates a strong link between demasculinization and negation of the look/the gaze.

Negation of the look/gaze relates both to Elvira and the one who looks at her, since she was never looked/gazed at in a way that confirmed her identity as a transsexual/as a woman by those around her.

Ironically, the sole person to address her as a woman does not look at her at all. This is the man fired by Saitz because of being ill with cancer, and whose powerless gaze at Saitz's office building went on daily for seventeen months. This all-day ritualistic act seeks hopelessly to restore the power to the look, to transform it to a gaze. As with each of the other secondary characters in the film, he too symbolizes a facet of Elvira's character.[17]

Extending this specular negation, there are only two prominent point of view shots in the film: Elvira's look at cattle being slaughtered and at the man who commits suicide in Saitz's building. The total absence of reaction shots of Elvira or Zora during the atrocious events in the slaughterhouse creates a strong opposition between the camera reflecting on events and an "unreflective" Elvira. The film creates a connection between dephallicization and negation of the look/gaze and these few subjective shots and death. That is, this look constitutes only momentary subjectivity.

Many scholars described Fassbinderian aesthetics as being based on display and on specularization. But this is not the case in *In a Year of Thirteen Moons*. In contrast to other Fassbinderian characters, Elvira is not positioned in front of mirrors (in the sense of a reversal shot like that taken of Hermann Braun on his return from Canada in *Maria Braun*, in the sense of the "simple" reflection in *Mother Kuster*, or in the *mise-en-scène* overloaded with mirrors in *Chinese Roulette*).[18] Similarly, the Fassbinderian style of photography does not block the spectator from Elvira, and Fassbinderian voyeurism à la Mayne[19] becomes one of Elvira's unfulfilled wishes: no one looks at her.

Fassbinder completely destroys the specular status associated with Elvira through the use of omnipresent objective photography in contrast to subjective photography, through the bond between subjective look and death-oriented object, and through undermining any gaze or look at Elvira by other characters (except when accompanied by violence, and even then photographed from a distance). The camera usually films

---

17 The man ill with cancer is similar to Elvira in a number of ways: there are parts within his body that are destructive and fatal; he is totally lacking social power, enslaved without purpose to a neurotic ritual, believes in magic powers of the look to return his previous identity to him, etc.

18 The sole *mise-en-scène* containing surrounding mirrors is in the restaurant toilet where Elvira and Zora go after Christoph's departure. The toilet is covered with black and white tiles the entire length of the walls and the ceiling. Elvira is reflected in them a great many times, primarily "parts" of her face. Of course, the "body in bits and pieces" is a metaphorical expression for what dramatically takes place in the scene. It is not specularization that constructs identity.

19 See e.g., Mayne on voyeurism in Fassbinder's films ("Fassbinder" 61-74).

Elvira from a fixed distance, with no movement, creating attraction-repulsion. This constantly positions the spectator among the other characters in the diegesis – including Elvira herself – who are forced to decide who she is/what she is and how they conceive their relationship. This is central to the process of negating the options of identity through destroying the look/gaze as a means of constituting identity.

In the convent scene, an additional strategy typical of NGC is derived from the absence of point of view shots: the nearly total absence of eye contact. When the nun stands facing Elvira, the latter raises her head for the first time and says, "How are you, Sister Gudrun, I am Erwin Weishaupt. Do you remember me?" (Fassbinder, "*In a Year of Thirteen Moons*" 23). There is a cut to a close-up of the nun's face, but from below, not from Elvira's point of view. Even if it were possible to explain this shot in terms of the plot (i.e., as expressing the nun's attempt to remember Erwin as a child, when he looked at her from below), the position of the camera fractures the look that would be expected from Elvira. From this moment on we are no longer closely attached to Elvira's consciousness as she becomes acquainted with her past, but rather to that of the nun.[20] In this way, the position of the camera has a critical role in fracturing any possibility of Elvira's establishing an identity.

Throughout the entire length of the scene in which the nun describes Erwin's history, there is no eye contact between her and Elvira (or Zora for that matter, a symbolic character who at this point emphasizes Elvira's difficulty in coping with her repression of her childhood and so is in a type of slumber). The scene is unrealistic in terms of sound. Most of the time the nun is standing at a distance from Elvira and Zora and speaks so softly they cannot hear her. Who, then, is listening to the story of Elvira's past? When Elvira is represented as coming close to fainting, it is clear that she can no longer sustain the repression of her childhood in the orphanage. While it appears that awareness of her personal history presents an option for constructing her subjectivity, the film undermines such a possibility through the positioning of the camera, lack of eye contact and the acoustic distance.

---

[20] Even if we interpret this shot as Elvira's point of view, as she sees herself as the small Erwin who looks up to the nun, this is after all the sole moment that represents Elvira's consciousness and which has no continuity in the scene. Since in this scene we are connected to the nun and Elvira is not present in it – physically or vocally – it seems to me that the first possibility I outlined – that the shot evolves from the nun's point of view – is more suitable. In any event, the absence of eye contact subverts the possibility of establishing Elvira's identity.

E. Lost Childhood as Performance

Norman Taurog's *You're Never Too Young* (1955) is a slapstick musical starring Dean Martin and Jerry Lewis. One of the numbers, "I Like to Hike," appears during a scene that takes place at a school party. At the conclusion, Lewis, who has been forced to impersonate a fourteen-year-old girl, is seen dancing in line and then jumping into the arms of Dean Martin. When Elvira enters Saitz's room, he and his employees are engrossed in a cultic performance of this scene. In my opinion, performing this number is Saitz's way of returning to a childhood he never had. In this sense, the scene parallels Elvira's visit to the convent, and the ritual involved is similar to the neurotic re-abandonment pattern which Elvira reproduces in each situation in her life, including the event under discussion. Saitz's emotional reaction to Lewis's jump and the imitative dancing being performed in the room is indicative of a repeated regression whose neurotic strength is similar to that of Elvira's. The performance, however, also sharpens the simulacric attachment between Elvira and Saitz: the sex change, after all, is also a simulation of what never took place. Ironically, the photo that Elvira shows Saitz of Erwin as a young adolescent to remind him who she is, strengthens the asymmetrical parallel between them: Anton Saitz is imitating an adolescent who is imitating an adolescent girl, while the gap between Erwin's photo and its "imitation," that is, Elvira, is too wide to be identified or accepted.

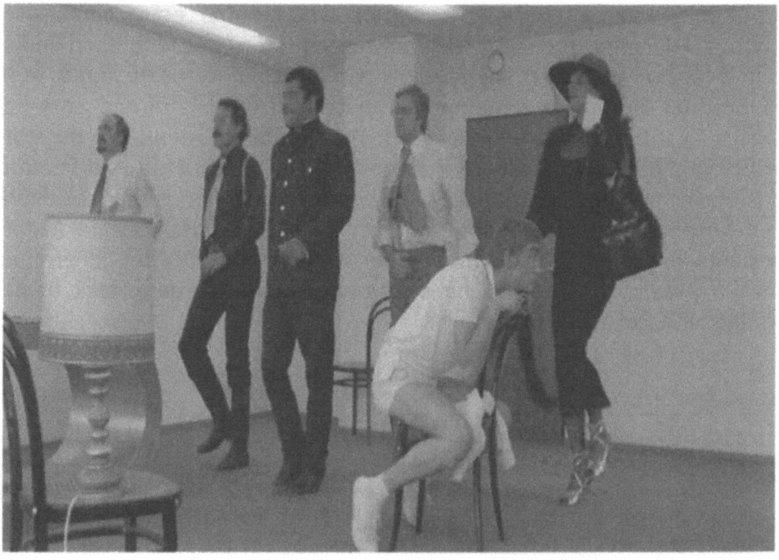

Reunion with Anton Saitz, *In a Year of Thirteen Moons*

F. Neither a Husband nor a Father

Most of the conversation in the scene in which Elvira meets his wife and daughter takes place without eye contact between any of the three protagonists. From the moment Elvira sits behind them, the camera is located at a fixed distance from the events taking place. When Irene first gets a glimpse at Elvira, her appearance evokes a laugh of mockery. Elvira's reproduction of the rejection neurosis is carried out in men's clothing and haircut. That is, when she attempts to adopt external phallic signs and to change, through them, her indistinguishable identity, it is apparent that she will lose her last patriarchal functions of husband and father, even if they were only a simulacra.

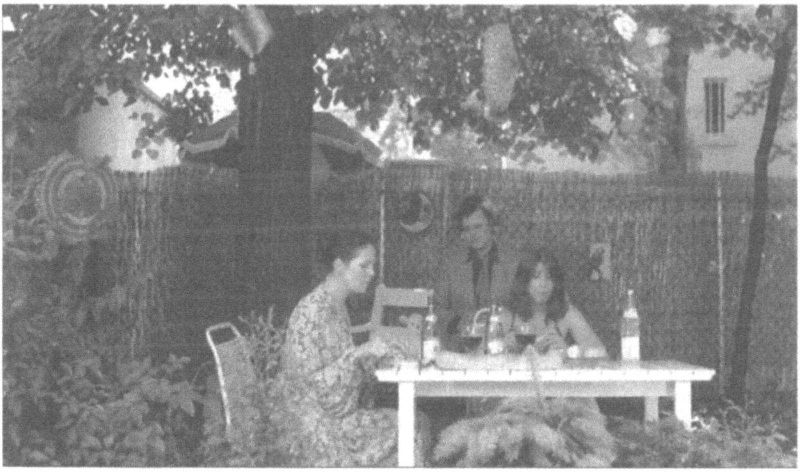

Elvira with her wife and daughter, *In a Year of Thirteen Moons*

I maintain that what characterizes Elvira, like all other NGC protagonists, is the irreversibility of their corporeal history which does not allow them to be part of the social body. This scene constructs irreversibility as leading to total loss: the following morning, in the last scene, what is left of her body is only a recording of her voice describing her previous suicide attempt.

II. Disembodied Voice

The presence of Elvira's recorded voice fills the void left by her body. This scene is highly reflexive since Nun Gudrun (who symbolizes Elvira's past) enters the apartment and circles all the characters – Saitz, Zora, Irene, Marie-Ann, the reporter and his wife – before she leaves. Of course, this metaphoric act expresses the influence of Elvira's past on her suicide. If during the scene at the convent Zora jumps and leaps when she approaches the nun (symbolically reiterating one aspect of Erwin's childish behavior in the past), a reversal takes place when the nun performs this ritual which connects all the characters through the crucial aspect of Elvira's life – abandonment and rejection.

Elvira's recorded monologue actually begins at the end of her visit to the reporter's house (the final rejection). In this monologue she tells him about her first suicide attempt following Saitz's rejection when she returned from Casablanca. The monologue appears to impose Elvira's audial presence on the people gathered in her apartment. In contrast to the multi-layered sound at the end of *Maria Braun*, for example, in which only diegetic voices are heard, at the end of *In a Year of Thirteen Moon*, Elvira's monologue is extra-diegetic in the dual sense of the term. As in *Maria Braun*, the recorded voice overcomes those of the protagonists (e.g. the anxious dialogue between Marie-Ann and her mother) and creates a conflict which intensifies because it is the (reconstructed) voice of the deceased. Intended to establish subjectivity, if even through memory, the narration undermines this very option. Separated from her body, Elvira's voice is the final expression of a split body, just as the recording is the final expression of simulacra.

In a Year of Thirteen Moons proves Gayle Rubin's statement that "sexual variation" is not a matter of binarism or of spectrum, but rather "a system of many differences" (qtd. in Butler, "Sexual Traffic" 44). The transsexual body in this film carries with it a humanistic subversion of any type of categorization, and a radical criticism of imposed heteronormativity. Clearly, this is not a case of undistinguished circulation of signs of sex à la Baudrillard. What was dubbed the unintelligible body in research is actually extremely distinctive and intelligible in its relation to the fascist-Nazi past. The film is radically subversive not because it presents impossible queerness, but because it demonstrates the impossibility of ignoring the presence of the body. As I claimed previously, Elvira's body symbolizes the total (irreversible) rupture of the Nazi trope of the son and total opposition to the male- and female-Nazi body. The total loss of sexuality (and the family unit) and the shattering of all phallic and patriarchal symbols in the end lead to the development of historical consciousness in the spectator.

CHAPTER 5

Post-Traumatic NGC Models

By the end of *Aguirre, Wrath of God*, all of his men have died during the quest for the legendary land of gold. Alone, Aguirre stands on the raft surrounded by corpses, hugging his dead daughter. The screech of monkeys fills the air and the current carries the raft down the Amazon; Aguirre's voiceover is heard: By marrying his daughter and establishing a "pure dynasty," he will seize Mexico from Cortez and rule over all of New Spain. As the editing cuts between his voice and the screeches, Aguirre holds a monkey in front of his face and declares himself "the wrath of God." In the last shot, the camera continuously circles the raft.

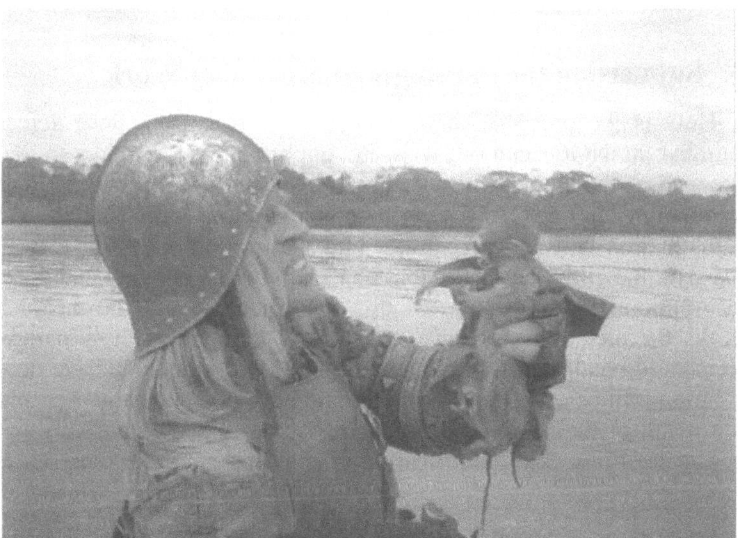

Aguirre, Wrath of God

I. Return of the Displaced

This scene not only allegorizes the connection between imperialistic murderous megalomania and the total denial of military defeat, as research until now has claimed, but also phantasmatic symbolic incest. The combination of these three structures demonstrates my claim that NGC turned to imaginary domains beyond Germany (physically, culturally, cinematically, and iconographically) to raise the imaginary domains of the German past in order to fracture them. NGC directors do not use displacement to present the other culture, but rather as a way to confront the presence of one of two others: either the "other who was the I until defeated" or the "other who was annihilated by that I." These classifications, first of all, indicate the deep indebtedness of NGC as a national cinema to its past; and second, reveals that NGC films define as "other" the German male who was defeated, and not the "other," the annihilated victims of the Nazi regime. The definition of the I (that is, including the intergenerational connection between NGC directors as representatives of the second generation and the first) and its multistrata attachment to the two "others" are, of course, at the heart of the present discussion.[1]

II. Subverting the Paradigm of Mourning Work

How is the presence of the "other who was the I until defeated" manifest in NGC, and what is its importance in relation to the a-presence of the "other who was annihilated by that I?" That is, what is the relationship between the absence of mourning work (including lack of distinction between perpetrator and victim) and work on identification with the Hitlerian imago that NGC offered its German audience? In my opinion, the subversion of this identification and the melancholy breaks the dichotomy of the mourning work or melancholy paradigm. We should recall that this subversion is present in an extensive number of canonic films of directors who to date have been prominent primarily as a result of their artistic differences. As described extensively in this section, work on past identification is embodied through representation

1 In regard to the layers of the trauma see, for example, Zimmerman: "There are two cores to the German trauma: the damage Germany caused itself and the damage it caused others – cause of Germany's disgrace. Rather than the thirteen years between 1933-1945 it was the seven years between 1941-1948 that are the years that traumatized Germany until today. *The totality of the war, Auschwitz, the collapse, the expulsion, the humiliation, sense of nothingness following the war and division of Germany are the traumatic foundations* of everyday life [...] it turns out that the *war* and the *defeat* are what is disgraceful about Nazism in the eyes of many Germans" (9, 30; Emphases in the original. My translation).

of three models of masculinity that undermine the trope of the son (i.e., identification with the Hitlerian imago); present counter images that oppose fascist-Nazi body/masculinity and its ideals of nationalism-respectability and racism (the remembering body); subvert the melancholy through showing its negative consequences, the enormous pain and tragedy of lost subjectivity;[2] characterize the defeated male as aphallic and apatriarchal (demasculinization, destruction of the gaze, breaking affiliation with the symbolic order, marginality, passivity, destruction of the family unit, couplehood and fatherhood); and present the social order as devoid of symbolic essence (without the Name of the Father, continuation of the family unit as representative of society, or the presence of the social body).

These strategies fracture the identifications that were transferred from the first to the second generation. The second generation inherited the lack of mourning work of the first, and NGC acted on its behalf to deconstruct the melancholic option. Of course, in such a manner, inter-generational transfer of identification was ruptured.

At this stage I wish to raise a hypothesis in regard to the question of the distinction between perpetrator and victim in NGC. Since the inception of the "inability to mourn" paradigm until the present day, scholars generally have accepted the claim that NGC films – including those by female directors – reflect the Germans' repudiation of responsibility as

---

2 There are an enormous number of films that describe the actual death of the protagonist as a result of the process of melancholy: e.g., Hermann (suicide) in *Despair*; Ricky (murder) in *The American Soldier*; Ariane and/or Gerhard Christ (murder or suicide) in *Chinese Roulette*; Kurt Raab (suicide) in *Why Does Herr R. Run Amok?*; Hermann and Maria Braun (suicide/murder?) in *Maria Braun*; and the industrialist (suicide) in *Wrong Movement*; Friedrich (murder) in *State of Things*; Gloria (murder) in *The Goalkeeper's Anxiety*.
There are also many cases of the symbolic death of the protagonist: e.g., Martha in *Martha*; Ali in *Fear Eats the Soul*; Bloch in *Goalkeeper's Anxiety*. Many of the protagonists die a symbolic death that is present in the film before their actual death. Symbolic death is prominent, as well, in the case of the abandoned children such as Oskar in *Tin Drum*, Angela in *Chinese Roulette*, Alice in *Alice*, and others. The number of secondary characters murdered is also high: For example, Gordon in *State of Things*, Traunitz in *Chinese Roulette*, and Rosa in *The American Soldier*.
In autobiographical films made by female directors the themes of loss are repeated as radical statements by way of corporeal embodiments. For example, in *Germany, Pale Mother* (hysterical paralysis); in *Marianne and Juliane* (the two sisters' self-imposed famine), in *Hunger Years* (bulimia). In my opinion, research carried out on these films to date (Kaplan, "Discourse," "Mother\Land"; Seiter; Knight; Liebman; Linville, "Mother-Daughter," *Feminism, Film*, "Retrieving History"; Byg; Kosta; McCarthy; Mouton; Keene) has failed to discuss the clear meaning of these phenomena. See my article "Not a Dirty Secret."

perpetrators and their adoption of victimhood. In his article on the survivor experience and trauma, Lifton writes:[3]

> [M]ore typical is the quest for vitality around direct biological continuity – the tendency of many survivors to reassert family ties and reproduce, and thereby assert biological and biosocial modes of symbolic immortality. In any case, the ultimate dimension, the struggle for resurgent modes of symbolic immortality, is crucial to the survivor, though rarely recognized as such. (177).

Earlier I hinted, without elaboration, that NGC made a distinction between the perpetrator and the victim. According to Lifton's description, the symbolic structures I have described – abandonment of the child, a-presence of fatherhood, mutant sexuality, destruction of the family unit and couplehood, etc. – are indicative of post-defeat trauma that is uncharacteristic of the survivor as victim. Applying Lifton's terminology, and in light of what he called the "psychic stigma of the annihilated" (176),[4] the German male is not presented in NGC as survivor-victim who does all he can to create "structures of symbolic immortality" (building close relationships, establishing a family). Even if NGC as post-traumatic cinema does not overtly accept the position of the perpetrator, it includes a repetitive symbolic structuring of subjectivity that is not characteristic of survivor-victim. Instead, it structures what I prefer to call the position of survivor-perpetrator.

III. NGC – Radicalism towards the Past

It is my contention, therefore, that academic research to date has not correctly assessed New German Cinema as a complete corpus. First, on the historical level, it focused only on such topics as its development from Young German Cinema through the Oberhausen Manifesto to the 1970s and interpretation of historical (de-Nazification) or cinematic (*The Holocaust*)[5] external events. On the theoretical, mainly psychoanalytical, level it limited itself to hegemonic paradigms that were obstructive,[6] prevalent conceptualizations,[7] and research questions that were

---

3 The article includes examples of traumatic reactions of soldiers from World War II and Vietnam, and Hiroshima and Buffalo Creek disasters.

4 "[…] [H]aving been annihilated and "killed," one feels oneself to have become part of the entire constellation of annihilation and destruction, to be identified with – live in the realm of – death and breakdown" (Lifton 176).

5 The perception that what inspired Germany directors to rethink the presentation of history in cinema was the enthusiastic reception of *The Holocaust* a year after the unenthusiastic reception of *Germany in Autumn*.

6 For example, the inability to mourn, displacement, oedipalization, and stranded objects.

established in the 1970s and 1980s.[8] On the narrow cinematic level, the research focused only on the auteurism of its directors, declarations of the directors themselves, and comparisons with parallel cinematic movements. Second, and consequently, academic research to date has not, in my opinion, correctly assessed the unique radicalism of NGC as national cinema with a moral orientation.

This radicalism is made explicit by the textual constructs analyzed in this section, which stand in complete contrast to the process of remasculinization[9] that characterized the cinema of the 1950s.[10] As I described in length, NGC consistently characterizes the German defeated male through desubjectivization, asexualization, and unrestorable loss of all previous affiliations, including fatherhood.[11]

It appears that NGC's deep moral stance towards the past was also unique in comparison with the "renewed essentialism of blood, race, and

---

7 Such as the general "narrative fetishism" (Santner, "History"); the textual "colonization of the unconscious"; or that connected with directors, for example, Herzog's "eccentric idiosyncratism," Wenders' "fraternal rivalries," and Fassbinder's "aesthetics of pessimism."

8 See Kaes's quote from *Hitler to Heimat* on page 141.

9 According to Fehrenbach, Jeffords, Moeller and Poiger in the issue of *Signs* (1998) devoted to this topic.

10 The framework of this study does not permit a discussion of NGC's role as a cultural agent of the historical past in comparison to the role of the media and public discourse in Germany from the 1970s to the 1990s. At the same time, a partial comparative analysis between the types of images represented in the media and in the public sphere (as analyzed by Linke and others) and between that of NGC reveals the difference regarding the definition of otherness. In my opinion, the metaphors of "skin," "blood," "whiteness," and "nudity" are not dominant metaphors in NGC. This is due to the fact noted previously that NGC does not apply latent symbolization in regard to the horror of the Holocaust, but rather the horror of the defeat.

11 The cinema of the 1950s that advances "remasculinization" is unusual in its ideological approach, even considering the background of other phenomena in public discourse. In *Fallen Soldiers*, Mosse described the decline of the war myth as early as the 1950s in various domains of the public sphere. He relates to "[G]ermany [...] where the Myth of the War Experiences had its deepest roots and the most important political consequences" (202), and points out different phenomena in the public discourse that preserve it (for example, war diaries of foot soldiers that appeared since the 1950s with millions of copies sold); other dominant phenomena that demonstrate its decline were the post-war policy of the German Democratic Republic in regard to monuments, gravestones, design of military cemeteries (in which the older design was preserved, "with their rows of crosses, while the inscription *invictis victi victori* – the unvanquished who will be victorious – often used after World War I, was now repudiated as irrelevant" [222]); and in the wording of eulogies. According to him, there was an enormous difference between the strength of the myth of the war experience prior to and after World War II.

body" that was typical of mass media and other phenomena in Germany's public sphere at that time.[12]

IV. Neither Betrayal of the Fatherland nor *Heimat*[13]

At this stage, I would like to recall two occurrences, each of which in its own way dramatizes my claims thus far – *The Sinner* (Willi Forst, 1951) and *Heimat*.

The Sinner was unusual in its presentation of the post-war German male as a victim, weak, impotent and one incapable of being rehabilitated.[14] The film thus aroused fear and strong opposition, primarily from the church.[15] Although by the end of the film traditional gender roles had been reconstructed – the sinner grants the man's request and gives him sleeping pills and after his death also takes them – the betrayal of the Fatherland, as described by Fehrenbach, was still shocking.

Heimat is noteworthy in contrast to the radicalism of NGC. Although this TV series (and its sequels broadcast in 1993 and 2004) aroused intense debate,[16] my intention here is only to point out the acute differences between it and NGC according to the paradigm offered in my study: The trauma of defeat is not present in any manner in *Heimat* – not in the narrative or representations of masculinity, the male body, male identity, sexuality, couplehood, family unit, or the symbolic order. The

---

12 Linke discussed the aesthetics of Nazi racism that structured identity in everyday life in Germany at that time: in the mass media (apart from the cinema), in politics, and in protests by the Left. She claimed that the racist aesthetics of the Nazis continues to influence German political thought until today; e.g., the continuation of prominent tropes such as "white skin," "nudity," "blood," and violence from Nazi literature to the body images used by the West German Left in contemporary documentation and the use of "purity of blood" images in contemporary media in relation to immigrants and refugees. Her discussion supports, albeit in a different direction altogether, my findings regarding NGC.

13 The first part of this title relates to Fehrenbach's article entitled: "*Die Sünderin* or Who Killed the German Male: Early Post-War German Cinema and Betrayal of Fatherland."

14 At the symbolic level he went blind, underwent an operation, and again lost his sight.

15 According to Fehrenbach, this included the Catholic and Protestant churches organizing protests against its screening, stink bombs thrown in movie theatres in many cities, screenings in Frankfurt and Mannheim interrupted by tear gas, pupils organizing protest marches in a number of cities, the archbishop of Cologne calling upon all Christians to boycott the film. The film was banned, hastily, in twelve cities throughout West Germany. The church was also angered by the unusual portrayal of the female character who survived the post-war activities, and even though she had to turn to prostitution, was not portrayed as a victim ("*Die Sünderin*" 136).

16 This debate erupted soon after its enormously successful initial screenings; e.g., in 1985 in the *New German Critique*'s dossier and afterwards.

veterans fit into the economic miracle (Anton), are depressed over the end of the war (Ernst), or continue with their Nazi activity (Wilfried). The shattered family unit so typical of NGC (the missing father/husband, the abandoned child, the self-destructive couple), becomes here its diametric opposite – a multigenerational family saga.[17] Furthermore, the series lacks any critical distancing from the characters (Koch, "Torments"). *Heimat*'s revisionism is revealed not only in its repression of the Holocaust and complete lack of Jewish characters (in a work lasting sixteen hours), but also in its repression of any post-war understanding of Nazism as an ideology, and its defeat. In contrast to the analytic approach I proposed in regard to NGC, in this case, the revisionism of the series does require identifying past traces, as is indeed was undertaken by a number of scholars.[18]

NGC, which deconstructs *papas kino* and offers Germany's first, but mainly second, generations new options for historical consciousness, constructs spectatorship that is the polar opposite to that which *Heimat*, as a return to *papas kino*, proposes to its audience.

---

17 Breaches in the family unit practically do not exist in so far as the first generation family of Katharina and Mathias is concerned. The sole exception is the flight of Paul, the World War I veteran, from Schabbach to the United States. In the transition to the second generation of the family, the instability of the Heimat is portrayed: Otto is killed, Ernst is divorced, and Hermann flees, and so too Apollonia and Klärchen (n.b. the second generation of the family saga consists solely of Hermann who left Schabbach and became a famous musician abroad. Horst died at a young age, and Anton's children live in Schabbach. That is, the issue of the second generation is repressed). This instability is not presented critically, but rather in a nostalgic light, as a result of modernization and as yearning for the Heimat of the grandparent's generation, as the film emphasizes that in spite of everything the family members remained part of it; that is, even the breaches in the family do not undermine the saga and its values.

18 For example, by Kaes and Rentschler. The comparison between the characteristics of veterans in *Heimat* and those in NGC films is instructive. Willi and Hermann Braun in *Maria Braun* or Hans in *The Merchant of Four Seasons* are not in any way like Anton, Ernst and Wilfried. Upon his return, Hermann in *Maria Braun* assumes responsibility for a murder he did not commit and is punished with death for the deal he made with Oswald, an event that the film connects through portraits of the German chancellors to the 1970s. Willi is not able to function in the family unit, and at Maria's birthday party, for example, he dances with Papa Berger (Anton Schiersner) in his arms, while his wife remains on the other side of the room. Hans in *The Merchant of Four Seasons* is unable to adjust to his life in any manner and in the end commits suicide.

V. Between Narrative Fetishism and Body Memory

In "History," Santner explained,

> By narrative fetishism I mean the construction and deployment of a narrative consciously or unconsciously designed to expunge the traces of the trauma or loss that called that narrative into being in the first place. The use of narrative as fetish may be contrasted with that rather different mode of symbolic behavior that Freud called *Trauerarbeit* or the "work of mourning." Both narrative fetishism and mourning are responses to loss, to a past that refuses to go away due to its traumatic impact. The work of mourning is a process of elaborating and integrating the reality of loss or traumatic shock by remembering and repeating it in symbolically and dialogically mediated doses [...] Narrative fetishism, by contrast, is the way an inability or refusal to mourn emplots traumatic events: it is a strategy of undoing, in fantasy, the need for mourning by simulating a condition of intactness, typically by situating the site and origin of loss elsewhere. (144).

Does Santner's "narrative fetishism" offer a new paradigm? In my view, although he does not refer here explicitly to the option of melancholy, his concept does preserve the dichotomy of mourning work or melancholy. Narrative fetishism is inherently connected to melancholy, as we can see, for example, in some well-known emplotments: the historiography written by Nolte and Hillgruber and Reitz's *Heimat* of 1984. In both cases, narrative fetishism denies the trauma (in the first case, it is compared to the Gulag; in the second case, it is tied to the longed-for region of the Heimat).

Is it possible that other paradigms deal with repetitiveness of trauma besides including it in a "symbolic space that allows for recuperation of anxiety" (Santner 147) or its denial (*Angstbereitschaft*[19])? Are the sole options for reconstructing post-traumatic identity mourning, working through, and narrative fetishism? In my opinion, the answer is no. As my reading of NGC canonic films proves, the corporeality of the body and mutant sexuality are post-traumatic symbolic strategies presented at every level of the cinematic text. NGC proposes substitutes for the mourning work or melancholy dichotomy through the (post-traumatic) memory of the Body.

The image of Lene's (Eva Mattes) paralyzed face in *Germany, Pale Mother* is especially conspicuous. After her husband, a Nazi soldier, returned from the war, she did not tell him of her rape by Allied soldiers and he accused her of taking lovers. This scene shows the first close-up of Lene's trembling cheek. The trembling becomes more pronounced and in the end half of her face is paralyzed. In an especially horrifying

---

[19] Unwillingness to feel anxiety.

scene, we are witness to the extraction of Lene's teeth, which her husband orders over her pleas and objections. From this scene onward we only see Lene when the length of her face is covered by a scarf. As a defeated male, overwhelmed with the sexual overtones of the Nazi defeat, Hans perceives Lene's vagina as *vagina dentate*, and so orders what I interpret as a (symbolic) extraction and suppression. The extreme desexualizaion of the German woman transforms the scarf, usually an accessory of the feminine temptress, into a symbol of the loss of sexuality, both feminine and masculine. Lene, like other protagonists (both male and female) featured in the prominent works of the canonical NGC directors, becomes asexual. Her body remembers.

VI. Multifaceted Reflexivity

I claim that the body that remembers, the convoluted German body, is not only anti-fetishistic, but as a broad symbolic strategy emphasizes the multifaceted reflexivity of NGC. I do not want to point out what is already known (the connection between alienating, non-nostalgic reflexivity and modernist aesthetics), but to propose the hypothesis that in this matter NGC created an alternative to Nazi anti-modernism.

NGC reflexivity is multifaceted and decisively facilitates the crucial shifts in the spectators' position (from identification to alienation). For example, Fassbinder's reflexivity strategies include using myriad mirrors, tablaux, and the same characters/names in different films, as well as acting in his own films and designing excessive *mise-en-scène*. Wenders' reflexivity strategies include using *mise-en-abyme* on all textual levels, showing the details of the cinematic apparatus, and shooting the films according to their linear chronological development. Herzog's reflexivity strategies include using the persona/biography of a permanent cast of actors (especially Bruno S. and Klaus Kinski), designing idiosyncratic images, and shooting in distant geographical regions. NGC multifaceted reflexivity is not undertaken in the name of *cinéphilic* playfulness, as in the case of the French New Wave; rather, it uses what Hansen and Huyssen called "generational memory" of the first and second generations in regard to past images, and ruptures it again and again. In this sense, NGC offers a kind of reversal of the displacement paradigm: the focus is no longer on the metonymic process (à la Laplanche and Pontalis). Generational memory, however, is focused on reflexivity which contrasts images of the fascist-Nazi past with those of gender-sexual counter images.

VII. Return of History as Body

Kaes summarizes his book *From Hitler to Heimat* in these words:

> [After the mid-1970's] [...] A new focus on individual life stories and the history of everyday life (rather than political history), an emphasis on subjective memory, a differently nuanced concern and empathy with the Germans as victims, and, connected with this, a characteristic shift from aggressive male protagonists to silently suffering female main characters, whose violated bodies stand as emblems of a devastated Germany – these are some of the most visible tendencies in the New German Cinema's recent attempts to reevaluate and reappropriate German history. (198).

I hope that the discussion undertaken in this section has revealed completely different tendencies than those indicated by Kaes in this citation. Indeed, a few years later, in "Distanced Observers" he claimed that the recent historical turn in cultural studies forced the reopening of issues regarding how cinema directs negotiations of national identity and operates in self-formation of national culture. A number of factors attach new meaning to these issues, given the myths at work in German memory culture and events such as the crisis in the West German historian community, the measured rehabilitation of "everyday life" historians, *Literaturstreit*,[20] and controversy regarding the Holocaust memorial in Berlin. But most importantly, although NGC addresses both German and international audiences, the above analysis proves its acute status as national cinema.

The decline of NGC following the death of Fassbinder in 1982 and the commercialization of post-unification cinema raises the question of which cultural products will be in a position to defend German and Western memory from memory culture mediated by the media in the absence of cinema with a clear ideology and a radical approach to the historical past.[21] In a period in which para-amnesia of the Nazi past is dominant in world cinema (*Schindler's List* [Steven Spielberg, 1993], *Life is Beautiful* [Roberto Benigni, 1997], and even *The Downfall* [Oliver Hirschbiegel, 2004]), there is a need to reconsider New German Cinema as post-traumatic cinema.

---

20 This term refers to the literary debate initiated by Martin Walser in relation to Goldhagen's book (Dinar; Levy; Korner).

21 See for example Rentschler's critique "The Use and Abuse of Memory" of NGC after Fassbinder's death (185), and especially his critique of the film *Das Boot* mentioned earlier. As claimed, Wenders' oeuvre of the 1990s is unusual in its relations with the past.

Part II

American Post-Traumatic Cinema in the Aftermath of the Vietnam War

CHAPTER 6

Captivity, Crisis, and Fantasy

Between the release of John Wayne's *The Green Berets* in 1968 and films such as Michael Cimino's *The Deer Hunter*, Francis Ford Coppola's *Apocalypse Now*, and Hal Ashby's *Coming Home* in 1978-1979, no canonic films directly addressing America's defeat in the Vietnam War were produced by the American film industry.[1] This ten-year exclusion was evident not only in Hollywood, but in cinematic research, as discussed in the Introduction.

Vietnam War films have not been directly treated until now as post-traumatic films. Prominent studies dealing with the representation of the Vietnam War and masculinity in Hollywood films (Jeffords, *Remasculinization of America* and *Hard Bodies*; Corrigan, *A Cinema Without Walls*; and Gibson),[2] major anthologies (by Gilman and Smith, Dittmar and Michaud, Berg and Rowe, and Anderegg); and writers who dedicated key chapters in their books to the subject (Wood, Easthope, Burgoyne [*Film Nation*] and Savran) have all ignored the trauma. Not even one of the sixty-seven contributors to these anthologies posited trauma as a central issue in their discussion. Gibson, for instance, argues that the war genre resulted from the defeat in Vietnam, but he never examines the trauma in his writings and he describes the war as "humiliation." From this perspective, *The Deer Hunter* is merely a masculine ritual of sacrifice for the future of the community, characteristic of the

---

1 In Part II I will analyze films that either present the trauma directly or in an indirect but obvious manner. For indirect expressions and allegorical interpretations see, for instance, Wood on the "Golden Age" of horror films in the 1970s, Slotkin (*Gunfighter Nation*) on the "Mexican Western" during 1965-1968, and Higashi on George Romero's 1968 *Night of the Living Dead*.

2 Looking at the similarities between cinema and other cultural products, such as TV programs or literary works (Jeffords, *Remasculinization of America*), or on a paramilitary culture celebrating "the new warrior" – comics, paramilitary magazines, paintball, and adult war game theme parks (Gibson), prevents both these writers from an in-depth cinematic analysis, while they impose a problematic set of generalizations. The examination of other cultural products is, of course, beyond the scope of the present study, but as far as the arguments of these two writers regarding the films discussed are concerned, in my opinion their conclusions contain fundamental inaccuracies and are incomplete.

new war culture in which the act of sacrifice is sacred in and of itself. As an extension of this problematic analysis, Gibson notes that the narrative of *Platoon* leads to "the platoon members' moral awakening and the hero's transformation into 'a man'" (45).[3]

In post-Vietnam War films, the drama of the defeated male is for the most part presented implicitly. The films are fraught with tension between the paternal and the fraternal orders.[4] Due to the failure of the patriarchal paternal order, as I shall describe in my discussion of father figures, the fraternal order is not merely its inevitable successor, but also its counterweight and substitute, both in battle and among veterans. Nevertheless, in all the films discussed here, brotherhood sooner or later breaks apart. The defeat is a performative failure in terms of gender, in terms of the institutions that characterize both patriarchy and the nation, and thus also in terms of possibilities for cultural-historical continuity. This destabilization is revealed first and foremost through breaking away from traditional affiliations, patricide, fratricide, and the demasculinization process expressed on all textual levels. This part of the book will describe the relationship between the structuring of masculinity in the text – which avoids any discussion or mention of the defeat – and the subtext, which subverts the war drama and reveals the undermining and destabilization of male identity.[5]

---

3 I wholly object to the manner in which Gibson uses a few select narrative events from the discussed films while totally ignoring the text as a whole. See my discussion of *The Deer Hunter* and *Platoon* below. Easthope, who offers a Freudian-Lacanian analysis of the myth of masculinity in popular culture, avoids any mention of the trauma and discusses *The Deer Hunter* only in the context of the castration threat (64). These examples highlight the general trend.

4 I use the terms fraternal/fraternity and brotherhood interchangeably, to denote the sense of camaraderie.

5 Analysis of films made in Vietnam about the war lies beyond the scope of this study. The modern Vietnamese film industry only began producing films in the mid-1970s, when the majority dealt with the Vietnam War and rehabilitation. Since the beginning of the 1980s the industry has produced about seventeen films per year; that is, we cannot identify a latency period. In addition, the representation of masculinity is totally different. *In Wide Field* (Nguyen Hong Sen, 1981), *The Return* (Dang What Minh, 1983), *When the Tenth Month Comes* (Dang What Minh, 1984), *The Little Girl from Hanoi* (Hay Ninh, 1973), *Wild Reed* (Vuong Duc, 1983), *My Sweetheart Got Married* (Vu Chau, 1994) and *Retired General* (Nguyen Khac Loi, 1988) even if the soldier who returns from the war is haunted by it, rehabilitation by the family, love, tradition and religion is central to the films; without a doubt these factors greatly assist the veteran in reconstruction of his identity.

I. Dialectics of Defeat: From Hunter to Captive

To the best of my knowledge, none of the scholars cited in this work has commented on a central feature of the diegesis depicted in these films: During the sixteen years of American involvement in Vietnam, most films, and certainly the canonic ones (except those belonging to the revisionist school, such as *Rambo: First Blood Part II* [George P. Cosmatos, 1985] or those by Chuck Norris), chose to describe the pre-1968 period; that is, they address the period prior to the Tet Offensive (and therefore, prior to popular American acknowledgement of the certainty of defeat), or at the latest, the Tet Offensive itself. Even such films as Oliver Stone's *Born on the 4th of July* (1989), which spans some nine years of the protagonist's life, returns through flashbacks to 1968, when he was injured.[6] The time span depicted in the film thus defines a potential for victory. But it is precisely against the background of this textual nonrecognition of the certain "future" of defeat and withdrawal from Vietnam that masculinity is so prominently vulnerable and lost, as I shall show below.

Victory movies are scarce among post-traumatic films.[7] Most do not suggest defeat as a signifying concept, but rather deny it altogether. At the most, they depict victory in a specific battle (John Irwine's *Hamburger Hill* [1987], Ted Post's *Go Tell the Spartans* [1978], or Oliver Stone's *Platoon* [1986]). In the majority, the victorious overtones of the closure, that partly stem from the choice of the pre-1968 time slot, imposes itself on the film text, thereby reconfirming the national consensus with its emphasis on manhood. This can be seen, for example, in the singing of *God Bless America* in the last scene of *The Deer Hunter* and the Mickey Mouse Club song in the final scenes of *Full Metal Jacket* (Stanley Kubrick, 1987). These characteristics (denial of defeat, a "freezing" of the period depicted, and an imposed, often phantasmatic representation of victory in the closure) define the contours of a dialectic textual pattern. In post-traumatic Vietnam War films from the mid-1970s to the early 2000s the recurring scenario was that of falling into a trap: being caught in a booby trap, being ambushed, or encountering Vietcong warriors lurking in the jungle. The films depict an invisible

6 Films made outside the American industry, such as *The Killing Fields* (Roland Joffe, 1984, Britain), depict the period differently. *The Killing Fields* takes place between 1973, the bombardment of Cambodia, and 1979. This film is unique in showing the consequences of US policy for the local population, which was long kept secret from the public. It is also unique in its continued representation of the viewpoint of Dith Pran (Dr. Haing S. Ngor), the Cambodian journalist taken into captivity by the *Khmer Rouge*.

7 On the revisionist approach in films see for instance Vlastos.

enemy, but the American soldiers are confronted with its almost tangible absence – through mines, traps, and snipers. Adding to this sense of being trapped is the fear of invisibility rising both out of the difficulty in distinguishing between South and North Vietnamese soldiers and the blurring of distinction between soldiers and civilians, both of which were so characteristic of this war.[8]

Whether the entire plot centers on a combative confrontation with the hidden Vietnamese other replete with bloodshed (*Hamburger Hill*), or a few battle scenes that appear as flashbacks within the post-war narrative (*Born on the 4th of July*), falling in a trap is a key determinant of the development of the drama, and unequivocally defines the depicted world as one of anxiety mixed with survivor's guilt ("The John Wayne Syndrome").[9] This emotional world is the polar opposite of Broyles' famous statement "Why Men Love War." Defeat means falling into captivity – whether real and/or metaphoric.

In my opinion, the recurring scenario of entering a death trap depicts masculinity as hanging between two possible subject positions: that of Hunter, that is, a victor, one whose subjectivity is realized according to the codes of dominance; and that of Captive, that is, the defeated, one whose subjectivity collapses, perpetuating helplessness. These options are distinctly mythic in nature. The mythicization, however, is not only a central means in the denial process of historical events, as developed by Levi Strauss, but also a means of inherently exposing the duality of masculinity: mythicization both preserves the male masquerade and exposes it as such. I will make use of Richard Slotkin's paradigmatic historical-cultural studies to discuss mythicization in order to reveal the subversion embodied in these options.

---

8 Cooke argues that "[W]hereas wars previously codified the binary structure of the world by designating gender-specific tasks and gender specific areas where these tasks might be executed, today's wars are represented as doing the opposite. Post-modern wars highlight and then parody those very binaries – war/peace, good/evil, front/home front, combatant/non-combatant, friend/foe, victory/defeat, patriotism/pacifism – which war had originally inspired" (182).

9 In *Gunfighter Nation*, Slotkin analyzes John Wayne's transformation from a Hollywood star into a cultural icon. The John Wayne Syndrome, a "complex of war-related stress disorders identified by Vietnam veterans and their doctors […] The common feature of the syndrome was the soldier's internalization of an ideal of superhuman military bravery, skill, and invulnerability to guilt and grief." According to Slotkin, "identification is not necessarily with a specific Wayne film or group of films, but with Wayne as a figure of speech, signifying the supposed perfection of soldierly masculinity. Since that ideal is, in fact, impossible to live up to, [the syndrome] often took the form of excessive guilt or shame for feelings of guilt or grief, or for responding to battlefield stress with a normal human mix of fear and bravery" (512-519).

In his books *Regeneration through Violence* and *Gunfighter Nation*, Slotkin describes the significance of the frontier myth in American history. The Hunter vs. Captive paradigm has defined the frontier hero from the Puritan era (circa 1682) through the Kennedy-style New Frontier.[10] The national hero has evolved from the farmer into the Hunter and then into the Native American. This is a mediating figure between the mythological concepts of "old" and "new" Americans: between farming and hunting, settling and wandering, races and cultures. It is full of contradictions, primarily the antinomy between the Native American and the White. The myth of the symbolic hero, according to Slotkin in *Regeneration through Violence*, had to combine the heroic attributes of various types of heroes created in diverse genres of colonial writing, "The explorer, the naturalist-surveyor, the farmer, the military hero-ranger or soldier, the captive partially adopted by the Native American, and the hunter of beasts and men" (267).

The dual paradigm of the link between Captive and Native American evolved in such a way that the experience of captivity (usually of a white woman in earlier myths), has been transformed into adoption or initiation into the Native American world. According to Slotkin, it was James Fenimore Cooper's hero of the Leatherstocking Myth who set the benchmark, "His stature as an American Hero depends on his uniting the characters of the hunter and the captive, since the captivity and the hunter myths together constitute the national myth of the frontier" (502).

The standard against which the hero is judged is his ability to assimilate opposing skills. In the circumstances existing during the Puritan era, however, as represented in literature from that period, he would first have to master the Native Americans' skills. The colonist needed a symbolic heroic figure to express his sense of history, attitude to the land, and detachment from Europe. The Native American became a model for American heroism, exactly the opposite of the British hero. In its later version, Slotkin suggests, Native American masculinity has become normative: hunting, capturing, victorious masculinity (564-594).

Slotkin regards American Vietnam War cinema as a direct continuation of the frontier myth. In my opinion, however, the films reveal a gender-sexual complexity that cannot be exhausted within the New Frontier and mythic continuity.[11] The Hunter vs. Captive paradigm also

---

[10] See the chapter on John F. Kennedy, John Wayne, and the New Frontier (*Gunfighter Nation* 489-533).

[11] In the war movie genre, Western style mythicization is related to oedipal tensions in the collapsing social order, and because of the pathology of the oedipal narrative in

characterizes the protagonist in post-traumatic films. These films offer two narrative alternatives. In one, the soldier who arrives in Vietnam inherently possesses the nature of the Native American Hunter (*The Deer Hunter*, *Rambo: First Blood Part II*, *Heaven and Earth* [Oliver Stone, 1993]); in the other, the soldier acquires these qualities during basic training (*Full Metal Jacket* and *Born on the 4th of July*).[12] But in all films, defeat repeatedly turns the Hunter into Captive, whether this captivity is real, as in *Rambo: First Blood Part II* (by the Russians) and *The Deer Hunter* (by the Vietcong); temporary voluntary, as in *Apocalypse Now* (Willard [Martin Sheen] at Kurtz's [Marlon Brando] headquarters), or metaphoric, as in *Coming Home* (Luke [Jon Voight] chained to the draft office, Billy [Robert Carradine] at the hospital, Bob [Bruce Dern] before the suicide) and *Birdy* [Alan Parker, 1984] (Birdy [Matthew Modine] in the mental hospital). Captivity is clearly a passive scenario that ends not in a victorious conquest but in surrender and returning home.

The two paradigms, Ranciére's "the birth of a nation" and Slotkin's "regeneration through violence,"[13] are thus subverted by this corpus. The crumbling social order determines "the decline of a nation" as the dominant fiction, and unlike colonial narratives,[14] the protagonist will not resolve the contradictions for a "noble cause" as defined by the social order. On one hand, the meanings embodied in the Vietnam War hero are indeed mythic. On the other, the psychohistorical situation of a war deemed unjustified by its fighters, as described in these films (except for revisionist films, which nevertheless still comply with the pattern, as shown below), has had a decisive role in the transformation

---

many of these films (*Full Metal Jacket* and *Platoon*, for example), the issue of patricide is inseparably linked to the issue of fratricide.

12 In confronting the father figure, the soldier is already a Hunter (Leonard in *Full Metal Jacket*, who murders Sgt. Hartman after becoming an expert sniper in boot camp, or Chris in *Platoon*, who murders Sgt. Barnes at the end of his tour of duty). In my opinion, the assimilation of the racial other's ability is replaced by a renewed discussion of the self in the context of father figures (the oedipal other). Having acquired the other's skills, confrontation with the father figure is depicted by the film as a violent, hunt-like encounter.

13 Post-traumatic cinema is unique in that it is stripped the trauma from the mythicization process that according to Slotkin (*Regeneration through Violence*) began during the Puritan period and continually through the 1970s. As indicated in this study, the traumatic event retrospectively transforms the mythicization; that is, the traumatic event is not an additional stage in the development of the paradigm from the gangster to the serial killer. In this sense, retaining the paradigm indicates that America's view of itself as a "gunfighter nation" is based on the repression of the trauma.

14 See also Hellman's "Vietnam," and Robert Warshow's classic essay on the tragedy inherent in the Western hero.

of the warrior from Hunter to Captive, on a realistic, metaphoric, and moral level.[15]

The central subversive element in these films is the transformation of Native American masculinity, along with its mythic and ideological implications, into an acoherent, volatile, unstable masculinity. That is, defeated. The films present a world that denies the defeat, but the gender-sexuality structure is inherently linked to the trauma of defeat and therefore lurks beneath the surface. According to Silverman in *Male Subjectivity at the Margins*, American World War II films have pointed to that historical moment in which the commensurability between the penis and the phallus was broken, causing a collective loss of trust in the dominant fiction. I argue that Vietnam War films involve a basic ideological distrust, which the subject experiences in the identity-crushing passage from Hunter to Captive. The traumatic splitting of the mythic paradigm is expressed in gender-sexuality and on all textual levels: geographic space (the split between America and Vietnam is presented as a geo-psychological chasm[16]), language (a split between the newly acquired language of basic training as "injurious speech" [Butler, *Excitable Speech*] and pre-army language), and within the paternal and fraternal figures.

II. Oedipal Structures, Fraternal Structures: Patricide, Fratricide

Post-traumatic American Vietnam films construct a split between positive and negative father figures. It is easy for the soldiers in the films to identify with the positive father figure because, in contrast to the negative father figure, he embodies traditional American values of morality. Positive father figures, however, are scarce, and their ability to influence the conflictual events that shape masculinity in crisis is minimal. The split therefore reflects the crisis of masculinity, which is fatherless and disconnected from intergenerational continuity.

Elias (Willem Dafoe), the humanitarian sergeant in *Platoon*, interferes with the massacre of the Vietnamese villagers and is murdered as a result. In Barry Levinson's *Good Morning, Vietnam* (1987), the positive

15 See, for instance, Eriksson's (Michael J. Fox) capture by his four comrades who kidnapped and raped a young Vietnamese girl despite his moral opposition, in Brian De Palma's 1989 *Casualties of War*.

16 See the following discussion of *The Deer Hunter*, for example, which is based on a total separation of scenes between America and Vietnam, while subversively suggesting linkage between the two spaces through intersecting motifs. See Wood, and also, for instance, the dialectic split in *Full Metal Jacket*.

father figure, Gen. Taylor (Noble Willingham), supports the DJ Adrian Cronauer (Robin Williams), but he is an outsider to the main events and eventually fails to prevent Cronauer's ousting. In Brian De Palma's *Casualties of War*, the only positive father figure is the priest, who appears in a very brief scene – the judges in the rape and murder trial are heard but never seen. In *Rambo: First Blood Part II*, Col. Trautman (Richard Crenna) is totally powerless against the negative father figure, Murdock (Charles Napier), who decides to desert Rambo and the POWs in the field. In *Apocalypse Now*, Col. Kilgore (Robert Duval) is presented as a split father figure – he both protects the soldiers and endangers them by going surfing.

Because the positive father figures depicted in the films are not dominant, they are excluded in various ways not only from the moral framework, but from history. The inevitable result is the collapse of the basic construction of the patriarchal order and the loss of its symbolic value, including intergenerational continuity.

The hero turns for help to characters who represent the military order, usually against the background of a psychological breakdown caused by an unresolved moral confrontation experienced during captivity (whether real or symbolic). In most cases, because the father figures have no moral perspective they lose their standing in the eyes of the hero who needs their support. So Kovic (Tom Cruise) in *Born on the 4th of July* vainly attempts to describe to his general how he accidentally killed his comrade Wilson; in *Casualties of War*, Eriksson unsuccessfully tries to enlist his commanders in his efforts to bring his comrades to justice for the rape and murder of a Vietnamese girl.

The culmination of the split is seen in patricide, which becomes a recurring motif in post-traumatic Vietnam War films. Gen. Kurtz in *Apocalypse Now* is finally murdered by Capt. Willard (Martin Sheen), who is commissioned by the social fathers to eliminate him. Gunnery Sgt. Hartman (Lee Ermey), the recruits' drill instructor in *Full Metal Jacket*, is murdered on the last night of boot camp by Pvt. Leonard (Vincent D'Onofrio), the most maladjusted soldier in the platoon. In *Platoon*, at the end of his tour of duty Chris Taylor (Charlie Sheen) murders Sgt. Barnes (Tom Berenger), who was involved in the massacre and who murdered the sergeant who opposed it.

In *Rambo: First Blood Part II*, when Rambo (Sylvester Stallone) returns from his mission, he spares Col. Murdock, who had left the former to his death and deserted the POWs, but warns that he will kill him if he does not act to return the POWs left in Vietnam. This metaphoric patricide is also seen when Eriksson informs on Capt. Hill (Dale Dye) and Lt. Reilly (Ving Rhames), the two father figures in *Casualties of War*, because they ignored the Vietnamese girl's rape and murder.[17] The failure of the father figure determines the course of the drama in many other films, including *Gardens of Stone* (Francis Ford Coppola, 1987), *Hamburger Hill*, *Off Limits* (Christopher Crowe, 1988), and *Heaven and Earth*. Only the Vietnam-related episodes in Robert Zemeckis' *Forrest Gump* (1994) depict the rescue of a father figure, Lt. Dan (Gary Sinise), by Forrest (Tom Hanks), as discussed below.

In these post-traumatic films patricide can be an oedipal murder and/or a political murder of a representative of the military establishment; in the Vietnam War it carries no tragic weight. Confrontations with negative father figures usually occur during crises, and their murders are perceived as necessary and inevitable, rather than a primal sin.

In contrast, a review of incidents of fratricide in the canonic films reveals that the phenomenon is widespread and diverse. Narratives centering on fratricide are divided into two categories, according to whether the murder is inadvertent or deliberate. Inadvertent murders play a major part in the PTSD suffered by the soldiers who committed them, and are thus a major factor in the transformation from Hunter to Captive: In *The Deer Hunter*, this occurs when Michael (Robert De Niro) says "one shot" during his last encounter with Nick (Christopher Walken) in burning Saigon, and causes Nick to repeat the phrase and shoot himself in the game of Russian roulette. In *Born on the 4th of July*, Ron Kovic inadvertently murders Wilson during the chaos of battle. In David Jones' *Jacknife* (1989), David (Ed Harris) has a breakdown after the war, feeling guilty for deserting the wounded Megessey (Robert De Niro) and for his friend Bobby's (Tom Isbell) death. In *Coming Home*, Luke plays a key role in Bob's suicide. The only time fratricide involves the symbolic rescue of a brother figure is in Jon Avnet's *The War* (1994). In this film Steven (Kevin Kostner), who during the war deserted the wounded Dodge in order to save his own life, saves a co-worker during a mining accident and consciously pays with his life.

In *The Deer Hunter*, Michael is deprived of his Hunter masculinity when he plays Russian roulette for the last time against Nick, as will be discussed below. The inadvertent murder in *Born on the 4th of July* haunts Kovic until he confesses to Wilson's family. David in *Jacknife* and Steven in *The War* also experience their involvement in the death of their comrades as the crucial event not only of the war, but their post-war lives.

17 A symbolic patricide also takes place in *Cutter's Way* (1981) by the Czech director Ivan Passer.

When fratricide is deliberate, the murder signifies the fall of the fraternal order, along with the disintegration of the patriarchal order. The fraternal order is not a substitute for masculinity that has lost its traditional affiliations: In *Platoon*, Sgt. Barnes murders his colleague Elias in order to cover up the village massacre. In *Apocalypse Now*, Capt. Willard murders Phillips (Albert Hall), the ship commander, when he refuses to proceed beyond the last army post on the way to Cambodia. At headquarters, Col. Kurtz murders Capt. Colby (Scott Glen), who was originally sent to kill Kurtz but joined his followers instead. In *Casualties of War*, Meserve (Sean Penn) attempts to murder Eriksson, the only soldier to disclose the atrocity when they returned to base. A murder attempt also takes place in *Good Morning, Vietnam*: Sgt. Maj. Dickerson (J. T. Walsh) knowingly sends Cronauer into territory recently captured by the Vietcong. The attempt to get rid of Cronauer, his colleague at the radio station, fails on the concrete level, but is realized symbolically when Cronauer is discharged and repatriated. In Robert Altman's *Streamers* (1983) fratricide also takes place at the recruits' camp before they are sent overseas.

Brotherhood disintegrates not only because of moral issues, but also as a result of defeat. The transformation from Hunter to Captive destroys fraternity, both during the war, and, metaphorically, afterwards. In *The Deer Hunter*, Michael suggests leaving Steven behind in the Vietcong cage and escaping without him. In *Coming Home*, Billy, "captive" in the hospital, commits suicide despite Luke's support. So does Bob, for whom coming home means symbolic captivity – no longer needed by the Army, unable to find himself in civilian life, he is held captive by his war memories and the absurdity of being decorated for his accidental self-inflicted wound. In *Apocalypse Now*, Willard is the physical and mental captive of a patricidal mission against Kurtz that leads to the fratricide of Phillips. In *Born on the 4th of July*, Ron Kovic and Charlie fight a wheelchair duel by the roadside in Mexico, having tortured each other with questions phrased in Hunter terms.[18]

[18] CHARLIE. You ever have to kill a baby? You ever have to kill a little gook baby? […] Don't shit me Kovic, you never killed a baby. You never had to kill a baby. You never put your soul in that war. You never put your soul on the line, man.
RON. How […] the fuck do you know? Maybe I killed babies […]
CHARLIE. What the fuck are you hiding? […] Don't shit me […] you never killed a baby, anybody, anything, did you, Kovic, did you?

III. Masculinity without Symbolization

Do these films offer the possibility of rebuilding the symbolic patriarchal and fraternal orders? According to Jeffords, remasculinization means, above all, the revival of patriarchy, including transformation of the veteran into a new social father. Is the fraternal order reinstated when, at the end of *Full Metal Jacket*, the soldiers overcome their disagreements and finally cooperate to kill the female sniper? Or when they march singing towards the Perfume River after the battle? Can Michael's actions in forcing Steven to discharge himself from the Veterans Hospital and return to his family, and Nick's wake at the end of *The Deer Hunter* be considered acts reinstating the symbolic order through a commitment to its rituals? Does joining the anti-war movement at the end of *Coming Home* and *Born on the 4th of July* constitute an attempt to join a new developing alternative order? In my opinion, the bitter irony of all the films' closures, including those not cited here, indicates, at best, a partial rebuilding of the symbolic order. Although having symbolic value, they are only single and highly ambivalent acts that are in contrast to the general depiction of the symbolic order in the films. In the majority of films discussed here – *Platoon*, *Casualties of War*, *Good Morning, Vietnam*, *Gardens of Stone* and others – there is no symbolic rebuilding of the fraternal order.

The result is a process of demasculinization that involves all aspects of the traumatic experience: performative, intergenerational, and fraternal. The masculine identity crisis is thus a crisis of the symbolic order and the impossibility of representing it in the films. The break in morality undermines masculinity's ability to be the obvious agent for representing the symbolic order. In Lasch's terms, the transformation is not merely from the "imperial self" to the "minimal self"; defeat means a transformation into a deconstructed self incapable of representing the symbolic order.

In her study *The Remasculinization of America*, Susan Jeffords describes the process of remasculinization in post-Vietnam War American culture. She suggests that representations of male bonding transcend all boundaries of race, ethnicity, class, age, and religion and reestablish relations between men in society. According to her, the soldier regains his status only in comparison to institutions which she defines as "feminine." As part of the total elimination of women from the masculine sphere, the veterans in these films take over reproduction as well, becoming the exclusive parent and father figures ("Reproducing Fathers").

So is this indeed remasculinization? Do these films actually depict the modification of gender relations in order to strengthen masculinity and patriarchy? Has remasculinization indeed become a decisive element in the more general process of ideological revisionism that Jeffords observes in contemporary culture? Are these processes so clear cut? In my opinion, Vietnam War films reveal a vast complexity regarding ideology and gender-sexuality and an ambivalent excess of contradictions and indeterminacies that can not be reduced to a unidirectional process, and certainly are not at the service of an unvanquished patriarchal image. Women's liberation, the anti-war, and other social protest movements all created a public sphere of resistance: this was an era of ongoing opposition to the patriarchal norms and the masculine-imperialist initiative.[19]

Jeffords analyzes the films as univocal and coherent, whereas they are actually fragmented and acoherent; the masculinity crisis they represent produces indeterminacy across all levels of the films' texts. The non-monolithic nature of masculinity is underscored by the defeat, which exposes the "mask" of masculinity. Jeffords, however, ignores the fact that these films were created following a decade of repression, which produced mostly indirect representations. Breaking this repression created symptomatic post-war representations, where the impact of trauma plays a more crucial role in constructing the male identity than the reconstruction motivated by patriarchal interests.

Post-traumatic films are non-hegemonic. Even when the reaffirmation of the social order is depicted, it is only temporary, and appears as an imposed closure, as described above. Most conspicuous is Jeffords' failure to analyze masculine construction (or actually deconstruction) processes in relation to traditional symbolic structures (fatherhood, brotherhood, history), sexuality, and the "feminine" in its diverse manifestations in these films. As I shall prove, the feminine (/the woman) is constructed as a counter image to the paternal/fraternal order, thereby constituting a dominant presence in many of the films discussed.

Studies of Vietnam War films that I have reviewed until now lack any reference to soldiers' sexuality. Is there an implied ideological assumption here that sexuality has no relevance on the battlefield except

---

19 To Martin, the new world order that Jeffords analyzes in *Remasculinization*, seems too similar to the old world order analyzed by leftist and feminist critics, that is, America at the time of the frontier period, after World War I and World War II (125). Martin's insistence on historical specificity and alternative readings is reinforced by feminist analysis. Howell argues that Jeffords' analysis is limited by the fact that "masculinity" and "femininity" in her terminology are constructed around a fixed, binary gender structure, and her methodology becomes part of the texts' depoliticization. As a result, she is unable to discuss specific historical constructions in the films. Moreover, her reading of the "feminization" process, for instance, is based on stereotypes, such as the feminine characteristics she attributes to the government – weakness, passivity, lack of aggression, negotiation (170).

in its displacement into homosocial relationships or through the usual contexts of prostitutes (*Full Metal Jacket*) and/or army nurses (Robert Altman's 1970 *M*A*S*H*)? In my opinion, avoiding examination of soldiers' masculinity in terms of sexuality is the same perspective that affected a concealment of the trauma; i.e., the desire to impose sexual potency even in contexts where all potency is undermined. The taking for granted of potent sexuality supports the taking for granted of victory. As I will show, in these films the implications of defeat affect masculinity in every conceivable realm, though I am not suggesting the usual analysis of the sexual impairment experienced by war veterans. In my opinion, an attempt to analyze post-traumatic masculinity in Vietnam War films demands deconstructing and examining this taken-for-granted heteronormativity and omnipotent sexuality. The obvious partnership between heteronormativity and patriarchy dissolves in these films. My description of masculinity thus includes on one hand the affinity between masculinity and symbolic structures, and on the other, sexuality. Through the following description I intend to prove that it is precisely by interpreting sexuality that the traces of the trauma are revealed. In other words, sexuality, supposedly the most taken for granted element in the construction of omnipotent militaristic masculinity, will be the most telling in terms of exposing the processes undermining this omnipotence. The discussion in this part of the book will focus on the dialectic relationship between devices of concealment and prove the power of the relationship between representations of sexuality and violence.

IV. Sexuality

Hetero-normative, stable, uniform, sexual masculinity as such does not appear in post-traumatic Vietnam War films, which fracture heteronormativity by subverting what Butler calls the "metaphysics of substance" (*Gender Trouble* 20).[20] Sexuality is apparent only in a few of these films, as the following representative examples will demonstrate.

In Ted Post's *Good Guys Wear Black* (1978), the Vietnam War is the setting for a Watergate-style thriller. The hero, John Booker (Chuck Norris), fights the corrupt military establishment responsible for deserting Special Forces during a POW/MIA rescue mission. Five years after the operation, he is apparently free of post-traumatic symptoms and the trauma of captivity is manifest only during a short nightmare scene. The film thus recreates the Special Forces veteran as hero – practically and morally.

---

[20] For a discussion of substance as an illusion see Butler (*Gender Trouble* 20-33).

In addition, the absence of any traumatic effects on male subjectivity is embodied in the construction of his sexuality – the less trauma depicted in the films, the stronger the sexuality of the hero. Even in the few films that present sexual relationships between the hero and a woman, they are temporary and doomed. In *Good Guys*, for instance, the hero's lover is killed in a terrorist attack as part of the military's cover up attempt. Trapped in an endless process of restructuring its identity (as performative, moral, and affiliated), the sexuality of post-traumatic masculinity is unstable, with the inevitable collapse of the heterosexual relationship evidence of the trauma lurking beneath the surface of heroism.

This correlation between the traumatic and the sexual can also be seen in *M*A*S*H*. Here too, the promise of sexuality, implied in the presentation of the protagonists in the opening scenes, is never realized. As is well known, in this film the trauma has been distanced from the protagonists (surgeons in a field hospital) in every possible way: in place and time (the setting is the Korean rather than the Vietnam War); in the invisibility of the war itself, other than through the casualties brought in to the hospital; and in genre (black comedy). The parodic tone intensifies the drama. In contrast to the palpable physicality of the injuries during the last battle for Hue in *Full Metal Jacket*, for instance, or in *Platoon*, in *M*A*S*H* the wounded soldiers are faceless and characterless. Distancing the trauma from the film and from the protagonists preserves the correlation between the weakened trauma and their intensified sexuality. Yet even in this case, as far as the two main protagonists, Hawkeye Pierce (Donald Sutherland) and Trapper John (Elliott Gould), are concerned, it is only pseudo-intensification: their relationships with women are only partial and temporary (for instance, a siren interrupts Hawkeye's tryst with a nurse). Moreover, casual sex is but one among the many rebellions against the military establishment depicted in the film, and while it does construct identity, it is episodic, part of the general anarchy. Its place in the world depicted in the film, an army base, grows increasingly less stable and safe. Not only is the power of heterosexual relationships too weak to pose a threat to brotherhood, for instance, but as the narrative proceeds, it is the fraternal order that prevails.

Despite its sexual potential, male subjectivity in the film evolves on the margins of the social order.[21] It is often depicted in childlike sexist ways, without any option for maturation (the Hot Lips scenes, for

---

21 On this see for instance Kolker (*A Cinema* 324-325), who does not address the film's conservative attitude to homosexuality, which is realized in scenes related to Walt, among others, as I will show below. The subversiveness of the film relates only to heterosexuality.

instance). Childlike sexual behavior is also part of the pseudo-carnivalesque world of the film, aimed at taunting the establishment in any way possible.[22] The anarchic reactions of the protagonists therefore represent a different mode of masculinity: carnival in the face of death. The constant presence of death makes survival under ongoing emergency conditions a celebration of death in all its forms, as illustrated in the take off on the Last Supper prior to the simulacra of suicide and burial, and the next scene when Painless (Walt [John Schuck]), describes his temporary impotence to Hawkeye. Shocked by the possibility of homosexuality, Hawkeye persuades a nurse to have sex with the "dead" Walt before she departs for the US. The film celebrates sex-in-death both as metonymic to the drama as a whole and to overcoming homosexuality; and parodies war film conventions regarding both the sexuality of nurses and their repatriation. Most importantly, the film preserves sexuality together with representation of trauma including its substitutes: Walt's "suicide," a substitute for the trauma of the casualties brought to the field hospital, is inseparably linked to sexuality.

Thus, a subversive construct haunts this film as well. Masculinity, and the femininity that serves as its counter image, are both fictitious: seemingly substantive, exaggerated sexuality is actually a masquerade. These expressions of sexuality are part of the heteroglossia inherent in the Altmanian text.[23] In the explicit text, casual sex is integral to other anti-establishment manifestations; but the celebration of sex, unlike that of death, is not just another act of rebellion. While the celebration of death takes place when they care for casualties, the celebration of sex takes place as an extension of that drama, but unlike it never fully materializes. It remains a mere simulacra of masculine substance under a crumbling order, whereas death-related simulations do not subvert the celebration of death, but are an integral part of it. Even films that portray sexuality in this way portray masculinity as defeated.

V. Motifs in Vietnam War Films

The following table illustrates the incidence of the central motifs that characterize canonic films as post-traumatic: The table shows that these motifs occur repeatedly, and do not vary during the entire period from the late-1970s until the 2000s, evidence of the intensity of the trauma, as will be discussed in the following chapters.

---

22 Hawkeye, Trapper, Radar and the others are the cinematic forefathers of Col. Kilgore (Robert Duval), who risks his soldiers' life to surf the waves in *Apocalypse*, and their spirit certainly inspired the character of DJ Adrian Cronauer in *Good Morning, Vietnam*.

23 See Kolker (*Cinema* 303-382); Wyatt.

Motifs / Films	Trap / Captivity	Patricide	Fratricide	Demasculin-ization	Tortured Body	Ahistoricity	Split identity
The Green Berets (1968)	+		Rescue	+		+	
The Deer Hunter (1978)	+		+ ++	+	+	+	+
Coming Home (1978)	+		+ ++	+	+	+	+
Apocalypse Now (1979)	+	+	+	+	+	+	+
Cutter's Way (1981)	+	+		+	+	+	+
Rambo: First Blood (1982)	+	+)		+	+	+	+
Streamers (1983)	+	+	+	+	+	+	+
Birdy (1984)	+		Rescue	+	+	+	+
MIA 1 (1984)	+	+)	Rescue	+	+	+	+
Rambo: First Blood Part II (1985)	+	+)	Rescue	+	+	+	+
MIA 2 (1985)	+	+)	+) Rescue	+	+	+	+
Platoon (1986)	+	+	+	+	+		+
Good Morning, Vietnam (1987)	+	+)	+)	+		+	+
Full Metal Jacket (1987)	+	+	++	+	+		+
Gardens of Stone (1987)	+		+)	+		+	+
Born on the 4th of July (1989)	+	+)	+	+	+	+	+
Casualties of War (1989)	+	+)	+		+		+
Heaven and Earth (1993)	+		++	+	+	+	+
The War (1994)	+		+ S. Rescue	+	+	+	+
Forrest Gump (1994)	+	Rescue		+	+	+	+
We Were Soldiers (2002)	+	+)	S. Rescue		+		+

+ Presence of motif   +) Symbolic murder   S. rescue – Symbolic rescue   ++ Suicide

VI. Three Models: Asexual Hyper-Masculine, Homoerotic, Impotent

Three models of masculinity characterize Vietnam War cinema: Asexual Hyper-Masculine, Homoerotic, and Impotent. In all three the masculine identity is analyzed in reference to the Hunter vs. Captive paradigm, paternal/fraternal orders, sexuality, characterizations of women/the feminine, and the use of language.

In her book *Gender Trouble*, Judith Butler describes gender's "appearance of substance."[24] Although Butler's writing is conceptually ahistorical, I do not find it so in terms of its basic assumptions. Her deconstruction of social and academic discourse on gender and sex conceptualizes gender not only as an illusion of substance, but also as a void that is filled by repetitive actions in various spheres. Butler does not identify these actions, so she never addresses psychohistorical conditions as factors in the creation of the infinite number of actions that constitute gender, but her analysis does imply their relevance. In my opinion, post-traumatic actions, being mostly unrelated to personal or social control and not constituted by the regulation of cultural-social mechanisms of the kind Butler describes, but occur as unconscious eruptions, are extremely relevant. The discontinuity, the randomness, the repetitiveness, and the arbitrariness that according to Butler characterize gender-generating actions, are uniquely intensified when post-traumatic actions are concerned. Butler argues that gender transformations too are related to this arbitrariness, to the failure to repeat these actions (and parodic repetition). Since gender identity is generated through compulsive socio-political performances (142-149), an examination of these actions (reactions during and after the battle) and transformations (from Hunter to Captive) as compared with compulsive performances (victorious imperialism, induction rituals, camaraderie, intergenerational affiliation, and heterosexuality) in this psychohistorical context, could illuminate the models under discussion.

The models differ in how they represent the dimensions of masculinity (violence, sexuality, and the conflict between them) in Vietnam War films. Violence in this context means murderous conduct towards the other, whether against a soldier or a civilian the film defines as the

---

24 "Significantly, if gender is instituted through acts which are internally discontinuous, then the *appearance of substance* is precisely that, a constructed identity, a performative accomplishment which the mundane social audience, including the actors themselves, come to believe and to perform in the mode of belief. Gender is also a norm that can never be fully internalized; 'the internal' is a surface signification, and gender norms are finally phantasmatic, impossible to embody" (*Gender Trouble* 14, Emphasis in the original).

enemy. Sexuality defines the power of the subject in the context of violence in its broad sense: it is not necessarily related to the other/enemy, but to significant others in terms of masculinity: brothers in arm and women.

How does the textual subversion manifest itself in these two dimensions? As noted, violence does not "win," and if the subject is victorious, it is only a temporary victory. Even in *Hamburger Hill*, the only distinctly combat film among these canonic films, and the only war movie to represent victory, the conquest of the hill comes only after a horrific scene of captivity.[25] Another tragic state of captivity is created when American helicopters mistakenly attack the American soldiers. In films where combat is only a part of the plot, the temporary victory is not even defined as such (for instance, the battle at the Cambodian border in *Platoon* or the escape from captivity in *The Deer Hunter*). The subversive uniqueness of post-traumatic films lies in the link they create between defeat and the negation of sexuality. The subject's sexual powerlessness, which the film regularly refers to in the context of the failure of victorious violence, undermines any possibility for the subject to attribute masculine power or phallic representability to himself. Even when sexuality is displaced into cathartic violence, as in *Rambo: First Blood Part II*, for instance, the dominant feature is the masquerade of the male character.[26]

The distinction made in research between war films based on their chronological appearance is relevant to examination of textual elements that deviate from the dominant pattern, which are then seen as the product of that specific period.[27] Palmer identifies three phases in cinematic representation of the Vietnam War, based on a chronology according to ideological issues raised during these phases and stylistic strategy: the Epic phase (1978-1979); the Comic Book phase (mid-1980s); and

---

25 "Soldiers coined the derisive term 'Hamburger Hill' for the site of bloody fighting along the A Shau Valley near the Laotian border. In a ten-day battle in May 1969, the 101st Airborne Division successfully overtook a well fortified North Vietnamese Army (NVA) position on Ap Bia Mountain. [...] The battle culminated in brutal bunker-to-bunker fighting. Fifty-six U.S. soldiers were killed, 420 were wounded; NVA loses were estimated at 505. The U.S. Forces abandoned the hill soon after the fighting, and the North Vietnamese retook the position a month later [...] The negative reaction by the U.S. public to the seemingly senseless bloodletting increased pressure on President Nixon and the U.S. military to reduce U.S. combat casualties" (Kutler 218).

26 See a detailed analysis of this argument in Chapter 7.

27 This may explain the rescue of the symbolic fathers and brothers in the postmodern context of the early 1990s (*Forrest Gump* and *The War* in particular). See Pfeil on the closed world of Vietnam War cinema in *Forrest Gump* (251-261).

the Symbolic Nihilist phase (mid-1980s on) (261).[28] It seems to me that his classification is based on two issues: historical authenticity (distortions, omissions) and the films' attitude towards the war (pro or anti), and consequently is limiting and misses the point.[29] The realistic depiction of events that are historically groundless, for instance, in *The Deer Hunter*, which falls into Palmer's Epic phase (the Vietcong did not play Russian roulette with their captives), is not so different from that in *Rambo: First Blood Part II*, which belongs to the Comic Book phase (no Special Forces entered Vietnam in 1985 to rescue POW/MIA). Such classification precludes tracing this compatibility between the two films in terms of the fantasy worlds they depict. Moreover, it fails to draw our attention to the connection between the similarity of fantasy in the two films and the model of masculinity. The Asexual Hyper-Masculine Model fits both films. The repetitive patterns of violence/sexuality in *The Deer Hunter* and *Rambo: First Blood Part II* prove the dominance of the post-traumatic reaction as the main factor in structuring masculinity through the decades.

The attitudes concealed in these films – best exposed through gender-sexual analysis – repeat themselves in a subversive manner that is independent of chronological appearance. They are valid in films from the 1970s and remain so in films through the 2000s, and during what I termed the "Vietnam Syndrome" stage.[30] The following descriptions of masculinity models are not based on the chronological evolution of Vietnam War representation and/or the varying political moods; rather, they are descriptions of the deep-seated subversive structure that coexists with the status quo but stands in opposition to it.

The following chapters will describe the three models of masculinity in post-traumatic Vietnam War films.

---

[28] To these phases we should add the postmodern, in the Baudriardian sense of the term (1990s films), and the Vietnam Syndrome phase in Gulf War and World War II films, which is characterized by a renewed denial of the past (from the late 1990s to early 2000s).

[29] This is the most prevalent methodological research question in Vietnam film studies. See for instance Tomasulo ("Politics") on *Apocalypse Now*.

[30] The scope of the present study precludes treatment of films I have described as belonging to the 2000s representation phase (The Vietnam Syndrome in Gulf War films) such as *Courage Under Fire* (Edward Zwick, 1996), *Three Kings* (David O. Russell, 1999), *Rules of Engagement* (William Friedkin, 2000), *Jarhead* (Sam Mendes, 2005), as well as the Vietnam Syndrome in World War II films such as *The Thin Red Line* (Terrence Malick 1998).

CHAPTER 7

The Asexual Hyper-Masculine Model

I. Description of the Model

The term asexual hyper-masculinity may superficially seem a contradiction in terms, but is actually appropriate for what the films affiliated with this model represent: a combination of intense murderous masculinity, pretence of sexual potency, and negation of sexuality. Post-traumatic masculine identity in these films is characterized mostly by its instability, with captivity the turning point in terms of constructing masculinity. To begin with, the model depicts murderous violence which intersects asymmetrically with sexuality: it is murderous-Hunting, but not sexual. The Hunter-Captive dialectic constructs masculinity as breaking away from captivity (real and/or metaphoric) through Native American skills and moral and patriotic values; however, during the period of captivity, when the subject is forced to channel his sexuality into (often cathartic) violence, sexuality is sabotaged. The result is a metaphoric return to captivity – by the end of the process the two are symmetrical: the Captive is completely powerless sexually.

On the narrative level, this process is expressed differently in the various films. In *Apocalypse Now*, for instance, violent events from the past (including six political assassinations by Special Forces), have forced Willard into a state of metaphoric captivity. Following a period of wavering between the two worlds he describes as "home" and "the jungle," he returns to Vietnam. This transition from Hunter to Captive and from sexuality to asexuality is presented in a voiceover during the first scenes in Saigon, which provides an ideological and psychological justification for returning. It exacerbates his symbolic post-traumatic sense of captivity and is the source of the patricide he commits against Kurtz.

This process also appears in *Gardens of Stone*, but unlike *Apocalypse Now*, the masculinity described in the narrative is not that of a Hunter in post-traumatic captivity. Here the protagonists define themselves as the nation's "toy soldiers" because of their posting at Arlington National Cemetery, so that the epitome of the masculine "mask," therefore, becomes the simulated combat that Hazard (James Caan) takes part in against orders, a desperate attempt to relive his heroism. In any case, following a brief heterosexual relationship, he returns to Vietnam. Despite the fact that *Apocalypse*, *Gardens of Stone*, *Heaven and Earth* and the rest of the films affiliated with this model present different narrative variations, the metaphoric return to captivity that occurs in all of them is evidence that masculinity is both hyper and asexual.

A close reading of *The Deer Hunter*, which I consider both the most post-traumatic of the films and the one that that best realizes the Asexual Hyper-Masculine Model, depicts victorious masculinity in the overt text as hyper-masculinity, and in the subtext exposes it as pretense, a mask.

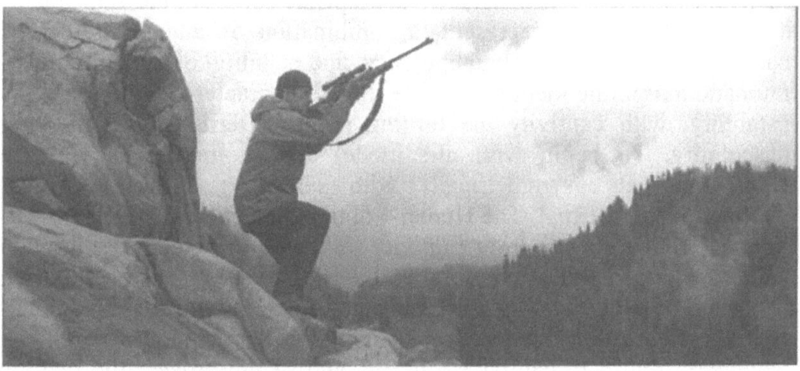

Asexual hyper-masculinity, Michael in *The Deer Hunter*

II. *The Deer Hunter*

The Deer Hunter (Michael Cimino, 1979).

A group of young Ukrainian-American friends from Pennsylvania who work in a steel mill are hanging out in a bar. Michael, Steven (John Savage), and Nick are leaving for Vietnam the day after Steven and Angela's (Rutanya Alda) wedding. During the deer hunt following the wedding, Michael kills a deer with one shot. In Vietnam, the three are captured by the Vietcong and are forced to play Russian roulette. Steven has a breakdown. Michael persuades Nick to kill their captors and they escape. Nick hides in a gambling house in Saigon. Unable to locate him, Michael returns to the US, where he tries to make amends through a relationship with Nick's girlfriend Linda (Meryl Streep) and a second deer hunt. He coerces Steven, whose feet were amputated, into leaving the Veterans Hospital and going back to his family. Then he returns to Vietnam to look for Nick, who forces him to play Russian roulette. When he begs Nick to come home, Nick repeats the phrase "one shot," and shoots himself. The film ends with Nick's funeral and the group singing "God Bless America" at the bar.

A. *Russian Roulette – Performance Conjures the Myth*

Michael's character resurrects the Puritan myth of the rescue of the Captive by the Hunter. It is fraught with ambivalence since Michael is both the Captive and the Hunter. His involuntary participation in Russian roulette during captivity and his escape consolidate both the myth of the hunt and the myth of captivity. Michael substitutes the "exorcism"[1] ritual of Russian roulette with initiation, and the character of the victim captive with that of the hunter-hero. From caged captive he becomes hunter,[2] and the totem figure of the deer, from which he got his nickname, leads to his being a mediator between the two myths.[3]

What is the meaning of such mediation? Racism and violence are inherent in the history of the American hero. In this film, he is like Slotkin's "man without a cross,"[4] who is transformed from deer hunter into Native American: After assimilating his heroic powers, by playing Russian roulette the hero symbolically scalps and annihilates the Native American. In essence, he exorcizes the demon after assimilating his natural heroic powers, and therefore becomes part of the myth of the White Man as Native American. According to Slotkin, this is the

---

1 The Puritans emphasized the character of the victim-captive, the wilderness as a chaotic and demonic environment, and the exorcism ritual. The quest of the Puritan hero involved an exorcism (and not a wedding, as in later narratives). According to the Puritan hunting myth, exorcism would lead the hunter to self-transcendence through an act of violence. Of course, this is not realized in Michael's case.

2 "Of beasts and men" (*Regeneration through Violence* 267).

3 In Slotkin's words: "Implicit in the myth is the rescue of the captive by the hunter, [who] […] becoming in the process a reflection or a double of his dark opponent […] in the hunter myth, the emigrant's sense of guilt for having broken the family circle by his departure is seen as the grounds for establishing a spiritual kinship with the Native Americans. But, this kinship is justified in that it makes the hunter more effective as the destroyer of the Native American, as the exorcist of the wilderness's darkness. He comes to know the Native American only in the act of destroying him" (563).

4 Both in terms of an interracial union and in the religious sense: "He is a purist in the related matters of morals and race. He will not mingle his blood with the Native Americans or with a woman whose character he sees as 'dark' or morally compromised. He wishes to remain a 'man without a cross'. To him this means in part a man without a crossing of Native American blood in his ancestry and with no desire to cross bloods in the future. It also implies his desire to preserve his pristine innocence: he is a man without a cross of sin to bear, a man exempted from the fall, a new Adam. Yet he is also, implicitly, a man beyond the pale of Christianity, a man without the Cross to guide him" (505).

American "cycle of the myth," because the destroyed demon is bound to rise again – it resides in the violent American psyche and erupts symptomatically. But in the film Russian roulette functions as a subversive element beyond reproducing the mythic scenario. This subversiveness is expressed in displacing the "one shot" all-American ethos from the Pennsylvania woods to the Vietnamese jungle, an unequivocal political statement. Yet in Russian roulette, a horrific realization of the American male ethos, the American hero is preempted from the possibility of representing history.

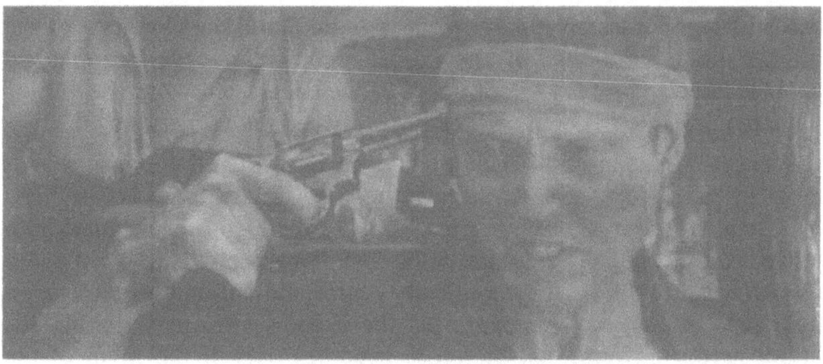

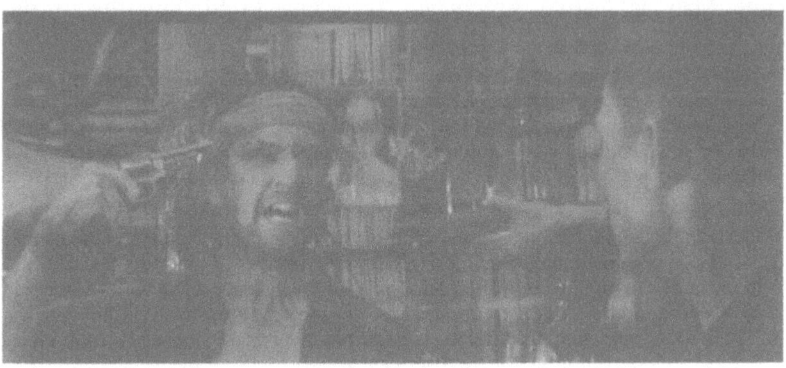

Horrific realization of the American male ethos, *The Deer Hunter*

The first game of roulette constitutes the subject through desubjectivization; that is, it constitutes the Corpse[5] as the "subject" of history (of historical trauma). This transition from subject to object, that is, to death, is as much at the center of the scene as is survival (Caruth's "double telling"). This state of limbo between subject and object (also, between reality and fantasy) is the result of the trauma, which prevents

[5] I use Corpse to denote that the corpse has taken on the status of subject.

any distinct identity. Through the horror of the limbo state, trauma questions the basis of such distinctions. According to Kristeva's canonic definition (*Powers of Horror: An Essay on Abjection*), the abject is a phantasmatic entity that is not only alien to the subject, but intimate with it – a bipolarity that causes the subject to panic. In this way the abject touches upon the fragility of the subject's boundaries between Inside and Outside, and the temporal transition from the "maternal body" to "paternal law." This roulette scene (which lasts for some fourteen minutes) reveals a gradual process of abjection among the protagonists. In both spatial and temporal terms, it is an abjected scene because it depicts the transition from the maternal body (anticipated death) to fraternal law (obeying orders from the negative father figure – the leader of the Vietcong).

This scene, which presents this process, is divided into three main stages, each comprising a game of roulette, imposing desubjectivization through sound and vision. In between the rounds are interim stages which highlight the physical elements of abjection.

At the beginning of the first stage, the camera reveals the prison camp in a long shot. On the right side of the frame is a straw hut where the game is taking place. The captives are being kept underneath the hut in half submerged cages and in another cage to the left of the hut. Only at the end of the first stage following four rounds of roulette, does the camera resume its movement. Between the first track and the second, the editing is based on quick cuts which alternate every 5-10 seconds between the objective point of view that reveals what is seen in the hut, and the reaction shots of the captives, who only hear the sounds of the gun hammer, the blast of the shots, and the shouts of the Vietcong leader and guards.

The tension between sound and image is not only dramatic tension caused by the fear of the unknown future, nor is it merely a pseudo-reflexive illustration of the realistic effect of popular cinema; rather, it is the tension between various elements of abjection that lead to the collapse of the subject. The sound range threatens the boundaries of identity and determines this stage as pre-object abjectness. Fear of the unknown is highlighted by the nature of the photography: the captives in their cages are only photographed in medium close-up or close-up, so that they are only seen from the waist up. This not only emphasizes the reaction shots of Steven, Nick, and Michael, but the close-up menacingly anticipates the process taking place over their heads; a latter-day reproduction in American history of the scalping ritual.

After the four rounds, with the cacophony of sound, the horror of the captives, and the glimpses they manage to catch as they look up, for the first time a corpse is seen falling. The first interim stage begins with a tilt-down that momentarily relieves the extreme suspense cutting, but its main function is to introduce the physical dimension of abjection in the context of an entire body. At this stage the elements of abjection are not only the breaching of the boundaries between subject and object, the blood and the Corpse, but the overall repulsive scene: the protagonists are immersed in water so that they are unidentifiable. Some are lying down, the water is full of blood, it's raining, bare feet stick out of the water detached from an invisible body, and rats are rushing about. The feelings of attraction-repulsion, fascination-disgust are intensified when the living-dead prisoners are tossed into the water, inside the cages.

According to Kristeva,

> The corpse [is] the most sickening of wastes [...] a border that has encroached upon everything. It is no longer 'I' who expels, 'I' is expelled. The border has become object [...] The corpse seen without God, and outside of science, is the utmost of abjection. It is death infecting life, abject. It is something rejected from which one does not part, from which one does not protect oneself as from an object. (*Powers of Horror: An Essay on Abjection* 3-4).

The Corpse as the "subject" of history (of historical trauma), universally associated with taboos and rituals to avoid contamination of the living, is deprived here of any symbolic order whatsoever. The living dead, neither object nor subject, are contaminated by the physical and sonic space symbolized by the Corpse. The intimacy of horror is not only between captives and captors, but mainly between the captives and the Corpse. Abjection, which generally establishes social order, is used here in reverse – as its destroyer.

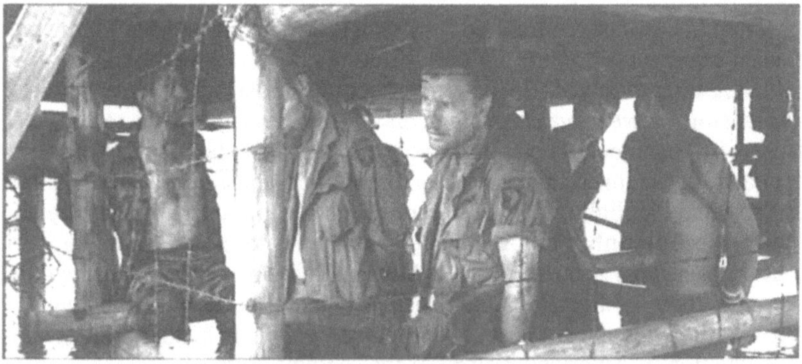

The tragic outcomes of conjuring the myth, Russian roulette in *The Deer Hunter*

In terms of screen time, this interim stage takes about ninety seconds. In terms of the sense of trauma, due to the multiplicity of suspense (with respect to the action, sound, relations between the "lower" and "upper" worlds, development of the drama, etc.), the time interval is indefinite, intensifying the traumatic time and its essential non-referentiality.

Most of the second stage still takes place on the aural level. The first round of roulette between Michael and Steven depicts Steven's breakdown, mainly against the backdrop of the polyphony (ecstatic roars, anxious utterances, crying, orders in untranslated Vietnamese, and soothing and encouraging English).

According to Kristeva,

> We may call it a border; abjection is above all ambiguity. Because, while releasing a hold, it does not radically cut off the subject from what threatens it – on the contrary, abjection acknowledges it to be in perpetual danger. But also because abjection itself is a composite of judgment and affect, of condemnation and yearning, of signs and drives. Abjection preserves what existed in the archaism of pre-objectal relationship, in the immemorial violence with which the body becomes separated from another body in order to be – maintaining that night in which the outline of the signified thing vanishes and where only the imponderable affect is carried out. (*Powers of Horror: An Essay on Abjection* 9-10).

The entire roulette scene, which opens with the above mentioned track, ends with the Vietcong guard spitting. His spitting actually signifies the beginning of abjection. Steven's cry when being thrown into the pit with rats, Michael and Nick's dive into the water of their cage, and Nick's spitting when he surfaces – all signify the interim stage, again, as a physical phase in the desubjectivization. It highlights the distance between the "inside" and "outside" of the body, the Lacanian rim.

The roulette achieves full realization on the dramatic, visual, audial and spatial levels in the forced confrontation between Michael and Nick. In terms of the process of abjection, the polyphony of sounds, three rounds of shots, mental disintegration (laughter/crying), and mimicry as quasi-language all attest to the culmination of the process that up to now has been conveyed only metonymically or partially. Cutting to Steven in the pit preserves the physical aspect (water, blood, rats) in the spectator's mind "within" the scene. Ho Chi Minh's photograph, cans of American beer, valuables and money on the table, are the only signifiers of a symbolic order beyond abjection. À la Hal Foster the scene depicts "[...] on the one hand an ecstasy in the imagined breakdown of the image screen and/or the symbolic order; on the other hand a horror at this breakdown followed by a despair about it" ("Obscene" 121).[6] The ecstasy resulting from the imagined breakdown of the image screen and the symbolic order, along with the horror and despair that accompany this breakdown, characterize the Russian roulette. Juxtaposed with this overwhelming process of abjection and the Corpse, a reversal takes place when Michael once again becomes Hunter.

Up to this point, the game has been conducted according to untranslated, symbolic ritualistic rules that derive their meaning from mimicry and repetitiveness. Accompanying these ritualistic rules by way of anticipation was the gaze of the Vietcong leader (multiplied by the gaze of those around him as a sort of extension), which functions as a violent force in the scene. The subject is trapped by that gaze, which anticipates death (and not merely symbolized castration). By murdering the Vietcong leader, Michael turns the one gazing into the object of the gaze. Because of his role as Hunter who rescues the prisoners from the roulette and from their abjective surroundings, Michael's physical performances signify the possibility of a reversal in representation.

Does the Hunter masculinity replace the Corpse as the subject that represents history (historical trauma)? Does Michael create a meaning that stands in opposition to the moment of forced suicide, the moment in which all "meaning collapses"?[7]

The tension between the Hunter and the Corpse structures masculinity as unstable, yet the trauma makes that tension irreversible. Michael's masculinity (as well as that of Steven and Nick) is horrifically exhausted during the displaced performance of the "one shot" ethos, resulting in a return to captivity (metaphoric and/or real).

B. *From Otherness to Interactivity*

During the abjection process, the male body becomes a metaphor for the Corpse instead of standing for masculinity. The tension expressed in the male body between these two options is also related to the buddy construct. In the film, the interaction between self and other among the buddies is broken off, a part of the desubjectivization process. For Michael, the other is not Steven or Nick,[8] but the deer. Since the images of the hunt are displaced into images of Russian roulette, the question is, who is the other? The opponent in the roulette game? Or the Vietcong

6 The article deals with post-modern art, but its definitions are applicable to *The Deer Hunter* because of its discussion of trauma.

7 Foster, Hall argues that "[...] abjection is a condition in which subjecthood is troubled, 'where meaning collapses'" ("Obscene" 114).

8 Steven is not a hunter, and Nick dissociates himself from the "one shot" performance.

leader? Within the rules of the ritual, the leader is indeed the negotiable other, but this sense of otherness is altered when he is murdered. Roulette as fetishization of racial difference (Baudrillard, *Transparency of Evil* 129) then becomes a manifestation of the same. On a deeper level, there is a recuperation of the other into the self, which is potentially annihilating for both.

The only element left to signify otherness is language. Language (alternately Vietnamese and English) is the other of the subject, but because it is but one component of the cacophony, its importance in signifying racial difference and otherness diminishes. Mimicry, which dominates the final confrontation phase (when Michael acts out the rules of the three bullet game to the Vietcong leader), substitutes language but lacks otherness. According to Baudrillard,[9] mimicry is part of the "psychodrama of otherness":[10]

> We are no longer living the drama of otherness. We are living the psychodrama of otherness, just as we are living the [...] psychodrama of sexuality, the psychodrama of the body and the melodrama of all the above [...] All we do in psychodrama [...] is acrobatically simulate and dramatize the absence of the other. (125).

The psychodrama of otherness is linked to simulation of the trauma and associated with the interaction created by this simulation: Nick turns Russian roulette into an unconventional interactive game that precludes all possibility for mutual relationships between the subject and the other. The result of being forced to play the game in captivity is for Nick both indifference to his own subjectivity and interactivity in which the (desubjectivized) subject is not the other of anyone else. It is the disappearance of otherness that creates recurrent interactivity with an infinite simulation of the trauma. In this case, the buddy construct is unviable as a counter structure for trauma and its collapse is the continuation of the collapse of otherness as a dialectic structure. Masculinity that has no other inevitably becomes the signifier of that Corpse and, at best, is suspended at the margins of the symbolic order like a kind of living dead. Trauma thus generates a new kind of cultural history that makes both the self and the other non-dialectic.

---

9 Baudrillard analyzes postmodernism, but his description of the indifference of the subject to her/his own subjectivity is valid for trauma as well (*Transparency of Evil* 124-125).

10 According to Baudrillard, the psychodrama of eternal introjection and rejection of the other is linked to racism. Does the roulette trauma simultaneously create a cultural reality of the death of otherness and its psychodramatic revival, à la Baudrillard? The answer is given in the film through the transformations the roulette undergoes until its final phase in Saigon. For Nick in Saigon, there is no other.

C. Compulsive Repetition

As mentioned above, there had been little historical or representational imagery of Russian roulette before *The Deer Hunter*.[11] The film, however, abounds with repetitions of the roulette and every subsequent round of the game is a repetition of the first instance during captivity: Michael watching Nick play in Saigon, the bowling scene in Clairton, in the cabin during the second hunt, the Bingo game at the hospital,[12] and again in Saigon – the original trauma is repeated thirteen times!

The compulsive nature of the power of repetition has been central to the discussion of trauma ever since Freud's "Beyond the Pleasure Principle." The paradoxes of repetition may be described as outlined in the following table:

Control, integration		Dissociation, disintegration
Bound energy		Unbound energy[13]
Demand by the ego for the "constancy principle"		Increase in psychic excitation[14]
Release		Shattering
Cognition		Affect
Access to trauma	Or	Fixation of image, fixation of interpellation
Creation of scheme, intelligibility		Lack of scheme, deconstruction
Associated with an instinct for control		Associated with the death drive
Secondary		Primordial
An experience related to the present		An experience "belonging" to the past
Enables narrative memory		Creates flooding, anti-narrativization
Active position		Passive position

But do these options exist in the film? As the following analysis will prove, the post-captivity construction of Michael, Nick, and Steven's male subjectivity is the frame of reference for examining the meaning of the repetition, since they are the performers in an "epidemic of simulations" (Baudrillard, *Transparency of Evil* 4). The repetitions reflect the disintegration of male subjectivity. The split between the Hunter and the Captive is inherent, and Michael's active performance as a Hunter (escaping from captivity, rescuing his buddies, releasing Steven from

11 In this matter, I totally disagree with Chong. The visuality of Eddie Adams' famous photo *Saigon Execution* (1968) has unmistakable effect on John Woo's 1990 remake of *The Deer Hunter*, *Bullet in the Head*, contrary to previous interpretations.

12 Wood claims that the sound of the tray falling from the nurse's hands at the Veterans Hospital where Michael goes to meet Steven is reminiscent of the sound of the roulette blasts, both for Michael and the spectator.

13 Silverman (*Male Subjectivity at the Margins* 61).

14 Laplanche (118, 122).

the hospital, returning to Vietnam to save Nick) is repeatedly subordinated to the roulette or its substitutes so that it never offers new options for identity. It is a simulated activity which intensifies seeing the subject as an effect. The compulsive element reappears in every repetition of the original traumatic event, both as opposition to being forced to play the game and as its continuation.

Lack of awareness is inherent in the psychiatric diagnosis of post-traumatic stress disorder. Although PTSD does not involve denial, as in Steven's case, it also does not necessarily involve awareness, as in Michael's case.[15] The only awareness he gains is knowledge of the rules of the game. Consequently, Michael remains at the margins of the symbolic order (of Clairton) and does not undergo post-captivity resubjectivization.[16]

The repetitions in *The Deer Hunter*, especially those that partially or completely simulate the suicidal obsession of the roulette ("one shot"), are not associated with control. The abyss Silverman observes beneath the male ego (*Male Subjectivity at the Margins* 121) finds a visual correlation in the film: upon returning to Clairton, Michael goes out on a second hunt but refrains from shooting: he spares the deer and does not carry out the "one shot" performance. Instead, he is seen sitting alone at the top of a waterfall and shouting.

This primal scream is soon replaced by repetition compulsion at the cabin and its instinctual basis is most obvious during the confrontation with Stanley. Michael's outburst and the likelihood of him killing Stanley with one shot indicate that this "edge of the abyss" male control is undermined by a primordial repetition associated with the death drive. The nature of the repetition on this instinctual level subverts subjectivity. Since post-captivity subjectivity in the three protagonists is characterized both by increased psychic excitation and a process of shattering, we must conclude that the repetitions impose a state of inescapable captivity.

---

15 This point has been missed in essays about the film. Writers such as Hellman ("Vietnam") and Burke describe Michael's awareness during the incident at the cabin or his metamorphose as a hunter as part of his becoming aware of his own obsession for control. I find no such references in the film itself. On the contrary, Michael's post-traumatic reactions are distinctly uncontrollable.

16 According to Kaja Silverman, "[O]nce removed from the battlefront, the traumatized veteran no longer enjoys the support of his comrades-in-arms. All that stands between him and the abyss is the paternal imago, within which he can no longer recognize himself. For the society to which he returns [...] he represents a sorry travesty of "our fighting men and boys," a living proof of the incommensurability of penis and phallus. Because of the resulting crisis of faith, "reality" itself is at least temporarily jeopardized" (*Male Subjectivity at the Margins* 63).

The cabin scene once again clarifies that male brotherhood is a construct that has collapsed under the burden of trauma and its repetitions. Steven's liberation from the hospital sets him free as a belated echo of the rescue act in Vietnam. The attempt to free Nick, who is more trapped than the others in the repetition compulsion complex, indicates that in its transference to the traumatic reality of Vietnam, Kracauer's "ideological fatigue" becomes death.

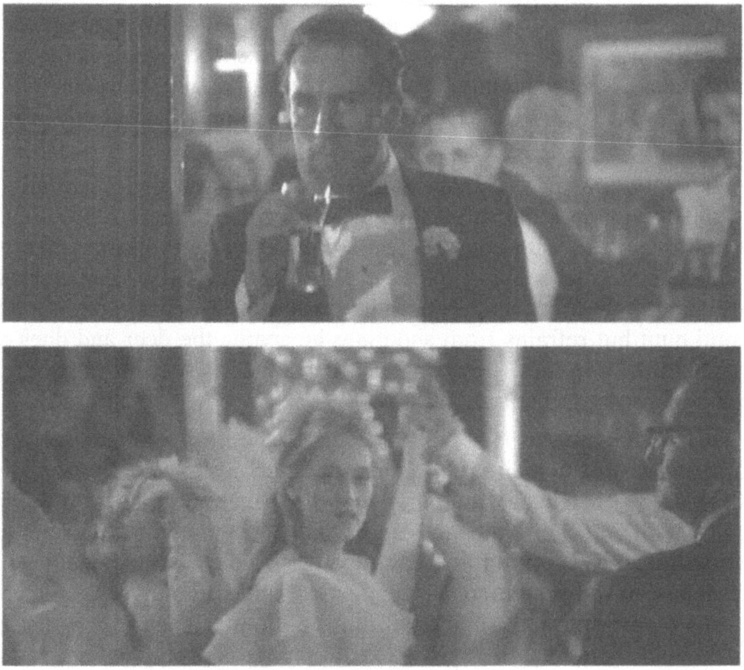

Gazing at the wedding scene, *The Deer Hunter*

D. *Loss of the Sexual Gaze*

How does the paradigm outlined here depict the Hunter's sexuality, and what transformation does this sexuality undergo from the film's mythogenic level to its psychodramatic superstructure?[17] From the subject position of Hunter to that of Captive and then to the horrific Hunter-Captive subject position?

17 The film's basic assumptions are phallocentric. The opening scene emphasizes the patriarchal institutions: the steel mills, drinking at the bar, Ukrainian traditions, the hunt, the church that consecrates marriage, etc. – all reaffirm the penis phallus commensurability at the heart of the world being depicted.

The three future soldiers are depicted at the outset of the narrative as alienated from their own bodies. Steven is uniquely positioned as he leaves for the traditional wedding night (although he is not the father of the child Angela is carrying). The two hunters – Michael and Nick – are characterized by varying levels of alienation from their bodies, which in Vietnam will evolve into a state of an "antibody to himself" (à la Baudrillard). Nick is characterized as accepting the convention of the wedding ceremony more than the "one shot" ethos of the hunt. Michael, in contrast, is described from the onset as being sexually alienated from his body (he does not join in the wedding festivities; Stanley calls him "faggot"). Alienation from the male body is a subversive element in the film, since it is unlike conventional representations of the male body in cinema – it creates a split between the body as performing in the soldierly sense and in the sexual sense. This last characteristic is linked to the Hunter on the mythogenic level of the film, on one hand, and to the self-negation that is the result of trauma, on the other. As Slotkin puts it,

> As a racial purist, Hawkeye is not given to the idea of marrying "a redskin." On the other hand, his way of life and his moral values make even white women unsuitable as mates; their natures are either too high for his manner of life or too low [...] for his respect [...] The code of the wilderness is also problematic. The hunter's violence, markedly sexual in its symbolic character, brings him into communion with the goddess of this world, the wilderness. Yet the violence itself and the consequent initiation into another identity violate the norms of European culture and of Christian morality and moralized sexuality. To accept wholeheartedly the wilderness marriage and Eucharist is to lose one's white soul; to hold back is to fail in America as an American. Leatherstocking's rationalizations save his purity but unsex him, render him permanently celibate. (*Regeneration through Violence* 505).[18]

The violent racist element of the hunter, according to Slotkin, precludes sexuality and family. The characterization of the hunter in *The Deer Hunter* is even more extreme than Slotkin's. Clearly, in this paradigm Michael, a "mere" hunter, is depicted as weighing the erotic

[18] Fenimore Cooper's hero (Leatherstocking in the novel cycle and Hawkeye as his later transformation in *The Deerslayer*) is a mixture of Puritan and Native American. According to Slotkin, this figure is based on Daniel Boone, who developed the "salvation through suffering" captivity narrative characteristic of the Puritan era (symbolized by the rescue of a white woman from Native American captivity by the hunter for the scenario of the victory of civilization over savagery). But even in his most extreme development, Fenimore Cooper's hero does not act as a mediator or interpreter between races and cultures, nor is he the most effective warrior, since he is Native American in his methods, but a "Native American-hater," who has been turned into an avenging savage as a result of suffering he underwent in captivity or when fighting Native Americans. He is now intent on "exterminating the brutes" at any cost (*Gunfighter* 16).

possibilities of a relationship with Linda during Steven and Angela's wedding. When Russian roulette creates the terrible encounter between Hunter and Captive within himself, the already subverted distinctions collapse.

The wedding scene is dominated by the gaze of men directed at women; the original roulette scene is dominated by the gaze of men directed at other men, the Vietcong's at the captives participating in the game and the captives at each other. The pattern of the male gaze with erotic overtones at the wedding ceremony, objectifying women, is thus replaced by a different pattern of the male gaze with violent overtones, leading to the most extreme objectification of the players: their death. The culmination of the process comes, of course, during the last confrontation with Nick in Saigon. In other words, trauma changes the nature of the gaze until it exists only in the murderous context. The sexual gaze is lost: post-traumatic masculinity lacks the power of the gaze and of sexuality.

Michael's sexuality as mentioned, changes with the split created by trauma, but upon returning from Vietnam he sleeps with Linda. Does that signify the breaking of the paradigm? I don't think so. The desubjectivization process in captivity does not destroy Michael's phallic sexuality, since it is not presented as such in the first place. The captivity trauma only ruins the possibility of potential sexuality that the hunter had in the pre-captivity phase; to be specific, before he realized the horror of being a Hunter-Captive. During the wedding, the film underlines the eroticism of Michael's attitude towards Linda and Nick. In a sense, as Nick's girlfriend, Linda is displaced as an object of desire. While during the first hunt Michael shoots a deer and Nick has a woman, in the second hunt, Michael does not shoot and the woman is a substitute for the deer.[19]

Male subjectivity is not only void à la Silverman, but is a very intense masquerade. Michael's momentary attempt to extract himself from his ruined sexuality through sleeping with Linda is doomed to fail. The gaze at Linda will be replaced by the gaze at Nick playing Russian roulette, and will become gazeless at the wake scene. In this respect, the

---

19 It should be noted that Michael goes to a motel with Linda and falls asleep with the disappointed Linda lying next to him. The camera shows Clairton Lake for the third time through an omniscient point of view, thereby stressing the presence of abjection, of the cages in Vietnam. Only after the second hunt and the roulette scene in the cabin (which cancels any possibility that post-war brotherhood could support his shattering masculinity), does Michael finally have sex with Linda. She alternately replaces Nick (as mentioned above, in the Puritan narrative the captive is always a woman), and the deer. Not surprisingly, a stuffed deer head is hanging on the wall during the scene.

pattern of gazing at the female body replaced by gazing at the Corpse determines masculinity as asexual. The failure to bring Nick back home finally makes the Hunter, forced to play Russian roulette against Nick, a Captive, and unwillingly complicit in fratricide.

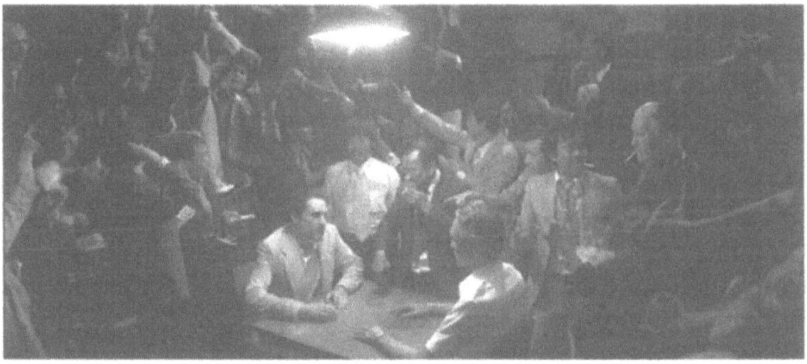

Inadvertent Fratricide, *The Deer Hunter*

E. *Exposing Mask-ulinity*

The inability to connect eroticism and sexuality, the confrontation with lack as a confrontation with death, the collapse of fraternity as defining a facet of masculinity, the fracturing of otherness and othering processes, the powerless gaze and the covered body[20] – all clearly suggest that the masculine model invoked by *The Deer Hunter* is that of asexual hyper-masculinity. Hyper-masculinity is pseudo-empowerment dominated by the violence at the heart of subjectivity, the latter making masculinity asexual, a fraud. The non-subject is determined by trauma through endless repetitions.

The main reason for *The Deer Hunter*'s uniqueness as a post-traumatic film distinctly affiliated with this model is the representation of the trauma of war and defeat through the experience of captivity and the roulette image. The roulette stands for the horror, the abjection, the repetition compulsion, the split of subjectivity and the male body, the unwilling fratricide, the collapse of otherness and of the symbolic order. Negating the sexual gaze, the Russian roulette image transforms the Corpse into the subject of the history of defeat.

[20] See the scene where Michael runs naked through the streets of Clairton the night of the wedding until Nick finds him and covers him up as an expression of blocking potential sexual tensions.

III. Defeated Masculinity and the Negation of History

This broad demasculinization has far-reaching ideological and historical implications. The events in *The Deer Hunter* have no historical referent, and the same is true of all other films affiliated with the Asexual Hyper-Masculine Model. Such a negation of history exists as one of two modes of representation: phantasmatic or distanced. In the first case, defeated masculinity is capable of representing only a history of fantasy – not the realization of its omnipotence (à la Jeffords), but pseudo-compensation for its impotence. Hence, *The Green Berets*, *Rambo* and Chuck Norris films, and *Forrest Gump* all present a fantasy of victory. In the second case, the films distance actual historical events, making them either a part of the protagonist's past or that of the Vietnamese other. For example, Willard's and Kurtz's military experience in *Apocalypse*, Hazard's (James Caan) and Jody's (James Earl Jones) in *Gardens of Stone*, Lawrence Dell's (Burt Lancaster) in *Twilight's Last Gleaming* (Robert Aldrich, 1977) or the story of Le Ly Hayslip (Hiep Thi Le) which dominates *Heaven and Earth*.

Such distancing does not undermine the masculine mask. The characterization of the protagonist calls for a historical structuring that would provide a space for legitimizing hyper-masculinity. Indeed, the victory fantasy (in the first case) and the glorious combat record (in the second) serve this need. The historical aspect thus becomes a part of the mask. In other words, violent defeated masculinity that negates its own sexuality produces history that by its very existence negates its existence.

The negation of history is not just a manifestation of ideological attitudes towards history as depicted in post-traumatic Vietnam War films, but is primarily the result of the confrontation between this ideological subordination and the films' faithfulness to representation of the trauma. The result – distortions, acontextuality, the pre-1968 time slot, avoidance of presenting issues regarding responsibility for the war, the lack of representation of the Vietnamese other than iconographically, disregard of the number of Vietnamese casualties and the physical damages incurred by the country – all stem from this confrontation and are replete with tension associated with it.

As discussed in the Introduction, in terms of the perception of time, it is impossible to simultaneously represent trauma and history using the same image. The image of trauma, in its post-traumatic sense, is the reenactment of an event that "never happened." Hence, by definition, that image cannot be a historical image, since the power of a historical image stems directly from the fact that it "did happen."

The nature of the cinematic post-traumatic image is thus multifaceted. First, the belated nature of trauma undermines historical representation because of the films' inability to cater to two separate foci in terms of representing time. Obviously, films do not create a split between personal history (of a certain soldier during and after war) and collective history (of the nation at war and afterwards). The cinematic historical narrative is depicted (and perceived) as a representative narrative (even if the personal story has no allegoric dimension, it has a representative value as the story of the nation). That is, the personal history and the collective history are inseparable. To this, the complexity of the relationship between the traumatic and the historical should be added. Despite the temporal gap (essential for the representation of trauma through the cinematic image) between the traumatic and the historical dimensions, invoking traumatic components of the war, a historical event (captivity, torture, fratricide, injury, disability) transforms the traumatic into the historical for the spectator (and the scholar as well, as indicated by the prevalence of neo-Marxist analyzes that discuss history as ideology). This is not merely the familiar identification of the personal with the national. The post-traumatic cinematic image based on the paradox of the two foci derives its power from its reference to history although, as stated above, there is irresolvable tension between traumatic and historical representation of events. (The roulette image, for instance, derives its historical power from the historical events presented in the film [the evacuation of the American embassy and Saigon in flames] although it is not defined temporally in relation to these events. Another historical point of reference relates to personal history. When Michael returns to Clairton he meets Angela and Steven's two-year-old son, which defines the general time span of their tour of duty at about three years, since Angela was in early pregnancy when they were drafted. These events, grounded in historical time, apply the broader historical context to the trauma [the roulette], while because of their precise temporal nature they highlight the absence of time and place in the representation of that trauma.) The result is that having drawn much of its power from the historical context, these films construct the post-traumatic image through emphasizing the symptomatic-psychological elements over the referential historical ones.

The post-traumatic image is not an ideological substitute for historical representation; therefore, it should not be viewed as replacing, transforming, or displacing the historical image of an event. It produces an inevitable symptomatic dominance, whose value derives precisely from its areferentiality. That is, the post-traumatic image is inherently ahistorical and areferential. Fantasy and the distancing of history are vital strategies in constructing post-trauma; therefore, they are prerequisite to the construction of post-traumatic masculinity. Defeated masculinity pretending to be hyper-masculine involves this negation of history. As already demonstrated at length, *The Deer Hunter* presents the Corpse as the subject of the history of defeat. As one of the paradigmatic films in the post-traumatic cinematic representation of the Vietnam War, it redefines the tense relationship between the historical and the traumatic aspects within the image of defeated masculinity.

IV. Rescue vs. Asexuality: Rambo, Braddock, Forrest

In films that depict history as fantasy (*Rambo: First Blood Part II,*[21] *Missing in Action, Missing in Action: The Beginning, The War,* and *Forrest Gump*), masculinity is constructed as victorious. The victory of the Hunter is only limited in the historical sense (the number of POWs or wounded soldiers rescued by the hero) and fixates masculinity on a compulsive repetition of the trauma of captivity, whether real or metaphoric. Yet, unlike the rest of the films affiliated with this model, which present a real and/or symbolic fratricide or patricide, these films present a real and/or symbolic rescue of the father/brother figure. Through this act, they restore the morality of soldiers in Vietnam.

Hyper-masculinity is realized both in the performance of rescue with its mythic overtones and through the shaping of the masculine body. Yet despite victory and rescue, the Name of the Father is not reinvoked; (as mentioned, negative father figures are not punished, and the only positive father figure presented is weak); the heroes remain outside the social order as a sort of reproduction of Ethan Edwards' mythic position;[22] there is no continuity of the fraternal order (the hero operates as a lone wolf); and the sexual encounter does not construct rescuing masculinity as phallic.

A number of studies that discuss the hero, particularly with regard to *Rambo* films, have focused on the Native American as the "noble savage," the "symbol of 1960s counter culture" (Studlar and Desser; Hellman, "Rambo's Vietnam"), the spectacle, the technologization and

---

21 *Rambo: First Blood* was the basis for the series, and thus primarily involves symbolic concepts associated with the veteran, the father figures, and initial construction of the *Rambo* iconography. The sequel develops the Captive-Hunter dialectic through a concrete and not merely symbolical return to Vietnam.

22 Ethan Edwards (played by John Wayne) is the hero of *The Searchers*, John Ford's 1956 Western, who, after years of searching for his niece, who had been kidnapped by Native Americans, finds that she has become the wife of the chief, and returns her to her family against her will. In the famous closing scene, this heroic and ambivalent rescue quest leaves Edwards outside the family home with the door closing behind him.

fetishization of the male body (Jeffords, *Remasculinization of America*; Williams; Savran), the "idealistic avenger" (Clark 203), "exhibitionistic patriotism" (Waller 125), and the male body as a realization of the national body (Jeffords *Hard Bodies*; Burgoyne, "National Identity"; Savran). None of these studies have discussed the issue of sexuality. Even for Forrest Gump, who rescues both his buddies and the father figure by running (his only expression of extraordinary physicality in battle), the relationship between this hyper-masculine performance and rescue and the negation of sexuality remains intact. Hyper-masculinity, which rekindles America's lost values, finds no phallic parallel. The collapsed patriarchal order that cannot be represented (or at best, represented only by Forrest lacking any historical dimension, or constituted by the death of the hero as a legacy to his son in *The War*), leaves the New American Hero (or his postmodern clones) asexual. Is this "the magical reconstruction of masculinity?"[23]

The explicit text describes the violent realization of masculinity and of undisputed and unquestionable sexuality, but in the subtext, gender is conspicuously unstable. It is precisely this incongruity between the rescue (as limited as it may be) and phallic failure (despite the extraordinary prowess of the masculine body) that emphasizes the mask; that is, it intensifies the films' level of subversion in regard to the pretense of omnipotent masculinity.

The four male characters discussed here all get involved in relationships with female characters. For example, *Rambo: First Blood Part II* structures Rambo's masculinity as phallic through the use of several strategies: a romantic mini-narrative, a tragic end to the romance, displacement of fetishization from his body to hers, and the revenge motif. When Co Bao (Julia Nickson-Soul) falls in love with Rambo she removes any doubts about his distorted exaggerated masculinity.[24] Exposing heterosexual potential shifts the fetishization of the male body to the body of the Vietnamese woman, which is intensified by her dressing as a prostitute. As a postmodern reference to the cooperation between Col. Kirby (John Wayne) and the Vietnamese woman Lin (Irene Tsu) in *The Green Berets*, here too, the woman is characterized as a soldier whore in a sexist hierarchical gender characterization that legitimizes masculinity under battle conditions. Co Bao's presence reveals "sensitivity behind the monster's physique," permitting the spectator to identify with the Frankenstein-like hero of the film. Her death serves to highlight the hero's single-minded determination to complete his mission and unwill-

---

[23] See Pfeil 251-260.

[24] Which raises the question if this could be a homosexual masquerade; see Holmlund.

ingness to succumb to romance in keeping with the paradigm of the Western hero. The racial text (Co Bao is rehabilitated when she asks Rambo to take her to America, after which she dies in his arms) is implied in the mini-narrative. The tragic end to the romance is also utilized to turn Rambo into an avenger. This is the dramatic stage in which Rambo becomes omnipotent (using arrows, knives, and his hands). His transformation into a veritable mud-covered monster during the climax of the battle does not undermine the boundaries of the body; on the contrary, his becomes the epitome of the ecological body. The woman soldier dies, but Rambo's masculinity in that battle becomes indestructible. Violence is compensation for the ruined prospect of realizing sexuality.

In this construction of ideal Hunter physicality, the absence of sexuality, despite being sublimated, is the subversive element that undermines its idealization. The absence of sexuality appears in the film as a textual gap. Its ideological functions, as I have described, actually contribute to making masculinity unstable. In the Chuck Norris films, Col. Braddock also avoids any contact with women (in *Missing in Action* he pretends to be Anne's [Lenore Kasdorf] lover, only to sneak out of her balcony to carry out his mission. After completing the mission, he returns to her bed only to provide himself an alibi for the Vietnamese [his former torturers in the prison camp]). This recurring asexuality leads to the conclusion that transformation into a Native American Hunter (whether in the Ramboistic or Chuck Norris martial arts versions) is, in Lacanian terms, a type of masquerade because of the lack of phallus and the desire for it. Aren't Forrest's various disguises but masks used by the body against the phallic lack? Forrest only sleeps with Jenny (Robin Wright) once, and is presented as an asexual idiot while the film is replete with his numerous masks, which suggest, in contrast, an extraordinary physicality (ping pong, running, shrimping). Unlike non post-traumatic cinematic representations, which often attribute the female-like masquerade to males, men in post-traumatic films do not posses the phallus.

> For women to "be" the Phallus means [...] to reflect the power of the Phallus, to signify that power, to "embody" the Phallus, to supply the site to which it penetrates, and to signify the Phallus through "being" its other, its absence, its lack, the dialectical confirmation of its identity [....] On the other hand, men are said to "have" the Phallus, yet never to "be" it, in the sense that the penis is not equivalent to that Law and can never fully symbolize that Law. Hence, there is a necessary [...] impossibility [...] to occupy[ing] the position of "having" the Phallus, with the consequence that both positions of "having" and "being" are [...] comedic failures that are

nevertheless compelled to articulate and enact these repeated impossibilities. (Butler, *Gender Trouble* 44-46).

Despite the attempt to break free of the trauma of defeat through rescue acts rooted in the preservation of paternal-fraternal relationships (such as Rambo and Trautman, Forrest and Benjamin-Bubba [Mykelti Williamson], Braddock and Jack Tucker [M. Emmet Walsh]), the rewriting of historical trauma is not sexual, and does not contain affiliation with or possession of the phallus. Rambo's Native Americanicity, Braddock's mastery of martial arts, and Forrest's running skills are but performances of split subjectivity that do not lead masculinity into physical integrity, into being a subject. And in fact, as I have suggested above, this is not a rewriting of historical trauma, but a reenactment of trauma. Devoid of patriarchal order and phallus, with father/brother figures in need of rescue, history functions as either a fantasy or a distancing representation, and more than anything else, indicates the collapse of masculinity.

Among the films under discussion, *The War* most explicitly reveals the impact of trauma on veterans. Consequently, in keeping with the parameters I outlined previously, there are few historical traces in the film. In addition, despite the fact that Steven rescues his symbolic brother in the mine, he is still deprived of sexuality. The film never alludes to any physical relationship between Steven and his wife, but focuses on the trauma of deserting a comrade and atonement for survival by sacrificing his life. The fraternal connection broken in war due to traumatic circumstances is symbolically reinstated, with its significance augmented by the message from father to son. But as this summary suggests, even when the hero is part of a family unit, the trauma leaves his masculinity merely symbolic. The act of self-sacrifice holds no redemptive value – not in terms of the past, his sexuality, or even his fatherhood, which remains only a legacy. The new masculine order is not depicted in this film.

V. Murderer vs. the Other: *Taxi Driver*

Taxi Driver (Martin Scorsese, 1976).

Travis Bickle (Robert De Niro), a former Marine who served in Vietnam, drives a taxi in New York, usually at night. He meets Betsy (Cybill Shepherd), who works for Palantine's presidential election campaign. Travis asks her out and is angered by her reaction to his taking her to a pornographic movie. When she breaks up with him, Travis's loneliness and isolation mount. He buys weapons and begins training, but his plan to assassinate Palantine is thwarted. Travis also meets Iris (Jodie

Foster), a thirteen-year-old prostitute who calls herself Easy. He decides to save her and murders her pimp Sport (Harvey Keitel), the guard, and the client in Iris's room. The newspaper clippings in Travis's room tell the rest of the story: Iris went back to her parents, who thanked Travis in a letter, and the media made him a crime-fighting hero. Travis is back to driving the taxi, and gives the admiring Betsy a free ride.

Taxi Driver was made before the first wave of Vietnam War films (*Apocalypse Now*; *Coming Home*), as part of the indirect cinematic articulations of the war through the horror film genre.[25] The film is not post-traumatic in the sense of films that directly evoke the Vietnam War trauma, but is relevant because its characterization of the Vietnam veteran reflects on later films affiliated with the Asexual Hyper-Masculine Model.[26] An analysis of the Hunter-Captive dialectic will shed light on the difference between it and purely post-traumatic films.

As Kolker argued, "Travis Bickle is the legitimate child of John Wayne and Norman Bates: pure, self-righteous, violent ego and grinning, homicidal lunatic; each the obverse of the other; each equally dangerous" (*A Cinema* 194). *Taxi Driver* creates a link between John Ford's 1956 Western *The Searchers* and Alfred Hitchcock's 1961 horror film *Psycho*, between the Western hero and the psychopath, a result of a culture founded on "regeneration through violence." To follow Kolker, who primarily emphasizes the violent elements common to these two apparently opposed archetypes, we must consider Travis Bickle not only the embodiment of the inevitable connection between the two in the violent sense, but also in the sexual sense; not only as a murderer, but as a sexual pervert, and examine the relationship between the two.

As a film that anticipated future representations of Vietnam veterans, *Taxi Driver* is radical in linking Travis's murderous hyper-masculinity with sexual perversion. While he himself declares that he wants to rescue Iris from prostitution and "clean the city" of filth, I see Travis's slaying of her pimp and his cohorts as a defense mechanism against her threat to his exclusively voyeuristic sexuality. She embodies the potential for his breaking out of his sexual repression, and therefore he must use extreme violence to rescue and consequently distance her. The violent act preserves the hero's distorted and unrealized sexuality; Iris's rescue is but Travis' mythical mask.

---

25 See Wood on the golden age of horror films in the 1970s (70-94).

26 On the rehabilitation of the veteran in Vietnam War films, see for instance Haines; and Clark. Bowen discusses how veterans received the films. He notes that since the end of the war, some 65,000 veterans have died of unnatural causes or committed suicide (235).

The closing scenes depict Travis alternating between Westerner and psychopath, but the media makes him a hero and only covers the John Wayne aspect of his character, completely ignoring his Norman Bates side. Disregard of Travis's psychopathy and the public sympathy he enjoys as Iris's savoir means his perverted sexuality, which he has repressed from the beginning, is also ignored by the media. Murder is not sublimated into sexuality and does not change Travis's attitude towards women, as his voyeuristic gaze at Betsy in the closing scene demonstrates. Travis's famous Native American haircut prior to the murders subverts the two binaries of White/Native American and Westerner/psychopath. The Native American could become the White and the Westerner could become the Psychopath only in a culture based on the massacre of Native Americans; and as Slotkin suggests, as a result of the internalization of the Native American demonic nature. Both Native American and White are cultural constructions derived from the same violent ethos.

In order for Travis to continue to treat women as objects of voyeurism, Iris must become the other that is not a prostitute, since prostitution makes her a mediator for his obsessive passive sexuality. Likewise, Travis treats Betsy in the only way he knows by attempting to include her in his voyeurism, first unsuccessfully by taking her to the porn film, and later, during their last meeting, as the object of his gaze. Returning Iris to her parents preserves Travis's perverted sexuality, since it perpetuates objectification as his only possible approach to women. Betsy's reappearance does more to reinforce the pattern of the veteran as a sexually perverted killer than to underline the irony of the media's interpretation of the events.[27] The media's preference for the Western hero over the psychopath is an ironic statement about Travis's sexuality, which is intensified by reference to the asexuality of Ethan Edwards (*The Searchers*). Travis's psychopathy is realized in the complex masculine model he represents: murderous violence that preserves sick voyeuristic sexuality masked as "pure" masculinity that rescues and redeems.

---

[27] As argued, for instance, by Kolker (*A Cinema of Loneliness*) and Wood.

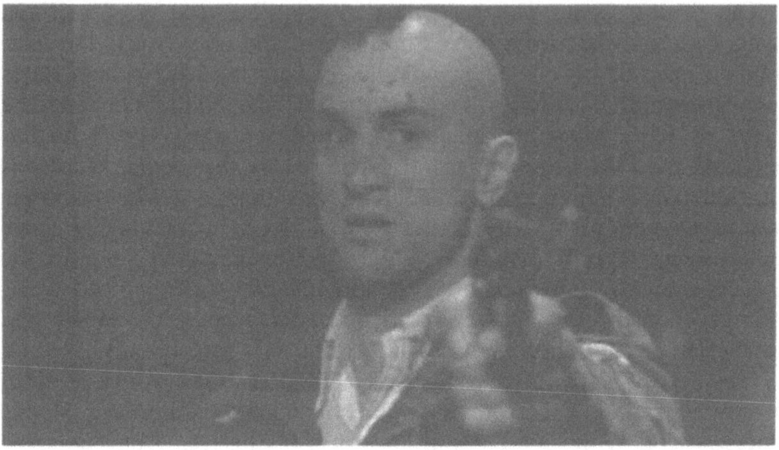

Saving voyeuristic asexuality by murder, Travis Bickle in *Taxi Driver*

According to Wood, "films [that] seem to crack open before our eyes" (50) are typical of American film texts from the 1970s. As he defines it, the "incoherent text" is based on experiences of contradiction, disillusion and despair, ambivalence towards the hero, and ambiguous closures. He contends that the impossibility of defining a coherent attitude towards the hero is a result of the turbulent times.

There is a crucial difference between the representation of asexual masculinity in purely post-traumatic films and those not purely post-traumatic. In *Taxi Driver*, the link between hyper-masculinity and voyeuristic asexuality is formed by the overt text, and not by the sub-text.[28] We can assume that Travis had experienced the trauma of realistic or metaphoric captivity because, like the hallmark of Special Units in Vietnam, he disguises himself as a Native American when he carries out his "mission"; and we can further assume that it undermined his sexuality. But this is a hypothesis that cannot be proven by what is seen in the film. Linda in *The Deer Hunter*, Co Bao in *Rambo: First Blood Part II*, and Le Ly in *Heaven and Earth* construct the sexual potential of masculinity, but as soon as they fulfill this role they are all dissociated from the hero (emotionally, symbolically, or physically). Moreover, in post-traumatic films, as already noted, the Hunter escapes from captivity

[28] Travis's relationship with Betsy is a voyeuristic process that begins with their first encounter, culminates in the killings and ends in their final encounter, which is entirely based on his fetishistic gaze at her. The film constructs the sexually perverted killer as the unambiguous product of a culture that was founded on violence and has produced various cultural "masks" (of which the sexual is the most prominent) in order to conceal it.

through violence, but captivity has sabotaged his sexuality. No woman supports Travis's sexuality in *Taxi Driver*, and, in contrast to the war trauma, the violence helps him defend his voyeuristic perverted sexuality. Therefore, while these films manifest asexual hyper-masculinity, the dialectic is totally different. In pure post-traumatic films violence is overt, Hunter becomes Captive; despite liberation, captivity negates sexuality and is one of the subversive elements in the text in terms of representing defeated masculinity; the film covers for its loss through various strategies (extraordinary physicality, fetishization, a romantic mini-narrative, rescue/salvation/revenge themes, mythical intertextuality). In not purely post-traumatic films, violence and sexuality are overt, and violence preserves sexuality. Because *Taxi Driver* does not attempt to conceal the defeat of masculinity, it has no latent subversiveness in terms of sexuality. It is not an incoherent text, but radically and openly constructs masculinity as inherently acoherent.

In *Heaven and Earth*, Steve (Tommy Lee Jones) saves the other, in the form of his Vietnamese wife, Le Ly Hayslip, by making the American dream come true for her: immigration and a new family unit. Here, as in *Taxi Driver*, the rescue is first of all an attempt at self-redemption. Despite this, Steve is still haunted by the trauma of his actions as an assassin, a metaphoric captivity that through recurrent nightmares defines his existence as one of inescapable violence. Unlike Travis, who is obsessed with protecting his own sexuality against a non-voyeuristic alternative that culminates in a serial killing, Steve is obsessed with preserving his uncontrollable violence that eventually culminates in his suicide. While Travis' physical vulnerability is never exposed, the camera exposes Steve's nudity as a symbol of that very vulnerability and defeat when he commits suicide in his car.

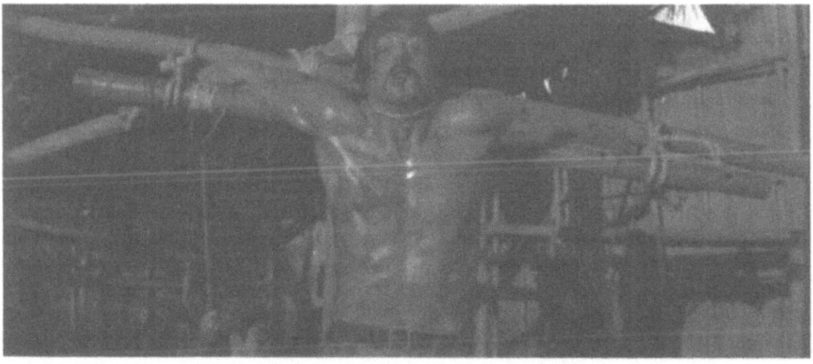

The tortured body, *Rambo First Blood Part II*

VI. The Tortured Body

Defeated masculinity does not manifest itself only in the transition from Hunter to Captive, from attempted victory to defeat, from wholeness to schizoidity, from representing the symbolic order to irrepresentability, from the father-son continuum to patricide, from fraternity to fratricide, but also in the transition from sexuality to asexuality.

Jeffords' "hard bodies" are not hard at all. She describes this image in films (particularly box office successes) made during the Reagan and H. W. Bush administrations and claimed that during Ronald Reagan's eight years in office the image of presidential machoism as the "hard body has remained a theme that epitomizes the national imaginary that made the Reagan Revolution possible" (192). This argument ignores the trauma of the 1970s in both historical-cultural and cinematic terms. It could be argued that the Reagan Revolution, symbolized by the hard body of Reagan-Rambo (and the "sensitive family man"),[29] is clearly a collective ideological reaction that preserves the repression of trauma, just as Jeffords's own research does. While she admits that not all films made in the 1980s are consistent with the model of cooperation between popular culture (Hollywood) and the Presidency (13), she argues that the most popular films[30] are part of that cooperation, and thus validate the model.[31] What is the meaning of popularity in this context? If it only means direct translation of prevailing sentiments in the collective unconscious, and never the sentiments that are repressed and that break the surface in the ways I have described, in blockbusters as well, then the cultural schizophrenia between the hard body and the "tortured body" must be deciphered. The hard body is not merely the opposite of the soft body. The former is, first and foremost, the opposite of the tortured body agonizing over the nightmares of the traumatic past and the hardships of post-war rehabilitation.

---

29 As opposed to the "soft body" model which she defines as characterizing Carter's Administration, women, and persons of color.

30 Not necessarily Vietnam War films. For instance, the *Star Wars*, *Indiana Jones*, and *Back to the Future* series (65).

31 Out of all Vietnam War films produced in the 1980s, Jeffords cites, without explanation, only *Hamburger Hill* as opposing the "hard body" model. As Palmer argues, between December 1986 and April 1988, that is, within sixteen months, at least six major Vietnam War films were released: *Platoon, Full Metal Jacket, Hamburger Hill, Off Limits, Gardens of Stone, Good Morning, Vietnam* (260-262). In my view, they all question the hard body concept. Palmer leaves out films such as *The Stunt Man* (Richard Rush, 1980), *Cutter's Way*, *The Big Chill* (Lawrence Kasdan, 1983), *Year of the Dragon* (Michael Cimino, 1985) and others created during this period, that present the veteran as the absolute antipode of the hard body. Savran's model of "new" white American masculinity also challenges the "macho."

The asexual hyper-masculinity model proves the existence of deep, irresolvable ambiguity in the masculinity of Vietnam War films. The relationship between the surface of the body and its secret (dys)functions subverts the hard body. The tortured body is trapped in perpetual trauma and its extraordinary performativity is a mask for its defeat.

CHAPTER 8

The Homoerotic Model[1]

I. Description of the Model

Fraternal relations define the nature of masculinity in the post-traumatic films affiliated with the Homoerotic Model. Butler claims that the performance of compulsive heterosexuality creates a "substantive effect" and "regulatory practices of gender coherence" (*Gender Trouble* 24-25); with that, fraternal relations are first and foremost dependent on the compulsive homoerotic male performance of brotherhood, and masculinity that is grounded in male bonding[2] is an alternative to the lone wolves found in the Asexual Hyper-Masculine Model. The laws of the symbolic order based on the Name of the Father are secondary to the laws of the fraternal order, and in defeat, the Law of the Father usually loses its moral and practical validity.

Laws of the fraternal order are not based on intergenerational relations, but rather on group ceremonies (induction and training) and moral values before and during battle.[3] Not only does the Law of the Father lose its validity, but the fraternal structure, revealing the absence of

---

1 Major canonic films affiliated with this model are *Streamers* (Robert Altman, 1983), *Birdy* (Alan Parker, 1984), *Platoon* (Oliver Stone, 1986), *Full Metal Jacket* (Stanley Kubrick, 1987), *Good Morning, Vietnam* (Barry Levinson, 1987) and *Casualties of War* (Brian De Palma, 1989).

2 In his well known 1991 essay "Why Men Love War," William Broyles, who served in Vietnam between 1969-1970, wrote, "A comrade in war is a man you can trust with anything, because you trust him with your life. [...] Unlike marriage, [this is] a bond that cannot be broken by a word, by boredom or divorce, or by anything other than death. [...] It [is] [...] a love that needs no reasons, that transcends race and personality and education [...] brotherly love" (73). Broyles makes no mention of the Vietnamese trauma or war crimes. It is paradoxically his one sided, nearly fascist analysis that provides a background against which to test the limits of the myth of brotherhood. The following analyzes of the canonic films affiliated with this model of masculinity will reveal how, in my opinion, even this mythic construct of brotherhood failed.

3 The films do not emphasize the national values of patriotism, anti-Communism, and helping the oppressed except when a conflictual situation tests them. See Tuchman and Chomsky for further discussion of these values.

moral partnership at the national-ideological level, is lost in the Hunter-Captive dialectic through disagreement on moral questions (such as how to treat villagers suspected of helping the Vietcong in *Platoon*, or the abduction and rape of a Vietnamese girl in *Casualties of War*). It is also lost as a result of moral betrayal. For example, in *Streamers*, Billy (Matthew Modine) and Roger (David Alan Greir) agree to Carlyle's (Michael Wright) offer of a visit to a whorehouse in exchange for tacit agreement to keep his homosexual relationship with Richie (Mitchell Lichtenstein) a secret, but in the end refuse to keep their part of the deal. The culmination of loss of brotherhood is fratricide. Carlyle cries and says that all he wanted was to be one big family and then murders Billy. The absence of ideological unity in this film is intensified because of the racial class differences that are emphasized by Carlyle, who describes himself as "a black street-kid" who "is not willing to die in Vietnam," in direct contrast to Richie, who is a white, upper class homosexual male. The trauma of defeat is not only depicted through the fears of the new recruits, but through the father figures as well. Sgt. Cokes (George Dzundza) and Sgt. Rooney (Guy Boyd) recount Vietnam battles and sing songs about death. These scenes are based on reaction shots of the recruits, who are the audience for Rooney and Cokes' simulations. Their fear is a portent of the events that will unfold: the murder of Sgt. Rooney by Carlyle and Sgt. Coke's breakdown after simulating another massacre he took part in.

A fragile fraternal structure is presented in the post-traumatic films affiliated with this model. The trauma reveals the ambivalent attitude held by the soldiers in regard to the war itself (is it justified, should field missions be carried out, and do they have moral significance); that is, there is an absence of moral solidarity. The tension between the physical intimacy of the closed, artificial world of the soldiers and the absence of moral solidarity and shared ideological goals is characteristic of Vietnam War films.[4]

The fear of loss of brotherhood is also the fear of loss of intimacy and of the danger of becoming a lone wolf. For example, Birdy in *Birdy* retreats to fantasies; Chris Taylor in *Platoon* participates in the group's ceremonies in an underground bunker; Joker murders the female sniper in *Full Metal Jacket* in order to be accepted as a killer.

Homoerotic masculinity in these films is based on historical events (the Tet Offensive and the battle for Hue in *Full Metal Jacket*, the My Lai massacre in *Platoon*) rather than the fantasy of the Asexual Hyper-Masculine Model. The undermining of masculinity in these films,

---

4 See Stanley Kubrick's film *Paths of Glory* (1957), which, though it shares *Full Metal Jacket's* anti-humanistic worldview, represents an unequivocal ethical model.

however, leads it to the same realm of fantasy (the masochistic fantasy at the end of *Full Metal Jacket*, Birdy's transformation into a bird; Adrian being saved from the Vietcong and the baseball game in *Good Morning, Vietnam*). The fantasy in these cases is not pseudo-historical (return to Vietnam and victory), but is overtly sexual, corporeal, and cultural, and compensates the protagonists for the tragic loss of fraternal intimacy.

In films that describe relationships between the protagonists before (*Streamers* or *The Deer Hunter*), during (*Full Metal Jacket*), or after (*Birdy* and *Jacknife*) army service, homoeroticism does not appear alone, but rather is a manifestation of homophobia and/or the fear of expression of overt homosexuality. In films that present battle scenes (*Platoon* and *Good Morning, Vietnam*) or field missions, homoeroticism appears alone – sexuality is displaced into violence.

Because of the trauma, masculinity, defined in these films through homoerotic brotherhood, is undermined. The trauma fractures the intimate connection, mutual responsibility, and fraternal partnership between the soldiers, and transforms homoeroticism into violence turned inward and/or outward (suicide and/or fratricide). *Full Metal Jacket* is analyzed here in detail because it uses the complex portrayal of homoerotic brotherhood as a subversive means of criticizing America's involvement and defeat in the Vietnam War. In contrast to other Vietnam War films, it deals with the ills of American society manifested in the protagonists as they go through basic training, and suggests that these ills are the cause of the defeat in Vietnam. This sharp criticism, however, is undermined by an imposed victorious closure.[5]

II. Patricide and Failure: *Full Metal Jacket*

Full Metal Jacket (Stanley Kubrick, 1987).

The first half of this film describes Marine boot camp at Parris Island. There, Sgt. Hartman (Lee Ermey) trains the recruits to be "killers." We follow the process primarily from the point of view of Joker (Matthew Modine). Leonard (Vincent D'Onofrio), a heavy-set soldier who has great difficulty adjusting, is abused by Hartman, who gives him the nickname Gomer Pyle. The last night of basic training Leonard kills Hartman and commits suicide. The second half of the film takes place in the Vietnamese city of Hue during the Tet Offensive. The platoon loses its way and is the target of an unseen sniper, who is finally discovered to

[5] This closure is similar to those of all the canonic Vietnam War films discussed in this book which present victorious overtones. The problematics of this closure is analyzed below.

be a young Vietnamese woman (Ngoc Le). Joker shoots her. After the battle, as evening falls, the soldiers walk to the river.

A. Dialectics of Defeat

The narrative structure of *Full Metal Jacket* creates, in the language of Hayden White, a dialectical tension between two plausible emplotments for presentation of the Vietnam War: basic training at Parris Island, focusing on how the recruits are turned into murderers-killers,[6] and the battle for Hue, focusing on the trauma of defeat.

The film describes the construction and the consequent failure of male brotherhood. On one hand, these two processes are divided by the psycho-geographic split between America and Vietnam; on the other, they are both complementary and dialectic, as seen through a series of parallels made between the two worlds. Thus, in contrast to all the other canonic films made about the Vietnam War discussed in this book, *Full Metal Jacket* is clearly subversive in terms of its structure, which requires the spectator compare the two emplotments and therefore come to terms with his/her stance regarding masculinity in war. The film claims that the source of America's illnesses lies at home – as revealed by the structuring process meant to transform the recruit into a killer during basic training – and not in the war or with the Vietnamese. The film's most prominent subversive strategies are the two emplotments, depiction of the symbiotic father, placement of the pivotal dramatic events in parallel structures, fracturing the point of view, close-up and slow motion shots of injury and death, and the relationship between history and fantasy.

B. Structuring Killers

The Law of the Father in regard to the masculinity of Marines, according to Sgt. Hartman, is a reductionist process that includes expropriation of the otherness from the self of the recruit in order to transform him into a killer. The process involves misogynism, sexism, homophobia, xenophobia, and racism.[7] Expropriation of the otherness also in-

---

6 HARTMAN. What makes the grass grow?
RECRUITS. Blood, Blood, Blood!
HARTMAN. What do we do for a living, ladies?
RECRUITS. Kill, Kill, Kill! (Kubrick, Herr and Hasford 38)
Hartman claims that Lee Harvey Oswald and Charles Whiteman are examples of the ideal Marine soldier (38-39).

7 Many scholars ignore the anti-Communist message that was a part of basic training at that time. See, for example, Willoquet-Maricondi, who only emphasizes its misogynic

volves negating the recruits' sexuality: Hartman emasculates the recruits by creating a distinction between the penis and the phallus and reserving sexual potential for himself alone. As he says, "Tonight [...] you pukes will sleep with your rifles! You will give your rifle a girl's name! Because this is the only pussy you people are going to get!" (Kubrick, Herr and Hasford 17) In this ritual, the weapon becomes a surrogate not for the phallus but for a woman (and her genitals), and is based on the gap between the penis and the substitute. Later, he makes the recruits march dressed only in their diaper-like underwear. Each Marine holds his rifle in one hand and his penis in the other:

HARTMAN. This is my rifle! This is my gun!
RECRUITS. This is for fighting! This is for fun! (18)

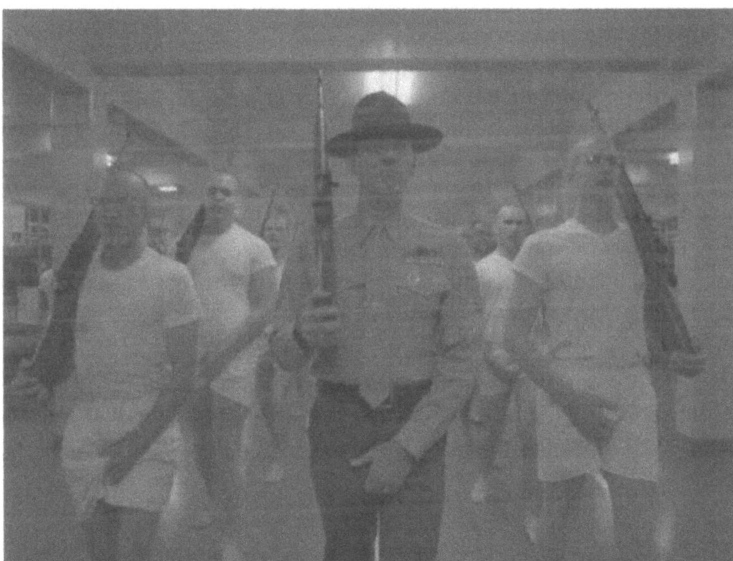

"This is my rifle, this is my gun," *Full Metal Jacket*

The anal infantile *mise-en-scène* intensifies the demasculinization of the male body, and the rituals emphasize the duality of the recruits' imitation of Hartman. On the one hand, as I will describe, the imitation includes pre-oedipal symbiosis; on the other, it does not allow the recruits to approximate Hartman's phallic masculinity: he is the only one to own both penis and phallus. This is the ironic meaning of the distinction he makes between the rifle and the gun (penis), suggesting a

---

and homophobic dimensions (17). See curses against Ho Chi Minh in the script (Kubrick, Herr and Hasford 12).

"shooting" that will not take place. It is actually the connection between violent sexist language and violent militaristic language that emphasizes the negation of sexuality. The recruits will soon take part in military violence, and sexist language is the principle means for constructing such violence. Channeling sexuality to militaristic violence involves sexual unfulfillment.

Hartman's giving the recruits nicknames like Joker, Cowboy, and Gomer Pyle, is "injurious":

> To be called a name is one of the first forms of linguistic injury that one learns. But not all name-calling is injurious. Being called a name is also one of the conditions by which a subject is constituted in language. (Butler, *Excitable Speech* 2).

In Butler's view, linguistic injury is a result not only of the words said, but also the mode of reference, which creates interpellation and names the subject. In this film, nicknames do not confer social recognition, but are a portent of the fate of the recruit. The suicide of Leonard/ Gomer Pyle[8] takes place in the latrine, like the "world of shit" Hartman constantly threatened them with. For Joker and Cowboy, their nicknames undermine subjectivity: Cowboy failed as platoon leader in battle and is killed by the sniper; Joker, named after the only card in the pack without identity, earned his identity as a killer only when he kills the sniper. Consequently, the names function injuriously, as part of the message that Hartmanian structuring of basic training led to failure under fire.

Through giving the recruits nicknames, their evening "prayers,"[9] verbal insults, and chanting and songs, Hartman directs the learning of a new language and establishes the process of constructing the recruit as a killer.

---

8 Susan White notes that Gomer Pyle, the nickname Hartman coined for Leonard, was taken from the popular 1968 television show by the same name. There were constant rumors concerning the homosexuality of star, Jim Nabors, who played the friendly but inept soldier (107).

9 The recruits snap their rifles to the port arms position over their chests.

HARTMAN. Pray!

RECRUITS. (in unison). This is my rifle. There are many like it, but this one is mine. My rifle is my best friend. It is my life. I must master it, as I master my life...I must shoot him (my enemy) before he shoots me. I will. Before God I swear this creed [...]. (Kubrick, Herr and Hasford 13-18)

C. *Law of the Father, Name of the Mother*[10]

Brotherhood is created through participation in Hartman's world of commands and injunctions, as well as through joining forces against him. Because Hartman establishes the character of basic training, he is part of an inevitable oedipal drama, but he also symbolizes the mother, the one who gives birth – and hence is part of a dyad. His infantilization of the recruits (forcing them to march in their underwear and forcing Leonard to march with his pants down sucking his thumb), expropriating their bodies,[11] teaching them elementary daily tasks from scratch (cleaning, buttoning buttons, tying shoelaces), and supervision of their oral pleasures all emphasize this dyad. Mixing the symbolic order with the imaginary order gives basic training – according to the Lacanian perspective – its pathological character. The oedipal father figure intricately channels identification with him through his demand for pre-oedipal symbiosis. Researchers who discuss the film (Rambuss, Willoquet-Maricondi, Modleski, Kolker, *A Cinema of Loneliness*, Fusch, Jeffords, Klein, and Susan White) miss, in my view, this complexity because they deal with Hartman character's only in the context of the oedipal.

Anti-humanistic reduction of otherness from the self, negation of sexuality, and imposition of injurious speech are processes of construction that connect oedipal with pre-oedipal identification. Leonard, however, represents one who is unable to adjust to the Marine "machine" (as it is called by Rambuss). His struggle during basic training is directed against dyad with Sgt. Hartman and for him, à la Girard, Hartman is the "monstrous double." According to Girard, desire is learned through imitation of the other and becomes desire to be like the other. The imitator of this "mechanism of mimetic desire" experiences adoration and rejection, imitation and differentiation. Therefore, the monstrous double erupts in "sacrificial crisis," in violence, when the group is unable to contend with this inherent conflict.[12] Leonard is not capable of opposing the dyad or the Law of the Father and is not ready for differentiation from Sgt. Hartman after he loses the homoerotic

---

10 The term "Name of the Mother" is, of course, not Lacan's. I coined it to describe the complexity of Sgt. Hartman, as will be discussed. As such, it also stands in contrast to Lacan's "Name of the Father" (Hartman/hard man) and provokes additional questions that contribute to the discussion.

11 "You can give your heart to Jesus, but your ass belongs to the Corps" (Kubrick, Herr and Hasford 40).

12 After being punished a number of times because of Leonard, the recruits gang up and beat him during a "blanket party." As a result, he loses his only remaining support – fraternity with his fellow recruits – and in their words, "went crazy." This event led him to become the outstanding sniper of the platoon; that is, to manifest the Hartmanian ideal killer.

brotherhood that had supported him. In this way, the sacrificial crisis was selected by the victim himself.

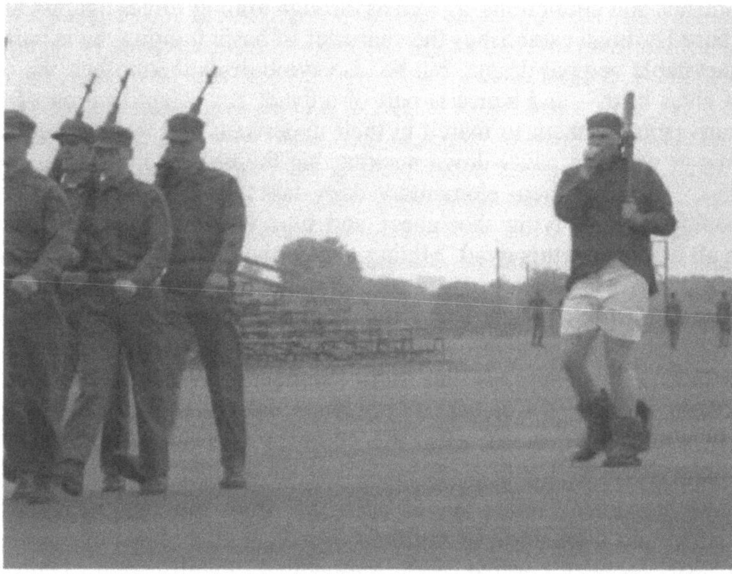

Infantilization by the symbiotic father, *Full Metal Jacket*

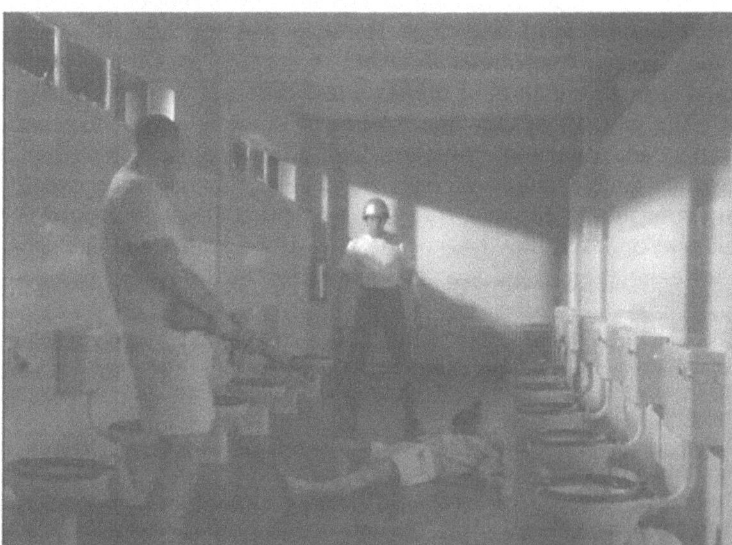

Patricide as adifferentiation, Leonard vs. Sgt. Hartman, *Full Metal Jacket*

Ironically, Leonard's murder of Hartman and consequent suicide are both realizations of the Marine killer ideal; that is, they are the realization of Leonard's identification with the father imago and destruction of this father, and a declaration about the impossibility of breaking the dyad. The double murder – of Hartman and of himself – takes place in the latrine, an anal *mise-en-scène* of pre-oedipal connotations.

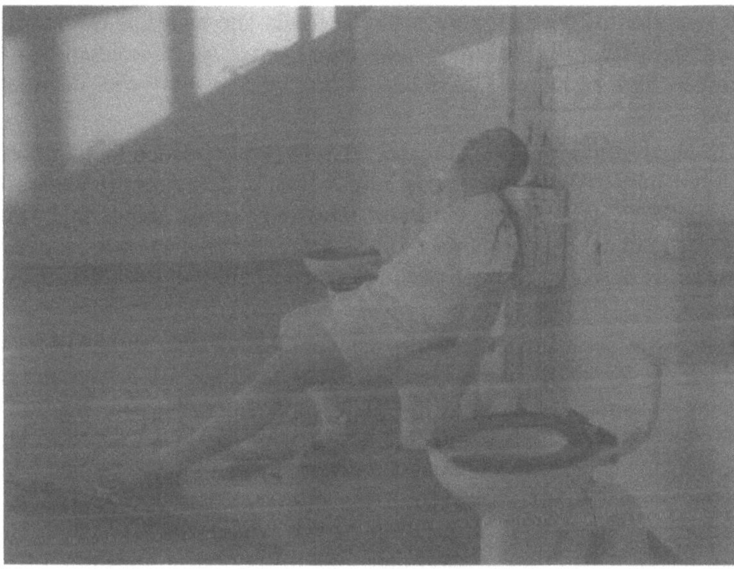

Sacrificial crisis, Gomer Pyle and the dehumanizing latrine, *Full Metal Jacket*

In *Full Metal Jacket* the dialectic of post-traumatic representation is realized through the representation of parallel events in the two parts of the film: because Hartman represents both the father and the dyad, the female sniper later replaces him. Leonard's inability to adjust leads to loss of brotherhood and consequently to Hartman's murder; later, the killing of the female sniper occurs following a loss of brotherhood (challenge to authority and conflict regarding saving the wounded; that is, the failure of comrades in arms). Thus, the film creates a parallel system between the two killings, and the circle – murder of the father and murder of the mother – is closed.

Negation of the feminine is realized not just symbolically during basic training, but concretely in battle, face to face with the female sniper. What had seemed to be banishment of the feminine from the self during basic training is in reality a reproduction of its presence through the demand for pre-oedipal identification, sexist language, female names for the rifles, and rituals. Endless attempts to banish the feminine are evidence of a binary gendered worldview; however, the appearance of the sniper has meaning beyond return of the repressed.

D. Loss of the Murderous Gaze

The ambiguous banishment-reproduction of the feminine as the significant other in the first half of the film leads to the violent and traumatic eruption of the feminine in the second. The anger of the recruits toward the father figure who stole their sexuality is directed to the feminine, and becomes traumatic confrontation with the disguised woman.

Through editing, Kubrick creates a connection between the platoon's encounter with a Vietnamese prostitute, which undermines the demasculinization process, and its encounter with the female sniper that takes place immediately afterwards. The editing intensifies the symbolic meaning of the connection between defeat in battle and castration by a woman.

The battle is based on the sniper's gaze (three cuts to her point of view before she fires), which is the gaze of a killer. As a woman, she does not become an object of the male gaze, since the soldiers fail to locate her. Though she is not seen,[13] her invisibility is not related to lack of power. In contrast to cinematic convention as described since Mulvey, the one with the view is not the one with the power. To gaze, according to Kubrick, is a question of life and death, of victory and defeat, of the realization of the killer masculinity or its negation, of the Law of the Father or the Name of the Mother. The sniper causes death, defeat, and collapse of the brotherhood because of the argument over saving the wounded, and undermines Hartmanian concepts of the soldier as the ultimate killer. In doing so, she reconstructs the horrific dyad unity. In other words, in Vietnam the Law of the Father does not exist and the dyad of boot camp becomes the horrific dyad of death at the hands of a woman.

The brotherhood collapses not only because of the dispute over the wounded and the trauma of being trapped by the female sniper, but also because the fraternal, constructed according to the Hartmanian legacy, is irrelevant when tested in battle. At the same time, the film transforms the social body of the brotherhood into the wounded body. The threat to intactness of the male body that the obsessive anality of basic training so

13 Visually, the rifle barrel, dominant in the frame when the editing takes us to the sniper's point of view, is a reminder of Hartman's order to give the rifle a woman's name.

tried to construct becomes real (the close-up, slow motion shot of injuries) and physically unbelievable (the powerless look toward the source of the threat). The physical body that is vulnerable to injury, castrated, and threatened by death is not the Marine machine. The wounded almost dead body is the polar opposite of the social body of the brotherhood.

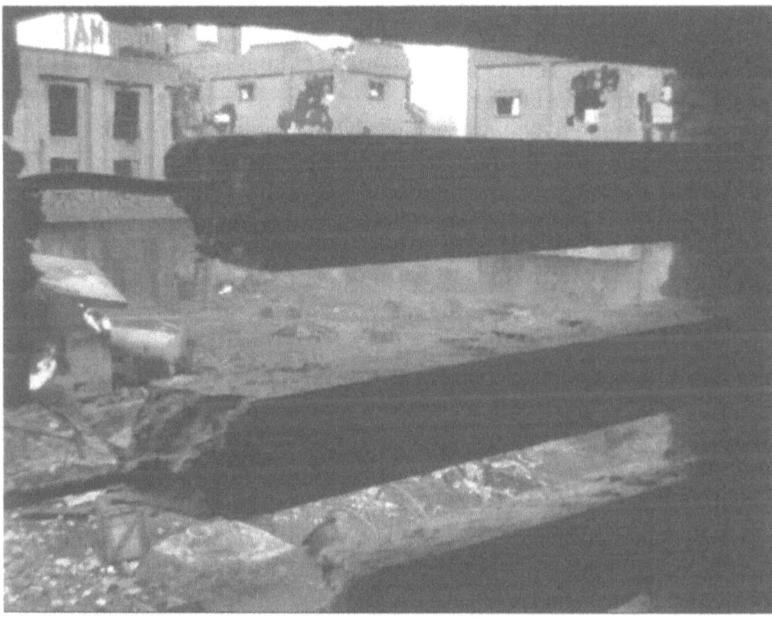

The name of the mother, the female gaze in *Full Metal Jacket*

E. *Post-Defeat Subjectivity*

At the end of the battle for the city of Hue[14] the soldiers finally shoot the sniper and Joker takes her out of her misery with one shot; in doing so he earns, apparently for the first time, his identity as a killer. Their walk to the river singing the Mickey Mouse Club song is not only an expression of nostalgia for their childhood mixed with the recent trauma, but an ironic statement about loss of leadership and identity.

[14] Many authors have commented on the fact that Kubrick located the fighting in the city rather than in the jungle. In my view, however, the importance of Hue as the former Imperial capital of Vietnam and a cultural and religious center has not been given its due. The city became a symbol of the battle for control of the country; see Olson (441). Accordingly, it is especially meaningful that the American forces met defeat there.

The song is used as a substitute for the irrepresentability of the symbolic order that has been undermined: "We play fair and we work hard and we're in harmony [...] Who's the leader of the club that's made for you and me? M-I-C-K-E-Y-M-O-U-S-E" (Kubrick, Herr, and Hasford 120).

Does the film's closure preserve a subversive stance in regard to fraternal masculinity and war? I don't believe so.[15] The surviving soldiers do not seem to be aware of the meaning of defeat (and, actually, awareness of any kind is not part of their military service – not even Leonard's suicide could prod its development). On the contrary, at the same time the soldiers are singing, we hear a voiceover of Joker's internal monologue, presented without irony: "My thoughts drift back to erect nipple wet dreams about Mary Jane Rottencrotch and the Great Homecoming Fuck Fantasy" (120). Shattered masculinity deprived of leadership still entails violent sexism. The sexist language the soldiers use when they finally discover the sniper is a woman is presented as a natural way to deal with the shock. Further, Joker is revealed to be the loyal son of Hartman by way of his thoughts about Mary Jane, which ignore the fact that Hartman's nickname for her is injurious. In this sense, when Joker returns home he will be the Travis of *Taxi Driver* who brings back to American society violence, asexuality (or sexist-voyeuristic sexuality), and a total lack of awareness. Like Travis Bickle, he is not only like John Wayne (whom he imitates, the source of his nickname Joker), but is also a psychopath.[16]

Trauma plays a decisive role in demasculinization: the sniper who castrated the soldiers is defeated in the end; that is, the trauma of battle does not transform the male order, which the soldiers reproduce in the homecoming fantasy. In a world in which it is impossible to achieve unanimity and phallic power, in which there is a tragic loss of male intimacy, all that remains is a sexist-misogynist fantasy.

F. Masochistic Fantasy and History; Sadistic Fantasy and Myth

The traumatic confrontation with the female sniper is based on falling into a trap – the transformation from Hunter to Captive that characterizes, as previously noted, post-traumatic Vietnam War films. It can also be described, however, as uncertainty: uncertainty about the attack,

15 For example, see Modleski in "A Father," where she appears to ignore the closure and views the film as entirely critical of the war (especially 73).

16 In my view this is Kubrick's variation on the paradigm of *Apocalypse Now*, in which after the murder of the father figure, Gen. Kurtz, Capt. Willard returns to American society with his gospel.

the involvement of the local population, the strength of the enemy, the location of the platoon and that of the sniper. The film makes the link between uncertainty based on actual historical events that took place during the Tet Offensive,[17] and the tension between knowing and unknowing that is at the heart of the masochistic fantasy. According to Reik (in Silverman, *Male Subjectivity at the Margins* 207), masochism is based on suspense; that is, it is built on the horrific expectations of the subject. In *Full Metal Jacket* the trauma combines historical uncertainty with masochistic fantasy: the soldiers are exposed to the next murderous attack in their (masochistic) expectation of uncertainty.

According to Deleuze,

> A contract is established between the hero and the woman, whereby at a precise point in time and for a determinate period she is given every right over him. By this means the masochist tries to exorcise the danger of the father and to ensure that the temporal order of reality and experience will be in conformity with the symbolic order, in which the father has been abolished for all time [...] Finally, he ensures that he will be beaten [...] what is beaten, humiliated and ridiculed in him is the image and likeness of the father, and the possibility of the father's aggressive return. (58).

According to Silverman, although Deleuze is aware of "exile of the father" from the symbolic order, his reading of masochism is utopian. She claims that masochism is actually an understanding between the oral mother and the son, according to which the father is expelled from his dominant position in culture and in masochism and is replaced by the mother (Silverman, *Male Subjectivity at the Margins* 211). In her view, all forms of masochism are a product of the existing symbolic order as well as a reaction against it. According to this interpretation, and in contrast to Studlar's, the sniper represents not the pre-oedipal mother but the oral mother.

Sgt. Hartman, as I have claimed, represents both the oedipal and the pre-oedipal; however, his command to give the rifles female names and

---

17 Immediately after the shock of the Tet Offensive in 1968, American forces re-established their control. Only in the city of Hue did the battle continue for several weeks, and there the Marines were engaged in face to face, house to house combat. As with the entire Tet Offensive, the battle for Hue was a tactical defeat for the Communists, but also a strategic victory. Their control of the city for several weeks proved that speculation about the nearing collapse of the Communists was baseless. The Tet Offensive in general, and the battle for Hue in particular, were decisive turning points both in the war and in American public opinion. The Tet Offensive was the reason President Lyndon B. Johnson decided not to seek re-election, and afterwards American foreign policy no longer sought victory in the war, but rather searched for an honorable solution and withdrawal. See Tuchman (364-365); Olson (441-442); and Kutler (536).

to relate to them as female genitals, together with his rejection of the feminine, are connected to the oedipal Law of the Father. It is clear that this naming of the rifles symbolically makes the female sniper the oral mother who possesses a phallus, and so the film expresses its subversiveness of the Hartmanian structuring of murderous masculinity. At the core of this textual subversiveness is the transition from the world of substitutes that characterized basic training to the real world. In contrast to the soldiers who undergo a regressive process in losing the gaze as well as the phallus (despite the fact they still have their rifles), the female sniper has the gaze, literally and metaphorically, as well as the phallus, and is the heir of the Father.

Consequently, the female sniper represents the expulsion of the father from his position of control as well as destruction of his legacy – the Marine heritage. The masochistic fantasy is not only the return of the repressed, but it transforms the Vietnamese woman into an other that is no less meaningful than the white Father,[18] and as such she is the cause of the soldiers' failed masculine subjectivity.

Modleski discussed the claims of Theweleit, Deleuze and Kristeva, who describe the transition from an emphasis on relations with the father to emphasis on relations with the mother as the reason for aggression against women in war; that is, they support the pre-oedipal masochistic model. Theweleit, who like Silverman, analyzes Deleuze, reached a different conclusion: he claims that the principle reason for aggression against women in war is not castration anxiety, but rather the fear of total disappearance, whose source is symbiosis with the mother during the pre-oedipal stage and during differentiation. According to Modleski, Kristeva claimed that rituals of defilement, such as war, are related to the subject's overcoming the threat that his identity will be absorbed within the mother. If so, both Theweleit and Kristeva emphasize that the reason for castration anxiety is the symbiotic relationship between mother and son. Modleski emphasizes the reversal of the Deleuzian concept of masochism in which the female becomes the master. Following Deleuze's, Theweleit's and Kristeva's depictions of symbiosis, I suggest that although the pre-oedipal Hartmanian aspect associated with the sniper certainly emphasizes symbiotic relations, the loss of sexuality, including the oedipal Hartmanian aspect, eventually brings the female sniper closer to the masochistic fantasy of the oral

---

[18] As part of his construction of the recruits, Hartman lectures about the eternal life of the Corps (Kubrick, Herr and Hasford 42). Saving the victim from his historical death destroys the experience of death, according to the Marine ethos. Death becomes symbolic; that is, eternal life. Of course, the cruel imagery of the sniper scene undermines this ethos of "fraternity even in death."

mother. As the oral mother, the sniper represents the various identifications characterizing Hartman and makes them exceedingly lethal. In Modleski's view, Kubrick's emphasis on masochism in the sniper scene enabled him to severely criticize the military: expulsion of the father and making the female the enemy highlight its absurdity. In contrast to her perspective, I do not view this film as totally critical of masculinity and the war in Vietnam, particularly because of its closure. I believe that the closure reproduces the Hartmanian ideology – albeit in an impaired and ironic manner – in order to reconstruct masculinity.

Because of its reliance on historical events, the phantasmatic aspect of the sniper scene is intensified. The turning point occurs when the masochistic fantasy reaches its nearly intolerable traumatic extreme (the third cut to the sniper's point of view) at the moment the soldiers locate the sniper and shoot her. The end of the masochistic fantasy changes the function of the historical in the scene. It seems as if this is a victory and the soldiers have managed to reestablish their identity as killers. The shift between the masochistic fantasy, which has historical context, and the Hartmanian sexist-misogynist fantasy of Mary Jane, which lacks any historical context, restores post-traumatic masculinity to mythic fraternal homoeroticism through the soldiers singing together after the battle.

G. *The Hartmanian Legacy*

Masculinity after the defeat at Hue preserves the identity constructed by Hartman during basic training:[19] stripping of the other from the self, demasculinization, injurious language, and unconscious symbiosis with the paternal heritage. Although the masochist fantasy of the defeat results in undermined brotherhood, the dead and wounded body, loss of the leader, masculine intimacy, and the gaze – the sexist and infantile fantasies of Mickey Mouse and Mary Jane restore the Hartmanian legacy to the soldiers.

This structuring of post-traumatic masculine identity includes not only the transition from homoeroticism to violence, but also from reproduction denial of the other to murder of the other, from murder of the father/brother to murder of the symbolic mother without taking possession of the phallus. Even after the sniper is killed, it is clear that recognition of the other as a victorious woman who defeated masculinity has also been preserved. The masks of the effeminate-homosexual-

---

[19] During negotiations just before the battle, the Vietnamese pimp uses the expression, "Boom-Boom, long time. Ten dolla" (86). Just before the sniper is finally killed, the dialogue reproduces the Hartmanian connection between misogyny, sexism, and racism: "No more boom-boom for this baby-san. There's nothing we can do for her. She's dead meat" (118).

inept-poorly adapted soldier and the (fe)male sniper, both removed so traumatically at the height of the drama, reproduces masculinity that wears the permanent mask of the murderer.[20] The outcome is masculinity deprived of values, sexuality, and historical context. What is left is only the readiness to kill.

Streamers, *Birdy*, *Casualties of War*, and *Good Morning, Vietnam*, like all of the other canonic films that present the defeat in war through failed homoerotic fraternal masculinity, raise moral questions as a way of defining masculinity. In *Streamers*, as described above, it is impossible for the brotherhood of the recruits to overcome divisions of class, race, and sexual orientation among the soldiers. The brotherhood between the two sergeants in this film is based upon their denial of the horrors of war and their war crimes. In *Good Morning, Vietnam*, Adrian Cronauer develops a seemingly close relationship with the Vietnamese other, much like his relationship with his listeners, but which breaks apart. The film enables "brotherly" recuperation only with his students, who are a substitute for comrades at arms, friends at the radio station, and meaningful others (Tuan and his sister). The uniqueness of *Platoon* in dealing with these issues will be discussed in the following.

III. Destroying Fraternal Masculinity in Order to Save It: *Platoon*[21]

Platoon (Oliver Stone, 1986).

Chris Taylor is a college graduate from a military family who volunteers to serve in Vietnam. He describes his experiences in letters to his grandmother, excerpts of which are heard in voiceovers. After being

---

20 HARTMAN. Private Joker, why did you join my beloved Corps?
JOKER. Sir, to kill, sir! [...]
HARTMAN. Let me see your war face!
JOKER. Sir?
HARTMAN. You've got a war face? Aaaaaaaagh! That's a war face. Now let me see your war face!
JOKER. Aaaaaaaagh!
HARTMAN. Bullshit! You didn't convince me! Let me see your real war face!
JOKER. Aaaaaaaaaaaaaaaagh!
HARTMAN. You didn't scare me! Work on it!
JOKER. Sir, yes, sir! (Kubrick, Herr and Hasford 5)

21 After the Tet Offensive, this was the most quoted phrase of the war: "It becomes necessary to destroy the town in order to save it" (Tuchman 349). The American major who first used it meant that the city had been completely destroyed in order to exterminate the Vietcong; but the phrase symbolizes how the Americans generally used force. He was actually referring to the city of Hue.

wounded he is accepted into Sgt. Elias's (Willem Dafoe) circle. The platoon, under the command of Sgt. Barnes (Tom Berenger), is outraged by the loss of comrades in a Vietcong ambush and massacres villagers and destroys their village. Elias arrives during the massacre, confronts Barnes, and orders the massacre stopped. In response, Barnes kills him during the battle with the Vietcong. Chris is the sole witness to the murder and after the last battle in the valley shoots the wounded Barnes. In the last scene Chris leaves Vietnam in a medivac helicopter.[22]

The first part of the film establishes that the soldiers need brotherhood in order to survive: they are seen teaching each other how to cope with the physical and mental challenges of everyday life (leeches, ants, snakes, mud, water and rain; mines, snares, ambushes and the invisible enemy in the jungle); and Gardner (Bob Orwig), the rookie soldier who had not been there long enough to learn, does not survive the night patrol. The antagonism between the two circles led by Barnes and Elias during the second part of the film is evidence that homoerotic fraternal masculinity helps the soldiers contend with their daily challenges, the sense of defeat, and the meaninglessness of being in Vietnam. Fraternal masculinity is tested in the third part of the film when, during events similar to the My Lai massacre,[23] the soldiers are divided between two approaches/two "fathers." The result is the collapse of brotherhood: Barnes murders Elias, an argument breaks out about whether the events

---

22 To the best of my knowledge no one who has discussed this film has commented on the phenomenon of American soldiers killing one another as a unique characteristic of the Vietnam War, including the specific period depicted in the film. According to MacLear, however, "incidents" in which officers were killed by enlisted men with grenades were first reported in 1969. Between 1969 and 1971 up to 730 such incidents took place; and altogether 831 officers were killed by their own forces. Violence against officers in Vietnam was fifteen times greater than during "war of the trenches" in World War I (305).

23 The war crimes that occurred in My Lai on March 16, 1968, enflamed public opinion in the United States. Four hundred villagers including women and children were killed; women were raped; property was destroyed, high-ranking officers refused to intervene; and falsified reports about the events were uncovered by investigative reporters. The trial of Lt. Calley, who was in command, took years. Though he was found guilty of twenty-two murders in 1971, his sentence was reduced by 20 years and he was released in 1975. See Olson (60-63). Klein is critical of *Platoon* for substituting a psychological and metaphysical discussion of the nature of human behavior in times of stress for a political analysis of war crimes (24 and beyond). For a view totally opposite to that of *Platoon*, see the documentary film directed by Kevin Sim, *Four Hours in My Lai* (1989) which includes testimonies from soldiers and from Pham Thi Tuan, who survived by hiding under dead bodies.
Rob Reiner's film *A Few Good Men* (1992) reconstructs the myth of the Marine's morality. In his arguments defending an officer in court, the lawyer mentions Calley in the same context as Nazi criminals. Oliver Stone's new film on My Lai, *Pinkville* (2008), is coming out as these lines are being written.

in the village were justified, and Elias' group raises the possibility of killing Barnes in revenge. Brotherhood and morality totally disintegrate during the fourth part of the film, the battle, climaxing with Chris's murder of Barnes the next morning.

The death of homoerotic fraternal masculinity is elegized by Chris, and he gives it an ambivalent moral meaning that finally restores brotherhood:

> I think now, looking back, we did not fight the enemy, we fought ourselves – and the enemy was in us. The war is over for me now, but it will always be there – the rest of my days. As I am sure Elias will be – fighting with Barnes for what Rhah called possession of my soul [...] There are times since I have felt like the child born of those two fathers [...] but be that as it may, those of us who did make it have an obligation to build again, to teach to others what we know and to try with what's left of our lives to find a goodness and meaning to this life. (<http://www.imsdb.com/scripts/Platoon.html>).

The textual strategies described below support his claim that "the enemy was in us" and include the use of *Bildungsroman* conventions (Klein; Kinney); symbolization of the fathers as good vs. evil[24] manifest in the confrontation between the humanitarian and the imperialistic approaches; cross cutting between the two groups of soldiers in the second half; suspense culminating in fratricide or murder of the other; symbolic murder of the father figure (Lt. Wolf [Mark Moses]); depiction of the underground bunker; Chris's internal monologue as testimony with concurrent blurring of temporality; and contrast staged between the primary and the secondary characters.[25]

---

24 Including the cinematic mythicization contained in this symbolization. In his discussion of the *Star Wars* trilogy, Palmer compares Chris Taylor to Luke Skywalker. He claims that Chris is a mediator between the light side of the Force represented by Obi-Wan Kenobi/Yodah and the Dark Side as represented by Darth Vader (264). Palmer, however, ignores the central scene in which Luke Skywalker removes Darth Vader's helmet by delivering a blow with his sword and sees his own face reflected in the helmet. I will describe how the film applies various strategies in order to facilitate Barnes evil and Chris's role of mediator.

25 Bunny (Kevin Dillon) is presented as a psychopath. Using the butt of his rifle, he joyfully crushes to death a young, mentally disabled Vietnamese villager and later is among the soldiers who rape young Vietnamese girls. In contrast to the explanation provided for Barnes' behavior, the film does not explain Bunny's in relation to survival in the chaos of Vietnam. His actions therefore diminish Barnes' standing as the epitome of evil.

A. The Bunker as a Homoerotic Site

Cross cutting between the "underground world," as the bunker is called, and the barracks, sharpens the difference between the two groups of soldiers and establishes homoerotic fraternal masculinity. *Platoon* proposes a homoerotic model that extends beyond the physical intimacy imposed by life in the field, in which the "You" in the "I Need You" of the song sung in the bunker is the comrades-in-arms and not necessarily a faraway sweetheart. In the scene in which Chris is accepted into Elias's camp, the underground bunker changes from a site used to hide from death[26] to one of security, support, belonging, partnership (smoking drugs, singing, couples dancing close) and shared values (poster of Ho Chi Minh above Elias's hammock). Lit by a variety of lights and candles, the intact half-naked bodies stand in contrast to the wounded body that characterizes life in the war taking place above ground.

The cut moves us sharply from Chris's point of view during the initiation ceremony into the world beyond this brotherhood in the barracks above, where Barnes and his group of soldiers remain. The camera moves back and forth between the two groups that are not in direct contact. In total contrast to the physical contact and the eroticism of the initiation in the bunker (Elias breathes smoke into Chris's mouth through the barrel of a rifle) Barnes and his soldiers are playing cards. The competition between the soldiers couldn't be more different than the collaboration in the bunker, just as the racist remarks in the barracks contrast with non-racist brotherhood in the bunker. The anxiety of dying in war is apparent in the dialogue between O'Neil and Barnes and stands in opposition to the happiness experienced by the bunker's "youth culture."

The film develops these contrasts to build up to a wider statement about the connection between homoerotic fraternal masculinity and morality. Not only Barnes, who murders both innocent Vietnamese and Elias, but those who identify with him, are representative of anti-fraternal and anti-humanitarian masculinity: Bunny; Junior (Reggae Johnson), who attempts to evade an order by spraying his feet with mosquito repellant; and O'Neil, who seeks to advance his R&R and, as noted, hides during the battle.

---

26 In the last battle scene, the underground bunker – with bodies of American and Vietnamese soldiers strewn about without distinction – is the site of defeat, fear, and death. It does not function as a fraternal site – the soldiers abandon their friends and wound one another. O'Neil (John C. Macginley), for example, covers himself with a body so he will not be discovered.

The murders of the two sergeants are not used to describe a nihilistic worldview (Palmer) or teach the protagonists lessons (Modleski; Jeffords [*Remasculinization of America*]). Nor do Elias and Barnes represent the confrontation with "the dark side of the human soul" (Klein 24-19) or the "battle between the feminine and the masculine" (Jeffords, "Reproducing" 209). Rather, Barnes represents a model of masculinity that denies the homoerotic, enabling him to be violent. Such an interpretation allows us to explain, in my view, his visit in the bunker following Elias's murder. Here he proclaims, "Kill me" and later wrestles with Chris, a physical struggle that replaces the denied homoerotic with fraternal punishment – a cut on the face, in accordance to the Mafia code for informants.[27]

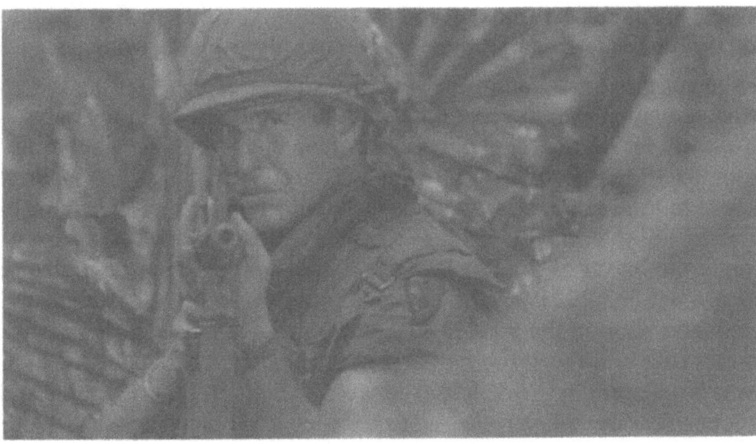

Fratricide, *Platoon*

B. Crisis of Testimony, Moral Instability

Chris's inner monologue on the way to the village, presented as if it were testimony after the fact, is the first sign of a transformative process from moral soldier to murderer.

> [...] the village, which had stood for maybe a thousand years, didn't know we were coming that day. If they had they would have run [...] Barnes was at the eye of our rage – and through him, our Captain Ahab – we would set things right again. That day we loved him.
> (<http://www.imsdb.com/scripts/Platoon.html>).

---

27 Homoerotic masculinity is also prominent in the hunting scenes and the bar in Clairton before the war in *The Deer Hunter*, but Michael denies it. Wood claimed there was a homosexual subtext between Michael and Nick. See Wood esp. 290-297.

This view of Barnes does not seem reasonable in light of what really took place, and broaches the question whether Chris is really making a retrospective statement intended to share the events with his grandmother, or if the film is using this blurring of temporality to present the turning point that results in the collapse of his moral subjectivity. Similar to what happened during the last battle, the departure scene reconstructs brotherhood and Chris's heroism through Rhah's imitation of Tarzan. Nevertheless, murderousness, ambivalent morality, and splitting of identity become inseparable from the reconstruction of masculinity.

Platoon is unique among post-traumatic films affiliated with the Homoerotic Model in that it kills the brotherhood at the center of fraternal homoerotic masculinity (Elias' murder) and restores it in a dehumanized version (Barnes' murder). The transformation from moral soldier to murderer begins with the murder of a traitor to brotherhood; and develops through concealment of the murder and a guiltless retrospective reflection masked as an elegy that makes use of initiation, human nature, and the reality of war as excuses for the transformation.

In "Why War" Jacqueline Rose says,

> For Money-Kyrle [...] there is a common myth [...] especially prevalent at the end of an unsuccessful war, that one had always wished to live in peace and treat the whole world as a brother: "In order to support this myth, the very limitations of our world are themselves denied. (qtd. in Rose 29-30).

As presented in Chris' final internal monologue, the all-encompassing myth of the fraternal in *Platoon*, à la Money-Kyrle, is a continuation of his elegy "we did not fight the enemy, we fought ourselves – and the enemy was in us." The film makes the connection between the enemy being in us and the transformation of Sgt. Barnes and Sgt. Elias, the two most notable examples of fraternity, into eternal father figures as a result of their deaths. In addition, the film emphasizes the myth of the split between the good father and the evil father. Do the initiation of Chris and the symbolic murder of the actual father figure (Lt. Wolf) make possible this transformation from the anti-oedipal to the death of the fraternal in the name of the revival of oedipality?

Further, Rose writes:

> For Franco Fornari, war is a "paranoid elaboration of mourning.' We project on to the alien, or other, the destructiveness we fear in the most intimate relations or parts of ourself. Instead of trying to repair it at home, we send it abroad. War makes the other accountable for a horror we can then wipe out with impunity, precisely because we have located it so firmly in the other's place. This saves us the effort of ambivalence, the hard work of recognizing

> that we love where we hate, that, in our minds at least, we kill those to whom we are most closely and intimately attached. (19).
>
> [...] It is the perfect image of the alien-ness that Freud places at the heart of human subjectivity, the alien-ness whose denial or projection leads us into war. (23) [...] Fornari writes: 'war serves to defend ourselves against the 'Terrifier' as an internal, absolute enemy [...] in this manner we arrive at the incredible paradox that the most important security function is not to defend ourselves from an external enemy but to find one.' (34).

The elegiac strategies, nostalgic songs in the bunker, Chris's pseudo-testimony about the village, and his internal monologue at the end of the film are manifestations of this denial. This is not hatred of the Vietnamese other but rather of oneself. In the Vietnam War, "finding the enemy" means making Communism and the otherness of the Vietnamese the alien described by Freud and Jacqueline Rose. The understanding that the "enemy is in us" means negating the denial process and denying the existence of the enemy; that is, ignoring the actual involvement in the war. Murderous aggression toward the Vietnamese other becomes secondary to finding the internal enemy that can be mourned without interruption, even if it is an ambivalent mourning. In this way, the elegiac process is not an extension of destructive aggression toward the other which characterizes intimate relations, but is the opposite: the denial of aggression towards the Vietnamese other by return to intimate relations.

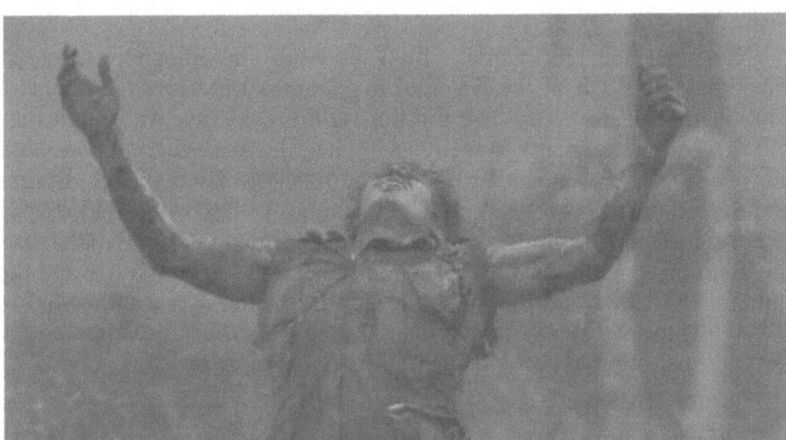

Fraternal violence under the guise of fraternal love, *Platoon*

No wonder, then, that in his final interior monologue the fraternal figures of Elias and Barnes become father figures: this reversal first serves the denials of self-hatred and then hatred of the other. In the internal reality that becomes primary, the fraternal characters easily become father figures. It is clear that this is the realm of fantasy and not reality, and therefore, it is possible to represent My Lai. Mourning takes place not in connection to the massacre, a realistic context, but rather in connection to a phantasmatic internal context that releases Chris and what he represents (patriotic, heroic, moral masculinity) from responsibility for the war. Thus, paradoxically, the conceptualization of masculine brotherhood permits fraternal violence under the guise of fraternal love.

CHAPTER 9

The Impotent Model[1]

In the Asexual Hyper-Masculine Model, masculinity is constructed in the tension between the ambiguity of the hyper-physicality of the Hunter and the asexuality of the Captive. Masculinity according to the Homoerotic Model is established through fraternal relations that are the target of both denial and preservation, resulting in immorality and fratricide. Both the physical-sexual fantasy of the Hyper-Masculine Model and the fraternal moral fantasy of the Homoerotic Model are ground in historical context, but fratricide and patricide eventually disconnect post-traumatic masculinity from physical, sexual, moral, and historical context. Performative, physical, sexual, homoerotic, and historical fantasy serve as an alternative to the identity void of defeated masculinity; but are not, however, a response to the failure to represent the symbolic order. The demasculated and aphallic masculinity represented by the tortured body is based upon masks that it fights to preserve. Trauma causes demythicization and results in masculinity split in terms of its identity. How is this fragile identity expressed in the case of films affiliated with the Impotent Model, which focuses on non-performative and impotent masculinity that fails to both represent the symbolic order and construct fantasy?

I. Description of the Model

Disabled veterans represented in post-traumatic Vietnam War cinema are limited to Steven in *The Deer Hunter*; Lt. Dan in *Forrest Gump*; and Alex (John Heard) in *Cutter's Way* (Ivan Passer, 1981); veterans who are both disabled and impotent are limited to Luke in *Coming Home* and Ron in *Born on the 4th of July* who literally embody the defeat. It is especially noteworthy that eleven years passed between the first representation of disabled and impotent masculinity in *Coming*

1 Major canonic films in this model are *Coming Home* (1978) and *Born on the 4th of July* (1989).

Home and the second, and last, in *Born on the 4th of July*.[2] These two films will be the focus of discussion in this chapter.

The aspects of post-traumatic masculinity already discussed (the Hunter-Captive dialectic, demasculinization, failure of performance and of the paternal and fraternal orders, inability to represent the symbolic order, patricide, and fratricide) are more extreme in the case of impotent masculinity and are intensely subversive, as the following analysis will demonstrate.

Susan Bordo wrote,

> Impotence. The word rings with disgrace and humiliation [...] unlike other disorders, impotence implicates the whole man, not merely the body part. He is impotent. Would we ever say about a person with a headache, "He is a headache"? Yet this is just what we do with impotence [...]. (59).

In phallocentric cultures, impotent masculinity is represented as physical loss of masculinity involving mental and physical states of total paralysis as part of an all-embracing castration anxiety.[3] The private body is no longer the social body and disability creates for the individual a new bodily order that is forced to contend with the failure of the symbolic order. Physical and mental confrontations between this new order and the unquestioned phallic order characterize the post-war period, as illustrated by Luke's clash with the police at the Marine Recruitment Center in *Coming Home* and Ron's with delegates to the 1972 Republican Convention in *Born on the 4th of July*.

The humanization and politicization of the protagonists of these films take place only during physical confrontations carried out by the body/wheelchair, and become possible only after the masculinity of the protagonist has been rehabilitated through sexual relations with a woman. Such rehabilitation, of course, is limited, so that only through politicization can the social father be established as a substitute for biological fatherhood. In this way the individual body allegedly be-

---

2 Despite the precedent set in *Coming Home*, Hollywood cinema followed contemporary social conventions regarding returning soldiers and for a decade did not deal with representation of impotence and disability. This having been said, it should be noted that though there were few representations of disabled veterans, these films were not a marginal phenomena. On the contrary, they were blockbusters with mass appeal as demonstrated by widespread discussion in the media. On the difficulties faced by returning soldiers and their representation, see Doherty; Haines.

3 According to *Webster's*, the definitions of impotence are lacking power or ability, utterly unable to do something, without force or effectiveness, lacking bodily strength, or physically helpless, and wholly lacking of sexual power; that is, only the fifth definition has a sexual physical connotation.

comes the social body once again, though at the price of sexuality, as will be discussed below.

In *Coming Home*, the impotent male is not rehabilitated by becoming a social father. Instead, the film suggests two other paths to rehabilitation: through political activism and personal relationships. These alternatives are distinct from the all-embracing rehabilitation of films from the 1990s in which becoming the social father, that is, displacement of lost sexuality, is the only possibility for rehabilitation of the impotent disabled veteran (*Born on the 4th of July*); or is even represented as unnecessary (*Forrest Gump*, in which Dan is rehabilitated by capitalism).

The two films affiliated with this model represent two subversive elements regarding the rehabilitation process: the nature of the sexual relations (*Coming Home*) and the visualization of impotence (*Born on the 4th of July*); however, the closures of both impose victorious overtones that do not allow the spectator to appreciate the utter subversiveness of this process. The reconstruction of masculinity does indeed result in self-awareness, but it is so rare in times of war that it is attained, at least in the films of the 1990s, at the cost of sexuality.

Brotherhood fills the central role in the rehabilitation process, and women only play a secondary role for the disabled veterans who are not impotent. Thus, for example, Steven in *The Deer Hunter* refuses to leave the Veterans Hospital because he claims he does not fit into society, while his wife Angela has been in a state of hysteria since his return, expressed through self-imposed silence and obsessive knitting of socks for his amputated legs. Michael's earlier refusal to include Steven in the escape from Vietcong captivity signifies the failure of brothers in arms (though later he does rescue him), but his subsequent rescue of Steven from the Veterans Hospital preserves the fraternal order, at least superficially.

The body of the disabled impotent veteran is continually in transition: it has been penetrated rather than being the one to penetrate; it has undergone abjectification;[4] and is split – the upper body is part of the bodybuilder subculture and the lower body is part of that of the paralyzed. The structuring of the body involves transition from being the historical body incorporating the history of the defeat, to reindividualization. The films define impotent masculinity as being established through tension not only between the new bodily order and the social

4 In Kristevian terms, the abject, incomplete, impure body cannot be part of the symbolic.

order, as indicated earlier, and between the historical body and individualization, but also within the body itself.

As defined by Eugene Monick, rage serves as a mediating stage between impotence as a total bodily order and reindividualization of the historical body. Being rescued from rage by realization of sexuality is the central subversive element of *Coming Home*.[5]

II. Radical Sexuality in *Coming Home*

Coming Home (Hal Ashby, 1978).

After Sally's (Jane Fonda) husband Bob leaves for Vietnam, she decides to volunteer in a hospital, unconventional behavior for an officer's wife. There she meets Luke (Jon Voight), who is paralyzed from the waist down, and they fall in love. Parallel to changes in her lifestyle (she buys a sports car, rents a house on the beach, changes her appearance), Luke undergoes rehabilitation, is released from the hospital, and becomes increasingly independent. After he chains himself to the doors of the Marine Recruitment Center in protest against the war and in mourning for the suicide of his fellow veteran Billy he is followed by the F.B.I. The photos and audio recordings of Sally and Luke's affair are shown to Bob when he returns home from Vietnam. He is awarded a medal and released from service. Suffering from the traumas of the war and the shame of his self-inflicted wound, he no longer feels he belongs either in the army or at home. In the final scenes, Bob is seen swimming naked out to sea, while Sally shops for a barbeque and Luke argues against the draft and the War in Vietnam in front of high school students.

Coming Home is subversive in terms of Luke's sexuality. In a culture that encourages men to think about themselves as their penis, that still confuses male sexuality with potency, and believes "sex which is not one" (Irigaray)[6] characterizes only women, Luke's sexuality is excep-

---

5 A comparison between the representation of masculinity in post-traumatic films and its representation in non post-traumatic films is beyond the scope of this book. Nonetheless, I would like to state that the trauma of defeat is a decisive variable in the difference in representation. In films of World War II, the hero was victorious in battle over the evil of Nazism and defeated it. The denial of impotency, like the sacrifice of sexuality, was perceived to be part of the woman's noble contribution to the war hero. *The Men*, Fred Zinnemann's well-known 1950 film, returned to the formula of the lover from the past who insists on contributing to the rehabilitation of the veteran. Her sexual sacrifice is hinted at in the angry outbursts between the couple on their wedding night, though it is not specifically stated.

6 See Bordo, who claims, brilliantly in my opinion, that the concepts used by Irigaray are appropriate to images and ideologies that are no longer relevant (42); Irigaray.

tional: his impotent masculinity is represented as sexual through oral sex with Sally and other sensual pleasures. Not only does Sally undergo emotional and sexual liberation (she has her first orgasm with Luke);[7] but Luke is also liberated from impotence. His sexual performance is a contra model to conventional masculinity: it is neither penetrating nor penetrated. Undermining the binarism that defines phallic masculinity subverts phallocentrism and changes its symbolic meaning to one of entrapment. Current research has reached the conclusion that femininity is implied when masculinity is lost as a result of impotency caused by paralysis (as claimed by Jeffords, *Remasculinization of America*; Norden; Selig; and Savran). On the contrary, Luke's masculinity presents the "new" male[8] not as a utopian dimension in popular culture (as Jameson claims in "Reification") but rather as a valuable strategy for both genders.

In *Coming Home* the phallus is not the preferred signifier (à la Lacan), rather it is a reversible symbolic code. Impotence challenges the accepted cultural code according to which the penis is hidden while the symbolism of the phallus is present everywhere. Bordo described the phallus as a construction that changes and develops over time, while the phallic ideology perceives it to be an atemporal universal symbol. In *Coming Home*, impotent defeated masculinity changes the phallus from a total, preferred, present symbol whose power is based on it being metonymic to the penis,[9] to a potentially radical construct.

Intimacy with the phallic wound provokes pseudo-phallic rage in the impotent veteran and becomes sexual energy, which changes castration to sexuality through sensuality. It leads masculinity to humanistic politicization based upon self-awareness. That is, *Coming Home* presents phallicization as a culturally dependent convention that must be undermined in order to create an alternative masculinity that is subver-

---

7 Theweleit ("Bomb's Wound") claimed that the concept of reproduction should be replaced with Ruddick's term "caring labor," which characterizes a way of life and thought that is unrelated to war (289). In my view, this term captures Sally's work in the hospital as well as her relationships with Luke and with Bob after his return. Theweleit cites Jefford's thesis regarding remasculinization without critiquing the nature of the discourse in her research, which stands in complete contrast to what he terms the peace discourse.

8 In "Masculine/Feminine," Tomasulo claims, for example, that the "new male" points to the gender crisis of the 1980s. He sees it as the alternative to "hard body" films, assuming that the masculinity represented between the rise of the feminist movement and the Reagan era of conservative-patriarchal discourse was full of contradictions. Sydney Pollack's film *Tootsie* (1982) points to a gender alternative. Regarding "sensitive masculinity," see also Pfeil (esp. 37-70); Savran.

9 See Butler (*Bodies That Matter* 57-91, esp. 83-84): "Indeed, the phallus would be nothing without the penis" (84).

sive of the symbolic order. These new sexual and political alternatives point to a new physical order for impotent masculinity.

According to Freud,

> The ego is first and foremost a bodily ego; it is [...] ultimately derived from bodily sensations, chiefly from those springing from the surface of the body. It may thus be regarded as a mental projection of the surface of the body. ("The Ego and the Id" 27).

De Lauretis responded in "Gender Symptoms" and claimed,

> As I read Freud, the body ego is a projected perceptual boundary that does not merely delimit or contain the imaginary morphology of an individual self, but actually enables the access to the symbolic [...] The body ego is a permeable boundary – an open border, so to speak – a site of incessant material negotiations between, on one side, the external world, the domain of the real, comprising other people, social institutions, etc., and, on the other, the internal world of the psyche, the drives, the unconscious, and the ego's mechanisms of defense-repression, disavowal, and so forth. (268).

In *Coming Home* the body ego mediates between external and internal realities, breaking the mental projection of the bodily morphology. The radicalism of the penis phallus relationship, however, extends beyond what I understand to be described by De Lauretis or by Lacan. Desire for Sally causes Luke to strengthen the split between the upper and lower parts of his body through body building: the surface of the body, the imaginary morphology, is multiplied by two. The radicalism derived is a portent of Luke's future sexual capability.

In *Bodies that Matter*, Butler deconstructs the latent, hegemonic relationship between the penis and the phallus, removes the phallus from its all-encompassing status, and instead emphasizes the possibility of more than one imaginary bodily ego. In her words:

> Consider that "having" the phallus can be symbolized by *an arm, a tongue, a hand (or two)*, a knee, a pelvic bone, an array of purposefully instrumentalized body-like things. And that this "having" exists in relation to a "being the phallus" [...] that being and having can be confounded, upset the logic of non-contradiction that serves the either-or of normative heterosexual exchange [...] The phantasmatic status of "having" is redelineated, rendered transferable, substitutable, plastic. (88-89, emphasis added).

Viewing the phallus as a transferable phantasm undermines the naturalization of the connection between the phallus and the morphology of masculinity. Butler stresses that the phallus is continually given new meaning. In *Coming Home*, the phantasmatic status of the phallus changes as a result of the representation of the many facets of pleasure that Luke and Sally derive from sexual relations.

Butler further writes,

> If what comes to signify under the sign of the phallus are a number of body parts, discursive performatives, [...] then the symbolic position of "having" has been dislodged from the penis as its privileged anatomical (or non-anatomical) occasion [....] And insofar as it operates at the site of anatomy, the phallus (re)produces the spectre of the penis only to enact its vanishing [...] This opens up anatomy [...] as a site of proliferative resignifications. (89).

Three aspects of Butler's insights are applicable to our analysis: dislodging the penis's status of "having" and transferring it to the mouth and the hands; regaining power through using the bodily split as imaginary; and Luke's use of his body and mouth against the war.

This symbolic displacement does not take place regarding Bob, whose situation is the polar opposite of Luke's: he has a penis, and therefore in the hegemonic imaginary world of the body, he also has a phallus (though he was unable to satisfy Sally sexually prior to the war and is emotionally unable to function afterwards). During the war, he shot himself in the foot, a symbolic self-castration, which is ironically intensified when in desperation he threatens Sally with his gun. It is no wonder that Luke is the one who disarms him, in accordance with the repeated textual symbolism of the film. The military context of receiving a medal for valor, that is, earning a phallus, expands the gap Bob feels between his defeated and wounded masculinity and the phantasmatic warrior masculinity he yearns for.

The subversive textuality of *Coming Home* is thus related to representation of an alternative sexuality; presentation of Sally's caring labor; the collapse of Bob's traditional, militaristic, and patriarchal masculinity; and the connection between bodily order continually given new meaning and Luke's struggle over resymbolization of the political order. Luke's politicization does not serve as a phallic substitute for the absence of sexuality as a means of rehabilitation, as we will see in *Born on the 4th of July*, and in this sense he is not a social father. In the social order presented in *Coming Home*, Billy's suicide in the hospital reconfirms the failure of the fraternal, and Bob's suicide the failure of the father figure. Thus, the film presents the new bodily order of the disabled impotent veteran and his partner as a radical corporeal alternative.[10]

---

10 Michel describes Luke's explicit sexuality and his use of oral sex as an alternative, but she overlooks the subversive nature of the film in relation to phallocentric ideology. Selig's analysis, in my view, is a limited perspective of the developmental potential of both Sally and Luke; see also Anderegg ("Hollywood") who claimed that although Fonda's character changes in *Coming Home*, eventually the political is re-

III. From the Abjected to the Symbolic Body: *Born on the 4th of July*

Born on the 4th of July (Oliver Stone, 1989).

In 1967, Ron Kovic, raised in 1950s small-town America, is encouraged by his mother to volunteer for service in Vietnam. During the chaos of battle he kills a comrade, Wilson, and his commanding officer denies the importance of the event and refuses to pursue it. In 1968, Ron is in the hospital coping with the reality of being paraplegic. At the University of Syracuse he meets his old girlfriend Darla (Kyra Sedgwick), an anti-war activist. At home, his mother cannot put up with his emasculated presence, and he leaves for Mexico. There, in the company of other disabled veterans, he clashes with Charlie (Willem Dafoe) and tries to have sex with a prostitute. When he returns to the US, he confesses to Wilson's family and is forgiven by Wilson's mother. He protests against the war during the 1972 Republican Party Convention and is expelled from the convention floor, only to return as the leader of a group of disabled soldiers who shout, "We are your 'Yankee Doodle Dandy!'" At the 1976 Democratic Party Convention he autographs copies of his book and prepares to speak to the convention.

Ron's defeated masculinity is based on transition between the fraternal structure (killing Wilson, wheelchair "duel" with Charlie in Mexico, and fraternity of the anti-war movement) and the maternal structure (his mother's ambivalent function as "blood seeker\milk giver" [Burgoyne, "National Identity"], the prostitute in Mexico, and Wilson's wife and mother). What is the meaning of transition between the anti-oedipal extreme that includes a negative father (the commanding officer), fratricide (in war), and brotherhood based on loss and guilt (in Mexico); and, at the other extreme, maternal ambivalence?

Ron is presented here as having tried to gain the phallus through war, but the familial pattern is tragically repeated (with his impotence presented as a continuation of his mother's symbolic emasculation of his father). When he returns from Vietnam his mother, the "blood seeker" who sent him off to war "against Communism and with God's will," is unable to forgive him for his failure and his impotence. In the heat of an

---

duced to the personal (20-21); in this respect, the film is a reminder and an opportunistic reinterpretation of Fonda's trip to Hanoi in 1972. In my view, Fonda's media persona served against her in regard to interpretations of the film. For attacks on Fonda see Jean-Luc Godard and Jean-Pierre Gorin's film *Letter to Jane* (1972) as well as MacCabe (49-76) and Slater.

argument, he rips out his catheter, for him a symbol of his invisible penis and loss, and her diverted look expresses her rejection of him.[11]

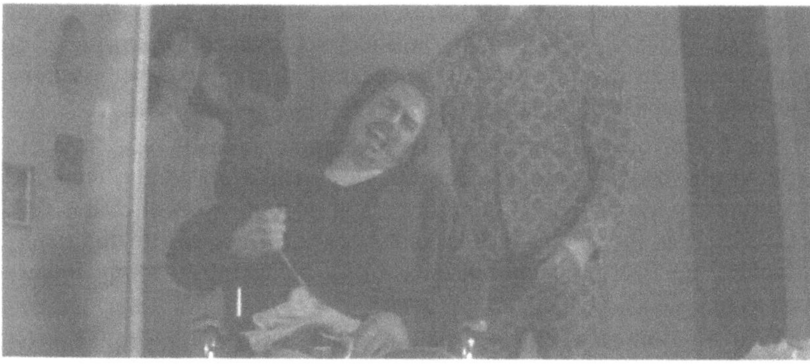

Visualizing the abject, *Born on the 4th of July*

In this scene, probably the most important in terms of visualization of the abject, the spectator is forced to face the abject (signified by the catheter). In this physical context, the horror results from the abject being not temporary, but a permanent fixture. As Ron's rehabilitation becomes more dominant in the film, the abjectiveness of his body becomes increasingly hidden until it becomes nonexistent.

11 THE MOTHER. I didn't force you to go!
RON. Yes you did force me! Yes! But it was for nothing […] (cries and shouts) only I am in this damn wheelchair for the rest of my life. For nothing. I am […] this […] penis (pulls out the catheter and waves it around)
THE MOTHER. My God! Not with the catheter!
RON. This dead penis!
THE MOTHER. I can't take this anymore.
RON. […] the church says it is sinful to play with your penis. I wish I could.
THE MOTHER. Never say "penis" in this house!
RON. Penis!
THE MOTHER. Enough!
RON. Penis! Big, fucking, erect penis, Mom!
THE MOTHER. Enough! Enough!
RON. Penis! Penis!
THE MOTHER. My god he won't stop, what can I do?
RON. I didn't have a chance to learn how to use it. Lost it in the jungle […] in the shitty jungle in Asia […]
The mother covers her face with her hands and cries.
RON. I'm really sorry that you are sad, Mom.

In contrast to the hyper-masculine and homoerotic masculinities that do not undergo external transformation,[12] impotent masculinity is constructed through the transition from symbolic body to abjected body. This transition creates a gap that is filled, as noted, either by sexual radicalism (*Coming Home*) or by political activism (*Born on the 4th of July*). These narrative processes are necessary to eliminate the transitory state, which lacks corporeal affiliation with the symbolic order.

The horror of *Born on the 4th of July* is also intensified because the male virgin body[13] remains so even after Ron's encounter with the prostitute in Mexico and, therefore, is based on objectification that preserves it as the "body in bits and pieces." In contrast to the latter, however, the film prevents any possibility of an intact bodily image, such as that depicted in *Coming Home*.

Transition between the fraternal and maternal structures takes place in the psycho-geographic split dividing Vietnam from America, but perhaps even more, in that dividing Mexico from the US. On one hand, the Mexican space as the alternative home for disabled Vietnam veterans rejected by American society stands in contrast to its role in the Mexican Western genre popular from 1965 to 1968, in which Mexico becomes what Slotkin describes in *Gunfighter Nation* as the symbolic, violent space of Vietnam. On the other hand, this space possesses mythic connotations that allow Ron to begin his rehabilitation through political activism.

Impotent masculinity displaces the weapon of the Hunter to the wheelchair, which in *Coming Home* becomes a subversive instrument. For Ron it becomes an extension of the self, in the sense of the objectification described earlier. Because of Ron's loss of sexuality, textual rehabilitation provides a multi-layered response to issues facing the male subject: he is rewarded with fraternity (anti-war movement) and a leadership role (Democratic Party Convention) and, consequently, his abjected body is transformed into the symbolic body. Forgiveness by Wilson's mother helps him realize the vision his mother had of him when he was a small boy, which although does not resolve the maternal ambiguity, serves as his redemption and that of his blood-seeking mother. The verbal mythicization "We're your 'Yankee Doodle Dandy,'" which connects two historical periods, is replaced with the rehabilitation process in which the dominance of the mother nation is renewed for the emasculated social father.

---

12 In contrast to cinematic monsters in, for example, horror films (Creed), Rambo does not undergo any physical transformation, rather is presented from the beginning as having possessing Frankenstein-like physicality.

13 The "innocent male virgin body," according to Theweleit ("Bomb's Wound" 285).

IV. Adaptation – Subversion

Ivan Passer's *Cutter's Way* does not allow rehabilitation – whether radical or conservative – of the impotent disabled veteran. Cutter's rage at his disability turns him into an "obsessive avenger" (Norden), but is of no avail. In contrast, Steven (*The Deer Hunter*), Luke (*Coming Home*), and Ron (*Born on the 4th of July*) adapt to the post-war order. In the latter two films, impotent masculinity describes how the protagonists adapt to various tensions: between the upper and lower bodies; between the symbolic and the abjected body; between objectification and radicalization of the bodies; between the permanent symbolization of the phallus and its transferability; between the loss of sexuality and its return; between the "milk giver" and the "blood seeker"; between historical and the individualized bodies; and between the guilty and the politicized bodies. These transitions were more radical in 1978 than they were in 1989, though in both films subversiveness is all-encompassing: the defeat is manifest on the broken bodies of the protagonists in the overt text and the status of the phallus as a hegemonic transferable signifier is discussed beyond the strategies of the subtext. As such, these films undermine the foundations of hegemonic masculinity and the patriarchal order.

It is interesting to note that *Forrest Gump*, made nearly twenty years after the end of the war, is different than these earlier representations in that it presents two protagonists with broken bodies. One, Forrest, handicapped from childhood, is paradoxically given the opportunity to realize his unusual physical capabilities during the war, while the other, Lt. Dan, an atypical war hero who was not involved in war crimes, undergoes complete rehabilitation after the war.[14] His rehabilitation is illustrated by the numerous scenes in which the camera focuses on his amputated legs but later shows his prosthesis during Forrest and Jenny's wedding ceremony. Moreover, the appearance of his fiancé, clearly of Asian origin, hints that he has reconciled with the past. Forrest relates to him as a father figure, a reversal in their power relationship that nevertheless preserves the fraternal and patriarchal orders without conflict between them. Thus, it appears that Dan embodies the relationship that existed between the male subject and the social order prior to the war.

---

14 See the Epilogue in which there is a short discussion of post-traumatic masculinity in films of the 1990s as part of the syndrome of the noble American male. See Magid and Parisi for discussions on the effects used to create Dan's disabilities. In contrast, for example, in the best tradition of Neorealism the director William Wyler gave the role of Homer, the handless soldier in *The Best Years of Our Lives* (1946), to the disabled veteran Harold Russell, who was not a professional actor.

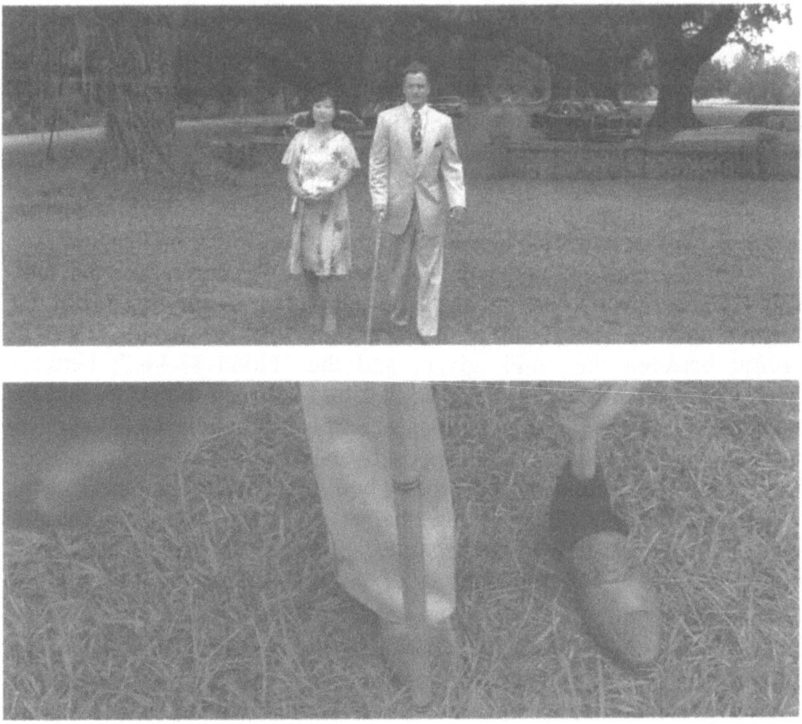

Rehabilitation of the rescued father, Lt. Dan in *Forrest Gump*

CHAPTER 10

Post-Traumatic Vietnam War Cinema Models

Why does canonic American Vietnam War Cinema differentiate between three distinct types of masculinity? After all, the models share prominent elements, such as the failure of the symbolic patriarchic and fraternal orders, patricide/fratricide, demasculinization, inability to represent the symbolic order, ahistoricity, split, mythicization, phantasmatization, and the tortured/abjected body.

The wide majority of the films are indeed affiliated with the Asexual Hyper-Masculine Model, evidence of a great need, lasting almost thirty years, to repress the defeat and create a counter image to it. This model also meets the needs of popular cinema to construct heroes, structure audience identification, and avoid questions of morality. It does so by using the centrality of the Hunter as the textual solution to the tension between depicting the protagonist as a hero (in the text) and recognition that, historically, he was defeated (in the subtext). The Asexual Hyper-Masculine Model therefore expresses the most extreme forms of denial – historical and moral.

Beneath the surface of Vietnam War films, however, are subversive forces that hinder all of the protagonists from becoming supermen in Vietnam (Quart)[1] The subversive construction of the desubjectivization processes of defeated masculinity in the three models exists in unrelenting tension with elements of denial. Exposing gender and sexuality is in conflict with narrative/dramatic/stylistic denial strategies, which have at their core mythicization that provides a broad historical canvas, a sym-

---

1 Quart claims, "The superman was an American soldier or officer who lived beyond conventional values, projecting an aura of almost superhuman courage and power and personal invulnerability" (159). In his analysis of *The Deer Hunter*, he described Michael as "a man-warrior committed to a code built on loyalty and Hemingway's notion of grace under pressure" (161). He interprets the one shot hunt as evidence of "purity of purpose" (160). The author does criticize the film because it "lacked just that historical and social imagination that would have allowed it to go beyond the superman conceit and evoke the political heart of Vietnam" (167). However, in my view, this is not a matter of "imagination" but rather the reality of the defeat and its influence on depiction on the protagonist. These references are representative, as I have claimed, of all the relevant academic research.

bolic system, and identity thematics. Despite the emphasis placed in the Hyper-Masculine and Homoerotic Models on heroism through mythicization of the Native American; the drama of rescue; construction of a chaotic context; rehabilitation processes; and textual strategies like imposed victorious closures, the subtexts of the films reveal that the protagonist is actually defeated. The two models that discuss moral issues, the Homoerotic and the Impotent, present an ambivalent morality and/or one that is irresolvable, as well as male identity that is clearly unstable.[2]

As presented in all three models, loss of masculinity does not require regeneration through violence. The symbolic order cannot be recouped when the characters that traditionally represent it lack the capability of representation; when violence negates intergenerational continuity and/ or brotherhood; when masculinity has no unified identity besides the compulsive reenactment of trauma; or when it is ahistorical. Imposed performances (victorious imperialism, national identity, brothers in arms, laws of the symbolic order, oedipalization, phallicization, heterosexuality) collapse, and therefore, redemption through a relationship with a woman, politicization, reenlistment, and brotherhood lead not to regeneration, but to decline.[3]

The canonic films mix power, intactness, activism, voyeurism, sadism, and fetishism with marginality, absence, passivity, exhibitionism, masochism, narcissism, and spectacle. They are rife with tension between these characteristics of masculinity, and create, as I have shown, novel ones. The latter are, on one hand, a result of a feminist reading of the films, which still relate, thirty-two years after Mulvey, to the "contemporary sexual regimes" (Butler, *Bodies that Matter* 85) and definitions that developed, as we know, from the psychoanalytic-phallocentric approach. On the other hand, it is apparent that markedly subversive feminist critique relating to women's sexuality, like that of Irigaray, limits the conceptualization of masculinity, and as such does not contribute to broadening the discourse. Markedly subversive feminist critique relating to male marginality, like that of Kaja Silverman in *Male*

2 Many veterans depicted in films that are not post-traumatic still present the desubjectivization of unstable, subversive masculinity. For example, Nick (William Hurt) in *The Big Chill* is a drug addict, unemployed, detached from life, with strong feelings of failure since his return from Vietnam; Stanley White (Mickey Rourke) in *Year of the Dragon* is a policeman who sees Chinatown as if it were Vietnam until his life is destroyed; or the paranoid-hysterical Walter (John Goodman) in *The Big Lebowski* (Cohen brothers, 1998).

3 The few films that either present a victorious story of battle, for example, *Hamburger Hill*; or are not considered canonic like *Go Tell the Spartans*; *Twilight's Last Gleaming*, and *Off Limits* are not exceptions to this rule.

Subjectivity at the Margins, is limited because her Lacanian analysis unavoidably lacks historical context. In contrast, by finally approaching defeat through the perspective of trauma, this book questions the place of basic definitions such as the symbolic order, phallicization, and the substance of powerless male subjectivity in historical context.

Such trauma discourse consequently contributes both to the understanding of this corpus and to expanding the Freudian-Lacanian conceptualization into specific historical context. This is exemplified by Di Piero's analysis of male hysteria, which he claims is a necessary element in the definition of masculinity, along with castration and the phallus. Since the patriarch is actually a phantom, an imaginary being, an ideal representation that sons create, à la Freud's *Totem and Taboo*, the male subject is not able to identify with it. Like the father who died in *Totem and Taboo*, the patriarch is beyond the symbolic order. The male subject must identify, paradoxically, with his actual father (at the expense of symbiotic relations with the mother) as well as with the patriarchal image. As a result, the continuous movement between genders creates hysteria; that is, the male subject is unable to identify with any of the culturally constructed genders. In my opinion, although Di Piero's analysis is replete with depoliticization of gender, it does bring into focus the phantasmatic qualities of the symbolic order and patriarchy. As claimed earlier, traditional sources of identification, like the father figure, were revealed to be without substance in the Vietnam War, making it impossible to idealize the phantom, as it too had been emptied of all content. Thus, it is not surprising that these post-traumatic films do not elegize or mourn the death of the father.

The logical conclusion is that the turmoil that trauma creates for the male subject is more grounded in the "mask" of hegemonic masculinity than described earlier. Following Di Piero's analysis, I claim that there is no greater anxiety for the male in war than the transformation that takes place when a woman is no longer the habitual, meaningful other, but rather the enemy; that is, another male. Any war damages relations with the other; but the threat to such relations (existing beneath the surface) becomes even more extreme in the case of a war without victory over the unfamiliar other. Further, post-traumatic cinema, which denied and repressed defeat, had no alternative but to confront the defeated soldier with a faceless, subjectless enemy. In my opinion this is a reaction to the trauma of the loss of American male substance rather than only a case of imperialistic-racist conceptions: it is impossible to have a soldier lacking identity confront an enemy with one.

Clearly, the diverse conceptualizations of masculinity developed in research carried out during recent decades indicate that masculinity is far more complex than assumed in feminist theory and masculinity studies. By definition, post-trauma includes mediation between the psychological and the historical and thus enables a connection between cultural-psychoanalytic concepts (attacked for being monolithic, universal, and depoliticized) and clearly historical context. Masculinity, in American Vietnam War cinema then, is a mediator defined by the effects of the connection between the psychological and the historical.

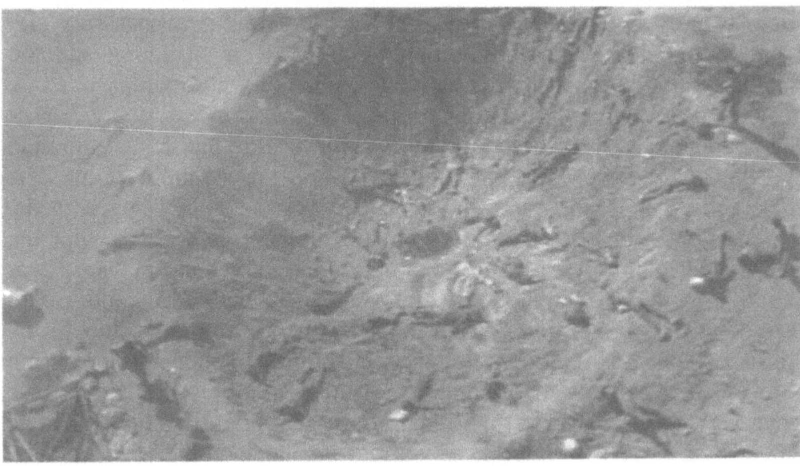

Imposed victorious closure, *Platoon*

Conclusion

I. A Special Truth

Foster writes,

> [A] special truth seems to reside in traumatic or abject states, in diseased or damaged bodies. To be sure, the violated body is often the evidentiary basis of important witnessing to truth, of necessary testimonials against power. ("Obscene" 123).

Adopting trauma discourse in cinema research indeed reveals a special truth that has been repressed in the overt, explicit, text of post-traumatic New German Cinema after World War II and American post-traumatic cinema in the aftermath of the Vietnam War, as well as in cinematic research dealing with the two. The essential claim is that in these two canonic cinemas the experience of the trauma of defeat is very similar – despite the fact that they are the product of two different historical periods, two different societies, two different wars, and two different cinematic cultures and industries. Engaging in an asymmetrical comparative study has proven that trauma is an organizing principle that intersects all the above differences; and moreover, that the collective unconscious that has undergone trauma is more dominant in the final product than any of these factors.[1] The post-traumatic subject is characterized first and foremost by the defeat, which is vastly more dominant than other characteristics, such as class or ethnicity.

The following criteria were compared in order to examine non-hegemonic defeated masculinity: the capacity of masculinity to represent the symbolic order; oedipalization; fraternal relations; sexuality including maturity, phallicization, and sexual relations; couplehood; existence of the family unit; intergenerational continuity; the body; the gaze; performance; the use of language; and the I-other relationship. Though each corpus requires a different mode of analysis, comparing the two showed that in both the features of the criteria were similar, and in most cases even identical. Post-traumatic masculinity in both corpora is defined by its inability to represent the symbolic order and lack of recognition of the Name of the Father; anti-oedipalization; anti-fraternal

1 For the advantage of comparison in comparative historical research, see Kocka and Lorenz.

structures; asexual or perverted sexuality; loss of all couplehood; destruction of the family unit; disruption of intergenerational continuity; the schizoid, convoluted, tortured body; negation of the gaze, of the look, the subjective point of view, and eye contact; passivity; counter-language (silence, injurious or regressive language); and radical change in the I-other dialectic.

II. Trauma and History

The realization that in both corpora the subtext undermines the text brings into question the validity of paradigms dominant in the relevant research. As a result, the "inability to mourn" paradigm of NGC is negated, as is the "regeneration through violence" paradigm of American cinema. That is, in both cases, trauma, as analyzed in this work, reveals radical opposition to the historical past. In both cases the prominent strategies – rupturing of the traditional affiliations of masculinity, demasculinization, incoherence at the gendered core of (masculine) identity – undermine the direct link between masculinity, heteronormativity, patriarchalism, and nationalism.

This work claims that there is an inevitable and immanent split between historical and traumatic representation of trauma that has distinctive textual outcomes: First, though historical trauma has no meaning without the historical events that created it, these events do not dominate the cinematic representation of the trauma; that is, the first actualization of the traumatic experience – the post-traumatic film – is subjugated to the processes of reenactment of the trauma and not to referential reliability. The original areferentialization destroys the attempt for referentiality through absence that is perceived as presence. A film that lacks any concrete traces of the historical event that originated the trauma will adhere to a more fully and reliably traumatic representation, and vice versa.

Second, post-traumatic films break the repression of the historical trauma through their subtexts. Post-traumatic imagery symbolizing the defeat in the two wars presents the trauma in the subtext by stripping the images of historical context. Instead, it structures a counter-history through post-traumatic corporeal images of the male body and sexuality.

Third, the spectator must contend with tensions between text and subtext, repression and breaking the repression, and trauma and historical context. S/he must recognize the trauma and possess extra textual knowledge of its historical context. In other words, the spectator is involved in a process that begins with loss of the (historical) referent because of the trauma, creates a new delayed (traumatic) referent, and ends with the recontextualization of the original historical event.[2]

Fourth, these tensions, including the inherent duality of the absence of the cinematic signifier, limit the spectator to hermeneutic interpretation in which symbolization becomes prominent. The symbol functions as one of the possible substitutes for the assimilation of the traumatic event. On one hand, it preserves the permanent distance that characterizes the representation of trauma; that is, it preserves the absence, the unrepresentable; on the other hand, it fills this gap through its inherent meaningfulness.

III. Post-Trauma and Gender

Does trauma discourse construct a close and inevitable connection with gender? Can gender be considered an analytic category when dealing with trauma discourse? We should deal with these crucial questions by first analyzing the metaphorization of these two concepts. According to Laplanche and Pontalis,

> In adopting the term [trauma], psycho-analysis carries the three ideas implicit in it over on to the psychical level: the idea of a violent shock, the idea of a wound and the idea of consequences affecting the whole organization. (465-466).

Both Hacking and Young discuss how the concept of trauma has changed from relating to the body to relating to the mind. According to Hacking, the original meaning of the word – from the Greek for wound, cut, or break – has long been forgotten, and what he calls the "transfer" between the two meanings, which took place at the metaphoric level, in time led to the death of the metaphor. According to Young, the accepted explanation that the two meanings of trauma are connected by analogy does not suffice. He believes the question should be "what actually was transferred?" (89) because the answer to this question determines how we understand the unique form of memory that is derived from psychogenic trauma.[3] In my opinion, the question should really be which power

---

2 See LaCapra's *Writing History* on contextual reductionism (181-220).
Obsessive transformation of the trauma from absent to present through repetitiveness and the continuous undermining of its presence by death-driven repetitiveness construct trauma discourse as the polar opposite of disaster-apocalyptic discourse. The latter is clearly representable and dependent on linear rather than vague temporality. By definition, it does not need to be stripped of context.

3 According to Young's claim, the first transfer was between types of physical mechanisms (surgical shock and neural shock) and not between different types of events (physical trauma and mental trauma). In addition, he claims that the historical relation between the physical mechanisms is genealogical and not analogical (89). If

mechanism is served by the transfer, which I answer by saying that the transfer serves to repress the trauma. Though as Hacking claims, the conventional meaning of trauma does not refer to a physical wound, this meaning is still relevant when speaking of mental trauma. The change in meaning conceals the tracks of the physical wound and enables the trauma to become invisible; consequently, it is possible to deny its existence. In my view, the power mechanism at work in this case is Herman's episodic amnesia (*Trauma and Recovery*). The transfer preserves the cultural binarism between the body and the mind by giving prominence to the mind at the expense of the body. In other words, if psychoanalysis had not adopted the concept of trauma and its implications, and if over the years the use of the metaphor had not led to its death, it would not have become possible to conceal trauma. The mechanisms of psychoanalysis and language, in this case, release the perpetrator from his deed. According to this hypothesis, Freud's early discussion of the etiology of neurosis included the concealment of the trauma even before he revised his conclusions regarding Dora's case. From the perspective of social power relations as they are represented by psychoanalysis and language, it is clear that transfer from the body to the mind enables concealment and repression of the trauma, consequently preserving the social body.

As indicated in the Introduction and throughout this book, Butler brought about a dramatic change when she challenged the distinction between gender and sex. If we extend the line of argument discussed above, she created a "transfer" between gender and sex. As a result of analogy, however, one is not concealing the other, but both are embedded in cultural construction, that is, they signify the mind and the body together. In relation to trauma and gender, the social power mechanism (concealing\repression and compulsive heterosexuality) makes a cultural distinction between the body and the mind. In both cases, the connection between the two is revealed to be a radical reaction against the powerful mechanism of social concealment that reveals the strength and extent of the trauma; and the strength and extent of non-binary, non heteronormative sexuality.

In light of the above, does trauma discourse indeed construct a close and inevitable connection with gender? Is the belated experience of trauma principally described through gender? My analysis of post-

---

speaking of an analogical connection, then in his opinion, a unique type of traumatic memory is created, one that includes images, feelings, sensations, and words that are in the psychological domain. If speaking of a genealogical connection, the result is an additional, less complex type of memory lodged in neuroanatomical, physiological, and developmental history.

traumatic cinema demonstrates that trauma can be described only through its (em)bodiment, as its symptoms are inscribed repeatedly upon the body. The correlation between trauma and gender leads to re-examination of other options: repression of the physical dimension of trauma is compensated by the link between gender and sex in the representation of trauma.

IV. The Spectator as the Moral Other

Because of the nature of the representation of trauma in post-traumatic cinema, the spectator is not the traumatized subject; rather, the subtexts demand that s/he become the moral other of the film texts. In contrast to the strong tension between the texts and the subtexts, the moral perspective provides him/her with a stable and coherent subject position. There is, however, a difference in what is demanded of the spectator in each of the two corpora: In NGC, s/he participates in the symbolic processes related to subversion of the Hitlerian trope of the son and undermining melancholia. This is the stronger demand because it is aimed not only at first generation Germany, but also at the third generation. In this sense, NGC is bi-directional. Addressing the past, NGC subverts first generation identification with Hitler, as I described in my analysis of the canonic films of the prominent directors. In addressing the future, NGC, as a part of the second generation, makes an addition demand from members of the third generation, which make up a portion of its German audience: its destructive stance toward couplehood and the family demands that the third generation take a sober look at its role in history and its place in society. The responsibility of NGC for transferring the trauma to future generations is revealed in its structuring the subject position of the third generation; that is, in its depiction of children.

In American Vietnam War cinema, spectator participation in the representational process of trauma is related to its imagery and to the imposed victorious closures of the films. Because they are members of the first generation, the directors who produced Vietnam War films, as mentioned previously, are fundamentally different from the German directors. It is clear that the way they experience the trauma of defeat is different, and therefore, so is their structuring of the trauma. The symbolic processes are only intergenerational when they refer in a mythical manner to the Native American. In most cases, the spectator is subject to the burden of the unconscious of the cinematic industry, which has a long history of collaboration with the patriotic tendencies that strive for victory. The "happy end," the result of this collaboration, again and again demands the spectator understand the textual gaps. Here also, because of the subtext, identification processes become part of the subject position of the moral other.

V. Six Models of Post-Traumatic Cinema

Post-traumatic cinema is characterized by its emergence after a latency period; the double absence of the cinematic signifier; subversion of the text (repression) by the subtext (breaking the repression); dual repetitiveness in the continuous production of films and the repetitive nature of the film texts; inherent ahistoricity; absence of the other (the other's presence as victor is expressed only in the collapse of the I); change in the relationship between the I and the other; construction of morality; demand on the spectator to become the moral other; the shattering of the war myth; and gender construction as an essential mechanism for undermining repression of the trauma of defeat – non-hegemonic demasculinized masculinity that symbolically carries with it ideological and political implications.

This book has described six models of masculinity: In NGC we find the Infantile Asexual, the Utopian Bisexual and the Transsexual; in American Vietnam War cinema we find the Asexual Hyper-Masculine, the Homoerotic, and the Impotent. Despite the differences between them, the models are grounded in the same characteristics delineated above; their similarities, however, extend beyond how masculinity is depicted in each of the two corpora. Asexuality is seen both in the Infantile and Hyper-Masculine Models and is the most common representation of masculinity in both cinematic cultures. Two other options of sexuality are represented, though they are much less common in the corpora: fraternal sexuality, as seen in the Utopian Bisexual and Homoerotic Models, and the loss of sexuality, as seen in the Transsexual and Impotent models. This suggests that sexuality is the focus of post-traumatic masculinity, overcomes cross-cultural differences, and gives meaning to the trauma; the materialization of the body becomes central to the discourse. According to Foucault (*Discipline and Punish*), the hysterization of the female body is a result of male power mechanisms analyzing, characterizing, and rejecting the female body as being entirely sexual. In my opinion, the hysterization of the male body is a result of these same male power mechanisms; however, in contrast to the former, it involves both denial and resexualization.

VI. Unresolved Issues

Consequent to the analysis of the two corpora, I would like to mention an important phenomenon that gradually began to emerge from the late 1980s: the syndrome of the noble male in American and German cinema, bringing to the fore the possibility that a new stage in the repression of trauma is unfolding. This evolution is intensified by the fading away of NGC since Fassbinder's death as part of the rebirth of current German cinema. It can be seen, for example, in the appearance of the American defeat in Vietnam in films about the Gulf Wars (*Jarhead* [Sam Mendes, 2005]).

Examples among NGC films are *Aimée and Jaguar* (Max Färberböck, 1999), though actually, Michael Verhoeven's *White Rose* (1982) was a portent of this trend, which he continued in *Nasty Girl* (1989), *My Mother's Courage* (1996), and even in his 2006 documentary debut *The Unknown Soldier*.[4] Examples of such American films are *Forrest Gump*, *The War*, Capt. Koons-"Nick's" (Christopher Walken) reappearance in *Pulp Fiction* (Quentin Tarantino, 1994),[5] *We Were Soldiers* (Randall Wallace, 2000), and *The Quiet American* (Phillip Noyce, 2002). What makes this phenomenon critical is that most of these films are based on actual historical events.[6]

Does the construction of the syndrome of the noble male prevent other historical representations? Does it suppress the majority in favor of an unusually small minority? Even if the answer to these questions is not unequivocal, posing them enables us to focus on the contribution of cinema made during the 1970s and 1980s to the two cultures in terms of the presentation of the trauma of defeat and subversion of the social/national order. In this respect, it is clear that as the process of this repression in the two cultures becomes increasingly dominant, the radicalism of 1970s and 1980s German and American cinema becomes

4 The strong commitment of Verhoeven to the making of his films is also noticeable in his biography (his father, Paul Verhoeven, was an actor and director working in Nazi Germany), in his choice of topics for his films, as well as the aesthetics of alienation which characterize his work. In my conversations with him in 1997 and in 2006, the director told me about the funding and distribution difficulties confronting those who seek to make films about Germany's past. Even as he achieved success, he was named best director at the Berlin Festival for *Nasty Girl*, there has been strong, open opposition in Germany to dealing with the topic.

5 The casting of Christopher Walken is a post-modern reference to his casting in *The Deer Hunter*.

6 For instance, the discovery of an anti-Nazi student underground in the film *White Rose*, the story of Anja Rosmus in *Nasty Girl*; and the controversy regarding the *Wehrmacht* exhibition in Germany in 1995 in *The Unknown Soldier*; and the Valley of Death in *We Were Soldiers*.

more of an anomaly that did not lead to further confrontation with the past.

The comparison between the two cultures raises another question that I think is important, though it is beyond the scope of this book: Why was there no parallel to *Heimat* – a revisionist production frozen in the repression stage – produced in America? Despite their clear ideological revisionist stance, films such as *Rambo: First Blood* and *Rambo: First Blood Part II* expose the trauma of the defeat. Does *Heimat*'s enormous and ongoing popular success indicate that the German social structure is still vulnerable to contradictory trends in processing the historical trauma of the past? What would a discussion comparing the collective unconscious of the two cinematic cultures reveal?

Epilogue

Eugene Ionesco's 1954 play *Amédée, or How to Get Rid of It* describes the life of Amédée, a failed playwright, and his wife Madeleine, a switchboard operator who for the past fifteen years has never left the four walls of their small apartment. All this time, however, a corpse has continually grown in the bedroom until its huge feet burst through the door and into the living room. The end of the play shows Amédée's attempts to drag the corpse to the window. As he pushes it out, however, the powerful corpse pulls Amédée along with it and as it flies into the distance, Amédée is seen hanging on.

In contrast to the conventions of the theater of the absurd, in which the audience is presented no clear reason for the presence of the corpse, in post-traumatic cinema, as this book demonstrates, the corpse itself announces its presence, and reveals both the reasons for its being there and the cultural and cinematic processes involved. Moreover, the omnipresent feeling of guilt typical of Ionesco's world is not even dealt with in post-traumatic cinema. Nevertheless, Ionesco's ever-expanding corpse is a rich metaphor for the ambivalent proliferation of the traumatic event in both corpora after the latency period. Both NGC and American Vietnam War cinema have represented the corpse's threatening asexual but bedroom-inhabiting presence, one that – as *Amédée* makes clear – could easily have turned into an ultimate triumph over the subject, but did not.

The enormous psychocultural difficulties the survivor-perpetrator faces in conquering the threatening corpse – that is, acknowledging defeat – is revealed in indirect and intriguing ways. The radicalism of NGC, like that of American Vietnam War cinema, is actually tied to repression, concealment, and misrepresentation, but paradoxically, because the reality of trauma – somehow unlike Ionesco's tenant but like the poisonous mushrooms sprouting throughout the apartment – escaped accessibility, recognition, and representation, the truth of the trauma emerged. The conclusions of this study show almost absurdly that if there had been no latency period and no repression of the trauma, it would have been impossible to come to terms with it. As Walter Benjamin rightly argues in "On the Concept of History," history is clearly written by the victors, and trauma by the defeated.

Filmography

Aguirre, Wrath of God [*Aguirre, der Zorn Gottes*]. Dir. Werner Herzog, 1972.
Aimée and Jaguar. Dir. Max Färberböck, 1999.
Alice in the Cities [*Alice in den Städten*]. Dir. Wim Wenders, 1974.
All about My Mother [*Todo Sobre mi Madre*]. Dir. Pedro Almodóvar, 1999.
The American Friend [*Der amerikanische Freund*]. Dir. Wim Wenders, 1977.
The American Soldier [*Der Amerikkanische Soldat*]. Dir. R.W. Fassbinder, 1979.
Apocalypse Now. Dir. Francis Ford Coppola, 1979.
Baptism of Fire [Der Feuerteufel]. Dir. Luis Trenker, 1940.
Berlin Alexanderplatz. Dir. R.W. Fassbinder, 1980.
The Best Years of Our Lives. Dir. William Wyler, 1946.
The Big Chil. Dir. Lawrence Kasdan, 1983.
The Big Lebowski. Dir. Joel Cohen, 1998.
Birdy. Dir. Alan Parker, 1984.
The Bitter Tears of Petra von Kant [Die bitteren Tränen der Petra von Kant]. Dir. R.W. Fassbinder, 1972.
Born on the 4th of July. Dir. Oliver Stone, 1989.
Braddock: Missing in Action 3. Dir. Aaron Norris, 1988.
Buena Vista Social Club. Dir. Wim Wenders, 1999.
Burden of Dreams. Dir. Les Blank and Maureen Gosling, 1982.
Casualties of War. Dir. Brian De Palma, 1989.
Chinese Roulette [*Chinesisches Roulette*]. Dir. R. W. Fassbinder, 1976.
Coming Home. Dir. Hal Ashby, 1978.
Courage Under Fire. Dir. Edward Zwick, 1996.
Cutter's Way. Dir. Ivan Passer, 1981.
The Damned. Dir. Joseph Losey, 1963.
Das Boot. Dir. Wolfgang Petersen, 1981.
Bullet in the Head. [*Die xue jie tou*]. Dir. John Woo, 1990.
The Deer Hunter. Dir. Michael Cimino, 1978.
Despair [*Eine Reise ins Licht*]. Dir. R.W. Fassbinder, 1978.
The Downfall [*Der Untergang*]. Dir. Oliver Hirschbiegel, 2004.
Duel in the Sun. Dir. King Vidor, 1946.
Even Dwarfs Started Small [*Auch Zwereg haben klein angefangen*]. Dir. Werner Herzog, 1970.
Every Man for Himself and God Against All, or the Mystery of Kaspar Hauser [*Jeder für sich und Gott gegen alle*]. Dir. Werner Herzog, 1974.
Faraway, So Close [*In weiter Ferne, so nah!*]. Dir. Wim Wenders, 1993.

Fear Eats the Soul [*Angst essen Seele auf*]. Dir. R.W. Fassbinder, 1974.
A Few Good Men. Dir. Rob Reiner, 1992.
Fitzcarraldo. Dir. Werner Herzog, 1982.
Forrest Gump. Dir. Robert Zemeckis. 1994.
Four Hours in My Lai. Dir. Kevin Sim, 1989.
Fox and His Friends [*Faustrecht der Freiheit*]. Dir. R.W. Fassbinder, 1975.
Full Metal Jacket. Dir. Stanley Kubrick, 1987.
Gardens of Stone. Dir. Francis Ford Coppola, 1987.
Germany in Autumn [*Deutschland im Herbst*]. Dir. Alf Brustellin, Hans Peter Cloos, R.W. Fassbinder, Alexander Kluge, Beate Mainka-Jellinghaus, Edgar Reitz, Katja Rupé, Volker Schlöndorff, Peter Schubert and Bernhard Sinkel, 1977.
Germany, Pale Mother [*Deutschland, bleiche Mutter*]. Dir. Helma Sanders-Brahms, 1980.
Go Tell the Spartans. Dir. Ted Post, 1986.
Goalkeeper's Anxiety of the Penalty Kick [*Die Angst des Tormanns beim Elfmeter*]. Dir. Wim Wenders, 1972.
Good Guys Wear Black. Dir. Ted Post, 1978.
Good Morning, Vietnam. Dir. Barry Levinson, 1987.
The Green Berets. Dir. John Wayne, 1968.
Greystoke: The Legend of Tarzan, Lord of the Apes. Dir. Hugh Hudson, 1984.
Hamburger Hill. Dir. John Irwine, 1987.
Hammett. Dir. Wim Wenders, 1981.
Haunted Screen: German Film after WWI. Dir. Peter Buchka, 1998.
Heaven and Earth. Dir. Oliver Stone, 1993.
Heimat [*Heimat – Eine deutsche Chronik*]. Dir. Edgar Reitz, 1984.
The Second Heimat [*Zweite Heimat – Chronik einer Jugend, Die*]. Dir. Edgar Reitz, 1993.
Heimat 3 [*Heimat 3 – Chronik einer Zeitenwende*]. Dir. Edgar Reitz, 2004.
Hitler, A Career [*Hitler – eine Karriere*]. Dir. Joachim Fest and Christian Herrendoerfer, 1977.
The Holocaust. Dir. Marvin J. C. Chomsky, 1979.
I Only Want You to Love Me [*Ich will doch nur, daß ihr mich liebt*]. Dir. R.W. Fassbinder, 1976.
In a Year of Thirteen Moons [*In einem Jahr mit Dreizehn Monden*]. Dir. R. W. Fassbinder, 1978.
In Wide Field [*Canh dong hoang*]. Dir. Nguyen Hong Sen, 1981.
Jacknife. Dir. David Jones, 1989.
Jail Bait [*Wildwechsel*]. Dir. R.W. Fassbinder, 1973.
Jarhead. Dir. Sam Mendes, 2005.
Kaspar Hauser – Crimes Against the Inner Life of a Human Being [*Verbrechen am Seelenleben eines Menschens*]. Dir. Peter Sehr, 1993.
The Killing Fields. Dir. Roland Joffe, 1984.

Kings of the Road [Im Lauf der Zeit]. Dir. Wim Wenders, 1976.
Klaus Kinski, My Friend [*Mein Liebster Feind – Klaus Kinski*]. Dir. Werner Herzog, 1999.
The Last Metro [*Le Dernier métro*]. Dir. François Truffaut, 1980.
Last Words [*Letzte Worte*]. Dir. Werner Herzog, 1968.
Letter to Jane. Dir. Jean-Luc Godard and Jean-Pierre Gorin. 1972.
Life is Beautiful [*La Vita è bella*]. Dir. Roberto Benigni, 1997.
Lili Marleen. Dir. R.W. Fassbinder, 1981.
Lisbon Story. Dir. Wim Wenders, 1994.
The Little Girl from Hanoi [*Em be ha noi*]. Dir. Hay Ninh, 1973.
Lola. Dir. R. W. Fassbinder, 1981.
The Lost Honor of Katharina Blum [*Der verlorene Ehre der Katharina Blum*]. Dir. Volker Schlöndorff and Magarethe von Trotta, 1975.
The Lusty Men. Dir. Nicholas Ray, 1952.
*M*A*S*H*. Dir. Robert Altman, 1970.
Marianne and Juliane [*Die Bleierne Zeit*]. Dir. Magarethe von Trotta, 1981.
The Marriage of Maria Braun [*Die Ehe der Maria Braun*]. Dir. R.W. Fassbinder, 1978.
Martha. Dir. R. W. Fassbinder, 1974.
Mediterraneo. Dir. Gabriel Salvatores, 1992.
The Men. Dir. Fred Zinnemann, 1950.
The Merchant of Four Seasons [*Händler der vier Jahreszeiten*]. Dir. R.W. Fassbinder, 1972.
Million Dollar Hotel. Dir. Wim Wenders, 2000.
Missing in Action. Dir. Joseph Zito, 1984.
Missing in Action 2 – The Beginning. Dir. Lance Hool, 1985.
Mother Kuster's Trip to Heaven [*Mutter Küsters Fahrt zum Himmel*]. Dir. R.W. Fassbinder, 1975.
My Fassbinder, The One and Only: The Willing Victims of Reiner Werner F. [*Für mich gab's nur noch Fassbinder*]. Dir. Rosa von Praunheim, 2002.
My Mother's Courage [*Mutters Courage*]. Dir. Michael Verhoeven, 1996.
My Sweetheart Got Married [*Nguoi Yen Di Lay Chong*]. Dir. Vu Chau, 1994.
Nasty Girl [*Das Schreckliche Mädchen*]. Dir. Michael Verhoeven, 1989.
Nibelungen: Kriemhild's Revenge [*Die Nibelungen: Kriemhilds Rache*]. Dir. Fritz Lang, 1924.
Nibelungen: Siegfried's Death [*Die Nibelungen: Siegfrieds Tod*]. Dir. Fritz Lang, 1924.
Nick's Film – Lightning Over Water. Dir. Nicolas Ray and Wim Wenders, 1980.
Night of the Living Dead. Dir. George Romero, 1968.
The Night Porter [*Il Portiere di notte*]. Dir. Liliana Cavani, 1974.
Nosferatu. Dir. Werner Herzog, 1979.

A Notebook on Cities and Clothes [*Aufzeichnungen zu Kleidern und Städten*]. Dir. Wim Wenders, 1990.
Off Limits. Dir. Christopher Crowe, 1988.
Olympia. Dir. Leni Riefenstahl, 1936.
Our Hitler [*Hitler-Ein Film aus Deutschland*]. Dir. Jürgen Syberberg, 1975.
Paris is Burning. Dir. Jennie Livingston, 1990.
Paris, Texas. Dir. Wim Wenders, 1984.
Paths of Glory. Dir. Stanley Kubrick, 1957.
The Patriot [*Die Patriotin*]. Dir. Alexander Kluge, 1979.
Pinkville. Dir. Oliver Stone, 2008.
Platoon. Dir. Oliver Stone, 1986.
Psycho. Dir. Alfred Hitchcock. 1961.
Pulp Fiction. Dir. Quentin Tarantino, 1994.
The Quiet American. Dir. Phillip Noyce, 2002.
Rambo: First Blood. Dir. Ted Kotcheff, 1982.
Rambo: First Blood Part II. Dir. George P. Cosmatos, 1985.
Retired General [*Tuong ve huu*]. Dir. Nguyen Khac Loi, 1988.
The Return. Dir. Dang What Minh, 1983.
Rules of Engagement. Dir. William Friedkin, 2000.
Schindler's List. Dir. Steven Spielberg, 1993.
The Searchers. Dir. John Ford, 1956.
Signs of Life [*Lebenszeichen*]. Dir. Werner Herzog, 1968.
The Sinner [*Die Sünderin*]. Dir. Willi Forst, 1951.
Soap [*Soap, En*]. Dir. Pernille Fischer Christense, 2006.
Southern Comfort. Dir. Kate Davis, 2000.
Star Wars. Dir. George Lucas, 1977.
Star Wars: Episode V – The Empire Strikes Back. Dir. George Lucas, 1980.
Star Wars: Episode VI – Return of the Jedi. Dir. George Lucas, 1983.
Star Wars: Episode I: The Phantom Menace. Dir. George Lucas, 1999.
The State of Things [*Der Stand der Dinge*]. Dir. Wim Wender, 1982.
Streamers. Dir. Robert Altman, 1983.
Stroszek. Dir. Werner Herzog, 1977.
The Stunt Man. Dir. Richard Rush, 1980.
Taxi Driver. Dir. Martin Scorsese, 1976.
The Thin Red Line. Dir. Terrence Malick, 1998.
Three Kings. Dir. David O. Russell, 1999.
The Tin Drum [*Die Blechtrommel*]. Dir.Volker Schlöndorff, 1979.
Tokyo-Ga. Dir. Wim Wenders, 1985.
Tootsie. Dir. Sydney Pollack, 1982.
Transamerica. Dir. Duncan Tucker, 2005.
Triumph of the Will [*Triumph des Willens*]. Dir. Leni Riefenstahl, 1935.
Twilight's Last Gleaming. Dir. Robert Aldrich, 1977.

The Unknown Soldier [*Der Unbekannte Soldat*]. Dir. Michael Verhoeven, 2006.
Until the End of the World [*Bis ans Ende der Welt*]. Dir. Wim Wenders, 1991.
Veronika Voss [*Die Sehnsucht der Veronika Voss*]. Dir. R.W. Fassbinder, 1981.
The War of the Bombers. Writer: Jochen von Lang, 1985.
The War. Dir. Jon Avnet, 1994.
We Were Soldiers. Dir. Randall Wallace, 2000.
When the Tenth Month Comes [*Bao gio cho den thang muoi*]. Dir. Dang What Minh, 1984.
Where the Green Ants Dream [*Wo die grünen Ameisen träumen*]. Dir. Werner Herzog, 1984.
White Rose [*Die Weiße Rose*]. Dir. Michael Verhoeven, 1982.
Why does Herr R Run Amok? [*Warum läuft Herr R. Amok?*]. Dir. R.W. Fassbinder, 1970.
The Wild Child [*L'Enfant Sauvage*]. Dir. François Truffaut, 1969.
Wild Reed. Dir. Vuong Duc, 1983.
Wings of Desire [*Der Himmel über Berlin*]. Dir. Wim Wenders, 1987.
Woyzeck. Dir. Werner Herzog, 1978.
Wrong Movement [*Falsche Bewegung*]. Dir. Wim Wenders, 1974.
Year of the Dragon. Dir. Michael Cimino, 1985.
Yesterday Girl [*Abschied von Gestern*]. Dir. Alexander Kluge, 1966.
You're Never Too Young. Dir. Norman Taurog, 1955.

Bibliography

Adams, Rachel, and David Savran, eds. *The Masculinity Studies Reader.* Malden, MA: Blackwell, 2002.

Adorno, Theodor. "On the Question: 'What is German?'" *New German Critique* 36 (1985): 121-131.

Alter, Nora M. "Documentary as Simulacrum: *Tokyo-Ga*." *The Cinema of Wim Wenders Image, Narrative, and the Postmodern Condition*. Ed. Roger F. Cook, and Gerd Gemunden. Detroit, MI: Wayne State UP, 1997. 136-162.

American Psychiatric Association. *Diagnostic and Statistical Manual of Mental Disorders DSM-IV-TR*. 4th ed. text revision. Washington D.C. 424-429.

Anderegg, Michael, ed. "Hollywood and Vietnam: John Wayne and Jane Fonda as Discourse." *Inventing Vietnam: The War in Film and Television*. Philadelphia, PA: Temple UP, 1991. 15-32.

———— ed. *Inventing Vietnam: The War in Film and Television*. Philadelphia, PA: Temple UP, 1991.

Baudrillard, Jean. *America*. Trans. Chris Turner. London: Verso, 1988.

———— "L'Esprit du Terrorism." *The South Atlantic Quarterly* 101 (2002): 403-415.

———— *The Transparency of Evil*. Trans. James Benedict. London: Verso, 1995.

Baudry, Jean-Louis. "The Apparatus: Metapsychological Approaches to the Impression of Reality in Cinema." *Film Theory and Criticism*. Ed. Gerald Mast, Marshall Cohen, Leo Braudy. 4th ed. 1975. New York: Oxford UP, 1992. 690-707.

———— "Ideological Effects of the Basic Cinematographic Apparatus." *Film Theory and Criticism*. Ed. Gerald Mast, Marshall Cohen, Leo Braudy. 4th ed. New York: Oxford UP, 1992. 301-312.

Benelli, Dana. "The Cosmos and Its Discontents." *The Films of Werner Herzog: Between Mirage and History*. Ed. Timothy Corrigan. New York: Methuen, 1986. 89-104.

Benjamin, Walter. "On the Concept of History." *Selected Writings 1933-1940*. Vol. 4. Ed. Marcus Bullock, and Michael W. Jennings. 1940 Cambridge, MA: Belknap P of Harvard U, 2003. 391.

Berg, Rick, and John Carlos Rowe, eds. *The Vietnam War and American Culture*. New York: Columbia UP, 1991.

Billings, Dwight B., and Thomas Urban. "The Socio-Medical Construction of Transsexualism: An Interpretation and Critique." *Blending Genders: Social Aspects of Cross-Dressing and Sex-Changing*. Ed. Richard Ekins, and Dave King. London: Routledge, 1995. 99-117.

Bordo, Susan. "What Is a Phallus?" *The Male Body: A New Look at Men in Public and in Private*. New York: Farrar, 1999. 84-104.

Bowen, Kevin. "'Strange Hells': Hollywood in Search of America's Lost War." *From Hanoi to Hollywood: The Vietnam War in American Film*. Ed. Linda Dittmar, and Gene Michaud. New Brunswick, NJ: Rutgers UP, 1990. 226-235.

Brown, Laura S. "Not Outside the Range: One Feminist Perspective on Psychic Trauma." *Trauma Explorations in Memory*. Ed. Caruth Cathy. Baltimore, MD: Johns Hopkins UP, 1995. 100-112.

Broyles, William Jr. "Why Men Love War." *The Vietnam Reader*. Ed. Walter Capps. New York: Routledge, 1991. 68-81.

Burgoyne, Robert. *Film Nation: Hollywood Looks at U.S. History*. Minneapolis: U of Minnesota P, 1997.

———— "Narrative and Sexual Excess." *October* 21 (1982): 51-61.

———— "National Identity, Gender Identity, and the Rescue Fantasy in *Born on the Fourth of July*." *Screen* 35.3 (1994): 211-234.

Burke, Frank. "Reading Michael Cimino's *The Deer Hunter*: Interpretation as Melting Pot." *Literature\ Film Quarterly* 20.3 (1992): 249-259.

Butler, Judith. *Bodies That Matter: On the Discursive Limits of 'Sex.'* New York: Routledge, 1993.

———— *Excitable Speech: A Politics of the Performative*. New York: Routledge, 1997.

———— *Gender Trouble: Feminism and the Subversion of Identity*. New York: Routledge, 1990.

———— "Sexual Traffic." Gayle Rubin interviewed by Judith Butler. *Coming Out of Feminism?* Ed. Mandy Merk, Naomi Segal, and Elizabeth Wright. Oxford: Blackwell, 1998. 36-73.

Byg, Barton "German History and Cinematic Convention Harmonized in Margarethe von Trotta's *Marianne and Juliane*." *Gender and German Cinema: Feminist Interventions*. Ed. S. Frieden, R. McCormick, V., Petersen, and L. Vogelsang. Vol. 2. Oxford: Berg, 1993: 259-271.

Caruth, Cathy, ed. *Trauma Explorations in Memory*. Baltimore, MD: Johns Hopkins UP, 1995.

———— *Unclaimed Experience: Trauma, Narrative and History*. Baltimore, MD: Johns Hopkins UP, 1996.

Chomsky, Noam. "Visions of Righteousness." *The Vietnam War and American Culture*. Ed. Rick Berg, and John Carlos Rowe. New York: Columbia UP, 1991. 21-51.

Chong, Sylvia Shin Huey. "Restaging the War: The Deer Hunter and the Primal Scene of Violence." *Cinema Journal* 44.2 (2005): 89-106.

Chouliaraki, Lilie. "Watching 11 September: The Politics of Pity." *Discourse & Society* 15 (2-3) 2004: 185-198.

Clark, Michael. "Remembering Vietnam." *The Vietnam War and American Culture*. Ed. Rick Berg and John Carlos Rowe. New York: Columbia UP, 1991. 177-207.

Cleere, Elizabeth. "Three Films by Werner Herzog Seen in the Light of the Grotesque." *Wide Angle* 3.4 (1980): 12-19.

Coates, Paul. *The Gorgon's Gaze: German Cinema, Expressionism, and the Image of Horror*. Cambridge: Cambridge UP, 1991.

Cook, Pam, ed. "The Western." *The Cinema Book*. London: BFI, 1996. 64-72.

Cook, Roger F., and Gerd Gemunden, ed. *The Cinema of Wim Wenders: Image, Narrative, and the Postmodern Condition*. Detroit, MI: Wayne State UP, 1997.

———— "Angels, Fiction, and History in Berlin: *Wings of Desire of Wim Wenders*: *Image, Narrative, and the Postmodern Condition*. Ed. Roger F. Cook, and Gerd Gemunden. Detroit, MI: Wayne State UP, 1997. 163-190.

Cooke, Miriam. "Wo-Man Retelling the War Myth." *Gendering War Talk*. Ed. Miriam Cooke, and Angela Woollacott. Princeton, NJ: Princeton UP, 1993. 177-205.

———— "Postmodern Culture and Film Narrative: *Paris, Texas* and Beyond." *The Cinema of Wim Wenders*: *Image, Narrative, and the Postmodern Condition*. Ed. Roger F. Cook, and Gerd Gemunden. Detroit, MI: Wayne State UP, 1997. 121-135.

Cooper, James Fenimore. *The Deerslayer*. New York: Heritage, 1961.

Corrigan, Timothy. *A Cinema Without Walls: Movies and Culture After Vietnam*. New Brunswick, NJ: Rutgers UP, 1991.

———— ed. *The Films of Werner Herzog: Between Mirage and History*. New York: Methuen, 1986.

———— "German Friends and Narrative Murder: *Lightning over Water*." *The Cinema of Wim Wenders*: *Image, Narrative, and the Postmodern Condition*. Ed. Roger F. Cook, Gerd Gemunden. Detroit, MI: Wayne State UP, 1997. 110-120.

———— *New German Cinema: The Displaced Image*. Rev. ed. Bloomington: Indiana UP, 1994.

———— "The Original Tradition: 'Hypnotic Space in Herzog's *The Mystery of Kaspar Hauser*.'" *New German Film: The Displaced Image*. Rev. ed. Bloomington: Indiana UP, 1994. 19-32.

———— "Producing Herzog from a Body of Images." *The Films of Werner Herzog: Between Mirage and History*. Ed. Timothy Corrigan. New York: Methuen, 1986. 3-22.

———— "Transformations in Fassbinder's *Bitter Tears of Petra Von Kant*." *New German Film: The Displaced Image*. Rev. ed. Bloomington: Indiana UP, 1994. 33-52.

———— "Wenders' 'Kings of the Road': The Voyage from Desire to Language." *New German Film: The Displaced Image*. Rev. ed. Bloomington: Indiana UP, 1994. 19-32.

Creed, Barbara. "Dark Desires: Male Masochism in the Horror Film." *Screening the Male: Exploring Masculinities in Hollywood Cinema*. Ed. Steven Cohan, and Rae Ina Hark. London: Routledge, 1992: 118-133.

De Lauretis, Teresa. "Gender Symptoms, Or, Peeing Like a Man." *Social Semiotics* 92 (1999): 257-270.

Deleuze, Gilles. *Masochism: An Interpretation of Coldness and Cruelty*. Trans. Jean McNeil. New York: Braziller, 1971.

Di Piero, Thomas. "The Patriarch is Not (Just) a Man" (Responses to "Male Trouble"). *Camera Obscura* 25-26 (1991): 101-124.

Dittmar, Linda, Gene Michaud, eds. *From Hanoi to Hollywood: The Vietnam War in American Film*. New Brunswick, NJ: Rutgers UP, 1990.

Doane, Ann Mary. "The Voice in the Cinema: The Articulation of Body and Space." *Movies & Methods*. Ed. Bill Nichols. 2nd ed. Berkeley: U of California P, 1985. 565-576.

Doherty, Thomas. "Witness to War: Oliver Stone, Ron Kovic, and *Born on the Fourth of July*." *Inventing Vietnam The War in Film and Television*. Ed. Michael Anderegg. Philadelphia, PA: Temple UP, 1990. 251-268.

Doty, Alexander. "Queer Theory." *The Oxford Guide to Film Studies*. Ed. John Hill, and Gibson Church. Oxford: Oxford UP, 1998. 148-152.

Easthope, Antony. *What a Man's Gotta Do: The Masculine Myth in Popular Culture*. New York: Routledge, 1992.

Ekins, Richard, and Dave King. "The Medicalisation of Gender Blending: Introduction." *Blending Genders: Social Aspects of Cross-dressing and Sex-changing*. London: Routledge, 1996. 75-77.

Elsaesser, Thomas. "An Anthropologist's Eye: *Where the Green Ants Dream*." *The Films of Werner Herzog: Between Mirage and History*. Ed. Timothy Corrigan. New York: Methuen, 1986. 133-156.

——— *Fassbinder's Germany: History, Identity, Subject*. Amsterdam: Amsterdam UP, Amsterdam, 1996.

——— *New German Cinema: A History*. London: BFI, 1989.

——— "The New German Cinema's Historical Imaginary." *Framing the Past: The Historiography of German Cinema and Television*. Ed. B.A. Murray, and C.J. Wickham. Carbondale: Southern Illinois UP, 1992. 280-307.

——— "Spectators of Life: Time, Place, and Self in the Films of Wim Wenders." *The Cinema of Wim Wenders: Image, Narrative, and the Post-modern Condition*. Ed. Roger F. Cook, and Gemunden Gerd. Detroit, MI: Wayne State UP, 1997. 240-256.

——— "Subject Positions, Speaking Positions: From 'Holocaust,' 'Our Hitler,' and 'Heimat' to 'Shoah' and 'Schindler's List.'" *The Persistence of History Cinema, Television, and the Modern Event*. Ed. Vivian Sobchack. New York: Routledge, 1996. 145-183.

Esslin, Martin. "Jean Genet: A Hall of Mirrors." *The Theatre of the Absurd*. New York: Doubleday, 1969. 166-197.

Evans, Richard J. *In Hitler's Shadow: West German Historians and the Attempt to Escape from the Nazi Past*. New York: Pantheon, 1989.

Everly, George S. Jr. "Psychotraumatology." *Psychotraumatology: Key Papers and Core Concepts in Post-Traumatic Stress*. Ed. George S. Everly Jr., and Jeffrey M. Lating. New York: Plenum, 1995: 3-8.

Farrell, Kirby. *Post-Traumatic Culture: Injury and Interpretation in the Nineties*. Baltimore, MD: Johns Hopkins UP, 1998.

Fassbinder, Werner Reiner. "*In a Year of Thirteen Moons*." October 21 (1978 rep. 1982): 5-50.

———— "In a Year of Thirteen Moons." 1978 *The Anarchy of the Imagination: Interviews, Essays, Notes Rainer Werner Fassbinder*. Ed. Micheal Toteberg, and Leo A. Lensing. Trans. Krishna Winston. Baltimore, MD: Johns Hopkins UP, 1992. 177-195.

Fehrenbach, Heide. "*Die Sunderin* or Who Killed the German Male: Early Postwar German Cinema and Betrayal of Fatherland." *Gender and German Cinema: Feminist Interventions*. Ed. S. Frieden, R. McCormick, V. Petersen, and L. Vogelsang. Vol. 2. Oxford: Berg, 1993. 135-160.

———— "Rehabilitating Fatherland: Race and German Remasculinization." *Signs* 24.1 (1998): 107-128.

Felman, Shoshana. "Education and Crisis, or the Vicissitudes of Teaching." *Trauma Explorations in Memory*. Ed. Cathy Caruth Baltimore, MD: Johns Hopkins UP, 1995. 13-59.

Felman, Shoshana, and Dori Laub. *Testimony: Crises of Witnessing in Literature, Psychoanalysis and History*. New York: Routledge, 1992.

Foster, Hall. "Obscene, Abject, Traumatic." *October* 78 (1996): 103-124.

———— "Death in America." *October* 75 (1996): 37-58.

Foucault, Michelle. *Discipline and Punish: The Birth of the Prison*. Trans. Alan Sheridan. 2nd ed. New York: Vintage, 1995.

———— *The History of Sexuality*. Trans. Robert Hurley. New York: Vintage, 1980.

Franklin, James C. *New German Cinema: From Oberhausen to Hamburg*. Boston, MA: Twayne, 1980. 21-56.

Freud, Sigmund. "Beyond the Pleasure Principle." *The Standard Edition of the Complete Psychological Works of Sigmund Freud*. Trans. James Strachey, Anna Freud, Alix Strachey, and Alan Tyson. 1920. Vol. 18. London: Hogarth, 1953-1974.

———— "The Ego and the Id." *The Standard Edition of the Complete Psychological Works of Sigmund Freud*. Trans. James Strachey, and Anna Freud, Alix Strachey, and Alan Tyson. 1920. Vol. 19. London: Hogarth, 1953-1974.

———— *Totem and Taboo*. Trans. James Strachery. New York: Norton, 1950.

Friedlander, Saul. "Some German Struggles with Memory." *Bitburg in Moral and Political Perspective*. Ed. Geoffrey Hartman. Bloomington: Indiana UP, 1986. 27-42.

Fulbrook, Mary. "The Two Germanies: 1945-1990." *A Concise History of Germany*. Cambridge: Cambridge UP, 1992. 204-248.

Fusch, Cynthia J. "'Vietnam and Sexual Violence': The Movie." *America Rediscovered Critical Essays on Literature and Film of the Vietnam War*. Ed. Owen Gilman, and Lorrie Smith. London: Garland, 1990. 120-133.

Garber, Marjorie. "Spare Parts: The Surgical Construction of Gender." *Vested Interests: Cross-Dressing and Cultural Anxiety*. New York: Routledge, 1991. 93-117.

Gardiner Kegan, Judith. *Masculinity Studies and Feminist Theory: New Directions*. New York: Columbia UP, 2002.

Geist, Kathe. *The Cinema of Wim Wenders from Paris, France to Paris, Texas*. Ann Arbor, MI: UMI Research P, 1988.

———— "Mothers and Children in the Films of Wim Wenders." *Gender and German Cinema: Feminist Interventions*. Ed. S. Frieden, R. McCormick, V. Petersen, and L. Vogelsang. Vol. 1. Providence, RI: Berg, 1993. 11-22.

Gemunden, Gerd. "Oedi-pal Travels: Gender in the Cinema of Wim Wenders." *The Cinema of Wim Wenders: Image, Narrative, and the Postmodern Condition*. Ed. Roger F. Cook, and Gemunden Gerd. Detroit, MI: Wayne State UP, 1997. 205-221.

Genet, Jean. *The Balcony*. Trans. Bernard Frechtman. New York: Grove, 1978.

Geyer, Michael. "The Place of the Second World War in German Memory and History." *New German Critique* 71 (1997): 5-40.

Gibson, James William. *Warrior Dreams: Violence and Manhood in Post-Vietnam America*. New York: Hill and Wang, 1994.

Gilman, Owen, and Lorrie Smith, eds. *America Rediscovered: Critical Essays on Literature and Film of the Vietnam War*. New York: Garland, 1990.

Ginsberg, Elaine K., ed. "Introduction: The Politics of Passing." *Passing and the Fictions of Identity*. Duram, NC: Duke UP, 1996, 1-18.

Girard, Rene. "Generative Scapegoating." *Violent Origins*. Ed. Robert Hamerton-Kelly. Stanford, CA: Stanford UP, 1987. 73-105.

Grass, Günter. *The Tin Drum*. Trans. Ralph Manheim. New York : Pantheon, 1999.

Griggs, Claudine. "Mind, Body, and Attributed Gender." *S/he Changing Sex and Changing Clothes*. Oxford: Berg, 1998. 1-23.

Grob, Norbert. "'Life Sneaks Out of Stories': *Until the End of the World*." *The Cinema of Wim Wenders: Image, Narrative, and the Postmodern Condition*. Ed. Roger F. Cook, and Gerd Gemunden. Detroit, MI: Wayne State UP, 1997. 191-204.

Grosz, Elizabeth. *Volatile Bodies: Toward a Corporeal Feminism*. Sydney: Allen and Unwin, 1994.

Hacking, Ian. "Memory Sciences, Memory Politics." *Tense Past: Cultural Essays in Trauma and Memory*. Ed. Paul Antze, and Michael Lambek. New York: Routledge, 1996. 67-88.

Haines, Harry W. "'They Were Called and They Went': The Political Rehabilitation of the Vietnam Veteran." *From Hanoi to Hollywood: The Vietnam War in American Film*. Ed. Linda Dittmar, and Gene Michaud. New Brunswick, NJ: Rutgers UP, 1990. 81-97.

Hall, Carol. "A Different Drummer: *The Tin Drum*: Film and Novel." *Literature/Film Quarterly* 18.4 (1990): 236-244.

Hansen, Miriam. "Dossier on Heimat." *New German Critique* 36 (1985): 3-23.

Hansen, Miriam, and Andreas Huyssen. "Introduction." *New German Critique* 71 (1997): 3-4.

Hartman, H. Geoffrey. "Introduction: 1985." *Bitburg in Moral and Political Perspective*. Ed. Geoffrey H. Hartman. Bloomington: Indiana UP, 1986. 1-12.

Hatty, Suzanne E. *Masculinities, Violence, and Culture*. Thousand Oaks, CA: Sage, 2000.

Haug, W. Fritz. *Critique of Commodity Aesthetics*. Trans. R. Bock. Cambridge,: Polity, 1986. 13-56.

Hausman, Bernice L. "Semiotic of Sex, Gender, and the Body." *Changing Sex: Transsexualism, Technology, and the Idea of Gender*. Durham, NC: Duke UP, 1995. 175-194.

Hawkesworth, Mary. "Confounding Gender." *Signs* 22.3 (1997): 649-685.

Hellman, John. "Rambo's Vietnam and Kennedy's New Frontier." *Inventing Vietnam: The War in Film and Television*. Ed. Michael Anderegg. Philadelphia, PA: Temple UP, 1990. 140-152.

———— "Vietnam and the Hollywood Genre Film: Inversions of American Mythology in *The Deer Hunter* and *Apocalypse Now*." *Inventing Vietnam: The War in Film and Television*. Ed. Michael Anderegg. Philadelphia, PA: Temple UP, 1990. 56-80.

Herman Judith Lewis. "Complex PTSD: A Syndrome in Survivors of Prolonged and Repeated Trauma." *Psychotraumatology Key Papers and Core Concepts in Post-Traumatic Stress*. Ed. George S. Everly Jr., and Jeffrey M. Lating. New York: Plenum, 1992. 87-100.

———— "Crime and Memory" *Trauma and Self*. Ed. Charles B. Strozier, and Michael Flynn. New York: Bowman, 1996. 3-17.

———— *Trauma and Recovery*. New York: Basic Books, 1992.

Herzog, Werner. *Of Walking in Ice*. New York: Tanam P, 1980.

Higashi, Sumiko. "*Night of the Living Dead*: A Horror Film about the Horrors of the Vietnam Era." *From Hanoi to Hollywood: The Vietnam War in American Film*. Ed. Linda Dittmar, and Gene Michaud. New Brunswick, NJ: Rutgers UP, 1990. 175-188.

Holmlund, Chris. "Masculinity as Multiple Masquerade: The 'Mature' Stallone and the Stallone Clone." *Screening the Male: Exploring Masculinities in*

Hollywood Cinema. Ed. Steven Cohan, and Ina Rae Hark. London: Routledge, 1993. 213-229.

Horak, Jan-Christopher. "W. H. or the Mysteries of Walking in Ice." *The Films of Werner Herzog: Between Mirage and History*. Ed. Timothy Corrigan. New York: Methuen, 1986. 23-42.

Howell, Amanda. "Susan Jeffords's *The Remasculinization of America*: Gender and the Vietnam War." *Camera Obscura* 27: 166-173.

Huston, Nancy. "The Matrix of War: Mothers and Heroes." *The Female Body in Western Culture*. Ed. Susan Rubin Suleiman. Cambridge, MA :Harvard UP, 1986. 119-136.

<http://www.imsdb.com/scripts/Platoon.html>.

Ionesco, Eugene. *Amédée: The New Tenant, Victims of Duty*. Trans. Donald Watson. New York: Grove, 1958.

Irigaray, Luce. "This Sex Which Is Not One." Trans. Claudia Reeder. *New French Feminisms*. Ed. Elaine Marks, and Isabelle de Courtivron. Brighton: Harvester, 1980. 99-106.

Jameson, Fredric. The Political Unconscious: Narrative as a Socially Symbolic Act. London: Methuen, 1981.

——— "Reification and Utopia in Mass Culture." Signatures of the Visible. New York: Routledge, 1992. 35-54.

Jeffords, Susan. *Hard Bodies: Hollywood Masculinity in the Reagan Era*. New Brunswick, NJ: Rutgers UP, 1994.

——— *The Remasculinization of America Gender and the Vietnam War*. Bloomington: Indiana UP, 1989.

——— "The 'Remasculinization' of Germany in the 1950s: Discussion." *Signs* 24.1 (1998): 163-170.

——— "Reproducing Fathers: Gender and the Vietnam War in U.S. Culture." *From Hanoi to Hollywood: The Vietnam War in American Film*. Ed. Linda Dittmar, and Gene Michaud. New Brunswick, NJ: Rutgers UP, 1990. 203-216.

Johnson, Catherine. "The Imaginary and *The Bitter Tears of Petra Von Kant*." *Wide Angle* 3-4 (1980): 20-25.

Kaes, Anton. *From Hitler to Heimat: The Return of History as Film*. 1989. Cambridge: Harvard UP, 1992.

——— "Distanced Observers: Perspectives on the New German Cinema." *Quarterly Review of Film Studies* 10.3 (1985): 239-245.

——— "History and Film: Public Memory in the Age of Electronic Dissemination." *Framing the Past: The Historiography of German Cinema and Television*. Ed. B.A. Murray, and C.J. Wickham. Carbondale: Southern Illinois UP, 1992. 308-323.

——— "The Presence of the Past: R. W. Fassbinder's *The Marriage of Maria Braun*." *From Hitler to Heimat: The Return of History as Film*. 1989. Cambridge: Harvard UP, 1992. 73-103.

Kaplan E. Ann. "Discourse of Terrorism: Feminism and the Family in von Trotta's *Marianne and Juliane*." *Persistence of Vision* 2 (1985): 61-68.

———— "The Search for the Mother\Land in Sanders-Brahms's *Germany Pale Mother*." *German Film and Literature*. Ed. Eric Rentschler. New York: Methuen, 1980. 289-304.

Keene, Judith. "Mothering Daughters: Subjectivity and History in the Work of Helma Sanders-Brahms's *Germany Pale Mother* (1970-1980)." *Film Historia* 7.1 (1997): 3-12.

Kinney, Judy Lee. "*Gardens of Stone, Platoon*, and *Hamburger Hill*: Ritual and Remembrance." *Inventing Vietnam: The War in Film and Television*. Ed. Michael Anderegg. Philadelphia, PA: Temple UP, 1990. 153-165.

Kirby, Lynne. "Fassbinder's Debt to Poussin." *Camera Obscura* 13-14 (1985): 5-27.

Klaus, Phillips, ed. *New German Filmmakers: From Oberhausen Through the 1970s*. New York: Ungar, 1984.

Klein, Michael. "Historical Memory, Film, and the Vietnam Era." *From Hanoi to Hollywood*: *The Vietnam War in American Film*. Ed. Linda Dittmar, and Gene Michaud. New Brunswick, NJ: Rutgers UP, 1990. 19-40.

Knight, Julia. *Women and the New German Cinema*. London: Verso, 1992.

Koch, Gertrud. "Blindness as Insight: Visions of the Unseen in *Land of Silence and Darkness*." *The Films of Werner Herzog: Between Mirage and History*. Ed. Timothy Corrigan. New York: Methuen, 1986. 73-86.

———— "Torments of the Flesh, Coldness of the Spirit." *New German Critique* 38 (1986): 28-38.

Kocka, Jurgen. "Asymmetrical Historical Comparison: The Case of the German *Sonderweg*." *History and Theory*. 38.1 (1999): 40-50.

Kolker, Robert P., Peter Beicken. *A Cinema of Loneliness*. 2nd ed. New York: Oxford UP, 1988.

———— *The Films of Wim Wenders: Cinema as Vision and Desire*. Cambridge: Cambridge UP, 1993.

Korner, Axel. "'The Arrogance of Youth' – A Metaphor for Social Change?: The Goldhagen-Debate in Germany as Generational Conflict." *New German Critique* 80 (2000): 59-76.

Kosta, Barbara. *Recasting Autobiography: Women's Counterfictions in Contemporary German Literature and Film*. Ithaca, NY: Cornell UP, 1994.

Kracauer, Siegfried. *From Caligari to Hitler: A Psychological History of the German Film*.1947 Princeton, NJ: Princeton UP, 1974.

Kristeva, Julia. *Powers of Horror: An Essay on Abjection*. Trans. Leon S. Roudiez. *European Perspectives*. New York: Columbia UP, 1982.

Kubrick, Stanley, Michael Herr, and Gustav Hasford. *Full Metal Jacket: The Screenplay*. London: Secker and Warburg, 1987.

Kutler, Stanley I., ed. *Encyclopedia of the Vietnam War*. New York: Macmillan Library Reference.

Laing, R.D. *The Divided Self*. Chicago, IL: Quadrangle P, 1969.

LaCapra, Dominick. "Trauma, Absence, Loss." *Critical Inquiry* 25.4 (1996): 626-727.

———— *Writing History, Writing Trauma*. Baltimore, MD: Johns Hopkins UP, 2001.

Laplanche, Jean. *Life and Death in Psychoanalysis*. Trans. Jeffrey Mehlman. Baltimore, MD: Johns Hopkins UP, 1976. 25-47.

Laplanche, Jean, and J.B. Pontalis. *The Language of Psychoanalysis*. Trans. Donald Nicholson-Smith. New York: Norton, 1973.

La Valley, Al. "The Gay Liberation of Rainer Werner Fassbinder: Male Subjectivity, Male Bodies, Male Lovers." *New German Critique* 63 (1994): 109-137.

Lehman, Peter. *Running Scared: Masculinity and the Representation of the Male Body*. Philadelphia, PA: Temple UP, 1993.

Levy, Daniel. "The Future of the Past: Historiographical Disputes and Competing Memories in Germany and Israel." *History and Theory* 38.1 (1999): 51-66.

Leys, Ruth. *Trauma: A Genealogy*. Chicago, IL: U of Chicago P, 2000.

———— "Traumatic Cures: Shell Shock, Janet, and the Question of Memory." *Tense Past: Cultural Essays in Trauma and Memory*. Ed. Paul Antze, and Michael Lambek. New York: Routledge, 1996. 103-150.

Liebman, Stuart and Annette Michelson. "After the Fall: Women in the House of the Hangman." *October* 72 (1995): 5-14.

Lifton, Robert Jay. *Home From the War: Vietnam Veterans, Neither Victims Nor Executioners*. New York: Simon, 1973.

———— "Home from the War: The Psychology of Survival." *The Vietnam Reader*. Ed. Walter Capps. New York: Routledge, 1991. 54-67.

———— "Survivor Experience and Traumatic Syndrome." *The Broken Connection On Death and the Continuity of Life*. New York: Simon, 1979. 163-178.

Linke, Uli. *German Bodies: Race and Representation after Hitler*. New York: Routledge, 1999.

Linville, Susan E. *Feminism, Film, Fascism: Women's Auto\biographical Film in Postwar Germany*. Austin: U of Texas P, 1998.

————"The Mother-Daughter Plot in History: Helma Sanders-Brahms's *Germany, Pale Mother*." *New German Critique* 55 (1992): 51-70.

———— "Retrieving History: Margarethe von Trotta's *Marriane and Juliane*." *Feminism, Film, Fascism: Women's Auto\biographical Film in Postwar Germany*. Austin: U of Texas P, 1998. 84-108.

Lorenz, Chris. "Comparative Historiography: Problems and Perspectives." *History and Theory*. 38.1 (1999): 25-39.

Ludtke, Alf. "'Coming to Terms with the Past': Illusions of Remembering, Ways of Forgetting Nazism in West Germany." *Journal of Modern History* 65 (1993): 542-572.

MacCabe, Colin. *Godard: Images, Sounds, Politics*. Bloomington: Indiana UP, 1980. 49-76.

MacLear, Michael. *Vietnam: The Ten Thousand Day War*. London: Thames, 1981.

Magid, Ron. "ILM Breaks New Digital Ground for *Gump*." *American Cinematographer*. 75.10 (1994): 44-53.

Mangan, J. A., ed. *Shaping the Superman: Fascist Body as Political Icon: Aryan Fascism*. London: Cass, 1999.

Martin, Andrew. Rev. of "*The Remasculinization of America: Gender and the Vietnam War*," by Susan Jeffords. *Discourse* 13.2 (1991): 123-125.

Mayne, Judith. "Fassbinder and Spectatorship." *New German Critique* 12 (1977): 61-74.

———— "Herzog, Murnau, and the Vampire." *The Films of Werner Herzog: Between Mirage and History*. Ed. Timothy Corrigan. New York: Methuen, 1986. 119-130.

McCarthy, Margaret. "Consolidating, Consuming, and Annulling Identity in Jutta Bruckner's *Hungerjahre*." *Women in German Yearbook* 11 (1995): 13-33.

McCormick, Richard W. *Politics of the Self: Feminism and the Postmodern in the West German Literature and Film*. Princeton, NJ: Princeton UP, 1991.

Meijer, Irene Costera, and Baukje Prins. "How Bodies Come to Matter: An Interview with Judith Butler." *Signs* 23.2 (1998): 275-286.

Merck, Mandy, Naomi Segal, and Elizabeth Wright. Introduction. *Coming Out of Feminism?* Oxford: Blackwell, 1998. 1-10.

Metz, Christian. *The Imaginary Signifier: Psychoanalysis and Cinema*. Bloomington: Indiana UP, 1982.

Michel, Sonya. "Danger on the Home Front: Motherhood, Sexuality, and Disabled Veterans in American Postwar Films." *Gendering War Talk*. Ed. Miriam Cooke and Angela Woollacott. Princeton, NJ: Princeton UP, 1993. 260-279.

Mitscherlich, Alexander. "Two Kinds of Fatherlessness." *Society without the Father: A Contribution to Social Psychology*. New York: Schocken, 1970. 268-304.

Mitscherlich, Alexander and Margarete. *The Inability to Mourn*. New York: Grove Press, 1975.

Modleski, Tania. "A Father Is Being Beaten: Male Feminism and the War Film." *Discourse* 10.2 (1988): 62-77.

Moeller, Robert G. "'The Last Soldiers of the Great War' and Tales of Family Reunions in the Federal Republic of Germany." *Signs* 24.1 (1998): 129-146.

———— "The Remasculinization of Germany in the 1950s: Introduction." *Signs* 24.1 (1998): 101-106.

Monick, Eugene. *Castrating and Male Rage: The Phallic Wound*. Toronto, Canada: Inner City Books, 1991.

Morag, Raya. "Defeated Masculinity: Post-Traumatic Cinema in the Aftermath of the Vietnam War." *The Communication Review* 9.3 (2006): 189-219.

———— "'Life-Taker Heart-Breaker': Mask-ulinity and/or Femininity in *Full Metal Jacket.*" *The Seeing Century: Film, Vision, and Identity*. Ed. Wendy Everett. Atlanta GA: Rodopi, 2000. 186-197.

———— "Not a Dirty Secret: On Some Cases of Bulimia in Cinema." *Camera Obscura* 61 21.1 (2006): 147-182.

———— "Unclaimed Masculinity: The New German Cinema as Post-Traumatic Cinema." *Babylon* (2008).

Mosse, George L. *Fallen Soldiers: Reshaping the Memory of the World Wars*. New York: Oxford UP, 1990.

———— *The Image of Man: The Creation of Modern Masculinity*. New York: Oxford UP, 1996.

———— *Nationalism and Sexuality: Respectability and Abnormal Sexuality in Modern Europe*. New York: Fertig, 1985.

Mouton, Janice. "Margarethe von Trotta's Sisters: Brides Under a Different Law." *Women in German Yearbook* 11 (1995): 35-47.

Mulvey, Laura. "Visual Pleasure and Narrative Cinema." *Screen* 16 (1975): 6-18.

———— "Afterthoughts on Visual Pleasure and Narrative Cinema Inspired by *Duel in the Sun.*" *Framework* 15-17 (1981): 12-15.

Neale, Steve. "Masculinity as Spectacle: Reflections on Men and Mainstream Cinema." *Screen* 24.6 (1983): 9-22.

Norden, Martin. "Portrait of a Disabled Vietnam Veteran: Alex Cutter of *Cutter's Way.*" *From Hanoi to Hollywood: The Vietnam War in American Film*. Ed. Linda Dittmar, and Gene Michaud. New Brunswick, NJ: Rutgers UP, 1990. 217-225.

Noy, Haim. *Traumatic Stress*. Tel Aviv: Schocken, 2000. (in Hebrew)

Olson, James S., ed. *Dictionary of the Vietnam War*. New York: Greenwood, 1988.

Overy, Richard. *The Penguin Historical Atlas of the Third Reich*. London: Penguin, 1996.

Palmer, William J. "Symbolic Nihilism in *Platoon.*" *America Rediscovered: Critical Essays on Literature and Film of the Vietnam War*. Ed. Owen Gilman, and Lorrie Smith. New York: Garland, 1990. 256-274.

"Para-amnesia." *Webster Encyclopedic Unabridged Dictionary*. 1996. 1047.

Parisi, Paula. "Forrest Gump Gallops Through Time." *American Cinematographer* 75.10 (1994): 38-42.

Penley, Constance. *The Future of an Illusion: Film, Feminism & Psychoanalysis*. London: Routledge, 1989.

Penley, Constance, and Sharon Willis, eds. "Male Trouble." *Camera Obscura* 17 (1988).

Pfeil, Fred. *White Guys: Studies in Postmodern Domination and Difference*. London: Verso, 1995.

Peucker, Brigitte. "The Invalidation of Arnim: Herzog's *Signs of Life* (1968)." *German Film & Literature: Adaptations and Transformations*. Ed. Eric Rentschler. New York: Methuen, 1986. 217-30.

———— "Literature and Writing in the Films of Werner Herzog." *The Films of Werner Herzog: Between Mirage and History*. Ed. Timothy Corrigan. New York: Methuen, 1986. 105-117.

Poiger, Uta G. "A New 'Western' Hero? Reconstructing German Masculinity in the 1950s." *Signs* 24.1 (1998): 147-162.

Prosser, Jay. *Second Skins: The Body Narratives of Transsexuality*. New York: Columbia UP, 1998. 1-17, 21-60.

Quart, Leonard. "*The Deer Hunter*: The Superman in Vietnam." *From Hanoi to Hollywood: The Vietnam War in American Film*. Ed. Linda Dittmar, and Gene Michaud. New Brunswick, NJ: Rutgers UP, 1990. 159-168.

Radstone, Susannah, ed. "Screening Trauma: *Forrest Gump*, Film and Memory." *Memory and Methodology*. Oxford: Berg, (2000). 79-107.

Rambuss, Richard. "Machinehead." *Camera Obscura* 42 (1999): 97-122.

Rentschler, Eric. "The Use and Abuse of Memory: New German Film and the Discourse of Bitburg." *New German Critique* 36 (1985): 67-90.

———— ed. *West German Filmmakers on Film: Vision and Voices*. New York: Holmes & Meier, 1988.

———— *West German Film in the Course of Time*. New York: Redgrave, 1984.

Rose, Jacqueline. "Why War?" *Why War? — Psychoanalysis, Politics, and the Return to Melanie Klein*. Oxford: Blackwell, 1993. 15-40.

Rosenfeld, Alvin H. "Another Revisionism: Popular Culture and the Changing Image of the Holocaust." *Bitburg in Moral and Political Perspective*. Ed. Geoffrey Hartman. Bloomington: Indiana UP, 1986. 90-102.

Sampath, Ursula. *Kaspar Hauser: A Modern Metaphor*. Rochester, New York: Camden House. 1991.

Sandford, John. *The New German Cinema*. New York: Da Capo Paperback, 1980.

Santner, Eric. "History Beyond the Pleasure Principle: Some Thoughts on the Representation of Trauma." *Probing the Limits of Representation: Nazism and the "Final Solution."* Ed. Saul Friedlander. Cambridge, MA: Harvard UP, 1992. 143-154.

———— *Stranded Objects: Mourning, Memory and Film in Postwar Germany*. Ithaca, NY: Cornell UP, 1980.

Savran, David. *Taking It Like a Man: White Masculinity, Masochism, and Contemporary American Culture*. Princeton, NJ: Princeton UP, 1998.

Schlöndorff, Volker. "David Bennet and Oskar Mazerath." *West German Filmmakers on Film Vision and Voices*. Ed. Eric Rentschler. 1978 New York: Holmes & Meier, 1988. 176-178.

Scott, Joan W. "Gender: A Useful Category of Historical Analysis." *American Historical Review* 91(1986): 1053-1075.

Seiter, Ellen. "The Political is Personal: Magarethe von Trotta's *Marianne and Juliane*." *Films for Women*. Ed. Charlotte Brunsdon. London: BFI, 1986. 109-116.

Selig, Michael. "Boys Will Be Men: Oedipal Drama in *Coming Home*." *From Hanoi to Hollywood: The Vietnam War in American Film*. Ed. Linda Dittmar, and Gene Michaud. New Brunswick, NJ: Rutgers UP, 1990. 189-202.

Seltzer, Mark. "Wound Culture: Trauma in the Pathological Public Sphere." *October* 80 (1997): 3-26.

Shapiro, Judith. "Transsexualism: Reflections on the Persistence of Gender and the Mutability of Sex." *Body Guards: The Cultural Politics of Gender Ambiguity*. Ed. Julia Epstein, and Kristina Straub. New York: Routledge, 1991. 248-279.

Shoham, Shlomo Giora. *Alienation and Deviance*. Tel Aviv: Ramot, 1993. (in Hebrew)

Showalter, Elaine. *Hystories, Hysterical Epidemics, and Modern Media*. New York: Columbia UP, 1997. 3-112.

———— "Male Hysteria: W. H. R. Rivers and the Lessons of Shell Shock." *The Female Malady Women, Madness, and English Culture, 1830-1980*. New York: Penguin, 1985. 167-194.

Silverman, Kaja. "Kaspar Hauser's 'Terrible Fall' into Narrative." *New German Critique* 24-25 (1981-2): 73-93.

———— *Male Subjectivity at the Margins*. New York: Routledge, 1992.

Slater, Thomas J. "Teaching Vietnam: The Politics of Documentary." *Inventing Vietnam: The War in Film and Television*. Ed. Michael Anderegg. Philadelphia, PA: Temple UP, 1990. 269-290.

Slotkin, Richard. *Gunfighter Nation: The Myth of the Frontier in Twentieth-Century America*. New York: Atheneum, 1992.

———— *Regeneration through Violence: The Mythology of the American Frontier 1600-1860*. Middletown, CT: Wesleyan UP, 1973.

Spivak, Gayatri Chakravorty. "A Speech after 9-11." *Boundary* 2 (2004): 81-111.

Stone, Sandy. "The Empire Strikes Back: A Posttranssexual Manifesto." *Body Guards: The Cultural Politics of Gender Ambiguity*. Ed. Julia Epstein and Kristina Straub. New York: Routledge, 1991. 280-304.

Studlar, Gaylyn and David Desser. "Never Having to Say You're Sorry: Rambo's Rewriting of the Vietnam War." *From Hanoi to Hollywood: The Vietnam War in American Film*. Ed. Linda Dittmar, and Gene Michaud. New Brunswick, NJ: Rutgers UP, 1990. 101-112.

Studlar, Gaylyn. "Masochism and the Perverse Pleasures of the Cinema." *Movies and Methods* II. Ed. Bill Nichols. Berkeley: U of California P, 1985. 602-621.

Theweleit, Klaus. "The Bomb's Womb and the Genders of War (War Goes on Preventing Women from Becoming the Mothers of Invention)." *Gendering*

War Talk. Ed. Miriam Cooke, and Angela Woollacott. Princeton, NJ: Princeton UP, 1993. 283-315.

Tomasulo, Frank P. "Masculine/Feminine: The 'New Masculinity' in *Tootsie* (1982)." *The Velvet Light Trap* 38 (1996): 4-13.

Tuchman, Barbara. *March of Folly: From Troy to Vietnam*. New York: Ballantine, 1985.

Van Der Kolk, Bessel, and Onno Van Der Hart. "The Intrusive Past: The Flexibility of Memory and the Engraving of Trauma." *Trauma Explorations in Memory*. Ed. Cathy Caruth. Baltimore, MD: Johns Hopkins UP, 1995. 158-181.

Van Wert, William. "Last Words: Observations on a New Language." *The Films of Werner Herzog: Between Mirage and History*. Ed. Timothy Corrigan. New York: Methuen, 1986. 51-71.

Vasterling, Veronica. "Butler's Sophisticated Constructivism: A Critical Assessment." *Hypatia* 14.3 (1999): 17-38.

Vlastos, Stephen. "Revisionist Vietnam History." *The Vietnam War and American Culture*. Ed. Rick Berg, and John Carlos Rowe. New York: Columbia UP, 1991. 52-74.

Von Saldern, Adelheid. "Victims or Perpetrators? Controversies About the Role of Women in the Nazi State." *Nazism and German Society 1933-1945*. Ed. David Crew. New York: Routledge, 1994. 141-165.

Von Weizacker, Richard. "Speech in the Bundestag during the Ceremony Commemorating the 40th Anniversary of the End of the War in Europe and of National Socialist Tyranny, May 8, 1985." *Bitburg in Moral and Political Perspective*. Ed. Geoffrey Hartman. Bloomington: Indiana UP, 1986. 262-273.

Walker, Janet. *Trauma Cinema: Documenting Incest and the Holocaust*. Berkeley: U of California P, 2005.

———— "The Traumatic Paradox: Documentary Films, Historical Fictions and Cataclysmic Past Events." *Signs* 22 (1997): 803-825.

Waller, Gregory A. "*Rambo*: Getting to Win This Time." *From Hanoi to Hollywood: The Vietnam War in American Film*. Ed. Linda Dittmar, and Gene Michaud. New Brunswick, NJ: Rutgers UP, 1990. 113-128.

Wege, Astrid. "Who Decided what is '*Hauptstadkultu*' and What is Not?" *October* 89 (1999): 127-138.

Wenders, Wim. *Emotion Pictures: Reflections on the Cinema*. Trans. Shaun Whiteside, and Michael Hofmann. London: Faber, 1991.

———— "Talking about Germany." *The Cinema of Wim Wenders: Image, Narrative, and the Postmodern Condition*. Ed. Roger F. Cook, and Gerd Gemunden. Detroit, MI: Wayne State UP, 1997. 51-59.

———— "That's Entertainment: Hitler." *Emotion Pictures: Reflections on the Cinema*. Trans. Shaun Whiteside in association with Michael Hofmann. London: Faber, 1991. 93-99.

White, Hayden. "Metahistory: The Historical Text as Literary Artifact." *Clio* 3.3 (1974): 277-303.

White, Susan. "Male Bonding, Hollywood Orientalism, and the Repression of the Feminine in Kubrick's *Full Metal Jacket*" *Inventing Vietnam: The War in Film and Television*. Ed. Michael Anderegg. Philadelphia, PA: Temple UP, 1990. 204-230.

Williams, Tony. "*Missing in Action* – The Vietnam Construction of the Movie Star," *From Hanoi to Hollywood: The Vietnam War in American Film*. Ed. Linda Dittmar, and Gene Michaud. New Brunswick, NJ: Rutgers UP, 1990. 129-144.

Willoquet-Maricondi, Paula. "Full Metal Jacketing, Or Masculinity in The Making." *Cinema Journal* 33.2 (1994): 5-21.

Wilson, John P. "The Historical Evolution of PTSD Diagnostic Criteria: From Freud to DSM-IV." *Psychotraumatology: Key Papers and Core Concepts in Post-Traumatic Stress*. Ed. George S. Everly Jr., and Jeffrey M. Lating. New York: Plenum, 1995. 9-26.

Wood, Robin. *Hollywood from Vietnam to Reagan*. New York: Columbia UP, 1986.

Wyatt, Justin. "Economic Constraints/Economic Opportunities: Robert Altman as Auteur." *The Velvet Light Trap* 38 (1996): 51-67.

Young, Allan. "Bodily Memory and Traumatic Memory." *Tense Past: Cultural Essays in Trauma and Memory*. Ed. Paul Antze, and Michael Lambek New York: Routledge, 1996. 89-102.

Zelizer, Barbie. "Photography, Journalism, and Trauma." *Journalism after September 11*. Ed. Barbie Zelizer, and Stuart Allan. New York: Routledge, 2003. 48-68.

Zimmerman, Moshe. "Phoenix and the Trauma – Federal Republic." *Germany after 1945*. Ed. Moshe Zimmerman, and Michael Toch. Jerusalem: Magnes, 1974. 9-36. (in Hebrew)

References

Adorno, Theodor. "What Does Coming to Terms with the Past Mean?" *Bitburg in Moral and Political Perspective*. Ed. Geoffrey Hartman. Bloomington: Indiana UP, 1986. 114-129.

Baudrillard, Jean. "The Precession of Simulacra." *Art after Modernism*. Ed. Brian Wallis. Boston, MA: Godine, 1984. 253-281.

Berg, Rick. "Losing Vietnam: Covering the War in an Age of Technology." *The Vietnam War and American Culture*. Ed. Rick Berg, and John Carlos Rowe. New York: Columbia UP, 1991. 115-147.

Berg, Rick and John Carlos Rowe, eds. "The Vietnam War and American Memory." *The Vietnam War and American Culture*. New York: Columbia UP, 1991, 1-17.

Bohrer, Karl H. "The Three Cultures." *Observations on 'The Spiritual Situation of the Age.' Contemporary German Perspectives*. Ed. Jurgen Habermas. Cambridge, MA: MIT P, 1984. 122-155.

Brustellin Alf, Rainer Werner Fassbinder, Alexander Kluge, Volker Schlondorff, Bernhard Sinkel. "*Germany in Autumn*: What Is the Film's Bias?" *West German Filmmakers on Film: Vision and Voices*. Ed. Eric Rentschler. New York: Holmes, 1988. 132-137.

Butler, Judith. *The Psychic Life of Power Theories in Subjection*. Stanford, CA: Stanford UP, 1997.

Capps, Walter, ed. *The Vietnam Reader*. New York: Routledge, 1991.

Caruth, Cathy. "An Interview with Robert Jay Lifton. *Trauma Explorations in Memory*. Ed. Cathy Caruth. Baltimore, MD: Johns Hopkins UP, 1995. 128-151.

———— "Traumatic Departures: Survival and History in Freud." *Trauma and Self*. Ed. Charles B. Strozier and Michael Flynn. Lanham, MD: Rowman, 1996. 29-43.

Cawley, Leo. "The War about the War: Vietnam Films and American Myth." *From Hanoi to Hollywood: The Vietnam War in American Film*. Ed. Linda Dittmar, and Gene Michaud. New Brunswick, NJ: Rutgers UP, 1990. 69-80.

Chase, Cynthia. "Oedipal Textuality Reading Freud's Reading of *Oedipus*." *Decomposing Figures: Rhetorical Readings in the Romantic Tradition*. Baltimore, MD: Johns Hopkins UP, 1986. 175-195.

Cixous, Helen. "The Laugh of the Medusa." *Signs* I (1976): 875-899.

Cohan, Steven and Ina Rae Hark, eds. *Screening the Male: Exploring Masculinities in Hollywood Cinema*. London: Routledge, 1992.

Conrad, Joseph. "Heart of Darkness." *Three Short Novels*. 1963 Toronto: Bantam, 1971.

Corrigan, Timothy. "Genre, Gender, and Hysteria: The Road Movie in Outer Space." *A Cinema Without Walls: Movies and Culture after Vietnam*. New Brunswick, NJ: Rutgers UP, 1991. 137-160.

Crimp, Douglas. "Fassbinder, Franz, Fox, Elvira, Erwin, Armin, and All the Others." *October* 21 (1982): 63-81.

Cunning, Kathleen. "The Body as Method? Reflections on the Place of the Body in Gender History." *Gender & History* 11.3 (1999): 499-513.

Czaplicka John, Andreas Huyssen, Anson Rabinbach. "Introduction: Cultural History and Cultural Studies: Reflections on a Symposium." *New German Critique* 65 (1995): 3-17.

Dean, Tim, Hal Foster, Kaja Silverman. "A Conversation with Leo Bersani." *October* 82 (1997): 3-16.

De Lauretis, Teresa. *Alice Doesn't: Feminism, Semiotics, Cinema*. Bloomington: Indiana UP, 1981.

Denzin, Norman. "*Paris, Texas* and Baudrillard on America." *Theory, Culture & Society* 8 (1991): 121-133.

Desser, David. "'Charlie Don't Surf': Race and Culture in the Vietnam War Films." *Inventing Vietnam: The War in Film and Television*. Ed. Michael Anderegg. Philadelphia, PA: Temple UP, 1990. 81-102.

Dittman, Linda and Gene Michaud, eds. "America's Vietnam War Films: Marching Toward Denial." *From Hanoi to Hollywood: The Vietnam War in American Film*. New Brunswick, NJ: Rutgers UP, 1990. 1-15.

Doane, Ann Mary. "Film and the Masquerade: Theorizing the Female Spectator." *Screen* 23.3: 1982.

Edelstein, Marilyn. "Metaphor, Meta-Narrative and Mater Narrative in Kristeva's 'Stabat Mater.'" *Body / Text in Julia Kristeva: Religion, Women and Psychoanalysis*. Ed. David Crownfield. Albany, State U of New York P, 1992. 27-56.

Elsaesser, Thomas. "Primary Identification and the Historical Subject: Fassbinder and Germany." *Narrative, Apparatus, Ideology*. Ed. Philip Rosen. New York: Columbia UP, 1986. 536-549.

———— "Postmodernism as Mourning Work." *Trauma and Screen Studies*. Spec. issue of *Screen* 42.2 (2001): 93-201.

Eng, David L. "Melancholia in the Late Twentieth Century." *Signs* 25.4 (2000): 1275-1281.

Erikson, Kai. "Notes on Trauma and Community." *Trauma Explorations in Memory*. Ed. Cathy CaruthBaltimore, MD: Johns Hopkins UP, 1995. 183-199.

Fehrenbach, Heide. *Cinema in Democratizing Germany: Reconstructing National Identity After Hitler*. Chapel Hill: U of North Carolina P, 1995.

Feinberg, Leslie. "International Bill of Gender Rights." *Trans Gender Warriors: Making History from Joan of Arc to Rupaul*. Boston, MA: Beacon, 1996. 165-169.

Felski, Rita. "*Fin de siecle, Fin de sexe*: Transsexuality, Postmodernism, and the Death of History." *New Literary History* 7.2 (1996): 337-349.

Flinn, Caryl. *The New German Cinema: Music, History, and the Matter of Style*. Berkeley: U of California P, 2000.

Foucault, Michelle. *The History of Sexuality*. Trans. Robert Hurley. New York: Vintage, 1980.

Freud, Sigmund. "Moses and Monotheism." *The Standard Edition of the Complete Psychological Works of Sigmund Freud*. Trans. James Strachey, Anna Freud, Alix Strachey, and Alan Tyson. 1939. Vol. 23. London: Hogarth 1953-1974.

———— "Studies on Hysteria" *The Standard Edition of the Complete Psychological Works of Sigmund Freud*. Trans. James Strachey, Anna Freud, Alix Strachey, and Alan Tyson. Vol. 2. 1895 London: Hogarth, 1953-1974.

———— "Psychoanalysis and War Neuroses." *Character and Culture*. Ed. Philip Rieff. New York: Collier Macmillan, 1963. 215-219.

———— "Why War?" *Character and Culture*. Ed. Philip Rieff. 1932 New York: Collier Macmillan, 1963. 134-147.

Frieden, Sandra. "In the Margins of Identity: Fassbinder's *In a Year of 13 Moons*." *Gender and German Cinema: Feminist Interventions*. Vol. 1, Providence, RI: Berg, 1993. 51-58.

Frieden, S., R. McCormick, V. Petersen, and L. Vogelsang, ed, *Gender and German Cinema: Feminist Interventions*. Vol. 1, 2. Providence, RI: Berg, 1993.

Friedlander, Saul. "Some German Struggles with Memory." *Bitburg in Moral and Political Perspective*. Ed. Geoffrey Hartman. Bloomington: Indiana UP, 1986. 27-42.

Friedman, Régine Mihal "Male Gaze and Female Reaction: Veit Harlan's *Jew Süss* (1940) "*Gender and German Cinema Feminist Interventions*. Ed. S. Frieden, R. McCormick, V. Petersen and L. Vogelsang, Vol. 2. Providence, RI: Berg, 1993. 117-133.

Fusch, Cynthia J. "'All the Animals Come Out at Night': Vietnam Meets Noir in *Taxi Driver*." *Inventing Vietnam: The War in Film and Television*. Ed. Michael Anderegg. Philadelphia, PA: Temple UP, 1990. 33-55.

Gallop, Jane. *Reading Lacan*. Ithaca, New York: Cornell UP, 1985.

———— "Phallus\ Penis: Same Difference." *Thinking Through the Body*. New York: Columbia UP, 1988. 124-133.

Geisler, Michael E. "'*Heimat*' and the German Left: The Anamnesis of a Trauma." *New German Critique* 36 (1985): 25-66.

Grasskamp, Walter. "The De-Nazification of Nazi Art: Arno Breker and Albert Speer Today." *The Nazification of Art: Art, Design, Music, Architecture & Film in the Third Reich*. Ed. Brandon Taylor, and Wilfried Van Der Will. Winchester, Hampshire, UK: Winchester Press, 1990. 231-248.

Grosz, Elizabeth. *Jacques Lacan: A Feminist Introduction*. London: Routledge, 1990.

Grosz, Elizabeth. "The Body of Signification." *Abjection, Melancholia & Love: The Work of Julia Kristeva*. Ed. John Fletcher, and Andrew Benjamin. London: Routledge, 1990. 80-103.

Habermas, Jürgen, ed. *Observation on "The Spiritual Situation of the Age": Contemporary German Perspectives*. Trans. Andrew Buchwalter. Cambridge MA.: The MIT P, 1984.

Hacking, Ian. "Trauma." *Rewriting the Soul: Multiple Personality and the Sciences of Memory*. Princeton, NJ: Princeton UP, 1995. 183-197.

Hake, Sabine. *German National Cinema*. 2nd ed. New York: Routledge, 2008.

Hall, Carol. "A Different Drummer: *The Tin Drum* Film and Novel." *Literature/ Film Quarterly* 18.4 (1990): 236-244.

Hartman, Geoffrey H. "On Traumatic Knowledge and Literary Studies." *New Literary History*. 26.3 (1995): 537-563.

Herzog, Werner. "Tribute to Lotte Eisner" *West German Filmmakers on Film Vision and Voices*. Ed. Eric Rentschler. New York: Holmes, 1988. 115-118.

Higonnet Margaret R., Jane Jenson, Margaret C Weitz, eds. Introduction. *Behind the Lines: Gender and the Two World Wars*. New Haven, CT: Yale UP, 1987. 1-17.

Higonnet Margaret R., & L. R. Patrice. "The Double Helix." *Behind the Lines: Gender and the Two World Wars*. Ed. Margaret R. Higonnet, Jane Jenson, and Margaret C. Weitz. New Haven, CT: Yale UP, 1987. 31-47.

Hirsch, Marianne. *The Mother\Daughter Plot: Narrative, Psychoanalysis, Feminism*. Bloomington: Indiana UP, 1989.

———— "Mothers and Daughters." *Ties that Bind: Essay on Mothering and Patriarchy*. Ed. J.O'Barr, D. Pope, and M. Wyer. Chicago, IL: U of Chicago P, 1990. 177-199.

Horak, Jan-Christopher. "Postwar Traumas in Klaren's *Wozzeck* (1947)." *German Film and Literature: Adaptations and Transformations*. Ed. Eric Rentschler. New York: Methuen, 1986. 132-145.

Hughes, John. "*The Tin Drum*: Volker Schlöndorff's 'Dream of Childhood.'" *Film Quarterly* 34.3 (1981): 2-10.

Hyams, Barbara. "Is the Apolitical Woman at Peace?: A Reading of the Fairy Tale in *Germany Pale Mother*." *Wide Angle* 10.3 (1988): 40-51.

Jacobs, Diane. "Hitler's Ungrateful Grandchildren." *American Film* (1980): 34-40.

Johnston, Sheila. *Wim Wenders*. BFI Dossier 10, 1981.

Kaes, Anton. "German Cultural History and the Study of Film: Ten Theses and a Postscript." *New German Critique* 65 (1995): 47-58.

Kahane, Claire. "Gender and Patrimony: Mourning the Dead Father." *Difference* 9.1 (1997): 49-67.

Kaplan E. Ann. *Women and Film: Both Sides of the Camera*. New York: Methuen, 1983.

———— "Melodrama, Cinema and Trauma." *Trauma and Screen Studies*. Spec. issue of *Screen* 42.2 (2001): 201-205.

————, ed. *Psychoanalysis and Cinema*. New York: Routledge, 1990.

Kaplan E. Ann, and Ban Wang, eds. *Trauma and Cinema: Cross-Cultural Explorations*. Hong Kong: Hong Kong UP, 2004.

Kirkham, Pat, and Janet Thumim, eds. *You Tarzan: Masculinity, Movies and Men*. New York: St. Martin, 1993.

Klaus, Phillips, ed. *New German Filmmakers: From Oberhausen Through the 1970s*. New York: Ungar, 1984.

Koch, Gertrud. "Blood, Sperm, and Tears." *October* 72 (1995): 27-41.

————"Torments of the Flesh, Coldness of the Spirit." *New German Critique* 38 (1986): 28-38.

Kristeva, Julia. "On the Melancholic Imaginary." *Discourse in Psychoanalysis and Literature*. Ed. Shlomith Rimmon-Kenan. London: Methuen, 1987. 104-123.

———— *Black Sun: Depression and Melancholia*. Trans. Leon S. Roudiez. New York: Columbia UP, 1989.

Kuzniar, Alice. "Wenders' Windshields." *The Cinema of Wim Wenders: Image, Narrative, and the Postmodern Condition*. Ed. Roger F. Cook, and Gerd Gemunden. Detroit, MI: Wayne State UP, 1997. 222-239.

————*The Queer German Cinema*. Stanford, CA: Stanford UP, 2004.

Lacan, Jacques. *Écrits: A Selection*. New York: Norton, 1977.

Laub, Dori. "Truth and Testimony: The Process and the Struggle." *Trauma Explorations in Memory*. Ed. Cathy CaruthBaltimore, MD: Johns Hopkins UP, 1995. 61-75.

Levin, Thomas. "Nationalities of Language: Adorno's *Fremdworter* An Introduction to 'On the Question: 'What is German?'" *New German Critique*. 36 (1985): 111-119.

Lovibond, Sabina. "'Gendering' as an Ethical Concept." *Feminist Theory* 2.2 (2001): 151-158.

Mack, Burton. "Introduction: Religion and Ritual." *Violent Origins*. Ed. Robert G. Hamerton-Kelly. Stanford, CA: Stanford UP, 1987. 1-70.

McCormick, Richard W. "The Writer in Film: *Wrong Move*." *The Cinema of Wim Wenders*: *Image, Narrative, and the Postmodern Condition*. Ed. Roger F. Cook, and Gerd Gemunden. Detroit, MI: Wayne State UP, 1997. 89-109.

Michaud, Eric. *The Cult of Art in Nazi Germany*. Trans. Janet Lloyd Staford, CA: Stanford UP, 2004.

Mithers, Carol Lynn. "Missing in Action: Women Warriors in Vietnam." *The Vietnam War and American Culture*. Ed. Rick Berg, and John Carlos Rowe. New York: Columbia UP, 1991. 75-91.

Moi, Toril. *Sexual/Textual Politics: Feminist Literary Theory*. London: Methuen, 1988.

Morrison, Toni. *Playing in the Dark: Whiteness and the Literary Imagination*. Cambridge, MA: Harvard UP, 1992.

Mosse, George L. *Nazi Culture: Intellectual, Cultural and Social Life in the Third Reich*. Trans. Salvator Attanasio and others. New York: Grosset. 1966.

Mouton, Jan. "The Absent Mother Makes an Appearance in the Films of West German Women Directors." *Women in German Yearbook: Feminist Studies in German Literature and Culture* 4 (1988): 69-81.

Muller, John P. *Lacan and Language: A Reader's Guide to Écrits*. New York: International UP, 1982.

Neale, Steve. "Aspects of Ideology and Narrative Form in the American War Film." *Screen* 32.1 (1991): 35-57.

O'Kane, John. "History, Performance, Counter-Cinema A Study of 'Die *Patriotin*'" *Screen* 26.6 (1985): 2-17.

Oliver, Kelly. "The Abject Mother." *Reading Kristeva: Unraveling the Double-Bind*. Bloomington: Indiana UP, 1993. 48-68.

Petro, Patrice. "Historical *Ennui*, Feminist Boredom." *The Persistence of History: Cinema, Television and the Modernist Event*. Ed. Vivian Sobchak. New York: Routledge, 1996. 187-199.

Peucker, Brigitte. "The Invalidation of Arnim: Herzog's *Signs of Life* (1968)." *German Film & Literature: Adaptations and Transformations*. Ed. Eric Rentschler. New York: Methuen, 1986. 217-230.

———— "Literature and Writing in the Films of Werner Herzog." *The Films of Werner: Herzog Between Mirage and History*. Ed. Timothy Corrigan. New York: Methuen, 1986. 105-117.

Polan, Dana. "Above All Else to Make You See: Cinema and the Ideology of Spectacle." *Postmodernism and Politics*. Ed. J. Arac. Minneapolis: U of Minnesota P, 1986. 55-69.

Radstone, Susannah. "Trauma and Screen Studies: Opening the Debate." *Trauma and Screen Studies*. Spec. issue of *Screen* 42.2 (2001): 188-193.

Randall, Halle. "'Happy Ends' to Crises of Heterosexual Desire: Toward a Social Psychology of Recent German Comedies." *Camera Obscura* 44 15.2 (2000): 1-39.

Rayns, Tony, ed. *Fassbinder*. London: BFI, 1980.

Reinke, Martha "The Mother in Mimesis: Kristeva and Girard on Violence and the Sacred." *Body/Text in Julia Kristeva: Religion, Women and Psychoanalysis*. Ed. David Crownfield. Albany: State U of New York P, 1992. 67-85.

Reitz, Edgar. "The Camera Is Not a Clock (Regarding My Experiences Telling Stories from German History)." *West German Filmmakers on Film: Vision and Voices*. Ed. Eric Rentschler. New York: Holmes, 1988.137-141.

Rentschler, Eric. "American Friends and New German Cinema: Patterns of Reception." *New German Critique* 24-25 (1981-2): 7-35.

———— "How American Is It: The U.S. as Image and Imaginary in German Film." *The German Quarterly* 57.4 (1984): 603-620.

———— ed. *German Film and Literature: Adaptations and Transformations*. New York: Methuen, 1986.

———— "The Politics of Vision: Herzog's *Heart of Glass*." *The Films of Werner Herzog: Between Mirage and History*. Ed. Timothy Corrigan. New York: Methuen, 1986. 159-181.

———— ed. *West German Filmmakers on Film Vision and Voices*. New York: Holmes, 1988.

Richardson, Annie. "The Nazification of Women in Art." *The Nazification of Art : Art, Design, Music, Architecture and Film in the Third Reich*. Ed. Taylor Brandon, and Wilfried Van Der Will. Winchester, Hampshire, UK: Winchester Press, 1990. 53-79.

Rowe, John Carlos. "Eyewitness: Documentary Styles in the American Representations of Vietnam." *The Vietnam War and American Culture*. Ed. Rick Berg and John Carlos Rowe. New York: Columbia UP, 1991. 148-174.

Sander, Helke. Introduction.*BeFreier und Befreite: Krieg, Vergewaltigungen, Kinder*. Trans. Stuart Liebman. *October* 72 (1995): 15-25.

Schatz, Thomas. "The Western." *Handbook of American Film Genres*. Ed. D. Gehring, New York: Greenwood, 1988. 25-46.

Schlöndorff, Volker. "Reading Kracauer's *From Cligari to Hitler*." *West German Filmmakers on Film: Vision and Voices*. Ed. Eric Rentschler. 1980 New York: Holmes, 1988. 104-111.

Scott, Joan W. "Rewriting History." *Behind the Lines: Gender and the Two World Wars*. Ed. Margaret R. Higonnet, Jane Jenson, and Margaret C. Weitz. New Haven, CT: Yale UP, 1987. 21-29.

Selig, Michael. "Genre, Gender and the Discourse of War: The A/historical and Vietnam Films." *Screen* 34.1 (1993): 1-18.

Shrader, Paul. *Taxi Driver*. London: Faber, 1990.

Singer, Alan. "Comprehending Appearances: Werner Herzog's Ironic Sublime." *The Films of Werner Herzog: Between Mirage and History*. Ed. Timothy Corrigan. New York: Methuen, 1986. 183-205.

Sobchack, Vivian, ed. "Introduction: History Happens." *The Persistence of History: Cinema, Television and the Modernist Event*. New York: Routledge, 1996. 1-14.

Sontag, Susan. "Fascinating Fascism." *Movies and Methods*. Vol. 1. Ed. Bill Nichols. Berkeley: U of California P, 1976. 31-43.

Springer, Claudia. "Military Propaganda: Defense Department Films from World War II and Vietnam." *The Vietnam War and American Culture*. Ed. Rick Berg, John Carlos Rowe. New York: Columbia UP, 1991. 95-114.

Staiger, Janet. "Cinematic Shots: The Narration of Violence." *The Persistence of History: Cinema, Television and the Modernist Event*. Ed. Vivian Sobchack. New York: Routledge, 1996. 39-54.

Stiles, Victoria M. "Fact and Fiction. Nature's Endgame in Werner Herzog's *Aguirre, the Wrath of God." Literature/Film Quarterly* 17:3(1989): 161-167.

Straub, Jean-Marie. "Bitburg: A Text." *West German Filmmakers on Film Vision and Voices*. Ed. Eric Rentschler. New York: Holmes, 1988, 146.

Syberberg, Hans Jürgen. "The Abode of the Gods." *West German Filmmakers on Film Vision and Voices*. Ed. Eric Rentschler. New York: Holmes, 1988. 145.

Taylor, Clyde. "The Colonialist Subtext in *Platoon*." *From Hanoi to Hollywood: The Vietnam War in American Film*. Ed. Linda Dittmar, and Gene Michaud. New Brunswick, NJ: Rutgers UP, 1990. 171-174.

Theweleit, Klaus. *Male Fantasies* I. trans. Stephen Conway. Cambridge. UK: Polity, 1987.

Thomson, David. "The Many Faces of Klaus Kinski." *American Film* (1980): 22-27.

Tomasulo, Frank P. "The Politics of Ambivalence: *Apocalypse Now* as Prowar and Antiwar Film." *From Hanoi to Hollywood: The Vietnam War in American Film*. Ed. Linda Dittmar, and Gene Michaud. New Brunswick, NJ: Rutgers UP, 1990. 145-158.

Toteberg, Michael and Lensing, Leo A., eds. *The Anarchy of the Imagination: Interviews, Essays, Notes Rainer Werner Fassbinder*. Trans. Krishna Winston. Baltimore, MD: Johns Hopkins UP, 1992.

Turim, Maureen. "The Trauma of History: Flashbacks upon Flashbacks." *Trauma and Screen Studies*. Spec. issue of *Screen* 42.2 (2001): 205-210.

Walker, Janet. "Trauma Cinema: False Memories and True Experience." *Trauma and Screen Studies*. Spec. issue of *Screen* 42.2 (2001): 211-216.

Weigel, Sigrid. "Notes on the Constellation of Gender and Cultural Identity in Contemporary Germany." *New German Critique* 55 (1992): 45-50.

Wenders, Wim. *The Logic of Images: Essays and Conversations*. Trans. Michael Hofman. London: Faber, 1991.

———— *Wim Wenders: Photos*. Heidelberg: Wim Wenders Produktion Verlag der Autoren Goethe-Institut, 1995.

———— "Talking about Germany." *The Cinema of Wim Wenders: Image, Narrative, and the Postmodern Condition*. Ed. Roger F. Cook, and Gerd Gemunden. Detroit, MI: Wayne State UP, 1996. 51-59.

———— *The Act of Seeing: Essays and Conversations*. trans. Michael Hofman. London: Faber, 1997.

Whillock, David Everett. "Narrative Structure in *Apocalypse Now*." *America Rediscovered: Critical Essays on Literature and Film of the Vietnam War*. Ed. Owen W. Gilman Jr., and Lorrie Smith. New York: Garland, 1990. 225-237.

Wilden, Anthony. "Lacan and the Discourse of the Other." The Language of the Self: The Function of Language in Psychoanalysis. Trans. A. Wilden Baltimore, MD: Johns Hopkins UP, 1974. 157-312.

Woodward, Kathleen. "Freud and Barthes: Theorizing Mourning, Sustaining Grief." *Discourse* 13.1 (1990-1): 93-110.

Wright, Elisabeth. *Psychoanalytic Criticism: Theory in Practice*. London: Methuen. 1985.

Index

A

B

C

D

E

F

G

H

I

J

K

L

M

N

R

S

T

U

V

W

X

Y

Z

Rethinking Cinema

The main purpose of the "Rethinking Cinema" series is to provide film scholars as well as professionals from the audiovisual field with innovative research material in the field of film aesthetics, theory and history. Many areas of last century's main attraction are still there to be rediscovered or have seldom been approached in the past. Consequently, priority is given to film concepts, genres, oeuvres or authors which have not been frequently dealt with. Conference proceedings, collections of essays, revised doctoral theses or monographs are published and have to distinguish themselves by a considerable degree of originality, audacity and scientific rigour, without neglecting the transdisciplinary and crosscultural aspects related to different branches from the Humanities such as Art History, Philosophy or Linguistics. The series welcomes manuscripts written in French and/or in English as well as translations of noteworthy texts from other foreign languages.

Series Editor: ***Dominique NASTA***,
Université Libre de Bruxelles (Belgium)

Series' Titles

No.4 – Raya MORAG, *Defeated Masculinity. Post-Traumatic Cinema in the Aftermath of War*, 2009, ISBN 978-90-5201-469-2

No.3 – Tarja LAINE, *Shame and Desire. Emotion, Intersubjectivity, Cinema*, 2007, ISBN 978-90-5201-062-5

N° 2 – Muriel ANDRIN, *Maléfiques. Le Mélodrame filmique américain et ses héroïnes (1940-1953)*, 2005 (2nd printing 2007), ISBN 978-90-5201-210-0

No.1 – Dominique NASTA & Didier HUVELLE (eds.), *Le son en perspective : nouvelles recherches / New Perspectives in Sound Studies*, 2004, ISBN 978-90-5201-208-7